A BOOK TO
BURN
AND A BOOK TO KEEP
(HIDDEN)

TRANSLATIONS FROM THE ASIAN CLASSICS

TRANSLATIONS FROM THE ASIAN CLASSICS

EDITORIAL BOARD

WM. THEODORE DE BARY, CHAIR

PAUL ANDERER

DONALD KEENE

GEORGE A. SALIBA

HARUO SHIRANE

BURTON WATSON

WEI SHANG

A BOOK TO BURN AND A BOOK TO KEEP (HIDDEN)

SELECTED WRITINGS

LI ZHI

EDITED AND TRANSLATED BY
RIVI HANDLER-SPITZ, PAULINE C. LEE,
AND HAUN SAUSSY

COLUMBIA UNIVERSITY PRESS
NEW YORK

Illuminating the Ming

This publication was made possible by a grant from the James P. Geiss Foundation, a private, non-profit operating foundation that sponsors research on China's Ming dynasty (1368–1644).

Columbia University Press
Publishers Since 1893
New York   Chichester, West Sussex
cup.columbia.edu
Copyright © 2016 Columbia University Press
All rights reserved

Library of Congress Cataloging-in-Publication Data
Names: Li, Zhi, 1527-1602, author. | Handler-Spitz, Rivi, editor. |
Lee, Pauline C. editor. | Saussy, Haun, 1960- editor.
Title: A book to burn and a book to keep (hidden) : selected writings
Li Zhi ; edited and translated by Rivi Handler-Spitz,
Pauline C. Lee, and Haun Saussy.
Description: New York : Columbia University Press, [2016] |
Series: Translations from the Asian classics | Includes bibliographical
references and index.
Identifiers: LCCN 2015027376 | ISBN 9780231166126 (cloth : acid-free paper) |
ISBN 9780231166133 (pbk. : acid-free paper) | ISBN 9780231541534 (e-book)
Classification: LCC PL2698.L45 A2 2016 | DDC 895.18/460—dc23
LC record available at http://lccn.loc.gov/2015027376

Columbia University Press books are printed on permanent
and durable acid-free paper.

Printed in the United States of America

Cover design: Jordan Wannemacher

CONTENTS

Acknowledgments xi
Conventions and Abbreviations xiii
Introduction xv

SELECTIONS FROM *A BOOK TO BURN* (*FENSHU*) 焚書 1

PART I: PREFACES 序引 3

1. Author's Preface 自序 3

PART II: LETTERS 書答 7

1. In Response to Deng Shiyang 答鄧石陽 7
2. To Yang Dingjian 與楊定見 10
3. To Zhuang Chunfu 與莊純夫 12
4. A Letter in Reply to Provincial Officer Liu 答劉方伯書 15
5. Letter to a Friend in the Capital 寄京友書 19
6. Three Essays for Two Monks of Huang'an 為黃安二上人三首 21
7. A Letter in Response to the Claim That Women Are Too Shortsighted to Understand the Dao 答以女人學道為見短書 29
8. Li Zhi and Geng Dingxiang 耿定向: Correspondence 34
9. To Yang Dingjian 與楊定見 63
10. A Response to Zhou Liutang 答周柳塘 65

PART III: MISCELLANEOUS WRITINGS 雜述: SHORT ESSAYS AND DISCOURSES 小品與論說 75

1. A Sketch of Zhuowu: Written in Yunnan 卓吾論略：滇中作 75
2. On He Xinyin 何心隱論 84
3. On the Warring States 戰國論 89
4. On Weapons and Food 兵食論 92
5. Discussion on Husband and Wife: Reflections After Long Contemplation 夫婦論：蓄有感 99
6. On Miscellaneous Matters 雜說 102
7. Explanation of the Childlike Heart-Mind 童心說 106
8. On the Childlike Mind 童心說 111
9. The Hub of *The Heart Sutra* 心經提綱 114
10. Notes on "The Hub" 提綱說 119
11. On Loftiness and Cleanliness 高潔說 121
12. Preface to *The Loyal and Righteous Outlaws of the Marsh* 忠義水滸傳序 125
13. Preface to Su Che's *Explication of Laozi* 子由解老序 129
14. Postface to *The Prose of Our Time* 時文後序 132
15. Mr. Li's Ten Kinds of Association 李生十交文 135
16. Self-Appraisal 自贊 138
17. An Appraisal of Liu Xie 贊劉諧 140
18. On a Scroll Painting of Square Bamboo 方竹圖卷文 142
19. In Memoriam, Master Wang Longxi 王龍溪先生告文 146
20. In Memoriam, Master Luo Jinxi 羅近溪先生告文 150
21. Afterword to *Journeying with Companions* 征途與共後語 158
22. Reading a Letter from Ruowu's Mother 讀若無母寄書 162
23. Record of Master Geng Dingli 耿楚倥先生傳 166
24. A Petition of Worship and Recitation to the Medicine Buddha 禮誦藥師告文 172
25. A Petition Upon Completion of Worshipful Recitation of *The Medicine Buddha Sutra* 禮誦藥師經畢告文 175

26. A Brief Introduction to *Resolving Doubts About the Pure Land* 淨土決前引 178
27. Disciplining the Sangha 戒衆僧 181
28. Reflections on My Life 感慨平生 185
29. *The Pavilion for Worshipping the Moon* 拜月 190
30. *Red Duster* 紅拂 192

PART IV: READINGS OF HISTORY 讀史 195

1. On the Letter Terminating Relations 絕交書 195
2. Dragonfly Ditty 蜻蛉謠 197
3. Biography of Bo Yi 伯夷傳 199
4. Adorned with Every Mark of Dignity 無所不佩 201
5. Xunzi, Li Si, and Master Wu 荀卿李斯吳公 204
6. People of the Song Dynasty Disparaged Xunzi 宋人譏荀卿 206
7. On Friendship 朋友篇 207

PART V: POETRY 詩 209

Introduction to Li Zhi's Poetry 209
1. "The Pleasure of Reading," with a Prologue 讀書樂並引 211
2. Ballad of the North Wind 朔風謠 215
3. Chrysanthemum Regrets 恨菊 217
4. Monastic Seclusion 閉關 218
5. Lantern Festival 元宵 219
6. Red and White Plum Blossoms Flourishing at the Lake—an Amusement 湖上紅白梅盛開戲題 220
7. At a Banquet on a Spring Evening, I Receive the Word "Lack" 春宵燕集得空字 221
8. Sending Off Zheng Zixuan, Also for Jiao Hong 送鄭子玄兼寄弱侯 222
9. To Matteo Ricci of the Far West 贈利西泰 223
10. Encountering Troops Marching East During a Morning Walk, I Send a Poem to Vice-Censor-in-Chief Mei 曉行逢征東將士卻寄梅中丞 225

11. Composed with Joy Upon Arriving at the Temple of Bliss on the Double Ninth Festival and Learning That Yuan Hongdao Would Soon Be Here 九日至極樂寺聞袁中郎且至因喜而賦 227

12. Heavy Rain and Snow at the Temple of Bliss on New Year's Day 元日極樂寺大雨雪 228

13. The Glazed Temple 琉璃寺 229

SELECTIONS FROM *ANOTHER BOOK TO BURN* (*XU FENSHU* 續焚書) 231

PART I: PREFACES 序引 233

1. Preface to Master Li's *Another Book to Burn*—by Jiao Hong 李氏續焚書序 233

2. Upon Reading Old Zhuowu's Writings—Zhang Nai 讀卓吾老子書述—張鼐 235

3. Preface to the Second Printing of Li Zhi's Writings 續刻李氏書序—汪本鈳 238

PART II: LETTERS 書答 241

1. To Ma Lishan 與馬歷山 241

2. Discussing Literature with a Friend 與友人論文 245

3. A Reply to Li Shilong 復李士龍 247

4. To Zhou Youshan 與周友山 249

5. To Geng Kenian 與耿克念 253

6. To Zeng Jiquan 與曾繼泉 255

7. Letter to a Friend 與友人書 256

PART III: MISCELLANEOUS WRITINGS 雜述: SHORT ESSAYS AND DISCOURSES 小品與論說 259

1. Preface to *Selections from "A Record of a Cart Full of Ghosts"* 選錄睽車志敍 259

2. Preface to the Anthology *Unstringing the Bow* 說弧集敍 263

3. A Brief Introduction to a Selection of Daoist Teachings 道教鈔小引 265

4. Written at the End of Yuan Zhongdao's Hand Scroll 書小修手卷後 267
5. On *The Lotus Sutra* Chapter on Expedient Devices 法華方便品説 270
    6. On *The Diamond Sutra* 金剛經説 273
    7. On Recluses 隱者説 276
8. How the Three Teachings Lead Back to Confucianism 三教歸儒説 278
    9. After Śākyamuni Buddha 釋迦佛後 282
10. Distribution of Work Assignments in the Sangha 列眾僧職事 286
11. An Inscription for the Image of Confucius in the Cloister
    of the Flourishing Buddha 題孔子像於芝佛院 289
    12. Master Li Zhuowu's Testament 李卓吾先生遺言 291

PART IV: POETRY 詩 295

1. On Reading Du Fu (Two Poems) 讀杜少陵二首 295
2. Watching the Army at the East Gate of the City 觀兵城東門 297
    3. Amitābha Temple 彌陀寺 298
4. Reading the Resignation Memorial of Gu Chong'an
    讀顧沖庵辭疏 299
    5. Spring Night 春夜 300
6. Listening to the Chanting of *The Lotus Sutra* 聽誦法華 301
    7. Eight Quatrains from Prison 系中八絕 302
8. Spring Rain on a Great House 樓頭春雨 305
9. My Feelings Upon Ascending the Mountain and Receiving a
    Letter from Jiao Hong 入山得焦弱侯書有感二首 306
    10. After the Snow 雪後 308
    11. Sitting Alone in Meditation 獨坐 309
    12. A Sudden Chill 乍寒 310
    13. Evening Rain 暮雨 311
14. Watching the Rain with Dazhi 大智對雨 312
    15. Hard Rain 雨甚 313
16. Viewing the Yellow Crane Pavilion from the River
    江上望黃鶴樓 314
17. Drifting on East Lake with Li Jiantian 李見田邀遊東湖 316

FROM *A BOOK TO KEEP (HIDDEN)* (*CANGSHU* 藏書) (1599) 317

1. Introduction to the Table of Contents of the Historical Annals and Biographies in *A Book to Keep (Hidden)* 藏書世紀列傳總目前論   317

2. Li Zhi on the First Emperor 秦始皇帝   320

THE HISTORICAL RECORD 史料 325

1. The Life of Li Wenling 李溫陵傳   325

2. Veritable Record of the Memorial Impeaching Li Zhi Submitted by Supervising Censor Zhang Wenda on the *Yimao* Day of the Second Intercalary Month of the Thirtieth Year of the Reign of Emperor Shenzong 神宗實錄萬曆三十年閏二月乙卯禮科給事中張問達疏劾李贄   334

Chronology of Li Zhi's Life   339
Bibliography   343
List of Contributors   351
Index   353

ACKNOWLEDGMENTS

MANY OF us who have contributed to this book first encountered Li Zhi in graduate school, during our initial forays into the fields of classical Chinese literature, religions, and intellectual history. Consequently, a considerable number of the translations in these pages represent extensive reworkings of material over many years as we have striven toward the elusive goal of achieving facility in classical Chinese. This process would not have been possible without the erudition, patience, and generosity of countless mentors, teachers, friends, and colleagues. We are most grateful for the guidance of our teacher-friends (*shiyou* 師友) Kang-i Sun Chang, Philip J. Ivanhoe, Andrew H-B Lo, Jacques Pimpaneau, Judith T. Zeitlin, and especially the late Anthony C. Yu, who did not live to see this book to publication. Equally important are our language teachers, Chou Chang-Jen, Chen Liyuan, Zhu Jinghua, Chen Yizhen, Yang Ningyuan, and Xu Zhicheng.

David (Bert) Westbrook sowed the seed of this book by asking a question: "Where can I find out more about the Chinese mandarin who abjured officialdom?" Among the friends, classmates, and colleagues whom we would particularly like to acknowledge are Stephen Angle, Tony Chang and the East Asian Library at Washington University in St. Louis, Lars Christensen, Rebecca Copeland, Dai Lianbin, Shari Epstein, T. Griffith Foulk, Gao Ruchen, Beata Grant, the Greater St. Louis Ming-Qing Reading Group, Zeynep Gürsel, Barend ter Haar, Robert Hegel, Irene Hsiao, Eric Hutton, Tao Jiang, Jiang Yuanxin, Jin Hui-han, Einor Keinan-Segev, Hillel Kieval, Stephen Lane, En Li, Li Kan, Li Sher-shiueh, Waiyee Li, Liu Chiung-yun, Filippo Marsili, Tobie Meyer-Fong, Steven B. Miles, Arthur Mitchell, On-cho Ng, John Renard, Katie Ryor, Robert Schine, Shao Dongfang, Reiko Shinno, Suyoung Son,

Louisa Stein, Justin Tiwald, Karin Velez, Ann Waltner, Yi-Li Wu, Xu Dongfeng, Xu Peng, Zhang Ying, and Zhu Tianxiao.

We are grateful to our editors at Columbia University Press, Jennifer Crewe and Jonathan Fiedler, for expertly shepherding the book through the production process. Mike Ashby was a strict and understanding copy editor—exactly what we needed. The book has also benefited from the meticulous commentary of several anonymous reviewers, as well as from institutional support and subvention funding from Saint Louis University, the University of Chicago, Macalester College, and the Mellon Foundation. We extend special thanks to the Department of Theological Studies at Saint Louis University, Kendrick Brown, Kathleen Murray, Satoko Suzuki, and Yang Xin of Macalester College. Andrew Notaras helped us to assemble the bibliography.

Earlier versions of Li Zhi's essays here titled "A Sketch of Zhuowu: Written in Yunnan," "On Miscellaneous Matters," and "Explanation of the Childlike Heart-Mind" were first published in Pauline C. Lee's *Li Zhi* 李贽, *Confucianism, and the Virtue of Desire* (Albany: SUNY Press, 2012). We thank SUNY Press for permission to reprint these translations.

Finally, we extend our profound gratitude to our closest friends and family members, who have sustained us with unwavering encouragement, strengthened our powers of self-discipline, instilled in us the love of language and literature, and endowed us with the conviction that we are, after all, engaged in meaningful work.

This book is dedicated to intellectuals everywhere who have the courage to speak their convictions.

CONVENTIONS AND ABBREVIATIONS

CHINESE NAMES and terms are transliterated according to the pinyin system. Exceptions are made for names that have become familiar in another style.

Chinese characters are given in their traditional (full) form.

The Buddhist meditative practice known in China as *chan* 禪 is sometimes styled Zen since the Japanese term has become familiar to readers of English.

Following the practice of the *Princeton Dictionary of Buddhism*, "Buddha" is capitalized only when the reference is to a specific buddha, bodhisattva, or divinity; when the reference is nonspecific, "buddha" is used.

Where applicable, classical Chinese works are cited by chapter and verse. Thus *Analects* 15.20 refers to chapter 15, section 20 of that work; *Mencius* 3B12 refers to verse 12 of the second half of chapter 3 of that work; *Zuozhuan* (Xiang, year 24), refers to the twenty-fourth year of the reign of Duke Xiang as recounted in the *Zuo Commentary* to the *Spring and Autumn Annals*; *Classic of Poetry*, Mao no. 260, "Sheng Min," refers to poem 260 of the *Shijing*, with its title given according to the Mao edition.

Sima Qian's *Shiji* (Records of the grand historian), frequently cited in Li Zhi's writings, exists in multiple English-language versions, all incomplete. Where the reference is to a chapter thus far untranslated into English, we cite the Zhonghua shuju edition (1962) of the *Shiji*; where translations by Burton Watson are available, we cite *Records of the Grand Historian* by its individual volume titles, *Qin Dynasty*, *Han Dynasty I*, and *Han Dynasty II* (thus, for example, Watson, *Records: Qin Dynasty*, 236), occasionally resorting to Watson's translation *Records of the Historian* of 1969; in other cases we cite the translation by William H. Nienhauser, *The Grand Scribe's Records*.

ABBREVIATIONS

- ch.: chapter
- CS: *Cangshu* [A book to keep (hidden)]
- DMB: *Dictionary of Ming Biography, 1368–1644*, ed. L. Carrington Goodrich and Chaoying Fang, 2 vols. (New York: Columbia University Press, 1976)
- FS: *Fenshu* [A book to burn]
- j.: *juan*, fascicle; chapterlike subunit of a traditional Chinese book
- LZQJZ: *Li Zhi quanji zhu* [The annotated complete works of Li Zhi], ed. Zhang Jianye and Zhang Dai, 26 vols. (Beijing: Shehui kexue wenxian chubanshe, 2010)
- MRXA: *Mingru xue an* [The records of Ming scholars], by Huang Zongxi, Wanyou wenku huiyao ed. (Taipei: Taiwan Shangwu yinshuguan, 1965)
- T: Tripiṭaka
- XCS: *Xu cangshu* [Another book to keep (hidden)]
- XFS: *Xu fenshu* [Another book to burn]

INTRODUCTION

THE TITLE of Li Zhi's best-known collection of writings, *A Book to Burn*, was both prescient and self-dramatizing, perhaps a self-confirming prophecy. On May 6, 1602, an elderly man being held for interrogation in a Beijing prison asked for a razor and shaving water. Before his jailers could stop him, he had slit his throat. Thus ended the life of "one of the most famous men of our time in China"[1] (according to a contemporary Italian observer), also described by the imperial censor Zhang Wenda 張問達 as a seditious author who "confuses and perplexes the minds of the people" with his "mad, flagitious, aberrant, and willful theses."[2] Li's teaching "must be abolished" and his books destroyed, Zhang had said, and with the emperor's accord, Li had been arrested at Tongzhou, roughly thirteen miles outside Beijing, and brought to the capital for questioning. The prediction or challenge in the title of Li's *Book to Burn* may then have seemed to come true—but the proof that it did not is in your hands.

One of the most strikingly original thinkers and prolific writers of his day, Li Zhi 李贄 (1527–1602; style name Zhuowu 卓吾) produced voluminous works in genres ranging from essays, letters, and commentaries to poetry, historiography, and philosophy. In his most famous works, *A Book to Burn* (*Fenshu* 焚書) and *Another Book to Burn* (*Xu fenshu* 續焚書),[3] Li expressed eccentric views that flouted ethical and aesthetic conventions. Brazenly provocative, his writings challenged authorities of all kinds and championed individual judgment and personal desires. Strong-willed and

---

1. D'Elia, *Fonti Ricciane*, 2:65.
2. Cited in Gu Yanwu, "Li Zhi," in *Rizhi lu*, 18/28b.
3. See notes 59 and 60 for bibliographic information on these two texts.

opinionated, wild and unrestrained, Li embraced contradiction and reveled in scandal and self-dramatization. An outspoken opponent of corruption in the Confucian, or Ru,[4] civil bureaucracy, Li nonetheless spent the better part of his adult life employed in this service. At the age of fifty-four, however, he resigned his post as prefect (1577–1580) of Yao'an, a remote outpost of the western province of Yunnan, and went to live with his friends and patrons the Geng family of Huang'an. As conflicts with the Gengs arose, Li departed and took up residence in a monastery, the Vimalakīrti Monastery in Macheng, Huguang, present-day Hubei. There and in the Cloister of the Flourishing Buddha (his dwelling place from 1588),[5] he retreated into a world of study, shaved off his hair in conformity with Buddhist practice—but grew a long and incongruous beard—strictly observed the morning and evening monastic rituals (but profaned the premises by consorting with widows and refusing to abstain from eating meat). As Li admitted himself, he "never liked the idea of having to take orders from another person."[6] Entering a monastery was a way for him to find freedom—or, his detractors would say, an alibi for his lawlessness. The literary record seems to indicate that he found there a rule he could obey. Unlike his essays on artistic, philosophical, and social issues, ever stirring up controversy and reversing consensus judgments, his writings on Buddhist topics are notably irenic.[7]

Li's outrageous appearance and shocking behavior, along with his bold opinions and incendiary writings, did not fail to attract attention. As his social criticism grew increasingly pointed, his writings spawned a conservative backlash, which began with slanderous rumors and escalated to outright violence.[8] In 1600, two years before his death, Li's residence was torched and the grave site he had prepared for himself desecrated. Shortly thereafter, a memorial was submitted to the throne charging Li with writing books that "throw men's minds into confusion."[9] Li was arrested and thrown into prison, where he abruptly committed suicide. The Wanli emperor ordered Li's books destroyed, along with the wood blocks used for

---

4. The character *ru* 儒, traditionally translated as "Confucian," is now often rendered through transliteration. See, for example, Csikszentmihalyi, *Material Virtue*, 15–22. In this book, we use "Ru" and "Confucian" interchangeably.
5. The monastery's name is, more precisely, the Cloister of the Buddha-Shaped Fungus (*Zhi fo yuan* 芝佛院), from a discovery made at the time of its building.
6. "Reflections on My Life," pp. 185–89.
7. See "A Petition of Worship and Recitation to the Medicine Buddha," "Disciplining the Sangha," "On *The Diamond Sutra*," pp. 172–74, 181–84, 273–75.
8. See Rowe, *Crimson Rain*, 17–42, and Jiang, "Heresy and Persecution."
9. "Veritable Record of the Memorial Impeaching Li Zhi . . . ," p. 335.

printing them, as seditious works that "dared to disrupt the Dao, to muddle a generation, and to deceive the people."[10] Yet despite the emperor's harsh decree, Li's *A Book to Burn* and other writings were not—and have never been—effectively suppressed.

Li's writings continued to circulate so widely in his generation that one late-Ming literatus surmised that virtually every educated man kept a copy of *A Book to Burn* stashed discreetly up his sleeves.[11] This statement, while obviously exaggerated, conveys the tremendous influence Li's writings exerted. For although scholars may have kept Li's books out of sight in certain company, they pored over them in moments of solitude, delighting in Li's candidly scathing criticisms of official culture and reveling in his incisive wit. Indeed, so great was the demand for writings by Li Zhi that many enterprising booksellers indiscriminately slapped this author's name on writings obviously composed by other people. And authors too, equally eager to enhance their profits, thought little of concealing their true identity and passing their writings off as the words of Li Zhi. The prefaces to *Another Book to Burn*, translated in this volume, attest that, despite (or because of) the official ban on Li's books, forged and contraband editions of works "by Li Zhi" were readily available throughout the late Ming.[12]

One of the reasons why Li's writings attracted such a wide readership was the tremendous variety of subjects on which he wrote and the kaleidoscopic array of perspectives his writings display. In addition to expressing his views on aesthetics, politics, historiography, ethics, and the relationship between the sexes, Li's writings weave together strands of Confucianism, Buddhism, and Daoism, along with other schools of thought.

As a young man, Li choked back his distaste for rote memorization, and for the sake of an official career committed to memory both the Confucian classics and the Cheng-Zhu commentaries on those classics, endorsed as the standard in orthodox interpretation.[13] In 1522, he proudly became

---

10. Ibid., p. 336.
11. Zhu Guozhen, "Li Zhuowu," in *Yong chuang xiaopin*, 365–68.
12. Li Zhi's name is attached to many kinds of texts—essays, letters, travel diaries, fiction commentaries, novels, histories, and so on. For more on forgeries of Li Zhi, see Rolston, *How to Read*, 356–63; see also Plaks, *Four Masterworks*, 513–18.
13. The Cheng-Zhu school, also called the Daoxue school or School of Principle, was made the standard of orthodox Confucian philosophy by the Yuan and Ming dynasties. Its leading figures, the Song-dynasty Confucians Cheng Yi 程頤 (1033–1107) and Zhu Xi 朱熹 (1130–1200), had written commentaries on the Confucian classics that had become required reading for all civil service examination candidates. Although these comments contain subtle and nuanced arguments, they had, by the late Ming, come to symbolize the pedantry of the examination system. For this reason, Li and many of his contemporaries regarded them with scorn.

the first member of his extended family to pass the provincial civil service examination. Having accepted official posts in both capitals of the Ming dynasty, Nanjing (briefly in 1560 and again from 1570 to 1577) and Beijing (in 1564), Li would later go on to publish commentaries on the texts that the Ming considered the core of the Confucian canon, the Four Books: the *Great Learning* (*Da xue* 大學), the *Analects* (*Lunyu* 論語), the *Doctrine of the Mean* (*Zhongyong* 中庸), and the *Mencius* (*Mengzi* 孟子).[14] But Li's studies did not end there. Spurred by insatiable intellectual curiosity, Li also explored both Daoist texts and arcana, and his published works include commentaries on the *Daodejing* 道德經 and *Zhuangzi* 莊子. Additionally, toward the end of his life he developed a profound fascination with Buddhism and, while residing in his monastic retreat, meditated on sutras and published a commentary on the *Yinguolu* 因果錄 (Records of karmic retribution).[15] Because he peppered his writings liberally with allusions to texts ranging from the familiar to the obscure, his writings exhibit to an extraordinary, indeed adventurous, degree a synthesis of divergent religious-philosophical traditions, including Confucianism, Buddhism, and Daoism.[16]

And even so, Li's erudition went beyond the Three Teachings. Born into a merchant family with Muslim ancestors in the thriving international port city of Quanzhou in the southern province of Fujian, Li was aware from an early age of the diversity of human beliefs.[17] Although few of his writings exhibit traces of the Islamic influences to which Li was likely exposed in his youth, his books do register the author's keen interest in a teacher from another faith, the renowned Jesuit missionary Matteo Ricci (1552–1610). The two men met in Beijing in 1599, and Ricci's erudition made a strong impression on Li;[18] in addition to exchanging gifts with this foreign visitor and engaging in scholarly discussions with him, Li composed a vivid description of this "man of the Great Western Regions," which he included

---

14. These works, a subset of the classics first treated as a unit by Zhu Xi, were central to the civil service examinations from the thirteenth through nineteenth centuries. For an introduction to these texts, see Gardner, *The Four Books*. See LZQJZ, vol. 21, for Li's commentaries on these classics.
15. LZQJZ 18:7–101.
16. For a discussion of the problem of cataloguing Chinese religious traditions as "Confucian," "Buddhist," "Daoist," and such, see Campany, "On the Very Idea of Religions."
17. For discussion of Muslim influences on Li, see Billeter, *Li Zhi*, 24; Cheng, "Reality and Imagination"; and Handler-Spitz, "Li Zhi's Relativism."
18. For more on this meeting, see Ricci, *On Friendship*. Traces of Li's Muslim identity are discernible in "Master Li Zhuowu's Testament," translated in this volume, pp. 291–93.

INTRODUCTION   XIX

in a "Letter to a Friend," translated in this volume.[19] Li's open-mindedness also extended to the ethnic minority peoples he governed while serving as prefect of Yao'an. The genuine interest he took in their beliefs and affairs along with the humane and tolerant attitude with which he regarded these non-Han peoples won him a reputation for fairness and compassion.[20] By juxtaposing material culled from diverse sources, Li's writings record the broad scope of his experience and showcase his eclectic tastes. And when, as inevitably happens, these sources come into conflict with one another, Li rarely attempts to reconcile them. Rather, he allows discrepant views to coexist in the pages of his texts and challenges readers to make of them whatever sense they will.

If Li seems unperturbed by inconsistency in his own writings, he held quite a different view of the discrepancies and contradictions he discovered in Confucian officialdom. Early in his career, Li served as an erudite of the Imperial Academy, and later he worked for the Nanjing Ministry of Justice.[21] The years he spent in the empire's two capitals afforded him many opportunities to witness firsthand the workings of government in an era that has become famous for pervasive fraud and corruption.[22] The gap between the lofty ideals that many officials *claimed* to embody and the reality of their venal, self-interested behavior disgusted Li and roused him to fits of rage.

By nature abrasive and direct, Li composed essays and open letters that unflinchingly exposed the hypocrisy he saw around him. His writings teem with examples of "phony Confucians"— to whom he also refers as "gentlemen of the Way"— individuals who pose as men of virtue and are recognized publicly as such but whose conduct betrays the very values they purport to uphold. Li's searing attacks on officials of this kind have led many modern scholars to interpret him as a fundamentally anti-Confucian thinker.[23] However, what troubled Li was not Confucian ethics per se but rather the rampant distortions and perversions of this philosophy. Thus Li was more

---

19. See "Letter to a Friend," pp. 256–57, and verses addressed to Ricci, pp. 223–24.
20. Liu Tong 劉侗 and Yu Yizheng 于奕正, *Dijing jingwu lue* 帝京景物略 [Sketches of scenery at the capital], j. 8, *Jifu mingji: Li Zhuowu mu* 畿輔名跡—李卓吾墓 [Notable vestiges near the capital: Li Zhuowu's tomb]; cited in Xiamen Daxue Lishi Xi, *Li Zhi yanjiu*, 1:76–78.
21. For biographical information on Li, see Rong, *Li Zhuowu ping zhuan*, and *Li Zhi nianpu*; See also Lin Haiquan, *Li Zhi nianpu kaolue*. Li's autobiographical accounts, "A Sketch of Zhuowu" and "Reflections on My Life," are translated in this volume, pp. 75–83, 185–89. See also, in this volume, Yuan Zhongdao, "The Life of Li Wenling," pp. 325–33.
22. Mote, "Political Decline."
23. See Wu Ze, *Rujia pantu Li Zhuowu*; Zhu Qianzhi, *Li Zhi*.

a reformer, even a restorer, than a revolutionary. By pointing out the moral failures of contemporary Confucians, he sought to transform the tradition from within and thereby to restore its ethical foundation.

One of the grave problems Li perceived among contemporary Confucians was their rigid conformity to a particular version of tradition. In his most widely read essay, "Explanation of the Childlike Heart-Mind," Li excoriates scholars of his day for having become so mired in orthodoxy that they forfeited their own creativity and interpretive agency.[24] Instead of assessing texts critically, as they ought, Li charges, his contemporaries—"scholars" in name only—"blindly" and "deafly" repeat the accepted interpretations. By making such formalism and hypocrisy the target of his attacks, Li hoped to incite readers to find ways of solving these problems by following their own hearts and minds.

Li's conviction that each individual owes it to himself to cultivate his sense of personal judgment grows out of a philosophical tradition stemming from the mid-Ming philosopher Wang Yangming 王陽明 (1472–1529) and his Song-dynasty forebear Lu Xiangshan 陸象山 (1139–1193).[25] The Lu-Wang school, identified with the Learning of the Heart-Mind (Xinxue 心學), advanced interpretations of Confucian ethics that focused on particular cases considered in context and for that reason often clashed with more mainstream, "orthodox" views held by the Cheng-Zhu school, adherents to what was known as the School of Principle (Daoxue 道學 or Lixue 理學). Because the latter interpretations had been canonized and made required reading for all students wishing to pass imperial examinations, they had, by the sixteenth century, come to be associated with pedantry and with the stifling, hierarchical, and homogenized culture of academia instantiated in the form of the eight-legged essay. Unlike these examination essays, which required students to conform to a rigid and predetermined structure of paired theses and antitheses and to "speak on behalf of the ancients," Wang's open-ended interpretations, which were not institutionally sanctioned, offered students more flexible and individualistic ways of approaching classical texts.[26]

---

24. We have provided two translations of this essay, one that is relatively free and another that cleaves more closely to the original text; see pp. 106–13.
25. For an introduction and translations of select writings of both thinkers, see Ivanhoe, *Readings*. Li Zhi's biography of Wang Yangming, "Xinjian hou Wang Wencheng gong" 新建侯王文成公 [On Wang Yangming, marquis of Xinjian], appears in *XCS*, *j*. 14, in *LZQJZ* 10:214–25.
26. For more on the eight-legged essay, see Elman, *Cultural History*, 383; Gong, *Mingdai baguwenshi tan*; and Plaks, "Prose."

Although Wang Yangming died in 1529, when Li was still a young child, Li later encountered several of Wang's most brilliant disciples, including Wang Longxi 王龍溪 (1498–1583), Luo Jinxi 羅近溪 (1515–1588), and Wang Bi 王襞 (1511–1587), son of Wang Gen 王艮 (1483–1541).[27] Posted to Nanjing, just across the Yangzi River from Wang Gen's hometown of Taizhou 泰州, Li came under the influence of what later became known as the Taizhou school, a branch of adherents to Wang Yangming's philosophy, who contended that moral authority lay in the individual conscience and that, in consequence, anyone might be a sage.[28]

Wang Yangming preached a lifestyle based on personal self-cultivation, cut loose from the dictates of orthodoxy. Deeply skeptical of codified guidelines for ethical practice, Wang called on individuals to make their "innate knowledge" (*liangzhi* 良知) of right and wrong—not the rules transmitted in authoritative texts—the touchstone of their behavior. This emphasis on personal agency is expressed succinctly in the following oft-cited passage:

> If words are examined in the mind and found to be wrong, I dare not accept them as correct, even if they have come from the mouth of Confucius. How much the less from people inferior to Confucius! If words are examined in the mind and found to be correct, I dare not regard them as wrong, even if they have come from the mouths of ordinary people. How much the less so if they have come from Confucius himself![29]

The egalitarian spirit of Wang Yangming's philosophy had potentially unsettling implications for a rigidly hierarchical society, and conservatives at times derided Wang as a "wild Zen Buddhist" whose teachings risked undermining social stability. As a case in point, the leading Taizhou thinker, Wang Gen, son of a salt worker, was famous for claiming that "the streets are full of sages!"[30] Drawing inspiration from both Wang's notion that the self is the basis of all moral action and the Buddhist idea that all sentient beings possess buddha-nature, this teacher of humble origins, who neither passed nor even sat for a single civil service examination, insisted that through ethical self-cultivation, any individual could attain the highest

---

27. Li's testimonials in memory of the former two are translated in this volume; see pp. 146–57. His biographies of all three appear in *XCS, j.* 22, in *LZQJZ* 11:102–9, 111–20, and 131–36.
28. On the Taizhou school, see de Bary, "Individualism," and *Learning for One's Self*, 155–202.
29. Wing-tsit Chan, *Instructions*, 159.
30. Ebrey, *Chinese Civilization*, 258; de Bary, "Individualism."

degree of wisdom.³¹ Under his message of personal self-realization lay the liberating—yet potentially disquieting—notion that those in positions of power did not necessarily possess greater merit than did ordinary members of society.

The implications of this suggestion ran deep, for they corresponded to shifts occurring throughout Chinese society in the late Ming, a time of rising class mobility and economic uncertainty. As interregional transportation improved, urban populations flourished, commerce thrived, and merchants' fortunes were made and lost, those who prospered often used their newfound riches to buy positions of privilege. By the Wanli period (1572–1620) toward the end of the Ming dynasty, wealthy families so frequently purchased official titles for their sons that one contemporary scholar remarked, "The status distinctions among scholars, peasants, and merchants are becoming blurred."³² By deploying their assets in this way, successful merchants could avoid devoting tedious hours to memorizing the classics yet insinuate themselves into the ranks of the literati class with its monopoly on prestige.

The blatant injustice of this behavior outraged Li. His writings seem to overflow with vituperation for these individuals' phoniness and hypocrisy. Yet Li's writings display considerable sensitivity toward merchants who plied their trade honestly. He narrates their tribulations with compassion and tells how they are "burdened with heavy loads, run great risks, and brave many dangers, endure many humiliations from the tax officers and insults in the marketplace."³³ Such burdens contrast with the security and status enjoyed by even middling scholar-officials. By championing the causes of merchants, commoners, and other sectors of the population often scorned by orthodox Confucians, Li both valorized the increasingly important role merchants were coming to play in late-Ming society and built upon the egalitarian principles that Wang and his disciples had laid out.

In addition to speaking on behalf of merchants and commoners, Li challenged Confucian scales of value in his writings on history. Though commentary on historical figures is found scattered throughout *A Book to Burn*,

---

31. Wang Gen, "Mingzhe baoshenlun" 明哲保身論 [Clear wisdom and self-preservation], cited in de Bary, "Individualism," 164–65.
32. Gui Youguang, ed., *Zhen Chuan Xiansheng ji* 震川先生集 [Mr. Zhen Chuan's collected writings], cited in Ho, *Ladder of Success*, 73.
33. "You yu Jiao Ruohou" 又與焦弱侯 [Another letter to Jiao Hong], in *FS*, *j*. 2, in *LZQJZ* 1:118–23.

Another Book to Burn, and other works, Li's most famous work of historiography is *A Book to Keep (Hidden)*. In this work, based on an earlier collection of excerpts by the Ming literatus Tang Shunzhi 唐順之 (1507–1560), *The Left Scribes' Record of Deeds and Personalities Through the Ages* (*Lidai shi ji zuobian* 歷代史籍左編), Li offered his personal judgment on figures from Chinese history, often overturning the standard opinion.[34] "In keeping with his basic views, Li Zhi's judgments on many historical figures necessarily contradicted the orthodox appraisal. For contrary to all Confucian historiography to the present day, Li Zhi esteemed [the First Emperor] Qin Shihuang, and rated him 'the greatest emperor of all ages.'"[35] The title *A Book to Burn* even alludes to this emperor's cruel policy of "burning books and burying [uncooperative] scholars alive." Yet when Li scrutinized the historical record, he found that although Qin Shihuang was arrogant and headstrong, his crimes were planned and carried out by his advisers.[36] By publicly defending such a figure, Li shocked readers. Indeed, as the 1602 indictment against Li affirms, in *A Book to Keep (Hidden)*

> [he] throws men's minds into confusion ... considers Lü Buwei and Li Yuan wise counselors, Li Si shrewd, and Feng Dao an official who possessed the moral fiber of a recluse; he estimates that Zhuo Wenjun excelled in choosing an outstanding mate and finds laughable Sima Guang's assertion that Sang Hongyang deceived Emperor Wu of Han; he deems Qin Shi Huang the greatest emperor of all time, and he maintains that Confucius's judgments need not be considered standard.

(Lü Buwei 呂不韋, the architect of the rise of the state of Qin in the third century B.C.E., was portrayed by the Han historian Sima Qian 司馬遷 as an unscrupulous profiteer; Li Yuan 李園 smuggled his sister into the harem of the king of Chu and thus exerted influence over the next king, his nephew; Li Si 李斯 was the mastermind of the Qin dynasty's bibliocaust and thus the object of centuries of literati hatred; Feng Dao's 馮道 ambition was proverbial: he served under ten different rulers and four dynastic houses despite the precept that "a scholar has but one master"; Zhuo Wenjun 卓文君, a young lady of good family, eloped with the penniless poet Sima Xiangru

---

34. The relation between the two texts was already remarked on in the Ming. On Li's debt to Tang Shunzhi, see Li Defeng, "Li Zhi." Tang's book takes its title from the ancient practice of having two historians attend the ruler's court: one, on the right, recorded the speeches, and the other, on the left, recorded deeds and individuals. The Qing editors of the *Siku quanshu* did not think much of Tang's compilation; see *Siku quanshu zongmu tiyao*, 2:417.
35. Franke, "Historical Writing," 733; romanization altered.
36. See "Li Zhi on the First Emperor," pp. 320–24.

司馬相如; Sang Hongyang 桑弘羊 devised a strategy based on arbitrage for augmenting the national wealth without impoverishing the taxpayers, which the Song historian Sima Guang found contrary to nature and reason; and Qin Shihuang 秦始皇, founder of the imperial system, was cast as a perverse and ruthless tyrant by the Han historians Sima Qian and Ban Gu 班固.) Despite the irritation of the orthodox, however, Li had a purpose in issuing these revisionary judgments, and they opened the way for later writers to question the evidence and justifications of inherited histories:

> Li Zhi used entirely new criteria and viewpoints to evaluate historical personalities. The introductory remarks in his [Book to Keep (Hidden)] begin with the words: "Human judgments are not fixed quantities. In passing judgments men do not hold settled views." According to Li Zhi, opinions and judgments held by different people at different times vary greatly. If Confucius were to return, he said, his views would be very different from those he expressed two thousand years ago. Such ideas do not provide sufficient grounds to classify Li Zhi as anti-Confucian, but they clearly indicate that he opposed the kind of official neo-Confucian orthodoxy established by the Zhu Xi school, according to which judgments actually or allegedly once expressed by Confucius had to be the only valid criteria for all times.[37]

If these views on history writing (traditionally the preserve of Confucian moralism) suggest the influence of Daoist and Buddhist notions of transience on Li's thought, they further illustrate Li's readiness to act on Wang Yangming's suggestion that if the words and ideas of the sages no longer prove applicable to current situations, one must be willing to abandon them and search for a more practicable truth. The boldness with which Li articulated these controversial views has led modern scholars to herald him as one of the most innovative historiographers of his day.[38]

Li's historiographical provocations were of a piece with his literary affinities: in both forms of writing, he espoused the method of *fan'an* 翻案 (reversing accepted judgments).[39] That habit of mind also allowed him to come to his own conclusions about gender. If Wang Gen had maintained

---

37. Franke, "Historical Writing," 732. For Li's preface to *A Book to Keep (Hidden)*, see pp. 317–19.
38. See Qian, *Mingdai shixue de licheng*, 336.
39. On *fan'an* as a literary practice common to many Ming outsider intellectuals and partly responsible for Li Zhi's appeal, see Lowry, *Popular Songs*, 66–67, 191.

that anyone could attain sagehood, Li made it explicit that this principle included women. Li argued that, from an ethical standpoint, women and men were fundamentally similar; any differences that arose between them were likely a result of women's having been confined to the inner chambers while men were allowed to roam freely and explore the world. In his "A Letter in Response to the Claim That Women Are Too Shortsighted to Understand the Dao" Li opines that only such physical and intellectual confinement to the inner chambers stunts their development and prevents them from nourishing their talents and achieving their potential. He even dares to imagine a female rival to Confucius, a "person with a woman's body and a man's vision . . . It may have been in hopes of encountering such a person that the Sage Confucius wandered the world, desiring to meet her just once but unable to find her."[40]

In an attempt to rectify the conditions that kept women from "understanding the Dao," Li took the unusual step of accepting a female disciple, Mei Danran 梅澹然, daughter of the prominent statesman Mei Guozhen 梅國禎. In their lengthy correspondence, Mei Danran posed questions about Buddhism and the Way, and Li responded in detail. When word of their teacher-student relationship leaked out, rumors began to fly. The memorial that led to Li's arrest contains the following lurid accusations:

> Particularly reprehensible is that when Li was lodging in Macheng, he gave free rein to his impulses and, together with his unsavory companions, frequented nunneries, fondled courtesans, and bathed with them in broad daylight. Moreover, he enticed the wives and daughters of literati into the nunneries to discuss the dharma. They even went so far as to bring their quilts and pillows and to spend the night there. The situation was out of control.
>
> What's more, he wrote a book called *Questioning Guanyin*. But by "Guanyin" he meant the wives and daughters of literati.[41] Young men took delight in his unrestrained wildness and goaded one another on to follow suit. They knew no shame and behaved like beasts, openly stealing money and violating other people's wives and daughters.[42]

---

40. See p. 31.
41. Guanyin, or Avalokiteśvara, is a bodhisattva (enlightened being) in the Buddhist tradition. Originally male, Guanyin took female form in China, lest representations of this bodhisattva endanger the purity of women's private quarters.
42. See p. 336.

These accusations—no doubt exaggerated—testify to the conservatism of contemporary society and the resistance that Li's egalitarian views on gender sparked. (Almost two hundred years later, the poet and critic Yuan Mei would undergo a similar barrage of criticism for taking on a group of "female disciples.")

In addition to advocating women's education, Li opposed the conventional hierarchy of the Five Relationships (*wulun* 五倫) articulated in the *Doctrine of the Mean*, a core text of the traditional syllabus. Whereas the ancient text ranks the relationships in the order "ruler and subject, father and son, husband and wife, older and younger brother, friend and friend."[43] Li proposed in his essay "Discussion on Husband and Wife"[44] that the relationship between husband and wife, marked by fecundity, ought to be considered primary. After all, Li argues, "only on the basis of husband and wife can there be father and son; only on the basis of father and son can there be elder and younger brother; only on the basis of elder and younger brother can there be superior and subordinate." Thus, he declares, the conjugal relationship is the "origin of humankind." This argument unsettled contemporary readers accustomed to viewing the political interaction between ruler and subject as the primordial relationship, the pivot of all social order.

Li further interfered with widespread interpretations of the Five Relationships by granting special attention to the relationship between friends, typically regarded as the least important Confucian relationship. Here he had immediate precedent from within the radical faction of Taizhou Learning of the Heart-Mind. The social reformer He Xinyin 何心隱 (1517–1579) had left his family behind, forsaken a career, and "broke[n] with four of [the Five Relationships] to live his life among friends, teachers, and other worthy people."[45] In the same fashion, Li took the controversial stance of declaring friendship the most fundamental of all relationships. (The contradiction implicit in the fact that elsewhere in his writings he reserved that position for the relationship between husband and wife troubled him not at all and evinces the nonsystematic nature of his writings, or perhaps implies the even more revolutionary notion that the relation of husband and wife should be based on friendship.) By elevating the status of the relationship between friends, Li took a leading role in shaping an emerging discourse that was generating intense interest and passionate debate among

---

43. *Doctrine of the Mean*, ch. 20, in Legge, *The Chinese Classics*, 1:406.
44. Translated in this volume; see pp. 99–101.
45. Li Zhi, "On He Xinyin"; see p. 87.

contemporary intellectuals. The theme of friendship may have attracted such attention in this period because the nonhierarchical (or only marginally hierarchical) nature of this relationship mirrored the leveling of other hierarchies occurring throughout late-Ming society, or because it compensated for the inequalities generated by new wealth, vibrant corruption, and the collapse of the official career ladder.[46] Whatever the reason, friendship was a favorite topic among Li and his contemporaries.

Many of the entries in *A Book to Burn* and *Another Book to Burn* address friendship. Not only were a great number of the entries in these volumes—letters and poems—initially addressed to particular named friends and acquaintances, but these writings also frequently address ethical questions regarding the qualities constitutive of meaningful friendships. As the numerous and varied recipients of his letters attest, Li cultivated a wide network of friends including individuals of all walks of life: Buddhist monks, obscure townspeople, and leading scholars and literati.[47] Yet maintaining the friendships he cultivated seems to have posed challenges for Li. This was because he firmly believed that friends have the moral responsibility to remonstrate sternly with one another whenever they observe a friend straying from the ethical path.

Opinionated by nature and endowed with a notoriously prickly personality, Li did not restrict this view to the theoretical plane; he acted on it compulsively and often to his own detriment. Undoubtedly the most striking example of Li's insuppressible urge to criticize those whom he considered his friends is the series of events that took place between him and Geng Dingxiang 耿定向 (ca. 1524–1597), who rose to be imperial vice-censor-in-chief. The correspondence between these two men is translated in this volume.[48] Geng Dingxiang was the elder brother of Li's close friend Geng Dingli 耿定理 (d. 1584). Having failed the provincial examination, Dingli opted to devote himself to the study of Zen Buddhism and to cultivate his authentic moral self in accord with Wang Yangming's philosophy. Geng Dingxiang went on to pursue an illustrious career in the civil bureaucracy. Nonetheless, Dingxiang, inspired by the strength of Dingli's convictions, also developed a deep interest in Wang Yangming's thought. But Dingxiang did not embrace the notion—advocated by both Dingli and Li Zhi—that virtually

---

46. For more on the discourse on friendship in the late Ming, see Timothy Billings's introduction to Ricci, *On Friendship*. See also Martin Huang, *Friendship*.
47. See "Mr. Li's Ten Kinds of Association" and "On Friendship," pp. 135–37, 207–8.
48. See pp. 34–62.

any action grounded in moral sentiment could constitute loyalty or filiality. Rather, Dingxiang persisted in the more orthodox Confucian belief that individuals must conform to strict codes of ethical conduct corresponding to their stations in life. Li was distressed by the discrepancy between Dingxiang's professed interest in the progressive moral philosophy of Wang Yangming and his conservative belief that individuals must abide by set rules of decorum. In a series of letters that began as personal exchanges between the two men but later circulated publicly in print and attracted a wide readership, Li accused Geng of the worst kind of hypocrisy—feigning moral rectitude on the outside but secretly harboring base, self-serving desires. In these letters, Li's rhetoric mounts to a feverish pitch and in time devolves into Li's spewing venom at his sometime "friend."

Unsurprisingly, Li's compulsion to criticize Geng Dingxiang's every peccadillo annoyed the latter and caused a rupture in the men's relationship. Yet as Li poignantly points out, beneath his scathing attacks on Geng lay the sincere desire to help and improve his friend. Li clearly recognized in Geng a man of prodigious talents and abilities and was frustrated and disappointed by what he viewed as Geng's obdurate refusal to free himself from restrictive conventions and embrace a more expansive ethical attitude. But Li's inability to control his tongue and his tendency to let flow streams of hurtful criticism and hyperbolic rhetoric succeeded only in alienating Geng. The pattern of Li's developing friendships with men of ability but later becoming disillusioned with their shortcomings and heaping abuse upon them was repeated many times throughout his life. *A Book to Burn* reports the recurrent bewilderment and loneliness Li experienced as one by one his friends grew tired of his relentless faultfinding and abandoned him.

Despite Li's abrasive personality and the casualties it caused him among his friends, his writings also record a number of fruitful and beneficial interactions. Li's letters, especially, show him constantly engaged in stimulating discussions and debates on ethics and aesthetics. Among Li's interlocutors were some of the most scintillating minds of the day, including Jiao Hong 焦竑 (1540–1620) and the Yuan brothers, Yuan Zongdao 袁宗道 (1560–1600), Yuan Hongdao 袁宏道 (1568–1610), and Yuan Zhongdao 袁中道 (1570–1623). Through both face-to-face conversations and epistolary exchanges, this group of friends together created new standards of aesthetic taste that would have wide circulation in the late Ming. Rejecting the aesthetics of imitation that had dominated the literary and artistic scene for decades, these avant-garde aesthetes promoted literary and artistic forms grounded in pure, spontaneous, and uncensored emotion.

Their advocacy of artistic productions that exude emotion and express the human spirit in creative, spontaneous ways was inspired in part by the teachings of Wang Yangming. Just as Wang had maintained that ethical judgments need not comply with ancient prescriptions—they must simply be rooted in the genuine convictions of each moral actor—Li extrapolated from this concept and applied it to the realm of aesthetics. His essays "Explanation of the Childlike Heart-Mind," "Afterword to *Journeying with Companions*," and "On Miscellaneous Matters" laud works of art that spring from the author's irrepressible sentiments, burst the confines of convention, and take original, organic forms. Any piece of art or literature that cleaves too closely to established norms Li derides as formulaic. Applauding the unmediated expression of emotion, he champions writings composed in the vernacular idiom and argues that even lowbrow genres such as fiction and drama are capable of stirring powerful emotional responses. Thus, although he himself wrote exclusively in classical Chinese, the opinions he voiced perturbed the literary establishment and proclaimed a new set of aesthetic values. His theoretical statements about literature and art were adopted by many of the best in the next generation of playwrights and critics: the Yuan brothers, the playwrights Tang Xianzu 湯顯祖 (1550–1616) and Xu Wei 徐渭 (1521–1593), and the fiction commentator Jin Shengtan 金聖歎 (1608–1661).[49]

Indeed, Li has much responsibility for shaping the world of feeling realized in some of the greatest literary products of late-imperial China, among them *Mudan ting* 牡丹亭 (The peony pavilion), by Tang Xianzu, and *Honglou meng* 紅樓夢 (Dream of the red chamber), by Cao Xueqin 曹雪芹 (1715–1763) and Gao E 高鶚 (1738–1815). The years following Li's death not only witnessed the development of a cult of sentiment (*qing* 情) evident in fiction, drama, and essays but also coincided with the emergence of a robust culture of literary commentary and critique. As printed books became more affordable and easier to come by and rates of literacy rose, greater numbers of readers dared to take upon themselves the authority and the responsibility to respond in writing to the texts they read. Inspired by Li's creativity as well as by his insatiably critical spirit, they jotted down their views in increasingly pointed and personal ways. These late-Ming and early-Qing fiction and drama commentaries, some of which (as mentioned) were even

---

49. On the influence of Li Zhi's critical essays in the late Ming and afterward, see Chang and Owen, *Cambridge History*, 2:78–87, 112–13, 160, 212–13.

passed off as having been composed by Li himself, demonstrate the appeal his writing held for contemporary readers and the extent to which it shaped aesthetic discourse.

In the early years of the Qing dynasty (1644–1911) Li's works took on a new valence: they were viewed by many as symptomatic of the decadence that had led to the fall of the Ming dynasty. Gu Yanwu 顧炎武 (1613–1682) said as much in blaming Li for a late-Ming trend of mixing Confucian, Daoist, and Buddhist references in examination essays and likened Li's writing to the promiscuous behavior of which Li had been accused.[50] In the same vein, the mid-Qing scholar Wang Hong 王弘 (fl. 1788) disdainfully dubbed Li an "unbridled villain,"[51] and the Qianlong emperor attempted to suppress Li's works in the course of his literary inquisition (1772–1793). While Li's texts survived these efforts to defame or destroy them, their author's popularity nonetheless waned. Never having sought or achieved the status of a canonical author, Li sank into relative obscurity. His books languished on library shelves gathering dust and generating little scholarly discussion until they were rediscovered in the final years of the dynasty.

Chinese intellectuals of the late Qing gravitated to Li because in his writings they found corroboration for some of their own deeply held convictions. Like them, Li had advocated equality between the sexes, and like them he had attacked the Confucian bureaucracy and taken a firm stance against corrupt authority figures. The anti-Manchu activist, anarchist, and male feminist Liu Shipei 劉師培 (1884–1919) wrote, "Li's teachings and ideals are exceedingly noble, refined, and independent from conventional views."[52] Other contemporaries at the turn of the twentieth century equally praised Li's "courage" in rejecting the outmoded teachings of the School of Principle.[53]

Following the establishment of the People's Republic of China in 1949, mainland scholars continued to hail Li as an initiator of anti-Confucian and antifeudal thought and authored monographs with titles like *Li Zhi: Rebel Against Confucian Ideology* and *Li Zhi, a Herald of Antifeudalism in*

---

50. Gu Yanwu, "Kechang jin yue" [A prohibition in the examination halls], in *Rizhi lu*, 18/21b–23a; Gu Yanwu, "Li Zhi," in *Rizhi lu*, 18/28b–29b. See also Chang and Owen, *Cambridge History*, 2:158–59.
51. Wang Hong, cited in Cheng, "Continuities," 4.
52. Liu Shipei in *Guocui xuebao*, 1909 bound edition of 1905 volume, tome 7, 11/3a; cited in Cheng, "Continuities," 9n22.
53. *Guocui xuebao*, 1905 volume, tome 3, back cover; cited in Cheng, "Continuities," 11n27.

*Sixteenth-Century China.*⁵⁴ His statements reversing the unfavorable judgment on the First Emperor's utilitarian philosophy of Legalism gained him a brief vogue in the last years of the Maoist era, when "criticizing Confucianism" entailed "praising Legalism."⁵⁵ Until recently, Li remained largely unstudied outside the Sinophone world.⁵⁶ Translated only in fragments, his works remained largely inaccessible to scholars working in Western languages. This volume marks the first time that significant portions of Li's writings have been rendered into English. By making these works available in English translation, we hope that they will stimulate interest in the history of resistance in China and will dispel any misconception that premodern China was static or monolithic. Li's writings reveal beyond a doubt that some bold individuals did indeed stand up to authority; they illuminate as well the complex and polyvocal literary and philosophical world of late-Ming China.

Li's unfortunate end, which he had often predicted in essays and letters, attests to the intensity with which ideas of reform were put forth and lived in late-Ming China. Many of the thinkers he most admired had come to a premature and unjust end, just as might be expected of righteous people in an unrighteous age. He Xinyin, a member of Wang Yangming's School of the Mind movement, who was arrested for banditry after attempting to organize communities against official high-handedness and was beaten to death in prison, served as a moral beacon for Li. Li's friendship with Geng Dingxiang foundered largely over Li's accusations that Geng could have acted to save He but faltered. Many essays and letters in Li's corpus express the conviction that the pursuit of the Way must be intrinsically agonistic, pitted against the selfishness and stupidity of those who style themselves its guardians—and that it has always been so. Against those who wrote a triumphal story of China as the "transmission of the Way" (*daotong* 道統), Li pointed to moments in that history where a righteous teaching failed to be passed down, as when Confucius could only stand by and watch his favorite disciple, Yan Hui 顏回, die in poverty.⁵⁷ For someone so generally thought to be an irreducible maverick and individualist, Li displays a touching attachment to the idea of scholarly filiation: joining Confucius in bemoaning the premature death of Yan Hui and trying through tributes, obituaries, and

---

54. Wu Ze, *Rujiao pantu Li Zhuowu*; Zhu Qianzhi, *Li Zhi*.
55. Billeter, *Li Zhi*, 292–93; Hok-lam Chan, *Li Chih*.
56. Exceptions include de Bary, "Individualism"; Ray Huang, *1587*; Billeter, *Li Zhi*; Lee, *Li Zhi*.
57. On the concept of *daotong*, see Wilson, *Genealogy of the Way*.

allusions to cement his own place in the genealogy of the Taizhou school. Though the Way was seemingly doomed to fail in the present generation, a critical reading of the past might recover the point at which it had gone astray. Similarly, Li is alert to lost opportunities in convincing people to listen to the egalitarian, individualistic message that he reads into the texts of the ancients. In women, for example, he sees a neglected pool of intelligence, moral discrimination, and talent.

Unlike some philosophers, Li does not build a system. He is always responding to something—to a letter, a play script, a provocation, a quotation. He does not systematize; he seizes on chance material to strike critical sparks. A crucial term of denunciation is "fake." But how to detect falsity? How to denounce hypocrisy without showing oneself hypocritical? In no regard is he more of his age than in his rejection of it. These writings are most valuable as evidence of the way a late-Ming scholar developed a critique of his tradition in its own terms, by exploiting the inner discrepancies among its parts. The syncretism for which Li and his friend Jiao Hong are often blamed or praised—their combining of the three major traditions of China, Confucianism, Daoism, and Buddhism—is for Li not an overall principle but a strategy.[58] A confrontation with Daoist or Buddhist texts can serve to bring out the core of what Confucius must have taught and to denounce the abuses of the "Confucianism" of Li's day. The obsessive need of the administrative and familial ethos to differentiate degrees of authority breaks down in a Buddhist perspective, where the recognized "emptiness" of all phenomena and the ideal of monastic living undercut hierarchy. Again and again Li uses the traditions against one another as a way of provoking critical thought. His inability to endure hypocrisy (a constant theme) stirs him to sing the virtues of spontaneity and equality. And there his critique comes to rest.

THE TEXTS AND TRANSLATIONS

The texts translated in this volume are culled primarily from Li's two best-known collections, *A Book to Burn*, likely first published in 1590,[59] and *Another Book to Burn*, first published posthumously in 1618. The volume also

---

58. On the "Unity of the Three Teachings," see Ch'ien, *Chiao Hung*.
59. Although most scholarship dates the original publication of *A Book to Burn* to 1590, Suzuki Torao and Huang Lin argue that a likelier date of first publication is 1592; see Huang Lin, "'Fenshu' yuanben." For a defense of the 1590 publication date, see Wu Guoping, "Ye tan 'Fenshu.'"

includes a handful of pieces selected from among Li's other works, as well as two supplementary texts: a biographical sketch of Li written by the prominent contemporary literary scholar Yuan Zhongdao and the 1602 memorial denouncing Li to the throne, composed by the censor Zhang Wenda (d. 1625). These supplementary texts will round out readers' impressions of Li and provide a sense of his place in late-Ming literary and political history.

Nonetheless, our focus is on *A Book to Burn* and *Another Book to Burn*. We have chosen these texts because, in addition to being the writings on which Li's literary reputation rests, their authenticity is least in doubt. A number of pre-twentieth-century editions of Li's texts are preserved in rare book libraries throughout Asia, Europe, and the United States.[60] However, we have taken as our standard the recently published twenty-six-volume collected works of Li Zhi edited by Zhang Jianye.[61] In assembling this monumental work, Zhang and his collaborators meticulously collated the various early editions against one another and provided invaluable footnotes. Rather than replicate his labors, we have relied on Zhang's careful annotations and supplemented them whenever necessary with investigations of our own.[62]

The presentation of entries in our translation derives largely from the organization of essays, letters, and poems in Zhang's annotated editions, which, in turn, is based on the format of early editions of Li's works. While these early editions differed from one another in the number of entries included, both *A Book to Burn* and *Another Book to Burn* were, in the manner of many premodern Chinese publications, collections of miscellaneous writings loosely organized by genre. *A Book to Burn* contains six fascicles: the first two are devoted to correspondence, the third and fourth hold miscellaneous writings including treatises, discourses, prefaces, appraisals, and eulogies, the fifth lodges historical writings, and the sixth comprises poetry. A similar generic logic organizes the presentation of chapters in *Another Book to Burn*. Here again the first fascicle is reserved for letters, the second for prefaces, postfaces, and other short prose writings, the third fascicle is filled with historical jottings, the fourth with further miscellaneous prose selections, and the fifth and final fascicle is consecrated to poetry.

Within these large groupings, no discernible logic seems to govern the presentation of material. Letters are neither arranged chronologically nor

---

60. For a list of extant editions of Li Zhi's works, see Hok-lam Chan, *Li Chih*, 155–82.
61. LZQJZ.
62. Other editions we have consulted include Li Zhi, *Li Zhi wenji*, ed. Zhang Jianye and Liu Yousheng; Li Zhi, *Fenshu, Xu fenshu* (Zhongguo sixiangshi ziliao congkan series); Li Zhi, *Li Zhi sanwen xuan zhu*, ed. Zhang Fan; and Li Zhi, *Fenshu, Xu fenshu*, ed. Zhang Jianye.

clumped together by recipient or theme. Instead, the chapters present an unruly hodgepodge of facts, opinions, and impressions, which readers must sort out for themselves. In an effort to make sense of this tangled mass of material, some modern scholars have used the contents of these essays and letters as the basis for reconstructing a chronology. Thus it would have been possible for us to arrange our translations in chronological order, and we considered doing so. But for reasons aesthetic as well as historical, we decided to adhere as strictly as possible to the presentation style of early Chinese editions. Our hope is that by retaining this order, we will preserve something of the disorienting experience that Ming-dynasty readers would likely have had if they attempted to read such books as these from cover to cover.

Most likely, however, the first readers of *A Book to Burn* and *Another Book to Burn* would not have read them straight through; they would have dipped into them and set them down by turns, reading an essay here and a poem there. Reading such collections from start to finish raises many questions and may provoke both frustration and exhilaration as themes are introduced glancingly, developed and seemingly abandoned, only to recur, in sometimes distorted form, dozens of pages later. In the headnotes that precede each entry of the translation, we have attempted to guide readers across these gaps in the original texts and help them to forge connections among entries. Drawing deeply on the meticulous scholarship of Zhang Jianye and his collaborators, among others, we have pointed out in the headnotes the year and location in which each piece was written, as far as can be determined, and highlighted thematic connections among essays.[63]

Needless to say, translating these texts has raised several challenges. Li's highly ironic style and his propensity to engage in wordplay have at times left us scratching our heads, wondering what he truly meant. In such instances, we have endeavored to keep the ambiguity of the original texts and leave readers to decipher it on their own. Another challenge we faced was the dazzling internal diversity of Li's writings, which span a great range of linguistic registers. At times he employs simple diction and earthy analogies that make his philosophical ideas simple and easy to grasp, but just as frequently his writings exhibit stunning erudition and are replete with arcane classical allusions. While educated readers among Li's contemporaries would likely have been familiar with a goodly number of these

---

63. We are particularly indebted to Lin Haiquan, *Li Zhi nianpu kaolue*, and Li Zhi, *Li Zhi sanwen xuan zhu*.

allusions, our author's comprehensive knowledge of Buddhist, Daoist, and Confucian traditions makes it implausible that even adept readers of his own day would have been capable of identifying every reference. Thus various styles of translation can be envisaged. In a spirit of experiment, we have provided one text, "Tongxin shuo," in two versions: one ("Explanation of the Childlike Heart-Mind") aiming at scholarly precision, the other ("On the Childlike Mind") at fluency. Readers can imagine us assessing the trade-offs we faced among the virtues of different renditions, selection by selection.

While the collaborators on this volume have all approached these challenges from slightly different angles, our overriding goal has been to render Li's texts maximally accessible to English-language readers who will have varying degrees of familiarity with the canons of Chinese literature, history, religion, and philosophy. In the main, we have endeavored to stay as close as possible to the original but have added footnotes to provide essential historical and cultural information. Occasionally we have paraphrased the original text or added contextual information directly into the body of the text. In every case, the reason motivating these changes has been the desire to ensure comprehensibility in English.

Finally, we must acknowledge the limitations of the volume: the texts presented here represent only a portion of the contents of *A Book to Burn* and *Another Book to Burn* and a tiny fraction of Li's complete literary output. In making these selections, we had to exclude a number of worthwhile and fascinating pieces. Thus, of necessity, these translations paint only an incomplete portrait of Li Zhi. However, we hope that the partial image evoked in these pages will nonetheless convey a sense of the multifaceted, irrepressibly creative, slyly humorous, and relentlessly critical personality of our erudite and irascible author.

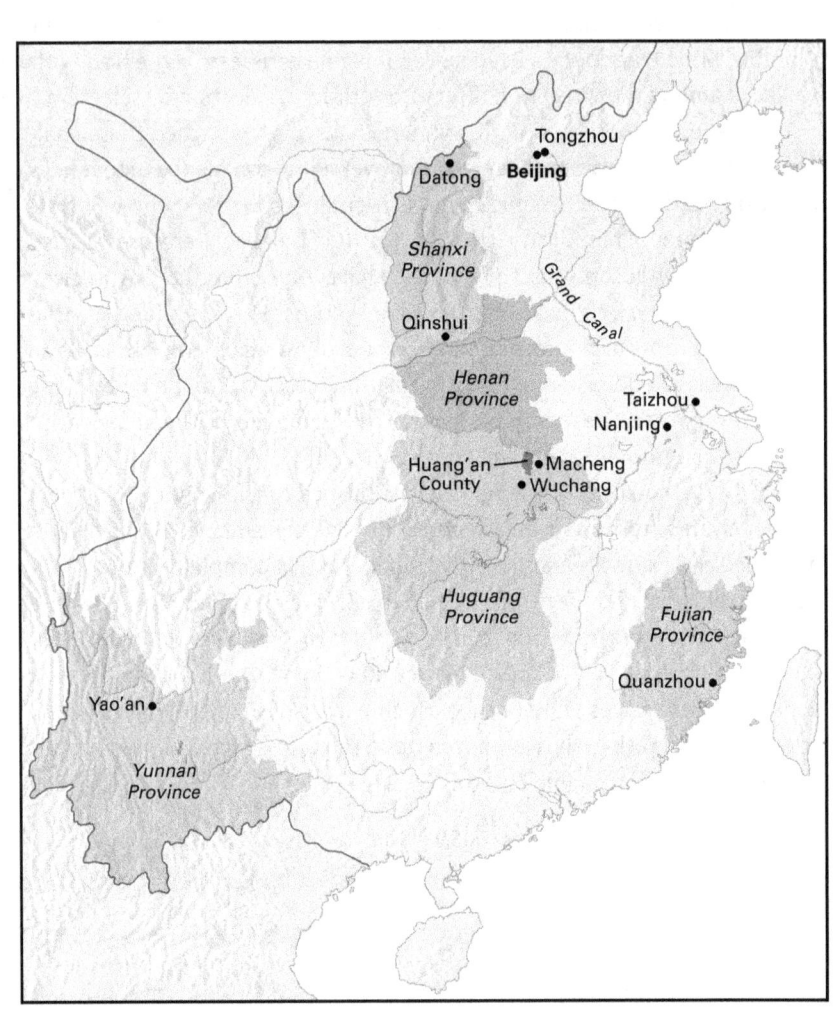

A BOOK TO
BURN
AND A BOOK TO KEEP
(HIDDEN)

SELECTIONS FROM
A BOOK TO BURN
(*FENSHU* 焚書)

PART I
PREFACES 序引

"AUTHOR'S PREFACE"
自序
"ZI XU"

The preface[1] to *A Book to Burn*, written in Macheng in 1590, encapsulates many of the salient stylistic features of Li Zhi's text: classical allusions, hyperbole, and self-contradiction, as well as many themes prominent throughout Li's writings—authenticity, friendship, and the quest for sagehood. In this short introduction, Li situates *A Book to Burn* in the context of his other literary works and explains the book's provocative title: he admits to hoping that the book be burned lest it offend readers' sensibilities. By sharing with readers his own ambivalence over the status and value of his book, Li creates an intimate bond between author and reader and challenges the reader to take a stand. His comment that readers "certainly will wish to kill me" resembles a self-confirming prophecy, for in 1602 Li Zhi was arrested on charges that his writings "threw men's minds into confusion," "disrupted the Dao," and "muddled a generation." He committed suicide in prison. (RHS)

---

1. *FS, j.* 1, in *LZQJZ* 1:1.

I have written four books. The first is called *A Book to Keep (Hidden)*. It records several thousands of years of good and bad deeds from ancient times to the present. It is not easy for common people with eyes of flesh to read, so I intended [at first] to hide it.[2] I meant for it to be hidden in a mountain to await someone of a later generation, a Ziyun to come.[3] The second book is called *A Book to Burn*; in it I reply to the questions posed by my soul friends. Its words get right to the point and criticize the intractable errors of today's scholars. Since I strike at the heart of their inveterate flaws, they certainly will wish to kill me. So I originally intended this book to be burned. I meant it to be burned and abandoned so that none of it would remain. At the back of *A Book to Burn* is an appendix called "The Suffering of Old Age."[4] Although it is part of *A Book to Burn*, I made it into a separate fascicle so that the people who want to burn my writings can burn it separately. Only *On the Four Books*, a work in forty-four chapters, truly brings delight.[5] It sheds light on the essence and inner riches of the sages and explains their applicability to everyday life. Readers who scan it will immediately understand that there is nothing difficult about becoming a sage, and nothing false about transcending the world of appearances. To be sure, writings such as commentaries and annotations exist to assist

---

2. The Buddhist term "eyes of flesh" (*rouyan* 肉眼, Skt. *māṃsacakṣus*) refers to the most mundane form of vision, which an utterly unenlightened person may possess. It represents the lowest point on a five-point scale. "Fleshy eyes" are followed by "heavenly eyes," "wisdom eyes," "dharma eyes," and finally "Buddha eyes."
3. Ziyun 子雲 refers to the philosopher Yang Xiong 揚雄 (53 B.C.E.–ca. 18 C.E.), who lived a half millennium after the time of Confucius. His *Fayan* 法言 [Model sayings] and *Taixuan* 太玄 [Ultimate mystery] are modeled on the Confucian *Analects* and the *Zhouyi*. Although Yang Xiong's reputation fell somewhat in late imperial times, Li Zhi thought highly of him and included his biography in the "Virtuous Confucian Ministers" section of *A Book to Keep (Hidden)*. Through the figure of Ziyun, Li invokes the image of an empathetic and understanding (but remote) reader. The idea of awaiting an appreciative reader has a long history; the locus classicus of this trope is the Han historian Sima Qian's declaration that he will hide his opus away in a mountain for readers of later generations to find; see his "Bao Ren An shu" 報任安書 [Letter to Ren An] in *Han shu, j.* 62; Watson, *Records: Qin Dynasty*, 236.
4. The title of this Buddhist-inspired text refers to the four types of suffering: birth, old age, illness, and death.
5. *On the Four Books* (*Shuo shu* 説書) is a collection of Li's critical essays on the *Analects*, the *Doctrine of the Mean*, the *Great Learning*, and the *Mencius* (a subset of the classics designated for special exegetical attention by Zhu Xi). These critical essays were later incorporated into Li's *Commentary on the Four Books* (*Sishu ping* 四書評). For further bibliographic information on these two texts of Li's, see Hok-lam Chan, *Li Chih*, 169–70.

people in becoming sages, but in fact they close the doors to sagehood; they do not draw people in but rather block the path. How lamentable! My *On the Four Books* says, "It was seeing my friends compose eight-legged essays that prompted to me to write *On the Four Books*.[6] So *On the Four Books* may bolster the writing of eight-legged essays, but there are plenty of pieces in it that will not have that effect."

Now *On the Four Books* has already been printed; *A Book to Burn* has also been printed; and one or two parts of *A Book to Keep (Hidden)* have been printed. What was to have been burned is no longer to be burned, and what was to have been hidden is no longer to be hidden.

Someone said, "If that's the case, it doesn't make sense to call your book *A Book to Burn*. Wouldn't using such a name produce a situation in which words and deeds no longer correspond and names can no longer be spoken?"

Alas! How would I know? And how would *you* possibly know? The reason to burn it is that [some claim] the book is grating to people's ears. The reason to print it is that [some claim] it enters people's minds. I fear that those who find my work grating to the ear will most certainly kill me. But I am sixty-four years old. If my writings should enter someone's mind, then perhaps I may find someone who understands me! I hope to be lucky enough to find even a few such people. Therefore I am letting it be printed.

TRANSLATED BY RIVI HANDLER-SPITZ

---

6. The eight-legged essay was a literary form required in writing answers to certain parts of the civil service examination and became the focus of much comparative evaluation and theory during the Ming. See the introduction, p. xxii, and "Postface to *The Prose of Our Time*," pp. 132–34.

PART II
LETTERS 書答

"IN RESPONSE TO DENG SHIYANG"
答鄧石陽
"DA DENG SHIYANG"

Written in 1585 in Macheng to Deng Lincai 鄧林材 (*juren* 1561), this letter[1] responds to Deng's advocacy of the Cheng-Zhu School of Principle. Li's focus on the corporeal, the material, and ever-changing daily bodily needs contrasts markedly with views of Cheng-Zhu neo-Confucians, who judged valuable only that which represented an immutable principle (*li* 理). For example, Cheng Yi (1033–1107), of that school, is known for remarking, "Starving to death is a small matter; losing one's chastity is a great matter." While at odds in their philosophical views, Deng and Li were close friends. In 1564 while Li was away and his wife and daughters were in the midst of a famine, Deng gave them money, keeping at least Li's wife and one daughter from starvation (see "A Sketch of Zhuowu: Written in Yunnan," pp. 75–83). (PCL)

---

1. *FS, j.* 1, in *LZQJZ* 1:8–9.

Wearing clothes and eating food constitute "human relations" [*renlun* 人倫][2] and the "principle of things" [*wuli* 物理].[3] There is nothing more to human relations and the principle of things than dressing and eating. In this world, everything is in the category of wearing clothes and eating food; if one speaks of wearing clothes and eating food, then without doubt one speaks of the various things in this world. Matters apart from wearing clothes and eating food are utterly severed from this world and separate from the lives of ordinary people. Scholars ought only to recognize the True Emptiness [*zhen kong* 真空][4] in human relations and the principle of things; they should not be creating distinctions within human relations and the principle of things. Therefore it is said [*Mencius* 4B19], "Shun had insight into the multitude of things; he scrutinized human relations." If one applies one's insight and scrutiny to the subjects of human relations and the principle of things, then one will be able to grasp what is fundamental and recognize the real source of all things. But if instead one spends all one's time bickering over speculations, in the end one will never reach the day of attaining one's own understanding.[5] Here then is the difference between focusing on "isolated details" and concentrating on work that is "easy and simple."[6] If by insight and scrutiny one perceives True Emptiness, one will naturally "act in accord with benevolence and righteousness."[7] If one does not use one's own insight and scrutinize the matter for oneself, one may outwardly appear to "walk the path of benevolence and righteousness" but

---

2. Referring to appropriate human relations between ruler and subject, father and son, husband and wife, elder and younger brother, and friends. For an early use of this term, see *Mencius* 3A4; here, the ancient virtuous and wise sage-king Shun appoints a minister to instruct the people regarding appropriate human relations.
3. A neo-Confucian term.
4. A Buddhist term.
5. On the motif of "attaining one's own understanding" (*zi de* 自得), see *Mencius* 3A4, as well as de Bary, *Learning for One's Self*, 43–70.
6. The value of "isolated details" (*zhili* 支離) and the "easy and simple" (*yijian* 易簡) was famously debated between the neo-Confucian philosophers Zhu Xi 朱熹 (1130–1200) and Lu Jiuyuan 陸九淵 (1139–1192) in a meeting in 1175 at Goose Lake Temple. On the way to the debate Lu wrote a poem capturing his views on these two concepts. The poem states, "Work that is easy and simple will in the end be lasting and great. Understanding that is devoted to isolated details will end up in aimless drifting." For a discussion of this episode, see Ching, "Goose Lake."
7. Li is quoting *Mencius* 4B19, referring to Shun.

in fact will have unwittingly entered into the search for "isolated details." How can we afford not to be cautious?

Yesterday I replied to you in regard to your composition "True Emptiness," a work consisting of sixteen characters. I have already thoroughly expressed my opinions. But now I'd like to add some comments and explanations because you requested that I correct your piece. How is that?

The phrase "emptiness cannot be emptied"[8] refers to the nature of Ultimate Emptiness; no human being can empty that. If people *could* empty it, it would not deserve to be called Ultimate Emptiness. How bizarre, then, that you wish scholars to regard "seeing one's own nature" [*jianxing* 見性][9] as the ultimate task. The phrase "what can never be emptied" refers to the fact that for every ounce of human effort one expends, one correspondingly obstructs a fraction of True Emptiness. And each obstruction of True Emptiness is like a polluting speck of dust. This speck of dust is like the fetters that bind one for a thousand kalpas. Never will one be free of it. Isn't there good reason to be fearful?

This broad and level path in this world—thousands of people together have followed it; tens of thousands together have stepped upon it. I am on this path; you, my friend, are as well. Everyone far and near is altogether here. If you continue to create distinctions in this world, wouldn't it be better for you to return to the quotidian considerations of ordinary people? Please, I hope you will ponder this!

I am old. I have written this letter in haste and it really does not adequately convey my thoughts. If you have your heart set on learning the principles of the "easy and simple" and do not wish to have spent this incarnation in vain, then I will gladly guide and correct you, even if doing so drives me to vomit up blood and spew bile. But if you persist in holding on to your contrary views and do not give thought to matters of life and death, then I beg you not to trouble yourself by offering me your "teachings"!

TRANSLATED BY PAULINE C. LEE

---

8. Zhang Jianye suggests that the quoted words in this paragraph are from Deng Shiyang's sixteen-word poem, now lost.
9. A Zen Buddhist term referring to seeing one's original nature and thereby attaining enlightenment.

"TO YANG DINGJIAN"
與楊定見
"YU YANG DINGJIAN"

Written in 1588 in Macheng.¹ Yang Dingjian was a Buddhist monk from Macheng and a devoted and favored student of Li Zhi's who, along with others, likely worked with Li Zhi on the so-called Li Zhuowu edition of the novel *Outlaws of the Marsh* (*Shuihu zhuan* 水滸傳). Yang also played a significant role in 1600: when mobs at the Cloister of the Flourishing Buddha were hounding Li Zhi, it was Yang who helped him escape to Beijing. For this Yang was arrested. (PCL)

This situation is truly not acceptable.² In this world judgments of right and wrong are countless. When people exist in a world ceaselessly debating right and wrong, how can they avoid taking sides? Take the desire to make judgments about right and wrong and add inclinations such as to ingratiate oneself to those in power, or to distance oneself from blame; you then have the general state of the petty man. This situation is not especially unusual. I don't know how many of the ancients shared their most genuine feelings with others, only to find in the end that they had fallen into a trap of their own making. The only thing to do is to have a good laugh and carry on as if nothing had happened.

Now that person³ spoke of right and wrong, and I responded and talked of right and wrong with him. We talked without stopping and our conversation developed into a contentious debate. Those who overheard us at first were not annoyed by our discussion on right and wrong. Rather, they grew weary of this heated disputation on right and wrong.

---

1. *FS, j.* 1, in *LZQJZ* 1:48–49.
2. Zhang Jianye suggests that the "situation" was the unfavorable response to Li's shaving his head in 1588, a gesture apparently signifying his taking the Buddhist tonsure.
3. The identity of this person is unknown.

The situation was clear, but buried in the midst of it we were simply unable to see it clearly.

On the one hand, I detest it when others speak of right and wrong. And yet I myself discuss right and wrong. This endless talking leads to conflict. And the endless conflicts cause me to lose my voice. Still I cry out, on and on, until my adversary becomes my enemy. Losing my voice harms my vital energy. Continuing to talk injures my body. Making enemies leads me to lose friends and family. How truly disadvantageous! In this world we live in, we do not even know how to seek one small bit of advantage for ourselves. How ever can we attain wisdom?

What's more, I abide by loyalty and righteousness when I interact with others; this is already unwise. But then, I upbraid others for turning their backs on loyalty and righteousness; this is deficiency of wisdom upon deficiency of wisdom, and foolishness followed by foolishness. If even those with only the scantiest understanding of how to care for the self do not behave in this manner, then for what reason do *I* act this way? If those with scanty understanding of what is advantageous to themselves laugh at me, shall I just sit here and allow them to ridicule me? I am constantly in this sort of situation, but when from time to time I reflect on matters and am again the master of myself, I am reluctant to allow others to take advantage of me.

You absolutely must laugh off this situation. Then you will immediately attain peace and feel settled, your spirits will be renewed, and your heart will return to its original state of openness. And anyway, whether they're studying or writing examination essays, it's only after a night of restful sleep that people are really able to show what they are capable of. If you have been losing sleep over these rumors, that is something worth sighing and feeling shame over! And the fact that people are creating a scandal and spreading rumors is not worth a sigh or a blush.

TRANSLATED BY PAULINE C. LEE

"TO ZHUANG CHUNFU"
與莊純夫
"YU ZHUANG CHUNFU"

Li Zhi wrote this letter[1] to Zhuang Chunfu, his son-in-law, in 1589, while in Macheng, after receiving news from Zhuang's cousin Rizai 日在 that Li's wife had been buried. Li's wife, née Huang, died in 1588 in her hometown of Quanzhou. Li, at that time in Macheng, did not travel back to bury her. In this letter we see Li expressing deep sorrow at his wife's death and appealing to Buddhist ideas of rebirth and karma. The situation also gives him an opportunity to condemn the hypocritical "gentlemen of the Way," whom Li compares unfavorably to his wife. (PCL)

Rizai came and told me that her burial has been completed. That is gratifying! Yes, that is gratifying! Our human lives are short—one generation, and it is over.[2] She and I lived together for over forty years; our lives were deeply intertwined. Just as we found it difficult to leave Bingzhou, having sojourned there for many years, so too do I now find it hard to be suddenly severed from her.[3] In relations between husband and wife, loving-kindness is especially profound. The relationship is not limited to the intimacies of pillow and mat; there are also conjugal advantages that derive from toil, and from economic and bodily sacrifice. Always as respectful as a guest, as sincere as a true wife,[4] filial to her parents, warm and loving with her

---

1. *FS, j.* 2, in *LZQJZ* 1:108–9. For an alternative translation, see Clara Yu, trans., "Letter to Zhuang Chunfu," in Ebrey, *Chinese Civilization*, 258–59.
2. From the common saying "Human life lasts but one generation; grass grows but one season."
3. Li echoes the phrasing of the poem "Crossing the Sangqian River," by the poet Jia Dao 賈島 (779–843), who had resided in a different Bingzhou for ten years, long enough that when it came time to leave, he felt homesickness for his acquired hometown.
4. Literally, "the sincerity of one who raises the serving plate to her eyebrows," signifying respect. The phrase refers to the *Hou Han shu* [History of the Later Han], ch. 83.

siblings, loyal to her superiors, and genuine with her friends, always sacrificing herself to benefit others, she surpassed those today who are admired as students of the Way. They possess a good reputation but lack any substance. So now that I must bid her farewell, I find it especially hard to be severed from her.

Why?

Along with her expression of loving friendship for me, she also demonstrated proper feminine comportment, engaged diligently in feminine work, exhibited appropriate feminine speech, and possessed feminine virtue,[5] which, combined, make one long for her even more: such was your mother-in-law Madame Huang. Only in intellectual matters did she not see eye to eye with me, and this is to be regretted. In every other respect, she surpassed the people of today. Even if I had a heart of stone or iron, how could I fail to be moved? How sad that we were separated from each other when on the verge of old age[6] and so were never able to bid a final farewell to one another. It is too much! Too much!

Since I learned of her death, she has appeared in my dreams every night. But in my dreams I do not know that she has died. Has she truly passed away? Or is it that I long for her, and so her soul naturally beckons to me? I recall that throughout her life she was cautious and did not easily enter a Buddhist monastery. What harm would there have been in entering a monastery? I assume she was not yet free from attachments. But once there is nothing more than soul and spirit, what is male and what is female? What is far and what is near? What are restraints and what are barriers? If we go on living as if restraints and barriers exist, then we will never even begin to free ourselves. Since spirit and soul subsist, we know that the self does not die and naturally no restraints or hindrances cling to us. Does it make sense for us to bind ourselves with our own restraints and hindrances? Once there are no restraints or barriers anymore, we find ourselves in the Western Pure Land, a world of bliss; and indeed there is no other Western Paradise but this.[7]

---

5. The four virtues important to cultivated women in Confucian society were womanly virtue, womanly speech, womanly appearance, and womanly work; see Ban Zhao 班昭 (45–ca. 116), *Nüjie* 女誡 [Instructions for women], in de Bary and Bloom, *Sources of Chinese Tradition*, 821–23.
6. In 1587 Li Zhi sent his wife and daughter back to their natal home in Quanzhou while he remained in Macheng.
7. Adherents of Pure Land Buddhism say that after death, a person who invokes the name of the bodhisattva Amitābha will be transported to the Western Pure Land, an idyllic world where one can devote oneself wholly to Buddhist practices and thereby attain enlightenment.

Chunfu, you can burn this letter and share it with the spirit of your mother-in-law so that she may know my intentions.

Do not seek the pleasures of being reborn. As soon as one is born into this world, the dusk of yet another world awaits. Do not covet the material goods of this world. As soon as one is born into the heavenly realm, one will receive sustenance and immediately forget all memories of one's previous incarnation. All rewards will be granted, karmic retribution will be fully expressed, and one will continue around the wheel of samsara reborn in the six realms of reincarnation. There will never be a time when one has exhausted one's karma [and thus attained nirvana].

In her daily life your mother-in-law comported herself as if she were in the Western Pure Land. There is no question but that she has been reborn there.

Remember my words and do not forget a single one. Even though you are now in the Pure Land, you must not forget these words for even a moment. Once I too have passed away, you will come and greet me, and we can then rely on each other and make no more mistakes.

Perhaps for the time being you can store her ashes in a hall where the name of the Buddha is recited. That would be especially wonderful. And it would be good if my lifelong companion, whom I have cherished, respected, and depended on throughout my entire life, could wait for me there. Above all, let her not seek to be reborn and live a new human life.

Chunfu, whatever you do please burn incense and paper money and earnestly recite this letter over and over several times. Repeat it to her soul until she understands the meaning of my words. Then she herself will be able to know my thoughts.

TRANSLATED BY PAULINE C. LEE

"A LETTER IN REPLY TO PROVINCIAL OFFICER LIU"
答劉方伯書
"DA LIU FANGBO SHU"

This letter,[1] written in 1591 to his friend Liu Dongxing 劉東星 (1538–1601) during Li's stay in Wuchang, contends that contemporary Confucians who desire to make a name for themselves or provide materially for their posterity are no better in the grand scheme of things than those who seek merely to fill their own bellies. Using transformations of scale reminiscent of Buddhist and Daoist thought along with gritty metaphors of food and drink inspired by the philosophy of Wang Yangming and his followers in the Taizhou school, Li highlights the unreliability of human perception and the ultimate vacuousness of all aspects of material life. The essay concludes paradoxically: that reputation has eclipsed substance, Li Zhi suggests, represents a departure from ancient values. But even in the time of Confucius, Li acknowledges, scarcely anyone was talented or insightful enough to fathom the teachings of the Sage. Implicit in these assertions is the arrogant claim that Li himself possesses such rare insight. (RHS)

It's like hunger and thirst. When hungry, of course a person will think of food; when thirsty, he will certainly yearn for drink. Has there ever been a person in this world who did not care for food and drink? If some people do not think about these matters, there is a reason: eating indiscriminately is

---

1. *FS, j. 2*, in *LZQJZ* 1:130–32. Liu Dongxing, to whom Li Zhi refers by his sobriquet, Fangbo, was an imperial censor and a close friend of Li's. He is the recipient of several letters included in *A Book to Burn*. Liu himself composed prefaces for Li's *A Book to Keep (Hidden)* and *The Shining Lamp of Records of the Antiquity of the Dao* (*Mingdeng daogu lu* 明燈道古錄). His biography is recorded in the Ming dynastic history.

their disease. Now when we consider all the sentient beings in our world, are any of them exempt from eating indiscriminately? But what is "eating indiscriminately"? People are shortsighted and their desires are pressing; they see only what affects their bodies and fail to see anything beyond their bodies. They project their desires a few dozen generations into the future, but as for what will happen several thousands of millions of generations from now, their desires do not extend that far.

Wealth and honor are what motivate the innumerable sentient beings in our world to serve their bodily needs. Since these things pertain to the body itself, it is appropriate that people regard them as matters of pressing concern. They devote their entire lives to striving for these things and labor with their hearts and minds until the end of their days to satisfy their hunger and thirst.[2] They spend their whole lives in pursuit of the food and drink they will consume in a lifetime. But people who are constitutionally greedy laugh at them and say, "How could this be enough? A man must establish for his sons and grandsons a foundation that cannot be uprooted. How can you fail to provide for them after your death?"

So people attempt to control the future; they seek to erect grave sites in elevated places and build homes in protected places, their strategy being to protect their descendants' good fortune by acquiring auspicious pieces of land. This might guarantee food and drink for ten or twenty generations. But avidity for food and drink, extended over so many generations, can satisfy the hunger and thirst of only those generations. Whether these people accumulate merit secretly or claim credit for their charitable deeds openly, they act with extreme meticulousness and care and take pains to ensure that their good deeds will extend to every corner of society. But all their endeavors stem from their craving for an endless supply of rice and tea to bequeath to their descendants.

A principled man, in turn, would laugh at these people and say, "How long could that last? How could it ever be enough? What about the things *beyond* our bodies? Exhausting the heart and mind to serve the body is not something a wise man would do, let alone exhausting the body in slaving away for one's sons and grandsons![3] A man is born into the world in order

---

2. The phrase "labor with their hearts and minds" alludes to *Mencius* 3A4, in which a distinction is made between the ruling classes, who labor with their hearts and minds, and the underclasses, who labor only with their physical bodies.
3. The phrase—literally, "to serve as a cow or horse for future generations"—alludes to the Buddhist belief in karmic retribution and the cycle of reincarnation.

to establish for himself a reputation that will not decay."[4] This type of person regards his reputation as food. And since his reputation feeds him, he hungers and thirsts for it and wears himself out trying to obtain it. But he forgets that although his reputation may last for a long time, it too will end when heaven and earth do. If heaven and earth have an end, his reputation too will have an end. How could it be eternal?

But then, those who have attained enlightenment laugh at men of principle and say, "Which is more precious, one's reputation or one's body? It is foolish enough to subordinate one's heart and mind to serving one's body, to say nothing of laboring one's mind to seek a reputation *beyond* one's body!" Obviously, one's reputation is no more precious than one's body. So why do people still say, "I fear that I will die without having left behind a name"?[5]

The malady afflicting the masses is fondness for profit. The malady afflicting men of principle is fondness for good reputation; if you don't use reputation to seduce them, your words will not penetrate their hearts. So the only way to teach them is to lead them gradually, to direct them back to reality. Once they've returned to reality, they will understand that a name is of no consequence. That's why it's said that the Master was "skilled at seduction."[6] But his pupil Yan Hui died, and that put an end to those who could truly understand the Master's skill at seduction. Thus, when Yan Hui died, the Master's method of seduction died along with him.

Alas! In the whole world, among all sentient beings, there are only shortsighted people with pressing desires; their appetites go no further than that. Are there any who have attained enlightenment? How difficult it is to make people long for what Confucius and Yan Hui ate and drank! I say that even if Confucius were to reappear on earth a thousand years from now and use his skill at seduction on such people, he would find it impossible to alter their appetites to make them correspond to what I eat and drink. So all I can do is just eat and drink alone, and sing and dance by myself. Especially since I have made my life "outside the bounds," fled the world and left the crowd behind,[7] and dare to jabber on noisily and without

---

4. The locus classicus for the concept "a reputation that will not decay" is the *Zuozhuan* (Xiang, year 24).
5. *Analects* 15.20.
6. In *Analects* 9.11 Confucius's most diligent and talented student, Yan Hui, praises the Master's skill in teaching in these terms.
7. For those who wander "outside the bounds," i.e., hermits and recluses, see *Zhuangzi*, ch. 6; Watson, *Chuang Tzu*, 86–87.

restraint, even to the point of violating conventions that are useless or downright harmful.[8]

But people today who take themselves for Confucius and want to seduce others and make followers of them are just absurd. Why? Because even Confucius had no success beyond Yan Hui. Is there anyone in the world who craves the same food as Confucius and Yan Hui, and would he eat and drink with me? I fear that even if I loaded up an entire tray with delicacies from the mountains and the sea—treats as rare as the marrow of dragons and phoenixes—and even if I knelt and presented this platter, it would be greeted with only anger, ridicule, and rejection. Even if occasionally hypocrites and flatterers lifted their chopsticks slightly, the sound of vomiting would immediately ensue. Why? Because these things are not what people eat and drink. So it would not be appropriate for me to call people over and seek to share these foods with them.

Having been born after the days of Confucius, I find scholarly discussions of no benefit whatever. Even if I had not aspired to shave off my hair and leave my family to become a monk, or to seek hermits and transcendents as my companions, I would have been compelled to do so. So is there anyone at all with whom I, born in this era, may eat and drink? No, there is truly no one at all fit to eat and drink with me.

TRANSLATED BY RIVI HANDLER-SPITZ

---

8. Li Zhi appears to be conflating accusations made against him with his own views on those accusations.

"LETTER TO A FRIEND IN THE CAPITAL"
寄京友書
"JI JING YOU SHU"

In this letter[1] written from Wuchang in 1592, Li Zhi addresses his friend the influential literary critic Yuan Zongdao. While convalescing from a severe illness, Li ruminates on Buddhist themes such as reincarnation, suffering, and the fallibility of human perception. In the final paragraph, the subject shifts abruptly from philosophical to mundane concerns. The concluding lines provide insight into Li's habit of editing and commenting on the books he read and allow us to glimpse the interactive reading culture of the late Ming. (RHS)

This autumn I had a bad case of dysentery that very nearly incapacitated me. From this I learned that having a body means suffering. This is why the Buddha Śākyamuni and the lofty immortals diligently studied the Way. Even though Śākyamuni possessed a hundred kinds of wealth and honor and could have ascended the throne of the Wheel-Turning Emperor, [he regarded such things as] unworthy of even a single contemptuous glance.[2] Instead, he considered the great calamities associated with this body that undergoes reincarnation; even a Wheel-Turning Emperor would be unable to avoid them. For this reason, he endured extreme bitterness and labored to the utmost, seeking enlightenment. Were it not for this reason, wouldn't Śākyamuni have been extremely stupid and inept to have given up wealth and easy living, renounced governmental rank, dwelt on snowcapped

---

1. *FS, j.* 2, in *LZQJZ* 1:171–72.
2. The Wheel-Turning Emperor, or Universal Monarch (*zhuanlun shengwang* 轉輪聖王, Skt. *cakravartin*), embodies the Buddhist ideals of kingship; his rule accords perfectly with the Way. It is said that had the Buddha Śākyamuni, Prince Siddhārtha Gautama (ca. 563 B.C.E.– 483 B.C.E.), not renounced the mundane world and opted to study the Way, he would have become the next Wheel-Turning Emperor. See Buswell and Lopez, *Princeton Dictionary*, 163–64.

mountains for twenty years wearing thin clothing and eating nothing but coarse grain, and sat and allowed birds to nest in his hair?! He thought studying the Way would surely bring extremes of wealth and honor such that nothing on earth could compare with them. For this reason, he devoted his whole life to seeking the Way. From the perspective of ordinary people who see only what is directly before their eyes, Śākyamuni's behavior appears extremely stupid. But the Buddha was not stupid. Today's scholars are not worthy of discussion. Some of them are highly praised as sincere and earnest, yet all day they frantically scheme to obtain profit and avoid harm. They have departed from the reality of things and cut off their faculties of perception, all in order to safeguard their "great worry of a body."[3] Do they still deserve to be called men of the Way who engage in study?

I have made corrections, excisions, and marginal notes in my copy of *The Collection of the Immortal of the Cliff*.[4] Every time I open it, I am filled with joy. This book would quicken my heart and banish the symptoms of my disease. There is no master copy left. By all means tell Shenyou[5] to return my copy to me. In general, I write only to amuse myself, not for other people.

TRANSLATED BY RIVI HANDLER-SPITZ

---

3. The word "faculties" (*gen* 根, Skt. *indriya*) refers to the sense perceptions as well as to the faculty of the mind. The phrase "great worry of a body" is borrowed from *Daodejing*, ch. 13; see *LZQJZ* 1:172nn12–13.
4. *Po xian ji* 坡仙集, by the Song literatus Su Shi 蘇軾 (1037–1101). Li Zhi annotated this text, and his friend Jiao Hong had the book printed in 1600.
5. Shenyou refers to the monk Wunian 無念, whose secular name was Xiong Shenyou 熊深有 (1544–1627). Wunian began serving as abbot of the Cloister of the Flourishing Buddha in Macheng in 1579, where he first met Li Zhi two years later, in 1581. He became Li's close companion and disciple during Li's epistolary debate with Geng Dingxiang in 1582; *LZQJZ* 1:172n15. For more on Wunian, see Rowe, *Crimson Rain*, 95, 97, 98, 115.

"THREE ESSAYS FOR TWO MONKS OF HUANG'AN"
為黃安二上人三首
"WEI HUANG'AN ER SHANGREN SAN SHOU"

These essays[1] were likely written in 1590 or 1591, after Li Zhi had moved from Huang'an to Macheng. The two monks referred to in the title are Wang Shiben 王世本, whose religious name was Ruowu 若無 (Apparent Emptiness), and Zeng Jiquan 曾繼泉, Li's student who lived with him at the Cloister of the Flourishing Buddha. The first essay blends Confucian and Buddhist discourse to extol the exemplary filiality of one of the monks. Religious syncretism was a common feature of Wang Yangming's philosophy and that of his followers in the Taizhou school, Li's intellectual lineage. The essay provides a lengthy rehearsal of this intellectual genealogy, sketches out the accomplishments of its major contributors, and ends by favorably assessing the monks' integrity and moral vision.

The second essay focuses on friendship, a theme of great moment in the late Ming, and a favorite subject among Li's contemporaries, including Matteo Ricci. Using the monks Ruowu and Zeng Jiquan as examples, Li criticizes the commonly held view that interactions with friends and teachers constitute two distinct types of relationships, each defined by its own rituals. By collapsing the categories of teacher and friend, Li demonstrates the identity of these roles and the misleading way in which language differentiates between them.

The third essay touches on Buddhist themes of cleanliness and purity. It begins with Li's humble admission that the two monks' purity far surpasses his own. Yet with a sleight of hand characteristic of Li's writings, the essay concludes by interrogating whether such purity is indeed necessary for attaining enlightenment. (RHS)

---

1. *FS, j.* 2, in *LZQJZ* 1:194–200.

"GREAT FILIAL PIETY"
大孝
"DA XIAO"

A monk of Huang'an had a loving mother who remained with her former husband's family as a widow.² Thinking again and again that he could never repay her, he cut his own flesh and made the blood flow, and with it wrote a statement declaring his intent [to be a perfectly filial son]. Moreover, he swore privately to the Buddha that he would devote his life to pursuing enlightenment in order to repay his mother's love. He considered that although keeping one's parents warm in winter and cool in summer is one way of exhibiting filiality,³ it is ultimately a lesser kind of filiality, insufficient for recompensing his mother. Even if he were to force himself to study diligently and achieve success, glory, and praise, that would only dazzle other people's eyes and ears; it would not enable him to rescue his loving mother from the sea of sorrows. Only by diligently refining his perception and attaining the Way of the Buddha could he come close to repaying her.

Compared with the emphasis that our Sage Confucius placed on repaying his parents, even the great filiality of King Wu and the Duke of Zhou—their ability to take upon themselves and further the aspirations of their parents—seems puny and insignificant.⁴ Now, as we see, our Sage's father and mother are revered even to this day, [and from this we can infer that] one cannot make good on one's obligation to repay one's mother merely by racking up a few trifling accomplishments. When the monk drew blood to write his [statement of] intent, he aimed, like [those who came before him, to demonstrate filial devotion], but as he did not dare to write down [his

---

2. Refers to Ruowu's mother, who did not remarry after her husband's death and instead dedicated her energies to raising her son. The tremendous value placed on widow chastity in the Ming period helps to explain why this young man found it so difficult to repay his mother's kindness and match her virtue. On widow chastity in late imperial China, see Mann, "Widows"; Sommer, "The Uses of Chastity."
3. The phrase "keeping one's parents warm in winter and cool in summer" comes from the *Li ji* 禮記 [Records of ritual], ch. 1; Legge, *The Li Ki*, 67. For Ming readers, the phrase would also recall the story of Huang Xiang, a filial son who took special precautions to cool his father's bedding in summer and warm it in winter. This tale is recorded in chapter 19 of the popular text *Ershisi xiao* 二十四孝 [Twenty-four tales of filial piety].
4. The *Doctrine of the Mean* (ch. 19) states, "How far-extending was the filial piety of King Wu and the Duke of Zhou [founders of the Zhou dynasty ca. 1046 B.C.E.]! Filial piety is seen in the skillful carrying out of the wishes of our forebears, and in the skillful carrying forward of their undertakings" (modified from Legge, *The Chinese Classics*, 1:402). Against this view, Li Zhi suggests that these figures actually exemplified a lesser sort of filial piety.

further purpose], one can only sigh and lament his unarticulated aspiration. So I have chosen to write his intention out for him and let it be known by all like-minded people.

When I first met him, he was still preparing for the civil service examinations. He had once told me that he was considering shaving off his hair, leaving his family, and becoming a monk. I strongly disapproved. This year when I encountered him, I saw that he had become a bald monk without a single hair on his head! Upon seeing him, I could not contain my surprise, but I realized that his intention had been sincere. For this reason, I did not dare to express myself openly, but I did occasionally hint at how I felt and let him decipher my meaning between the lines. However, he remained resolute. In the end I could not dissuade him. If today he still feels the same way, he must be a true ascetic; could anyone compare to him? So I sigh with emotion because the ancients said all people who study the Way must be heroic, spirited men. Is not this monk precisely such a heroic, spirited man?

Though the students of Wang Yangming filled the world, only Wang Gen[5] was exceedingly heroic and spirited. Wang Gen was an illiterate stove worker who didn't know even a single character. When he heard someone reading aloud, he experienced a sudden awakening. His path took him to Jiangxi province, where he met the executive censor Wang Yangming. He wanted to discuss and debate with him the nature of his enlightenment.[6] At that time, the two treated each other as friends. But later Wang Gen realized that he was not Wang Yangming's equal, so he completed his studies as his disciple. In this way, Wang Gen obtained the opportunity to hear the Dao of the sages; this shows his great integrity and moral fiber.[7]

---

5. Wang Gen, the most radical disciple of Wang Yangming, was the founder of the Taizhou school, with which Li Zhi was associated. Contending that "the streets are full of sages," he accepted students from all social classes and espoused the radical view that the Dao could be attained through participation in mundane activities. He further believed that ethical decisions should be rooted in an individual's personal sense of right and wrong, not derived from book learning or based on ancient authority. The intellectual historian Huang Zongxi 黃宗羲 (1610–1695) blamed Wang Gen for perverting Wang Yangming's philosophy and pressing it into the service of Buddhism. Li Zhi, however, greatly admired this thinker.
6. According to Wang Gen's own account, he visited Wang Yangming in 1520 in Jiangxi, at which time he debated with the teacher and raised many doubts and objections. Although Wang Gen eventually accepted Wang Yangming as his teacher, he never relinquished his critical spirit. See *LZQJZ* 1:196n15.
7. Literally, "breath and bone." These concepts refer both to an individual's inner sense of ethics and to the corresponding manifestation of these values in writing. For a discussion of this subject, see Owen, *Readings*, 218–23.

After Wang Gen came Xu Boshi 徐波石[8] and Yan Shannong 顏山農.[9] Yan Shannong wore commoners' clothes and spoke of the Dao. He possessed the kind of heroic vision that appears only once in a generation. But in the end he fell prey to slander. Xu Boshi, as provincial administration commissioner, mustered troops and supervised an assault, but he died in the southwest. "Clouds follow the dragon; wind follows the tiger; each according to its own kind."[10] This is how it is. Wang Gen was a true hero, so his disciples were heroic too. After Xu Boshi came Zhao Dazhou 趙大洲,[11] and after Zhao Dazhou came Deng Huoqu 鄧豁渠.[12] After Yan Shannong came Luo Rufang 羅汝芳[13] and He Xinyin.[14] After He Xinyin came Qian Huaisu 錢懷蘇 and Cheng Houtai 程後台.[15] One generation was nobler than the last. They say "the great ocean is not home to dead bodies and the Dragon Gate does not admit those with smashed-in heads."[16] How true! He Xinyin, dressed in commoners' clothes, stuck out his neck and promoted the Dao, but he died a violent death. Luo Rufang avoided disaster, but only by pure chance.

---

8. Xu Boshi (d. 1551) was a student of Wang Gen's who rose to the position of administration commissioner in Yunnan province. In an effort to quell a violent uprising of aborigines, Boshi fell in battle; see *MRXA*, ch. 32.
9. Yan Shannong refers to Yan Jun 鈞 (1504–1596). Yan was a student of Xu Boshi's and himself one of the leading members of the Taizhou school. Like Wang Gen, he taught students from the lower classes of society, was mistrustful of scholastic authority, and believed in following nature. In his "A Response to Zhou Liutang" (pp. 65–74), Li cites a letter from Geng Dingxiang in which Geng condemns Yan's wild antics, which included rolling around on the floor during an academic study session. Geng charges that Yan's unruly behavior provided a model that Li Zhi later imitated.
10. The commentary to "Qian," the first hexagram in the *Classic of Changes*, states, "Clouds follow the dragon; wind follows the tiger. . . . What is rooted in Heaven draws close to what is above; what is rooted in Earth draws close to what is below. Thus each thing follows its own kind" (Lynn, *The Classic of Changes*, 137).
11. Zhao Dazhou refers to Zhao Zhenji 貞吉 (1508–1576), a member of the Taizhou school.
12. Deng Huoqu (1498–1569), a member of the Taizhou school, was an itinerant teacher who cultivated a deep interest in Buddhism and studied under Zhao Dazhou. However, he later provoked Zhao's anger by adopting extreme positions. Li Zhi mentions Deng Huoqu frequently in *A Book to Burn*.
13. Luo Rufang (1515–1588) was one of the most prominent members of the Taizhou school. Li Zhi had the utmost respect for him, as is evident in the obituary Li Zhi wrote in his honor (pp. 150–57). For selected translations of texts by Luo Rufang, see Mann and Cheng, *Under Confucian Eyes*.
14. See "On He Xinyin," pp. 84–88.
15. Qian Tongwen (Huaisu) and Cheng Xueyan (Houtai) were students of He Xinyin's.
16. According to legend, every year in the third month fish would assemble in the Yellow River and attempt to leap over the Dragon Gate: those that succeeded were transformed into dragons, while those that failed smashed their heads in the effort. In late imperial times, the term "Dragon Gate" was used to refer to the examination system. Here Li Zhi implies that Wang Yangming and the rest were like fish that had successfully leapt over the gate. Or perhaps he is commiserating with those who, like He Xinyin, failed to attain official positions and were punished for their zeal. See *LZQJZ* 1:197.

In the end he lost his official position on account of Zhang Juzheng's 張居正 intolerance.[17] It seems that heroic men cannot avoid encountering bad luck, but they can make progress along the Dao. Now since this monk has made such progress along the Dao, who could surpass him? This is why I praise him as a man of great filial piety.

"TRUE TEACHERS"
真師
"ZHEN SHI"

When the two monks of Huang'an came here [to Dragon Lake], they often spoke of the importance of teachers and friends. Huailin 懷林 said, "Based on what monks generally say about teachers and friends, I think they are identical."[18] I say that teachers and friends are essentially the same. How could the two be different? But people these days do not realize that friends are precisely teachers. They only call "teacher" those to whom they have bowed four times and from whom they receive assignments. They also do not recognize that teachers are precisely friends. They only call "friend" those with whom they have a close relationship. Now if someone is your friend but you would not bow to him four times or accept assignments from him, then you really can't interact with him as a friend. And if someone is your teacher but you can't confide in him your heart's deepest feelings, then you can't serve him as a student. The ancients understood the importance of friends' attachment to one another, so they specially added the word "teacher" to "friend" to show that those who can be considered friends must also be considered teachers. He who cannot be considered a teacher cannot be considered a friend. Basically, this whole discussion can be summed up in the one word "friend." So when the word "friend" is uttered, the meaning of "teacher" is included within it.

As for these two monks, they are friends to each other and so they are teachers to each other. The older one often feared that the younger one's emotions might drag him down and that he might find it hard to extricate himself. So he took his younger brother teacher far away to strengthen his

---

17. Zhang Juzheng (1525–1582) was the powerful grand secretary who had Luo Rufang removed from office after the latter's lectures just outside the capital attracted large and unruly crowds. See *MRXA*, ch. 34. Li also blamed him for He Xinyin's death.
18. Huailin appears to have been one of the monks living at the Cloister of the Flourishing Buddha; see *LZQJZ* 1:198.

true heart and mind.[19] The younger brother teacher knew that the older brother teacher truly loved him, so he accompanied the older brother teacher far away and expressed to the Buddha his great aspirations. This shows the way in which he considered the older brother teacher both his friend and his teacher. Is it not an instance of being both teacher and friend?

The younger brother teacher feared that the older brother teacher recognized only one way of attaining the Western Paradise, joining the community of the sangha,[20] and that he did not recognize personal enlightenment. For this reason, in the presence of his older brother teacher, the younger brother teacher often spoke of his own teacher's praise of Deng Huoqu. Understanding the subtle meaning of the younger brother teacher's words, the older brother teacher came to believe that reciting the name of the Buddha was identical to practicing Zen, but merely reciting the name of the Buddha was not sufficient.[21] This is an example of the older brother teacher's treating the younger brother teacher as a friend and also as a teacher. Is it not an instance of the younger brother teacher's being both friend and teacher? This is why I say that the two exemplary men can be called true teacher-friends. What would be the point of merely drifting about, associating with the crowd? From such an experience, how could one learn the value of a teacher-friend?

For this reason, I often spoke of Deng Huoqu and traced the source of his ideas to his teacher-friends. The two monks were delighted. Although they had the honor of being descendants of Deng Huoqu, they realized, to their surprise, that they did not know Deng Huoqu's origins. Having heard my explanation, their minds were opened and they felt as if Grandfather Master Huoqu were right by their side. Since they also got the chance to hear the teachings transmitted by Wang Yangming and Wang Gen, their joy knew no bounds! But, they said, we have not heard where *your* teacher-friend is.

I said in studying, there is no constant teacher. "What did Confucius *not* study?"[22] This phrase has become a cliché, but it's nonetheless true. Although I have never bowed four times and accepted assignments from a single teacher, nor have I ever received four bows and officially taken

---

19. Literally, his "Dao heart-mind," meaning a truly selfless heart that is at one with the Dao.
20. Buddhist community of believers.
21. Whereas Pure Land Buddhism emphasizes the recitation of the Buddha's name, Zen Buddhism includes a variety of other practices, including discussing "cases" (*gong'an* 公案, Jpn. *kōan*) and sitting in meditation.
22. Citing *Analects* 19.22.

on a friend, I am so different from most people these days, who are constantly bowing four times to others or receiving four bows from others, that we cannot even be mentioned on the same day. I have inquired into this with people who have accepted four bows. These people who have accepted four bows are neither deaf nor mute, yet they told me nothing. I have also inquired widely among people who have bowed four times to others. They too are neither deaf nor mute, but they did not know how to answer me. The definition of teacher does not lie in four bows; that much is clear. But who knows whether in my heart I am constantly bowing four times or even a hundred times? I do not have enough fingers to count the number of times I have bowed, nor would grains of sand at the seashore suffice to reach such a number.[23] How could I possibly discuss my teacher-friends with the two monks?

"WASTING WORDS"
失言
"SHI YAN"

When I first met the two monks, I saw that they diligently recited the Buddha's name.[24] So, seeking advice from them, I told them that all my life I've loved loftiness and cleanliness.[25] Now having spent a long time together with them, I see that since the two monks' loftiness and cleanliness exceed mine by ten, a hundred, or even a thousand times, I had no business discussing loftiness and cleanliness with them. To speak of loftiness and cleanliness with the dejected and filthy of the world is to match the treatment to the disease. I have observed that people of this generation lack sincere aspirations; they have sunk into dejection and filth. That's why they say yes when they mean no; their words may be pure, but their actions are tainted. I have yet to encounter a single person who actually exemplifies fondness for loftiness or cleanliness, and yet people say that I am afflicted by an obsession with loftiness and cleanliness. I have meditated on this with intense sorrow.

---

23. Buddhist sutras often allude to the grains of sand along the Ganges River to indicate numbers of enormous magnitude.
24. The title phrase "Wasting Words" comes from *Analects* 15.8: "To fail to speak with someone capable of understanding is to waste human ability; to speak with a person incapable of understanding is to waste words. The wise man wastes neither human ability nor words." For related material, see "On Loftiness and Cleanliness," pp. 121–24.
25. See also "On Loftiness and Cleanliness."

How could it have been appropriate for me to speak of loftiness and cleanliness with the two monks? To speak of loftiness and cleanliness with a lofty or clean person is like trying to keep a pot from boiling while adding fuel to the fire. And how much the more so when the listener is ten times loftier and cleaner than the speaker. How stupid I was! "Overshooting the target is as bad as not reaching it."[26] Confucius discussed this in detail. To fail to advance on account of one's dejection and filth is to fall short of the mark. To be excessively fond of loftiness and cleanliness is to overshoot the mark. The Dao admits neither.

The two monks should do the following things: they should recite the Buddha's name just so, practice self-cultivation just so, and observe the prohibitions just so. By following these rules they may endure and may attain greatness; they may effortlessly ascend the Lotus Platform, experience the True Vehicle firsthand, and achieve Buddhahood. They must be wary of overindulgence. When it is time to recite the name of the Buddha, they should simply recite the name of the Buddha, and when they wish to see the loving mother, they should simply go and see the loving mother. They need not affect emotion, oppose their inner nature, obscure their own hearts, or suppress their aspirations. He who acts from the heart is a true Buddha. That's why reciting the name of the Buddha is sufficient; one need not be too lofty or clean.

TRANSLATED BY RIVI HANDLER-SPITZ

---

26. *Analects* 11.16.

"A LETTER IN RESPONSE TO THE CLAIM THAT WOMEN ARE TOO SHORTSIGHTED TO UNDERSTAND THE DAO"
答以女人學道為見短書
"DA YI NÜREN XUE DAO WEI JIANDUAN SHU"

This letter[1] expresses Li Zhi's views—radical for his time and place—on women. He begins by endorsing his interlocutor's low opinion of women's capacity for philosophical thought, citing the *Book of Rites* in support of the view that "women live within the inner chambers while men wander throughout the world." But as so often happens in Li Zhi's works, the citation is the occasion for a reversal of implications: Li concedes that women are shortsighted (*duanjian* 短見)—though not essentially but merely because their movements are restricted. In traditional China upper-class women were physically contained within the "inner chambers," rooms in the back of a family home. To Li, this cloistering of women stunts their education and blunts their insight. Women, Li argues, possess the same intellectual, moral, and spiritual capacities as men. They merely lack conditions that would enable these abilities to flourish.

Written soon after Li Zhi had shaved his head and retreated to the Cloister of the Flourishing Buddha, this letter may reflect the correspondence on scholarly topics that Li began at about this time with a number of female pupils, among them the widowed Mei Danran, daughter of Mei Guozhen (1542–1605), patriarch of one of the most affluent and socially esteemed families in Macheng. Li's relationship with Danran and other female pupils was the pretext invoked to accuse Li of immorality and lewdness, charges that played a part in the burning down of the cloister (1600) and his arrest (1602). Li's writings explicitly on women are few but influential. See also "Discussion on Husband and Wife" in this volume. (PCL)

---

1. *FS, j.* 2, in *LZQJZ* 1:143–47.

Yesterday I had the opportunity to hear your esteemed teaching wherein you proclaimed that women, being shortsighted, are incapable of understanding the Dao. Indeed this is so! Indeed this is so!

Women never cross the threshold of their reserved domain, while men wander freely throughout the world's four quarters.[2] That there exists vision that is shortsighted and vision that is farsighted is self-evident. But what is called shortsightedness comes about when one has not seen anything beyond the inner chambers. In contrast, the farsighted deeply investigate vast and open plains of light. The shortsighted perceive only what happens within a hundred-year span—what will happen in the lifespan of their children and grandchildren or what affects their own bodies. The farsighted see beyond their own physical bodies, transcend the superficial appearances of life and death, and reach into a realm that is immeasurably, incomparably large, larger than can be measured by numbers such as a hundred, a thousand, a million, a billion, or a kalpa. The shortsighted hear only the chatter in the streets, the viewpoints of those in the alleys, and the talk of children in the marketplace. The farsighted are able to hold great men in deep awe; they dare not disrespect the words of the sages, and, moreover, they are unmoved by the dislikes and prejudices that come from the mouths of commoners.[3]

I humbly propose that those who desire to discourse on shortsightedness and farsightedness should do as I have done. One must not stop at the observation that women's vision is shortsighted. To say that male and female *people* exist is acceptable. But to say that male and female *vision* exist—how can that be acceptable? To say that shortsightedness and farsightedness exist is acceptable. But to say that a man's vision is entirely farsighted and a woman's vision is wholly shortsighted, once again, how can that be acceptable?

Suppose there exists a person with a woman's body and a man's vision. Suppose she delights in hearing upright discourse and knows that uncultivated speech is not worth listening to; she delights in learning about the transcendent and understands that the ephemeral world is not worth becoming attached to. If men of today were to meet with such a woman,

---

2. Alluding to the *Li ji* [Records of ritual], ch. 12, "Neize" 內則 [Pattern of the family].
3. Quoting *Analects* 16.8.

I fear that they would all feel shame and remorse, sweat profusely, and be unable to utter a single syllable. It may have been in hopes of encountering such a person that the Sage Confucius wandered the world, desiring to meet her just once but unable to find her; and for such a person to be dismissed as a "shortsighted creature," isn't this unjust? However, why should such a person care about our treating her justly or unjustly? I suppose the disinterested observer would find the question ridiculous.

From our present perspective we can observe the following: Yi Jiang, a woman, "filled in the ranks" alongside King Wu's nine ministers. Nothing hindered her counting as one of the "ten able ministers" alongside Zhou, Shao, and Taigong.[4] King Wen's mother, a sagely woman, rectified the customs of the southern regions.[5] Nothing prevented her from being praised along with San Yisheng and Tai Dian as one of the "four friends" who helped King Wu in his difficulties.[6] These limited, mundane actions responded to the needs of the time: the concern of Kings Wu and Wen was no more than to establish one era of peace, and yet they dared not link shortsightedness with women and farsightedness with men. Those who study the transcendent Dao and desire to be like Śākyamuni and Confucius—people who, having heard the Dao in the morning, could die contentedly in the evening[7]—have even less reason to draw this distinction.

If a small-minded man in the street were to hear about women of their kind, he would scold them violently for having dared to peek out of their inner chambers, and in the name of "favoring the purity of women,"

---

4. Yi Jiang was the consort of King Wu, the founder of the Zhou dynasty, and she is sometimes said to have taken part in the council of ministers. *Analects* 8.20 records Confucius as saying, "Talent is hard to find—true, is it not? . . . [As for King Wu's ten ministers,] one was a woman, so he had only nine men" (Watson, *The Analects of Confucius*, 56–57). *The Book of Documents* refers to the "ten able ministers" of King Wu (see Legge, *The Chinese Classics*, 3:292). Dukes Zhou and Shao were brothers of King Wu who assisted in the founding of the dynasty; Taigong was a disaffected general of the Shang who came over to the Zhou. Li Zhi combines the two passages.
5. The ancient commentaries to the *Classic of Poetry* credit Tai Si, the consort of King Wen and mother of King Wu, with having given such a standard of virtuous behavior that the customs of the southern regions were "rectified."
6. King Wu was imprisoned by his sovereign, who was jealous of his subordinate's greater reputation. According to the *Zuozhuan* (Xiang, year 31), Wu's "four friends" paid a ransom to free him. The four named in *The Book of Documents* were Taigong, Nan Gongshi, San Yisheng, and Hong Yao—all male. Li Zhi may be misremembering, intentionally misquoting the passage, or relying on a different interpretation.
7. Quoting *Analects* 4.8.

consider King Wen's mother and Yi Jiang to be criminals.⁸ Isn't this unjust in the extreme? Rather, gentlemen who credit themselves with farsightedness should neither behave in such a way as to incite the ridicule of their betters nor strive to gain the approval or affection of small-minded men of the marketplace. If one desires to be admired by small-minded men of the marketplace, then one is just another such small-minded creature. Is this farsightedness, or is this shortsightedness? One needs to decide this for oneself. I say that a farsighted woman who can rectify human relations and serve as a propitious example of excellence is the sort of person who is born only once in several hundred years and comes as the result of accumulated virtue.

There once was a woman named Xue Tao who came from the city of Chang'an.⁹ Yuan Zhen¹⁰ heard about her and requested a posting in Sichuan so that he could meet her. Before Yuan Zhen's departure, Tao wrote a poem, "In Praise of Four Friends," to reciprocate his good intentions.¹¹ Yuan Zhen acknowledged her as his superior by far. Yuan Zhen was an outstanding poet in his day. Was it easy for him to acknowledge anyone as his superior? Ah! A literary talent such as Tao's can attract the admiration of people a thousand miles away. What if there were a woman wandering through this world with an understanding achieved by studying the Buddha's teachings? If one were to meet a woman who transcended this material world, could anyone possibly refuse to admire her greatly? But there has never been such a thing, you say. Have you not heard the story of Layman Pang?¹²

---

8. The phrase *kui guan* 窺觀 (peeking out [from the inner chambers]) comes from the *Classic of Changes*, hexagram 20, "Guan," second commentary, where such behavior is said to be permissible in children, tolerable in women so long as they are chaste, and reprehensible in men.
9. Xue Tao (768–ca. 831), honorary title "Lady Collator of Books," was one of the most distinguished women poets of her day and a famous courtesan of the Tang dynasty. Although born in the Tang capital of Chang'an, she spent most of her life in Sichuan. She shared her poetry with eminent poets such as Du Fu, Bai Juyi, and Yuan Zhen. For a biography and selections of her poetry, see Chang and Saussy, *Women Writers*, 59–66.
10. Yuan Zhen (779–831) was a government official, poet, and supposed author of "The Story of Yingying," much later adapted as the Yuan drama *The Story of the Western Wing* (*Xixiang ji* 西廂記). For Li Zhi's assessment of this play, see "On Miscellaneous Matters," pp. 102–5. See also "On the Childlike Mind," pp. 111–13.
11. The "Four Friends" in this instance are the four constant companions of the scholar: paper, ink, brush, and inkstone.
12. Pang Yun, often referred to as Pang Gong (ca. 740–ca. 808), turned in the middle of his life to Chan Buddhism and was said to have attained the ultimate spiritual enlightenment. His poems are found in *Pang jushi yulu* 龐居士語錄 [The recorded sayings of Layman Pang]. For an English translation, see Sasaki, Iriya, and Fraser, *Recorded Sayings*.

Layman Pang came from the city of Hengyang in the Chu region. He and his wife, Mother Pang, and their daughter, Ling Zhao, revered the Chan master Mazu[13] and made him their teacher. They sought to transcend the material world, and one day they escaped the cycle of rebirth. By putting aside the things of this world, they gave inspiration for all humanity. I hope, sir, that this man's story can stand as an example of what it is to be a far-sighted person. If you tell me, "I must wait to discuss this issue with the likes of a small-minded person from the marketplace," then I am at a loss for words.

TRANSLATED BY PAULINE C. LEE,
RIVI HANDLER-SPITZ, AND HAUN SAUSSY

---

13. Mazu (709–788), a native of Sichuan, is one of the most renowned Chan sages. For further biographical details, see Sasaki, Iriya, and Fraser, *Recorded Sayings*, 95; Poceski, *Records of Mazu*.

LI ZHI AND GENG DINGXIANG 耿定向: CORRESPONDENCE

The letter was a favorite genre for late-Ming authors. As the recipients are usually named, we can use them—as their contemporaries did—to follow the philosophical friendships and disputes of the famous. The collected exchanges of Li Zhi and Geng Dingxiang 耿定向 (1524–1596) are typical of the late-Ming fashion of including letters to named correspondents in their published works. *The Collected Writings of Mr. Geng Tiantai* 耿天台先生文集 (*Geng Tiantai xiansheng wenji*), published posthumously in 1598, includes seven letters addressed to Li Zhi, while *A Book to Burn*, which Li published eight years earlier, includes eight to Geng, with a fragmentary ninth in his posthumous *Another Book to Burn*. These letters are not direct transcripts of originals. The conventional salutations at the start and end have been omitted for publication, but beyond that, most read as either truncated or composite texts. This is particularly so with regard to Li's fifth letter, by far his longest, the first half of which I have broken up into four separate letters (5A, 5B, 5C, and 5D) on the basis of what appear to be responses in four separate letters from Geng (note that the second half of this long composite text remains untranslated). The letters are undated, so I have estimated dates in order to reconstruct the sequence and chronology of their correspondence. The numbers in brackets give their position in the sequence in which they were originally published. [TB].

"REPLY TO CENSOR GENG" [LETTER 8]
復耿中丞
"FU GENG ZHONGCHENG"

Though the space within the four seas is great, finding a friend is difficult: great men are not numerous.[1] Those who love learning are even more rare.

---

1. *FS, j.* 2, in *LZQJZ* 1:212–14. Composed in autumn 1584, this is Li's letter of condolence to Geng on the death of his brother Geng Dingli, who died on the twenty-third day of the seventh month in 1584. Li refers to him by his honorific, Ziyong. Geng left Huang'an that same

If one goes in search of someone who can pass on learning, the onus is on [the searcher] to get hold of what he has learned as though it were "within himself,"[2] so zealously that "he can experience disapproval without trouble of mind,"[3] and "who feels no discomposure though others may take no note of him."[4] Your younger brother Dingli certainly embodied those merits, but now sadly he is dead. I have made friends in all four directions[5] and had hoped to live and die in the hands of my friends but now cannot. Once I had met Dingli, I told myself that I could die without regret, but contrary to my expectation, he preceded me in death. Having written these words, how troubled I feel.

You have innocently pledged yourself to adhere to Heaven's ethics. [Your brother's death] has wounded you deeply, and I can understand that [your sorrow is so great that] you are unable to speak of it. Moreover, without seeking afar you have been able to gather like-minded friends [like your younger brother] inside your home. How could your cry of "[Heaven is] cutting me off" be empty?[6] Several times I have wanted to send you a letter offering my condolences, but my emotions were in turmoil and my mind could not calm itself. How could I dare present you with commonplace prose? Today at last I am ready. I bear in mind that the task of seeking after learning is not something that a person of "tiny capacity"[7] is able to attain. The ancients had a clear understanding that such learning is great learning, and such a man, a great man. How could an ordinary person understand a great man? In the time of Laozi, the only person who recognized him was Confucius himself. In the time of Confucius, the only person who recognized him was the one man, Yan Hui.[8] It is difficult to find a bosom friend. Was there anyone who knew Dingli while he was alive as well as I did?

---

      month to take up his post as senior censor-in-chief in Nanjing, hence Li's use of *zhongcheng*, the Han-dynasty title for censor.
2. *Mencius* 4B14; Legge, *The Chinese Classics*, 2:322.
3. Quoting Confucius's description of the man of noble character in the *Classic of Changes*, hexagram 1, "Qian"; see Legge, *The Chinese Classics*, 2:409.
4. *Doctrine of the Mean*, ch. 11; Legge, *The Chinese Classics*, 1:390. Translation modified.
5. *Mencius* 5B8; Legge, *The Chinese Classics*, 2:392, following the adaptation by Zhu Xi.
6. *Tian zhu yu* 天祝予 was Confucius's utterance of despair on the death of his prized disciple Yan Hui, according to the *Gongyang Commentary on the Spring and Autumn Annals* (Ai, year 14). See *Gongyang zhuan* 公羊傳, in Ruan, *Shisanjing zhu shu*, 28.11a.
7. The expression *genqi* 根器, used in the *Da ri jing shu* 大日經疏 [Great commentary on *The Sun Sutra*] and *Chuandeng lu* 傳灯錄 [Transmission of the lamp], expresses the Mahayana notion that people have different capacities for enlightenment.
8. *Analects* 11:6; Legge, *The Chinese Classics*, 1:239.

Alas, I can't speak of this. Having come a thousand *li* for you and your brother, I am saddened by the knowledge that you are back at court. Being now so isolated, who will mold me? To study and not to seek friends, rather than seeking friends and not devoting oneself to finding someone greater than oneself, is unbearable. You may call willingly submitting yourself to service to the realm an expression of your love of learning, but I don't believe it. You wish to become something of great use, to be a great man, all the while calling this great learning, but is this something you can achieve?

GENG TO LI [1]

Your letter inquired whether or not in my daily activities I was really able to avoid sticking to the model of the ancients and relying on principles based on what I have seen and heard from others.[9] I venture to say that the ancients had a model that altered with the age and changed in accordance with the times; and they had a model that over the thousands of years from the birth of humankind up to the present could not be changed. That is, they had principles relating to names and forms that were derived from what they saw and heard, and they had principles on which their own minds obliged them to act. This model, unchangeable over thousands of years, consists of the so-called regulations of Heaven and rules of the mind, which the ancients originally brought forth from the principles on which their minds felt obliged to act. This is not only what we are required to imitate but also what we cannot but imitate, what we cannot bear not to imitate.

Since the beginning of creation, all living creatures have been shaped and cast in this model of the ancients. They are born and nourished but perceive nothing of this in their daily activities. Yi Yin delighted in the way of Yao and Shun but was incapable of imitating their model of humble deference. Mencius devotedly learned from Confucius but was incapable of imitating his model of venerating the Zhou dynasty. Why is this? The times were different. That it is painful to be struck or hurt, or miserable to be starved or drowned, is a pattern that has existed for thousands of years. That it is calamitous to be orphaned or rulerless, or sinful to be an unruly subject or an unprincipled son, is also a pattern that has existed for thousands of years. The ancients expended great effort and thought to create a model so that you and I might have adequate shelter and be sufficient in food and

---

9. Geng, *Geng Tiantai xiansheng wenji* [1598], 4.40a–41b; written in 1585.

clothing, and they instructed us in ethics so that we might avoid being like wild animals. Being without position, Confucius and Mencius wrote tracts so that people would clearly recognize rebellious subjects and unprincipled sons, "extravagant words"[10] and extreme actions. Was there anything these sages imitated [outside themselves]? It is said: when a spring silkworm spins its cocoon, it takes its shape from the thing to which it attaches itself. This tells us that the inability to stop itself comes from its basic mind. So how could that which one's own mind feels obliged to act on really be like the "emotional affinity" that heterodox teachings go on about? "How profound and unceasing are the ordinances of Heaven!"[11] Accepting Heaven's [ordinance] not to stop was the mind of the ancients, such that though they might wish to stop, they could not. Those who don't act when they should end up stopping in all matters. Those who pursue the practice of silent self-annihilation may be capable of this, but I cannot learn from them.

I suspect that when you peruse these words of mine, you will say that I am proceeding from principles. You have never designed to comprehend this feeling in my mind of being obliged to act. I am like a mute who eats bitter melon: even he who cannot speak can have something to say. You do not embrace this commitment and are committed to leaving the world. But he who leaves the world also has a model for leaving the world. How can you bend words in this way? Admittedly I am an ignorant man. All I know is that between coming into life and leaving the world, one falls short of his duty by so much and never becomes a model himself. From what I have seen recently, study has become devalued and people's hearts are sunk into depravity. I dare not presume to measure up to the model of Confucius, yet I carry pessimistic feelings about humankind and the world.

"REPLY TO CENSOR GENG" [1]
答耿中丞
"DA GENG ZHONGCHENG"

Yesterday I received your letter in which you so penetratingly identified my errors of impetuosity and ignorance.[12] Extending and broadening the genuineness that comes from following one's own disposition and then joining with the world to fashion our common concern: only this we can call the

---

10. *Mencius* 2A2; Legge, *The Chinese Classics*, 2:191, 283.
11. *Doctrine of the Mean*, 16:10; Legge, *The Chinese Classics*, 1:421, quoting the *Classic of Poetry*.
12. *FS, j.* 1, in *LZQJZ* 1:40–41. Fragments of this letter are translated in Lee, *Li Zhi*, 85; our renderings vary slightly. Zhang Jianye proposes a date of 1584 for this letter; however, I date it to 1585.

Way. Once having desired to promote [the Way] together with this age and these people, one's success in using it to take control and straighten out what was crooked must be great.

"How can study be without a method?" These words of yours are excellent: you have taken them from Confucius and so deeply believe them that you have adopted this as the principle of your school of learning. What can I possibly say to this? Yet these are Confucius's words, not ours. When Heaven gives birth to someone, then that person naturally has the functionality of a complete person. He doesn't need to wait to be made complete by Confucius. If everyone needed to be made complete by Confucius, then wouldn't that mean that people in the time before there was Confucius ended up unable to attain personhood? Thus, as one who devotedly learned from Confucius, even Mencius got to his own level only by following Confucius.[13] I am deeply troubled by the cowardice [of this attitude], and yet you tell me to follow it blindly!

Actually Confucius never told anyone to learn from Confucius. Had Confucius really instructed others to learn from Confucius, then why, when Yan Hui asked about benevolence, did he say, "The practice of benevolence comes from oneself" and not from others?[14] Why did he say, "The scholar of ancient times acted for himself"; and also, "The gentleman seeks all from within himself"? Since it comes from oneself, Confucius's disciples of course didn't need to ask Confucius about benevolence. And since one acts for oneself, Confucius had no method to pass on to his disciples. His method depended on there being neither self nor other. To be independent of the self, the most important thing to learn is to control the self. To be independent of others, what is most important in teaching is in working with the person being taught.

Let me offer one or two examples by way of explanation. Ran Yong was a man of reverent disposition and careful practice.[15] When he asked Confucius about benevolence, Confucius pointed directly to him and said that it is nothing but reverence and generosity. Ran Yong was smart. Realizing Confucius's meaning, he requested to go into service. Sima Geng was under constant anxiety on account of his brother, which made him careful in word and cautious in deed.[16] When he asked about benevolence, Confucius

---

13. *Mencius* 2A2; Legge, *The Chinese Classics*, 2:194.
14. *Analects* 12.1; Legge, *The Chinese Classics*, 1:250.
15. *Analects* 6.1; Legge, *The Chinese Classics*, 1:184.
16. *Analects* 12.5; Legge, *The Chinese Classics*, 1:252.

pointed directly to him and said, "He is cautious and slow in his speech."[17] Sima Geng was not so smart. He doubted what he was told and felt that this was insufficient. From this perspective, when did Confucius ever teach others to learn from Confucius? Yet though Confucius never instructed anyone to learn from Confucius, those who claim to learn from Confucius are intent on setting aside their own [interests] and insist that they have to take Confucius as their object of study. Even you must find this really funny!

It is because Confucius never instructed others to learn from him that he was able to attain his purpose. He most certainly did not use himself to teach everyone in the world. For this reason, when the sage occupies the highest position, the ten thousand things find their proper places and everything follows as it should. Thus the people of this world are able to hold to their places permanently. What causes them to lose their places are when violent men trouble them and "benevolent" men harm them. When the people of the world lose their places, "benevolent" men trouble them and fuss over wanting to force them into the zone where they can find their places. Accordingly, they use virtuous conduct and ritual to restrain their minds and administration and punishments to constrain their bodies. Only then do people really begin to lose their places in a big way.

The people and things of the realm are so numerous. If you desire them all to act according to your dogma, then the world would certainly not be able to manage it. Cold can prevent glue from sticking, but it is not enough to prevent people from rushing off to the court or the market. Heat can melt metal, but it is not enough to melt the hearts of competitive people. Why is this? Wealth, honor, and success are means that satisfy the senses we were born with: the tendency of things is such that this is so. For this reason the sage accords with these, and when he accords with them, pacifies them. For this reason, those greedy for wealth he endows with emolument, and those pursuing opportunity he endows with rank; the strong he endows with authority, the capable he assigns suitable posts, and the weak he assigns tasks. The virtuous he honors with ceremonial positions so that all might regard them with respect. The talented he invests with serious responsibilities without close scrutiny of their comings and goings. If everyone pursues what he likes, everyone undertakes what he is good at, and there is not a single person who is without his function, then how easy it would be to put people to work! He might want everyone to engage in deception in order to

---

17. *Analects* 12.3; Legge, *The Chinese Classics*, 1:251.

win his favor, but suppose I have no favor to win? He might want everyone to hide his faults in order to put his own excellence on display, but suppose I have no faults to hide? How difficult then to convince people! Is this not the way of truly illuminating bright virtue for the whole world and bringing everyone to a state of eternal peace? Is this not the method of achieving a state of ease without displaying a single shred of action? If you really think Confucius's method of learning is amazing, then you could say that Confucius had a method of learning that he instructed people to follow. But if you are one of the people without a method of learning [like me], what need is there for Confucius's method?

What you deeply believe and earnestly put into practice can be said to be your method of learning, but not everyone is as you are. Whatever you do is of course good, how you put things to use is of course broadly applied, and what you study is of course apt, so of course I respect you, but I don't have to be just like you. You of course can show concern for me, but you are not necessarily any wiser than me. If this is the case, then when you go this time to the capital, everyone will flatter you on taking office. If you don't go, you may find that those who agree with you are few and those who differ from you are many, that the wise are few and the ignorant and unrighteous are many, in which case, when will there be peace in the world?

"ANOTHER REPLY TO CENSOR GENG" [2]
又答耿中丞
"YOU DA GENG ZHONGCHENG"

When the mind wants to do something, the ear doesn't have to hear it spoken by others.[18] It's not that it does not want to hear; it just doesn't. If it wants not to hear, what is better than not doing it? All you have done is to divide these off from each other.

This world is filled with so many marvelous things. How can one do them all one by one and ever finish? What binds my body to the realm is great. The gentlemen of ancient times lived peaceably at their leisure. It's not that they could not surpass others, but rather that they lacked the [motivation] even to measure up to them. Then suddenly one day because of the death of a ruler, despite living peaceably at their leisure, they made the conspicuous choice to appear. No matter how many millions there were, no one dared come forward, only such a gentleman. He briefly picks up the threads and

---

18. *FS, j.* 1, in *LZQJZ* 1:46–48; composed 1585–1586?

puts matters back in order. His work is done and yet the people do not know, and thus he far surpasses others. He is like the legendary swords Dragon Spring and Tai'a: unless you are decapitating a dragon or lopping off its horn, you don't lightly put them to the test. Trying them out on something small is of no interest; using them for a small task produces nothing special. When the right time comes, then everyone knows.

How can you bear to repeat conventional gossip and marketplace chatter? As he got to know you, Deng Huoqu set high expectations of you. In his relations with others, Huoqu values knowing their minds. If among those within the four seas who know me there was but one who cherished me, that would be enough and I wouldn't need anyone else. Looking at you today, you really weren't qualified to be Huoqu's close friend. Huoqu wanted you to lead each other beyond the corporeal realm, yet you bound him to the corporeal realm. You got argumentative disputing doctrine with Huoqu and regarded that as sufficient to honor your friendship. This is the way you responded to the profound character of your friend, who had high expectations of you. What a great error!

The judgments of ordinary people today are insufficient to affect what Huoqu values: that's the truth. Yet right from the beginning Huoqu never took the judgments of ordinary people as his own. Had he taken others' judgments as his own, Huoqu would never have acted as he did. This much is completely clear. Huoqu's doctrine was based on withdrawing from the world, so in everything he did, he conducted himself flawlessly. Your doctrine is based on being useful to the world, so it is even more apt that you let him hide himself away, shut his gate, and dwell in deep retirement. The actions of the two of you are opposite and yet your intentions complete each other. Why did you not value him on this point? I have touched upon him here because you wrote of him in your letter. Yet our arguing achieves nothing.

"SENT IN REPLY TO SENIOR CENSOR GENG" [6]
寄答耿大中丞
"JIDA GENG DA ZHONGCHENG"

Consider the discourses of two men:[19] The one is pleasant to listen to yet cannot necessarily be put entirely into practice, while the other does not

---

19. This letter (in *FS, j.* 1, in *LZQJZ* 1:103–7) was written perhaps sometime during 1585–1586; Zhang Jianye dates it to 1588. The "two men" mentioned are Zhou Youshan 周友山, given name Zhou Sijing 周思敬 (1527–1592), and Yang Qiyuan 楊起元 (1547–1599), a student of Luo Rufang and great admirer of Li Zhi.

strike the ear as pleasantly but can be entirely put into practice. Not only is he able to put it into practice, but the people can also put it into practice. Being able to put something into practice and only thereafter talk about it is what is called carrying out what beforehand has been said. Not being able to put something into practice but to talk about it first can be called "words having no respect to actions."[20] I follow only those whose doctrines I can put into practice. I follow only doctrines that others can put into practice.

To know what one can do oneself, and as well what others can do, is a case of recognizing that what is good for oneself is good for others.[21] Thus no one's self differs from the self of any other, so how could one not abandon his self? To know that others are able to do something and that one is also able to do it is a case of recognizing that what is good for others is good for oneself. Thus no others differ from oneself, so how is there anyone who cannot be followed? This is the doctrine of no others and no self, the accomplishment of "assisting in the nourishing powers [of Heaven and Earth],"[22] the purpose of aiding the era and establishing a doctrine, all of which are ultimately because of truly being able to see that what is good for oneself is the same for others. Today, not knowing the doctrine that what is good for oneself is the same for others but being single-minded in pursuing a reputation for setting aside [the interests of] oneself and pursuing [the interests of] others is a case of focusing one's intention on setting aside one's own interests. Focusing one's intention on setting aside one's own interests amounts to there being a self. Focusing one's intention on pursuing the interests of others amounts to there being others. Isn't it worse to not set aside one's own interests but teach others that you are setting aside your own interests? If you really want to set aside your own interests, then the positions of both men [Zhou and Yang] should be abandoned. Today no one is able to set aside his own interests and pursue others', so what is this incessant talk about setting aside one's own interests? Teaching people to set aside their interests when you yourself cannot

---

20. Li offers the negative corollary to the passage, "His words have respect to his actions" (*yan gu xing* 言顧行), in the *Doctrine of the Mean*, 13:4; Legge, *The Chinese Classics*, 1:395. Li's previous adage may be a variation on the phrase that follows: "His actions have respect to his words" (*xing gu yan* 行顧言).
21. This sentence alludes to Mencius's description of the sage-ruler Shun: "The great Shun had a still greater delight in what was good. He regarded virtue as the common property of himself and others, giving up his own way to follow that of others, and delighting to learn from others to practice what was good" (*Mencius* 2A8; Legge, *The Chinese Classics*, 2:205).
22. *Doctrine of the Mean*, ch. 23; Legge, *The Chinese Classics*, 1:416.

is the perversion of declaring that you are setting aside your interests and pursing others'. Setting aside his own delight in what was good and only encouraging virtue in others is not what Mencius claimed for the great sage Shun. When someone says he is setting aside his own interests, you have to pause and think about it.

He who truly sets aside his own interests does not view himself as having a self. Not viewing himself as having a self, he has no self whose interests he needs to set aside. Having no interests he needs to set aside is what can be called setting aside one's own interests. We know this is so by studying previous cases of those who knew themselves.[23] He who truly pursues the interests of others does not view others as existing. By not viewing others as existing, there is no one whose interests he needs to pursue. Having no interests he needs to set aside is what can be called setting aside his own interests. We know this is so by studying previous cases of those who knew others. To not know oneself and just talk about setting aside one's own interests, to not know others and just talk about pursuing the interests of others, it is hardly surprising that people today are miserly and set aside nothing, resolutely resisting the pursuit of anyone else's interests and instead going on and on about setting aside their own interests and pursuing those of others, for no other reason than to deceive others. Are others really being deceived? This is merely deceiving yourself. Espousing this notion rests precisely on espousing the idea of aiding the age by establishing a doctrine. The idea of aiding the age by establishing a doctrine must be preceded by the duty of being "first informed" and having "first apprehended."[24] The duty of being "first informed" and having "first apprehended" needs to be motivated by the mind that "loves to make ministers of those whom they teach."[25] For this reason, to talk endlessly about aiding the age without ever aiding one moment is equivalent to never having taken on aiding the age as one's duty. To talk endlessly about establishing a doctrine without ever

---

23. I have translated *zhiji* 知己 as "knew themselves," in contrast to the phrase *zhiren* 知人, "knew others," which Li uses four sentences later. The usual meaning of the term *zhiji* is of course someone who knows another well—i.e., an intimate friend.
24. *Mencius* 5A7; Legge, *The Chinese Classics*, 2:363, repeated at *Mencius* 5B1; Legge, *The Chinese Classics*, 2:370: "Heaven's plan in the production of mankind is this: that they who are first informed should instruct those who are later in being informed, and they who first apprehend principles should instruct those who are slower to do so. I am one of Heaven's people who have first apprehended; I will take these principles and instruct this people in them."
25. *Mencius* 2B2; Legge, *The Chinese Classics*, 2:215.

having taught one person is the same as never having taken on establishing a doctrine as one's duty. How shameful! Isn't this the opposite of what is called "being ashamed of saying too much and yet going above and beyond in one's actions"?[26] Isn't this also the opposite of what Mencius said: "When one differs from other men in not having this sense of shame, what will he have in common with them?"[27]

He who wishes to aid the age must be like Hai Rui in his sympathizing with the world: only then can he claim truly to aid the age. He who wishes to establish a doctrine must be like Yan Qing in his conduct; only then can he claim truly to establish a doctrine.[28] These two gentlemen were successful in aiding the age and establishing a doctrine without once saying that this is what they were doing; even though they did not once say that this is what they were doing, no one failed to acknowledge that they aided the age and established a doctrine. Is it permissible today to lack the accomplishment and yet elevate oneself with that title?

What is called aiding the age and establishing a doctrine is something that anyone who has received counsel and revered instruction can manage even if he is crippled, deaf, or blind. What your younger brother [Dingli] said must be taken to heart. Being able to aid the age and establish a doctrine is nothing more than doing what any deaf, blind, and crippled person can do once he has received counsel and revered instruction. So what is so remarkable about having to take on the burdens of the realm and make them your responsibility? If you don't believe that a crippled, deaf, or blind person can receive counsel and revere instruction and look elsewhere for a better case of receiving counsel and revering instruction, holding that those who study the way today are entirely devoted to their own interests and advantage and not like this, then you certainly won't end up with anything that can be called receiving counsel and revering instruction. This is a case of revering instruction and receiving counsel that would be beyond even a sage.

---

26. *Analects* 14.29; Legge, *The Chinese Classics*, 1:286: "modest in his speech but exceeds in his actions."
27. *Mencius* 7A7; Legge, *The Chinese Classics*, 2:452.
28. The official Hai Rui 海瑞 (1514–1587) was demoted many times for investigating corruption and at one point took a sixteen-year leave of absence but was reinstated and became a folk hero for his fearless honesty. Yan Qing 顏清 (1524–1590), despite his many high appointments, dressed and ate in the plainest manner, "like a servant" (according to Li Zhi in *XCS*; see *LZQJZ* 11:55–58).

GENG TO LI [LETTER 3]

In my view, he who returns to his original mind and cannot stop himself from acting, even if he desires to practice forbearance and nonaction will not be able to do so should something compel him otherwise.[29] He who returns to his original mind and cannot rest content, even if he desires to go ahead and act without hesitation will not dare to do so should something restrain him. This is a program that is simple: nothing more than striving not to lose one's own mind.[30] How can you consider this as being fettered to a teaching, as failing to attain to your lofty doctrine?[31]

"REPLY TO CENSOR GENG ON THE SUBJECT OF MILDNESS" [3]
答耿中丞論淡
"DA GENG ZHONGCHENG LUN DAN"

People of this age talk in broad daylight as though they were asleep, whereas you alone talk as though you were in broad daylight when you are sound asleep: this could be called staying constantly alert.[32] Could this be what is meant by saying that Zhou Youshan knows the principle of moral cultivation well but is ignorant of how to practice wiping and polishing? The sages of the past applied themselves to the task of wiping and polishing. What is called "wiping" has to do with scrubbing [ordinary?] consciousness, and what is called "polishing" has to do with cleaning sense perception [from the external?]. If you do not put your consciousness into action or establish your senses [in function right now], you are doing nothing [with wiping and polishing] but talking in your sleep. Even if you have little capacity for making distinctions, that is not mildness. This is not a method for staying constantly alert. Only after never getting to the point of being sated can one speak of mildness. Thus it is said, "The way of the gentleman is, appearing mild, never to become sated."[33] If there be something one covets, then certainly one will become sated and discard it, and that is not mildness. Furthermore,

---

29. Geng, *Geng Tiantai xiansheng wenji*, 4.42b–43a; written 1585–1586?
30. Geng alludes here to Mencius's statement that "the Way of learning consists in nothing other than seeking the mind that has been lost" (*Mencius* 6A11; Legge, *The Chinese Classics*, 2:414; translation modified).
31. "Lofty doctrine" (*shangcheng* 上乘) may refer to Mahayana Buddhism (*dacheng* 大乘).
32. *FS*, *j.* 1, in *LZQJZ* 1:58; composed 1585–1586? Zhang Jianye dates this letter to 1585.
33. *Doctrine of the Mean*, 33:1; Legge, *The Chinese Classics*, 1:431.

mildness is something that will sate you if you remain mild. Thus [Confucius] said, "I learn without satiety."[34] If one takes not being sated as the goal of learning and devotes oneself to study this to the point of achieving nonsatiety, then one cannot avoid a time of being sated, and that is not mildness; that is not Yu's achievement of "being discriminating and undivided" in the pursuit of the Way.[35] Discriminate and unity is achieved; be undivided and purity is attained; without discrimination there is no unity; without unity there is miscellaneity; and miscellaneity does not breed mildness.

From this can you not see how difficult it is to speak of mildness? This is why the sages of the past devoted their entire lives to the practice of seeking after learning. Lecturing and discussing, energetically carrying out what the mind has understood, to the point of giving no thought to sleeping or eating: this is mildness. Mildness is not something that can be sought after energetically through knowledge, nor is it something that can be grasped by the mind. There are reasons why it cannot be attained. Now gentlemen of this generation who tire of the ordinary invariably delight in the new, while those who disapprove of the different take no pleasure in discussing the strange. Surely someone who can open his eyes should be able to realize that if he doesn't look for what is normal, then he will find nothing strange, and if there is nothing strange, then he will not seek what is normal. Is there some separate place beyond statecraft that is withdrawal? How could the teaching of withdrawal exist somewhere apart from the business of statecraft? Thus when the accomplished man has attained vast knowledge, a glimpse of Shun yielding his power to Yu would be a sight no more remarkable than the sight of them downing three cups of wine. Eminent indeed were the undertakings of Yao and Shun, but they were no more long-lived than floating clouds in the great void.[36] It is for no other reason than taking a broad perspective. Having a broad perspective, the mind is vast; the mind being vast, nothing is lacking; and with nothing lacking, what further is there to covet? If you treat the rumors and common views of everyday life as normal and the rarely heard and fleetingly visible as strange, then strangeness and normality become two separate things, and statecraft and withdrawal, two separate states of mind. If you regard

---

34. *Analects* 7.2; Legge, *The Chinese Classics*, 1:195.
35. The legendary ruler Shun 舜 advised his successor, Yu 禹, "Be discriminating, be undivided [in the pursuit of what is right], that you may sincerely hold fast the Mean" (*Shang shu* 尚書 [Book of documents], 4:13; Legge, *The Chinese Classics*, 3:61–62).
36. "For the sage-king Yao, ceding the throne to Shun was no greater a matter than offering three cups of wine," said the Song-dynasty philosopher Shao Yong 邵雍 (1011–1077); and his contemporary Cheng Hao 程顥 (1032–1085) wondered whether "the deeds of Yao and Shun were any different from floating clouds in the sky."

Yao and Shun as being the sort who did not swig from an old jug in Three Family Village, then while you may wish to be mild, can you? And while you may wish to be free of covetousness, will you be able to manage it? This is due to nothing other than taking a narrow perspective.

What I wish is that you give up discussing the merits of wiping and polishing and speak only of the benefits of seeking after learning and taking the great path. Even less do you need to be concerned with the inveterateness of empty opinions and cumulative habits; better just to concentrate your efforts on the natural impulse to engage teachers and friends. Then, if you can achieve what Shao Yong meant when he wrote the lines, "The dark water is mild / The great sound fades away," you will achieve mildness without even trying to achieve mildness. Isn't this close to your instruction for being a person, yet you mislead with talk of "being constantly alert"?

"TO MY OLD FRIEND GENG DINGXIANG" [9]
答耿楚倜
"DA GENG CHUTONG"

Someone who can open his eyes should be able to realize that if he doesn't look for what is normal, then he will find nothing strange.[37] When the accomplished man has attained vast knowledge, a glimpse of Shun yielding his power to Yu would be a sight no more remarkable than downing three cups of wine. Eminent indeed were the undertakings of Yao and Shun, but they were no more long-lived than floating clouds in the great void. It is for no other reason than taking a long perspective.

"ANOTHER REPLY TO MY OLD FRIEND GENG DINGXIANG" [7]
復耿侗老書
"FU GENG TONG LAO SHU"

People of this age detest the ordinary and delight in the new and strange, though when speaking of what is newest and strangest in the realm, nothing can outdo the ordinary.[38] The sun and the moon are ordinary, and yet from ancient times they constantly renew themselves. Cloth and grain are

---

37. *XFS, j.* 1, in *LZQJZ* 3:143; composed sometime during 1585–1586. Here Li Zhi refers to Geng by his formal name, Chutong. As the reader will observe, this is a fragment taken from the preceding letter. Zhang Jianye dates this letter to 1585.
38. *FS, j.* 2, in *LZQJZ* 1:147–48; composed in 1585 or 1586.

ordinary, and yet when we're cold they warm us and when we're hungry they feed us. How strange is that! The new and strange are precisely within the ordinary. People of this age don't look closely but instead go off in search of the new and strange outside the ordinary. How can any of it be called new and strange? The Heavenly Maiden of Sichuan is a case in point. The masses all say she is able to know events in the future and the past, so they consider her a marvel equal to the gods. Well, what is past even I can know about—why wait for her to tell me? As for what is yet to come, there is no need to know it, so what is the point of having her expound it? Thus it is said, "The knowledgeable are free from perplexities."[39] Not perplexed by the new and strange, one cannot be troubled by disasters that have yet to come. Thus it is also said, "The benevolent are free from anxiety." Having no anxiety about the disasters yet to come, one does not seek foreknowledge or become perplexed by the new and strange. Is this not truly being able to see an advantage without hastening toward it, or see a danger without having to avoid it? It is like what Confucius said about "the determined officer never forgetting that his end may be in a ditch or a stream; the brave officer never forgetting that he may lose his head."[40] But who can measure up to that? Thus it is said, "The brave are free from fear." Only after combining the three virtues of knowledge, benevolence, and bravery can one not be bored by the ordinary or deluded by the new and strange. As for the people of this age wanting to know the future and therefore regarding the Sichuan maiden as strange and also new, how is that something to be marveled at? And why? For reason of ignorance. If ignorant, then malevolent; if malevolent, then cowardly; but really it is knowledge that is prior to benevolence and courage.

"REPLY TO JUSTICE MINISTER GENG" [5A]
答耿司寇
"DA GENG SIKOU"

Your last letter can be called true teaching on the one hand and, on the other, true friendship.[41] You wish to instruct me without knowing why, and I wish to receive your instruction without knowing why: these both could

---

39. This and the two following phrases ("The benevolent are free from anxiety," "The brave are free from fear") are taken from *Analects* 9.28; see Legge, *The Chinese Classics*, 1:225.
40. *Mencius* 3A1; Legge, *The Chinese Classics*, 2:261–62, repeated in *Mencius* 5B7; Legge, *The Chinese Classics*, 2:389–90.
41. *FS, j.* 1, in *LZQJZ*, 1:71–72; composed in 1587. Zhang Jianye dates this letter to 1586, yet Geng was not appointed minister of justice in Nanjing until the third month of 1587, where he was involved in the publication of the Wanli edition of the Ming Code.

be called the genuine impulse of compulsion to act. Things are the way they are without our knowing why.

Alas, the way of friendship has been long disrupted! Once I exaggerated by saying that in ancient times there were rulers and subjects but no friends. Indeed this is not an overstatement! The ruler, like a dragon, has reversed scales under his throat: he who goes against them will surely die. Still, there may be a rapid succession of those who choose to censure their ruler with their deaths. Why is this? The reputation got by censuring with death is something that determined gentlemen willingly gamble for. How much more gladly would they seek such great fortune without having to die for it! A mind set on avoiding harm is no match for a mind set on honor and advantage, and so they harm themselves without a second thought. How much more would they appreciate this great advantage without suffering harm! With friends it is different. Between those who have the fortune of becoming friends there is not the slightest desire for selfish benefit. Those who do not have the fortune of becoming friends will quarrel over minor matters and indulge in feuds over great affairs. Our cherished He Xinyin died because of this sort of situation, yet it is clear to all that his name was not established through dying.[42] Therefore, when I said that in ancient times there was no friendship, I should have said that there was no advantage sought. Hence it is clear that disapproving and censuring gentlemen are often seen in the relation between ruler and subject, but I have certainly never heard of them as having friends.

How fortunate that recently I have been able to present myself to you: this I value highly. And how fortunate I am to receive your instruction: for this I have longed. To have returned after all to see this place that is so important to me makes me happy and pleased. But how is it that you alone love to model yourself on Confucius, whereas I have never wished to? Your compulsion to act consists of indiscriminately loving people without addressing them individually. My compulsion to act involves finding people in the course of practicing my Way, and not treating them lightly. I suspect that these are different. Your compulsion to act amounts to the "be filial at home and deferential when abroad" teaching of *The Vocation of Younger Brothers and Sons* for those who are under fifteen years of age.[43] My compulsion to act amounts to adults over the age of fifteen understanding the

---

42. He Xinyin (1517–1579), a figure whom Li greatly respected, died in prison. Li blamed Geng for failing to intercede with Grand Secretary Zhang Juzheng on He's behalf. For Li's essay on He Xinyin, see pp. 84–88.
43. The text of the *Dizi shi* 弟子職 [The vocation of younger brothers and sons] survives in the *Guanzi*.

Great Learning and then seeking to go out and illuminate bright virtue for all people. Your compulsion to act is broad but only marginally addresses pressing problems. My compulsion to act is discriminating, directly receiving the good results of my own enlightenment. Your compulsion to act is like the rain that soaks everything, arriving without being asked; or like the local village schoolmaster who teaches schoolchildren in great numbers and gets few results despite very great efforts. My compulsion to act is like the shock of cold snow: I wait till the price is right before I sell; I am like the general who deploys his soldiers to first of all capture the king, getting great results while using little effort.

Though our methods are different, we have the same basic idea of being compelled to act. If our minds were at one, I could completely forget your theory about compulsion to act as though you had never uttered it. If you say that your compulsion is right and mine is wrong, that yours is the learning of the sages and mine is heterodox learning, then I cannot attest to your knowledge. Your compulsion to act is a case of knowing that you are not permitted to halt, but the true compulsion to act depends on really desiring not to halt. My compulsion to act is a case of not knowing that I am obliged to act. Naturally being obliged to act may not be the compulsion to act of the Sage Confucius, but I cannot attest to his knowledge either.

I fear that in this debate you are afflicted with self-righteousness. You cannot hastily assume that others take delight in this, I fear, yet you go ahead and consider yourself right and hastily claim that others are not. I am also afraid that you cannot hastily assume that your contemporaries must listen to you while "resting in your character without any doubts about yourself."[44] Furthermore, you assume that everyone else is involved in heterodox learning and laugh at them for being conversant in something that is not the orthodox tradition of Confucius and Mencius. I say that if your compulsion to act is in fact the real thing, then the compulsion to act of the people of this age is as well. If their compulsion to act is really not so, then yours also is not. This may be true of mine as well. Please tell me whether I'm right or wrong.

GENG TO LI [4]

You say that my compulsion to act amounts merely to the teaching of "be filial at home and deferential when abroad" in *The Vocation of Younger*

---

44. *Analects* 12.20; Legge, *The Chinese Classics*, 1:260.

Brothers and Sons, whereas your compulsion to act is the great man illuminating bright virtue for the whole world.[45] This is not how I understand it. Take away filial piety and deference, and what virtue is left to illuminate? I suspect that what you call illuminating virtue is watching for the evanescent principle of nonbirth from the vantage point of perfect silent self-annihilation and then saying that is bright. What I call compulsion to act is nothing other than that the minds of sons, subjects, younger brothers, and friends grasp the constant way of living.[46] As you know, twenty years ago I wiped the slate clean. As I would phrase it, I broke through that barrier.[47] I was then able to ground myself in everyday reality to cultivate [my self] and verify [my knowledge]. Only then was I able to understand Confucius's remark, "I am not equal to it" or believe that Shun "regarded virtue as the common property of himself and others."[48] You say that the great person has his own bright virtue, but no great man has surpassed Confucius or Shun. You used to quote at length from Confucius and Shun. So why do you perversely turn your back on them now?

"REPLY TO JUSTICE MINISTER GENG" [5B]
答耿司寇
"DA GENG SIKOU"

When I look at what you do, there is little to differentiate you from others.[49] Everyone is the same; I am, and you are too. From the time people come to the age of reason, morning to night they plow in order to get food, buy land in order to plant, build houses in order to find shelter, study in order to pass the examinations, hold office in order to win honor and fame, and search for propitious sites in order to provide good fortune for sons and grandsons. The daily round of tasks is done for the benefit of oneself and one's family, and not a bit for others. Yet whenever you start talking about

---

45. Geng, *Geng Tiantai xiansheng wenji*, 4.43a–b; composed in 1587.
46. In naming these four cardinal relationships (minus the bond between husband and wife), Geng is alluding to a passage in the *Doctrine of the Mean*, ch. 13; Legge, *The Chinese Classics*, 1:394.
47. Geng refers here to his disagreement with his middle brother, Dingli, and such friends as Li Zhi and Jiao Hong over the relevance of Zen Buddhism to Confucian knowledge. Geng notes this disagreement in the entry for 1566 in his memoir *Guansheng ji* 觀生記 [Contemplating my life], though I have not seen this text.
48. *Analects* 14.30; Legge, *The Chinese Classics*, 1:286; *Mencius* 2A8; Legge, *The Chinese Classics*, 2:205.
49. *FS, j.* 1, in *LZQJZ* 1:72; composed in 1587.

learning, you say, "You are for yourself alone, whereas I am for others; you are out for your own advantage, whereas I wish to benefit others. I pity my neighbors to the east who may be suffering from hunger; I regret the unbearable cold for my neighbors to the west. Some, like Confucius and Mencius, go out to teach, whereas some will have nothing to do with others: they are the slaves of self-advantage. Some may not be scrupulous in their actions but do good for others; whereas some may be perfectly proper but enjoy using Buddhist dharma to harm others." When you look at this, you may see that what you say is not necessarily what you do, and what you do is not necessarily what you say. How unlike [the maxim that] "speech should reflect action, action should reflect speech."[50] Is it right to say that this is the teaching of the Sage Confucius? As I think this over, I feel that you are not the equal of peasants in the marketplace talking about what they do. Those who do business say it is business; those who do farmwork say it is farmwork. Their talk really has substance, words that are truly virtuous, so that when others hear them, they forget their cares.

What is this "in speaking think of acting" that Confucius mentioned? He said that he himself was not capable of attaining to all the Ways of son, subject, younger brother, and friend.[51] He was not really capable; this was not false modesty. How could anyone born into this world ever exhaust these four even if they were at it all their lives? To say that you are capable is to stop and not advance. The Sage knew that these [ways] were the most difficult to execute and therefore said he was not capable. If when you are not capable you say that you are not, that is "speech that reflects action." If you say you are not capable and you really are not, that is "action that reflects one's speech." Thereby you are reliable, constant, loyal, and honest with yourself: a true sage. Ignorant of what they are not capable of, people today use these four qualities to reprimand and tutor others. Setting heavy demands on others, they take only light responsibilities on themselves. How can anyone believe them?

Sages do not demand of others that they be capable, hence all people can become sages. Accordingly, Wang Yangming said, "The streets are full of sages." The Buddha said, "Mind is Buddha, all men are Buddhas." If everyone is a sage, then sages do not distinguish different principles about

---

50. *Doctrine of the Mean*, ch. 13; Legge, *The Chinese Classics*, 1:395.
51. *Doctrine of the Mean*, ch. 13; Legge, *The Chinese Classics*, 1:394.

compulsion to act to display to others. Hence Confucius said, "I wish to do without speaking."⁵² Since everyone is a Buddha, there has never been a Buddha who has saved all living creatures. Without the phenomenon of living creatures, how can there be the phenomenon of people? Without the phenomenon of principles, how can there be the phenomenon of self? Without the phenomenon of self, I can discard myself; without the phenomenon of others, I can follow others. This is not forced, because I see myself that everyone is a Buddha, and that my goodness is the same as everyone else's. If my goodness really is the same, how can there be goodness only in myself? How can there be a good person from whom I cannot learn?

GENG TO LI [5]

"Holding to a course without doubting": this is merely "assuming the appearance of benevolence."⁵³ He who assumes the appearance of benevolence does so only from his recollection of what he knows and witnesses: this is not the genuine tradition of benevolence. As Master Cheng said, "In the end, it becomes separated into two [substance and name]." Such a man sets off in the wrong direction and holds to his course without doubting. The tradition of benevolence of Confucius and Mencius is consciously grasped from the position of being unable to stop oneself. Unable to do otherwise than "attend to other people's words and observe their countenances," one is "anxious to humble himself to others."⁵⁴ Those who are addicted to emptiness and hold on to appearances may see all the way to the ultimate absolute, but in the end they grasp merely the appearance of things. If you are done with just one glance, then where is there any doubt, and how can you bear to "humble yourself before others"? By starting from the true impulse of being obliged to act, once one thinks about being a son, subject, younger brother, or friend, one realizes by how much he falls short of his duty. "Not attaining to it in personal conduct":⁵⁵ even Confucius reproached himself on this point. How can you not doubt and not humble yourself before others?

---

52. Analects 17.19; Legge, *The Chinese Classics*, 1:326.
53. This letter was written in 1587; Geng, *Geng Tiantai xiansheng wenji*, 4.43b–44a. The quote is from Analects 12.20; Legge, *The Chinese Classics*, 1:259–60.
54. Analects 12.20; Legge, *The Chinese Classics*, 1:259–60.
55. Analects 7.32, Legge, *The Chinese Classics*, 1:206.

"REPLY TO JUSTICE MINISTER GENG" [5C]
答耿司寇
"DA GENG SIKOU"

If there is no person from whom one cannot take something good, then is there nothing good that I can give and no Way that I can speak of?[56] If this is so, then isn't the story about Zhou Youshan's not allowing the lecture too distressing? How is it that while opposing Zhou Youshan you insisted that you were making an effort on Youshan's behalf, and even protecting him? How is it that when Youshan misspoke, you still desired to shelter him? Dispensing your concern in this way is just too trifling! Your writings circulate in large luxury editions, yet you tell others they may not disseminate them. How can you be so contrary? Going over this back and forth, I think that what you give your attention to is really too twisted. Zhou Youshan did not regard himself to be at fault. If he did commit an error, he did not cover it up, yet you on the other hand did. What sort of concern are you really expressing? "The errors of the superior men of old were like eclipses of the sun and moon. All the people witnessed them, and when they had reformed them, all the people looked up to them with their former admiration. But do the superior men of the present day only persist in their errors? They go on to apologize for them likewise."[57] What do you think?

Zhou Liutang conducted his life in plain and quiet dignity and did not busy himself with [learning and government service] and for that reason did not advance far. You alone seem to think that Liutang was boastful, but how so? How is it that you felt so strongly about Liutang and yet did not wish him to advance? Zhou Youshan's love for Zhou Liutang was in his bones, whereas your love for Liutang was only skin-deep. You may not admit it, but this is well known. Liutang was like an older brother to Youshan. Youshan has other brothers and cousins besides Liutang, yet he lavished all his attention on Liutang. Liutang did not pursue a civil service career, nor is his residence or his land adjoining Youshan's, so neither of them has anything over which to dispute with each other. Youshan had no

---

56. *FS*, *j.* 1, in *LZQJZ* 1:73–74. In this letter, written in 1587, Li discusses a dispute between two brothers, Zhou Sijing 周思敬 (courtesy name Youshan 友山, d. 1597) and Zhou Sijiu 周思久 (Liutang 柳塘, 1527–1592). The Zhou lineage and the Geng lineage were closely interrelated in the politics and culture of Huang'an county; members of both groups were befriended and scathingly criticized by Li Zhi. See Rowe, *Crimson Rain*, 94–103.
57. *Mencius* 2B9; Legge, *The Chinese Classics*, 2:225.

reason to destroy Liutang in order to benefit himself; this is well known. Having not a speck of private interest, everything Youshan has said comes from his pure heart. You are certainly intelligent, so how is it that you alone were unclear about this? Even if what Youshan said was wrong, you should have compassion for Liutang and not bring trouble on him. If what Youshan said was right, you should have compassion for Liutang, who strives in daily life to accord with the correct tradition of the Confucian sages. If you are truly motivated by the obligation to act, then you should go to great lengths to point out the right way to Liutang. Liutang knows to respect and trust you; no matter what you say, he will not disagree. Matters being thus, how does this benefit Liutang? Besides, what does Liutang value more than his relationship with you? If that is the case, then Youshan's comment was a slip of the tongue. He said it merely in order to evade his responsibility as an official. As Liutang's scholastic achievement is indeed profound and not easy to detect, you should have continued to be pleased with him and would not have been troubled by his indifference to public service. Why is this? Withdrawing from the world and being unknown is not something to regret. Is this the goal of learning? I become a genius because people do not know the things I have learned: that would be pleasing. I become a sage because geniuses do not know the things I have learned: wouldn't that be even more pleasing? I become a god because the sages do not know the things I have learned: wouldn't that be more pleasing still?

In the time of Confucius, only Yan Hui understood him. Even though he had disciples like Zigong, they didn't understand him. This is truly what made him Confucius. So how can you expect Youshan to understand Liutang? And how can you know that he tried to obstruct Liutang, thereby causing Commander Liu Shouyou and his colleagues to disparage us?[58] I declare that I am not troubled by our being disparaged by others, for we disparage ourselves. No point trying to protect your name, for when will the protection ever finish? I have heard that Commander Liu is an outstanding man, but what is your purpose in urgently desiring that he lecture? How could your actions exceed in respect to Commander Liu's? If they can, please lay out these additions for me one by one. If not, can you explain why you wanted him to discuss with me this useless claptrap? I am afraid that I cannot deceive a small child, so how could I mislead a gentleman as outstanding as this?

---

58. Li refers to Commander Liu Shouyou 劉守有 as Jinwu 金吾, which is a literary term for the Embroidered Guard.

Wasn't Confucius's lecturing just the opposite? Confucius spoke bluntly of one rule for both the wise and the ignorant, without allowing for any adding or taking away. It is said that "the unicorn runs with ordinary beasts and the phoenix flies with ordinary birds" because they are "the same in kind."[59] This is also expressed by the saying "All things and I share one body." Only Confucius understood learning that stood apart from its kind, so it is interesting to note how Mencius spoke of him.[60] Still, when you examine the means by which someone can stand apart from his kind, it is in the aspect of wisdom, which is not something that can be got through strength.[61] If you do not approach this from the standpoint of its inaccessibility through effort but only try to get at it by the application of more effort, then you will have already lost the secret that even Confucius and Mencius could not hand down. What sort of thing is this, and how can it be treated so lightly when talking with others?

GENG TO LI [6]

In earlier days Zhao Dazhou said, "I care only that your eyes are bright; I do not place great value on what you do."[62] I on the other hand say: eyes are easy to open, but bones are hard to change. In assessing others, you rely on their eyes, whereas I rely entirely on their bones. In your letter you say, "The unicorn runs with ordinary beasts and the phoenix flies with ordinary birds because they are the same in kind." The reason why these two creatures are outside the category of birds and beasts is not their feathers, fur, or scales. It is because the unicorn and phoenix do what other animals cannot do, or warble more harmoniously, that they are outside the category of birds and beasts. Although monkeys are grasping, lions and tigers ferocious, and parrots and orangutans endowed with powers of speech, all these animals in the end have the bones of birds and beasts and cannot depart

---

59. *Mencius* 2A2; Legge, *The Chinese Classics*, 2:196.
60. "The sages among the people are also the same in kind. They stand out from their fellows and rise above the ordinary level, but none has been as great as Confucius" (*Mencius* 2A2; Legge, *The Chinese Classics*, 2:196; translation altered).
61. *Mencius* 5B1; Legge, *The Chinese Classics*, 2:372.
62. This letter was written in 1587; Geng, *Geng Tiantai xiansheng wenji*, 4.44a–b. Geng's relationship with the syncretic philosopher Zhao Dazhou 趙大洲 (courtesy name Zhenji 貞吉, 1508–1576) is discussed in Araki, *Chūgoku shingaku*. Li Zhi began to explore the affinities of Confucianism with Buddhism and Daoism as a result of meeting Xu Yongjian 徐用檢 (*jinshi* 1562), who invited him to attend Zhao's lectures in the capital in 1566 (*MRXA*, 14.7b; see also Billeter, *Li Zhi*, 67–68). Zhao's biography appears in *j.* 29 of the collection of laymen's biographies, *Jushi zhuan* 居士傳. Geng addressed several letters to him.

from their category. Looking from this perspective at Confucius and Mencius, we see that in lofty transcendence they are not the equals of Zhuangzi or Liezi, nor in political scheming are they the equals of Su Qin or Zhang Yi, nor in military strength the equals of Sun Wu or Wu Qi.[63] Where they do depart from their category is in the tradition of benevolence that obliged them to act. This has penetrated the world to ten thousand generations. Please consider this carefully. Is it so, or is it not?

"REPLY TO JUSTICE MINISTER GENG" [5D]
答耿司寇
"DA GENG SIKOU"

When you hear these words, you will surely think that heterodox thinkers are suitable only as teachers of young children, who might borrow the theme of "illuminating bright virtue" as an essay topic, and that there is no point propagating this doctrine of emptiness and self-annihilation to delude the people.[64] Daoist, Buddhist, and Confucian are all just names. Confucius knew that people cared for reputation, so he enticed them with his doctrine of differentiated names [i.e., Confucianism].[65] The Buddha knew that people feared death, so he terrified them with dying. Laozi knew that people were eager for life, so he drew them on with longevity. None could avoid setting up names and appearances to change those who came after them. But these were not true reality. Only Yan Hui understood this and therefore said that Confucius was "good at enticing."[66]

Am I in my actions so unlike you? You enjoy office and wealth, have a family and home, receive guests and friends, but does that make you better than me? How is it that only you should have learning enough to lecture, that only you are compelled to act? If I am the same as you, then you can forget everything you have ever said about my discarding ethics, leaving my wife and family, shaving my head, and wearing Buddhist robes. What do

---

63. Zhuangzi 莊子 and Liezi 列子 were the putative authors of two early Daoist books that described ways of transcending the narrow bounds of interest and obligation. Su Qin 蘇秦 and Zhang Yi 張儀 were political advisers during the hazardous Warring States epoch. Sun Wu 孫武 is best known as the author of the *Art of War*; Wu Qi 吳起 is the author of another ancient military treatise.
64. *FS*, *j*. 1, in *LZQJZ* 1:74; written in 1588, the year in which Li Zhi took the Buddhist tonsure.
65. It is difficult to capture in English the punning going on in this passage among "name," "reputation" (both *ming* 名), and Confucian ethics (*mingjiao* 名教).
66. *Analects* 9.10; Legge, *The Chinese Classics*, 1:220.

you think? There has never been anything in which I have not been the same as you, except for your being a high official. How can your learning be superior to mine because of your high office? If it is, then Confucius and Mencius would not have dared open their mouths!

GENG TO LI [7]

Your letter said, "Daoist, Buddhist, and Confucian are all just names.[67] Confucius knew that people cared for reputation, so he enticed them with his doctrine of differentiated names. The Buddha knew that people feared death, so he terrified them with dying. Laozi knew that people were eager for life, so he drew them in with longevity. None of them could avoid setting up names and appearances to change those who came after them." This statement has been true since the most ancient of times. Even if the three sages were to come back to life, they would all nod in agreement. But consider with what mind the three sages used these methods to entice people, and to what end they desired to do so. This is worth thinking about.

"BIDDING FAREWELL TO JUSTICE MINISTER GENG" [4]
與耿司寇告別
"YU GENG SIKOU GAOBIE"

Scholars in your new county are smart, but there are only two or three of advanced learning with whom I am able to speak.[68] To be able to speak to someone and yet not speak to him is an instance of losing a friend, but this is entirely my fault. The others were all young men, some as yet unenlightened and some lacking in purpose. As it is said, "Speaking to someone who should not be spoken to is a waste of words."[69] Although this is something of which I do not approve, I would rather waste words than lose a friend. Wasting words may be acceptable, but how can losing friends be? Human talent from ancient times has been rare. When talent is this hard to find,

---

67. Geng, *Geng Tiantai xiansheng wenji*, 4.45a; written in 1588.
68. This letter was written in 1588; *FS*, *j*. 1, in *LZQJZ* 1:66–68. Zhang Jianye dates it to 1587. The "new county" was Huang'an, formed in 1563 in large part through the efforts of Geng Dingxiang, who wanted this territory carved off from Macheng and given its own county-level jurisdiction. Twenty-five years later the locals were still calling it the new county. Geng returned to Huang'an early in 1588 to bury his brother Dingli in the second month and his wife, née Peng, who had died two years earlier, in the third, returning to Nanjing in the fifth month; see Xiamen Daxue Lishi Xi, *Li Zhi yanjiu*, 114.
69. *Analects* 15.8; Legge, *The Chinese Classics*, 1:297.

how can one not be distressed at the fortune of finding a talented person and then losing him?

Alas, as Confucius said of Yan Hui, "Now there is not such another. I have not yet heard of anyone who loves to learn as he did."[70] Confucius in his time certainly realized how hard it is to find a friend. How much harder is it today! He searched through his seventy disciples and found no one, so he turned to the crowd of three thousand. Not finding anyone there, he had no choice but to wander in all directions searching. Having looked everywhere without success, he decided to go back, sighing and saying, "Let me return! Let me return! The petty ones of my school are still in need of being shaped."[71] Confucius's being this distressed over not having friends, we can understand that those "pursuing the due medium" are not easily found.[72] An impetuous person does not follow old paths nor tread in old footprints, so he sees and knows much. He is like the phoenix flying at a great height. Who can stop him? So he does not believe that he is of the same category as ordinary birds. Even though he sees from a lofty height, if he is not practical, he will fail to "pursue the due medium." An uncompromising person "will not commit one act of unrighteousness, or put to death one innocent person."[73] Those like Yi and Qi are unshakable in their conduct. When the tiger is in the mountains, all animals quake with fear, for none dares oppose him, so he does not believe that he and all moving creatures are alike beasts. Even though he is unshakable, if he is not modest, then he cannot attain to "pursuing the due medium." Hence, [Confucius's disciple] Zeng Dian was in the end impetuous and impractical, while [another disciple,] Zeng Shen, after believing in the Way, was able to achieve modesty without wavering throughout his life.[74] This was the man Confucius found when he returned home. How distressing it would have been to lose this man!

As for those thieves of virtue, though the "sanctimoniously orthodox" passed his gate, he [i.e., Confucius] would not let them enter.[75] His rejection of them was deep-seated. How was he nonetheless able to see them as people? Today one has no choice but to take the sanctimoniously orthodox

---

70. *Analects* 6.2; Legge, *The Chinese Classics*, 1:185.
71. *Analects* 5.21; Legge, *The Chinese Classics*, 1:181.
72. *Analects* 13.21; Legge, *The Chinese Classics*, 1:272.
73. *Mencius* 2A2; Legge, *The Chinese Classics*, 2:194.
74. Zeng Dian 曾蒧 appears in *Analects* 11.26 as the disciple with the most modest ambitions; his son Zeng Shen 曾參, or Zengzi 曾子, was one of the main transmitters of Confucius's teaching to later eras.
75. *Analects* 17.13, Legge, *The Chinese Classics*, 1:324. Legge translates the phrase as "the good, careful people of the villages."

as companions, acting with loyal sincerity for the time being in the hope of bringing them to the Way. It is no surprise that they hate him, for he wastes his words. Still, what does wasting words matter? What is more troubling is the fear of losing people. If one has the tiniest bit of regret over losing someone, then he will carry this sorrow to the end of his life and die without peace. If we talk about admiring virtuous examples or liking good company, then the sanctimoniously orthodox are number one; if we talk about traveling in the Way and receiving the teachings of a thousand sages, then why bother about getting rid of the sanctimoniously orthodox?

You have traveled as an official over half the empire. The two capital cities are reservoirs of people. With all your looking and doing, have you ever found the talented person you seek? Have you sought for him and not found him? Have you even sought for him at all? None of those you have sought and found are impetuous or uncompromising. Had they been so, they would have been rejected for not being reliable, yet has there been any whose honesty matched the purity of Bo Yi? When you look at it like this, there is no way you can avoid the regret of losing someone. Bo Yi and Shu Qi were fed by the Western Earl and could not bear having their lives under King Wu's rule. When King Wen was the Western Earl, Bo Yi and Shu Qi traveled a thousand *li* to receive employment and were content to be retainers so as to serve the Shang. When his son King Wu ascended, they would rather starve to death and were unwilling to eat one grain from that earth on the grounds that King Wu had "exchanged cruelty for cruelty."[76]

Zeng Yuan said to Zeng Shen, "Your illness is critical. Hopefully at dawn we will change the bamboo mat." Zeng Shen replied, "The superior person loves others by treating them with virtue; the ordinary person loves others by indulging them. Which would I choose? To achieve correctness and then die. That is all." Zeng Yuan rose to change his mat, and before he had settled back in his place, he died.[77] How is this any different from Bo Yi's starving himself to death? Can you compare the sanctimoniously orthodox to this? Thus, studying the Way without such people will not lead to achieving the Way, and transmitting the Way without such people will prevent you from expressing the Way. There exist impetuous and uncompromising people

---

76. On the legend of Bo Yi and Shu Qi, martyrs for dynastic fidelity, see Sima Qian, *Shi ji*, ch. 61.
77. This story is from the first part of the "Tangong" 檀弓上 section of the *Li ji* [Records of ritual].

who have not heard the Way, but never has there existed anyone who could hear the Way but was not impetuous or uncompromising.

Today as I bid you farewell, I have pondered the questions of the impetuous and the uncompromising, of wasting words and losing people. What I have just written is, I think, all I can do to return my brief thanks to you. My dependents wanted to go home, and I had no choice but to send them.[78] Now I will travel in all directions as the ancients did in search of friends. Confucius looked for friends greater than himself to whom he could transmit the Way. Only when one's knowledge is greater than his teacher's is transmission possible. People like us seek friends greater than ourselves to verify the Way. This is what is meant by thrice going up to the Monastery of Dong Mountain or visiting the Mountain of Touzi nine times.[79]

GENG TO LI [2]

In your letter you use the "sanctimoniously orthodox" as evidence [for your position].[80] On careful examination, I am not convinced. I said that the model of the sanctimoniously orthodox is largely the same as "pursuing the due medium."[81] If Confucius and Mencius ridiculed these people, it is because they felt that acting in this way was insufficient for entering the way of Yao and Shun. If we give some thought to the way of Yao and Shun, what sort of a way is it? It is simply the tradition of benevolence by which these men felt a compulsion to act. It passed down to Confucius and Mencius, and their model has been visible for thousands of years. The Zen fanatics of this era neither cultivate [themselves] nor verify [their knowledge]. With twinkling eyes and laughing mouths, they declare their method subtle and mysterious. Although I do not understand their model, I have a general idea of it. I recognize that the way of Śākyamuni is certainly difficult to penetrate, yet isn't forcing it into being also the way of Yao, Shun, Confucius, and Mencius beyond credible? How is it possible for them to digest what they have heard?

In ancient times Zai Wo wanted to shorten the period of mourning. How could he bear to do this, to the point of considering returning to the world

---

78. Li sent his wife and daughter home to Fujian in 1587.
79. Li has taken this reference from the *Zhiyue lu* 指月錄 [Record of pointing at the moon], the sayings of the Song Zen Master Zonggao 宗杲 of Jingshan Monastery, Hangzhou.
80. Geng, *Geng Tiantai xiansheng wenji*, 4.41b–42b; written in 1588.
81. *Analects* 13.21; Legge, *The Chinese Classics*, 1:272.

and pursuing pleasures? Confucius answered him by saying, "If now you feel at ease, you may do it."[82] This would be to regard the matter only from the point of view of the compulsion to act. Yi Zhi thought to change the world with his way. His perspective was broad and his intentions great, but when he heard Mencius's statement about "perspiration on their foreheads," he "was thoughtful."[83] This was because he was thinking over in his mind his compulsion to act. So it is that the model of the ancients is such that it could not be changed even if a sage were to reappear. Current doctrine picks this up as a principle but commonly reduces it to karmic affinity. Doesn't this block benevolence and righteousness, mislead the age, and deceive the people?

Were I not to open my heart and speak bluntly, that would be a case of "not correcting errors and so not making the Way fully evident."[84] I hope you will think this over.

TRANSLATED BY TIMOTHY BROOK

---

82. *Analects* 17.21; Legge, *The Chinese Classics*, 1:328. After their conversation, Confucius criticized his disciple Zai Wo to those present for his lack of virtue.
83. *Mencius* 3A5; Legge, *The Chinese Classics*, 2:259–60. In a continuation of his famous passage about how people are hardwired to act when they see an infant crawling toward a well, Mencius here provides examples of what he regards as the natural human instinct of shame by way of rebutting the imputed Mohist views of Yi Zhi 夷之.
84. *Mencius* 3A5; Legge, *The Chinese Classics*, 2:257.

"TO YANG DINGJIAN"
與楊定見
"YU YANG DINGJIAN"

In 1588, Li Zhi moved to the Cloister of the Flourishing Buddha, shaved off his hair, and adopted the incongruous appearance of a "Confucian monk."[1] Three years later, he traveled with Yuan Hongdao from Dragon Lake to Wuchang to visit the scenic Yellow Crane Pavilion. Immediately upon arrival, however, he was accosted by an angry mob that accused him of "perverting the Dao and misguiding people" and promptly drove him out. This letter, written shortly after this ordeal, is addressed to Li's loyal companion Yang Dingjian, a monk from the Cloister of the Flourishing Buddha. The text alludes briefly to Li's decision to don once again the cap worn by members of the civil bureaucracy. Another letter composed in the same year declares his intention to let his hair grow back.[2]

If Li's stance on his appearance appeared conciliatory, his rhetoric remained unyielding. The letter blames Geng Dingxiang and his supporters for the attacks Li experienced and threatens that unless their behavior improves, there may be serious repercussions for the Geng family's reputation as one of the leading lineages in Macheng County.[3]

By the time this letter was written, the conflict between Geng and Li had been simmering for several years. Friction developed between the two men after the death, in 1584, of Geng Dingli, younger brother of Dingxiang and intimate friend of Li Zhi. At the time of Dingli's death, Li was residing at the Geng household in Huang'an, and Dingxiang was away serving as vice-censor-in-chief of the Censorate. Unable to supervise his own sons' education, Geng entrusted this matter to Li Zhi. Yet Dingxiang worried that Li's peculiar

---

1. *FS, j.* 2, in *LZQJZ* 1:157–58. A truncated version of this letter also appears in *XFS, j.* 1, in *LZQJZ* 3:148. For another letter to Yang, see pp. 10–11.
2. *FS, j.* 2, in *LZQJZ* 1:133–35.
3. For more on the Geng family's position in Macheng, see Rowe, *Crimson Rain*, 90–94.

thoughts and actions might lead his children astray. In this letter, Li makes clear that even in 1591 he was still in communication with Geng's eldest son, Geng Guyu, and, indirectly, with the others as well. (RHS)

People in this world who love me do not love me because I am an official. Nor do they love me because I am a monk. They love *me*. People in this world who want to kill me do not dare kill an official. Nor do they dare kill a monk. They dare kill *me*.

If nothing about me is deserving of love, then I am simply an unlovable man. But what's to stop people from loving me? If it is not acceptable for me to be killed, then surely I ought to receive the protection due a person whom Heaven will not kill. Aren't those who are trying to kill me taxing themselves unnecessarily?

The reason why I have donned an official cap is not that I am concerned lest people kill a monk. *That's* not the reason I'm wearing an official cap.

I recognize Geng Dingxiang as my senior, but he is inclined to believe what he hears. And indeed, for this reason none of the people living in his household wishes that he and I resume our previous relationship. Day and night in Wuchang they even take the lead in spreading groundless rumors about me because their basic wish is to amplify my wrongdoings. They do not realize that in doing so they are actually enhancing my fame!

I fear that the old codger does not understand that from the start he has been misled and exploited by those fellows. You must speedily relate this fact to Guyu and his brothers. Otherwise, should the situation change, Old Geng will be at fault as the prime instigator. And this could have serious implications for the Geng lineage.

As always, it does not do to get too close to people of the lesser sort. I am particularly saddened to see Old Geng so unaware. I am afraid that when he wakes up, though he may gnash his teeth, it may be too late.

When you have finished reading this letter, pass it immediately to Zhou Youshan and copy it to send directly to Guyu and his brothers.

TRANSLATED BY RIVI HANDLER-SPITZ

"A RESPONSE TO ZHOU LIUTANG"
答周柳塘
"DA ZHOU LIUTANG"

Writing in Macheng in 1588 at the height of his literary career, Li Zhi begins this convoluted letter[1] by quoting in detail a letter written by his nemesis, Geng Dingxiang. Geng's letter, not originally intended for Li's eyes, accuses Li of imitating the wild antics of the philosopher Yan Shannong (1504–1596), an influential member of the Taizhou branch of Wang Yangming's School of the Heart-Mind. Yan reputedly scandalized contemporaries when he started turning somersaults during an academic study session. Geng's letter likens Li's scandalous relationships with actors, prostitutes, and widows to Yan's putatively Zen-like and inappropriate behavior. Such insinuations foreshadow the accusations made against Li Zhi in Zhang Wenda's memorial to the throne (see pp. 334–37). Li replies with what we would call a public letter, not specifically directed to Zhou Liutang but defending his own reputation against all comers.

Among the salient themes in the letter is Li's contention that individuals of great insight can and should express themselves in unconventional ways, since doing so is often a mark of profound understanding. (RHS)

Our old friend Geng wrote a letter to Zhou[2] saying, "You once mentioned that Zhuowu consorts with prostitutes. That letter is still in my possession. But a little later you asserted that I did not catch the meaning of Zhuowu's Zen tricks. Once Yan Shannong suddenly rose from his seat in the middle of

---

1. *FS, j.* 2, in *LZQJZ* 1:218–26.
2. "Zhou" is presumably Zhou Liutang (formal name Sijiu), a native of Macheng and elder brother of Zhou Sijing. Late in life he lived at Dragon Lake and interacted with both Li Zhi and Geng Dingxiang. Geng's letter no longer exists. See *LZQJZ* 1:116n35; *LZQJZ* 1:222n2. To refer to the recipient by his family name alone, as Li does here, is odd and may indicate that this letter is designed for public consumption, hence its designation here as a "response" rather than a "reply."

an academic study session, got down on the floor, and began to do somersaults, declaring, 'Look at my innate knowledge!'³ To this day, scholars and friends have passed on this story, and Shannong has become a laughingstock. In all his sallies Li Zhi behaves just like Shannong doing somersaults. I only regret that he has expressed himself in inappropriate ways and that his sharp words have been so tactless."⁴

Geng Dingxiang also said, "When [Liu] Luqiao [劉魯橋] and several others invited County Magistrate Deng [Dingshi 鄧鼎石] to a banquet, Li Zhi engaged in some shenanigans involving a female impersonator.⁵ This was another 'Zen trick,' just like 'doing somersaults.' Presumably Li Zhi was trying to suggest that Luqiao's studies emphasized excessively strict rules for personal conduct, and he thought it was time to break free of those shackles. But Luqiao's learning originated in seeking benevolence through reverence and respect; that is the standard he upheld. When I hear of Li Zhi comporting himself in this manner, I feel only more adamant that his contemptuous and disrespectful treatment of both guests and host was a disgrace. Since he does not inspire trust but simply lashes out at people, how can he possibly enlighten them or lead them to nirvana?"

Geng Dingxiang also said, "Li Zhi has been known to drag his students along with him to whorehouses. This was another of his 'Zen tricks.'"

And Geng Dingxiang further said, "Li Zhi once led a gang of monks to a widow's house to beg for a vegetarian meal, and in the end they compelled this lady to commit the impropriety of venturing outside her curtain.⁶ Most local officials found this behavior disgraceful. Yet another 'Zen trick.' Now Confucius did meet Nanzi.⁷ But when Nanzi heard the sound of

---

3. "Innate knowledge" (*liangzhi* 良知) is Wang Yangming's term of art for the moral heart-mind.
4. The term "sharp words" (*jifeng* 機鋒) derives from Buddhist discourse and refers to a penetrating answer to a Zen riddle.
5. Luqiao refers to Liu Shishao (d. 1593), a scholar and native of Macheng. Additionally, the village of Luqiao, in Shandong province, was a hotbed of activity for students of the Taizhou school; Li Zhi, *Li Zhi sanwen xuan zhu*, 87n6. The female impersonator was a male actor who played women's roles. According to the dramatic conventions of the day, operas were performed by all-male casts. Until the middle Qing dynasty, actors and prostitutes belonged to the same category of "debased persons," and so even their presence at an official gathering might have been considered inappropriate.
6. Chaste women were supposed to remain concealed demurely within the inner chambers of the home. They might, if necessary, speak to outsiders through a curtain.
7. Confucius's meeting with Nanzi 南子, the wife of Duke Ling of Wei, is recounted briefly in *Analects* 6.28 but receives a fuller narration in Sima Qian's biography of Confucius ("Kongzi shijia" 孔子世家 [The hereditary house of Confucius], *Shi ji*, ch. 17). According to the latter source, when Confucius visited Wei, Duke Ling's alluring wife sent a message to the Sage asking him to call on her. Confucius first declined, then reluctantly accepted, claiming he did so only for the sake of propriety. For a humorous modern adaptation, see Lin Yutang, *Confucius Saw Nancy*.

Boyu's carriage, she recognized the man's worthiness. From this we can see that she was the type of person to whom one could speak without wasting words.[8] Li Zhi scorns people like me for being incapable of understanding his intentions; instead, he seeks students among women. My followers and I do not regard this behavior as disgraceful to ourselves, rather we consider Li Zhi a disgrace and his actions excessive! I fear that the woman he visited may not have been as intelligent as Nanzi, in which case his sharp words once again may have fallen wide of the mark."

I have seen this letter from Geng. In every way, he has covered up my blemishes. He deliberately described me in these extremely flattering terms in order to conceal my faults. He does not realize that throughout my life I have incurred shame precisely when I have tried to mask my unseemliness and emphasize my good qualities. People who cover over their blemishes in order to accentuate their good qualities—who descend to the point that they embody the dictum "When small-minded people are alone, there is no limit to what they will do"[9]—may claim to fool other people, but in the end they sink so low as to deceive even themselves. Luckily, I have relied on sincere friends, who have pointed out my errors as if with acupuncture needles and have spread salve on the wounds. Thanks to their help, I am beginning to gain insight into my errors. I deeply regret my past behavior and am seeking to reflect upon it. Gradually my original, true nature is coming into view. If other people call me unseemly, I dare not object. But these days I fear that I am still on the path of feigning goodness and covering over my bad deeds; I have not yet returned to my original state of wholeness and genuineness. Meanwhile our friend Geng persists in believing that I am unseemly and distorts his account so as to cover my flaws. It was not for this that I decided to study together with my friends, nor was it for this that I came ten thousand *li* to seek counsel. When I consider the care with which he criticizes me, I know that he is not disloyal or insincere; rather, my disease is incurable.

---

8. According to legend, Nanzi was sitting up at night with her husband. Outside, they heard a carriage approach, then stop. Nanzi surmised that the rider must be Qu Boyu, since only he would be courteous enough to dismount when passing the home of a superior. Scholars have questioned whether the wife of the Duke of Wei recorded in this anecdote is truly the same Nanzi referred to in the *Analects*, but Li Zhi treats them as the same person; see *Lienü zhuan* 列女傳, ch. 3.7; Kinney, *Exemplary Women*, 52–53, esp. n. 45. In *Analects* 15.8, Confucius declares that to speak with someone who is unable to understand amounts to wasting words, but not to speak with someone who is able to listen amounts to wasting a human being.
9. Li Zhi slightly misquotes the *Great Learning*, ch. 6: "When small-minded men are alone, they do no good; there is no limit to what they will do." For an alternative translation, see Legge, *The Chinese Classics*, 1:366.

What he calls "blemishes" are considered so from the perspective of common custom. Whatever vulgar people consider a blemish, everyone collectively considers unseemly. Whatever vulgar people deem beautiful, everyone deems exquisite. But common custom cannot truly distinguish the unseemly from the beautiful; it depends on what one has become accustomed to seeing and hearing. When what we have heard and seen governs us from within, our conceptions of what is unseemly and beautiful become fixed to external standards: they stick like glue and cannot be dissolved.[10] Thus even a wise person would not be able to break the mental habit of pointing to a "this" or a "that"—let alone a person as stupid, stubborn, and worthless as I am![11] Vulgar people may be of the confirmed opinion that these distinctions exist; noble and ethical people may consider their existence a settled matter, but if they were to examine their original hearts, they would find that there is a part of themselves that truly cannot be deceived. Since they cannot be deceived, they must emerge from the dark corners where they have been hiding and expose themselves. For only what is seen can be deemed unseemly. So they must bring their "unseemly" actions into the light and declare them openly in the great hall before the multitude; [these deeds will likely be exposed] sooner or later anyway.

This is precisely what Confucius meant when he said that when alone, one must be especially vigilant about one's moral rectitude.[12] The *Great Learning* mentions this "solitary vigilance" so that people will not deceive themselves. He who does not deceive himself can be content with himself; he who is content with himself can "make his will sincere." He who "makes his will sincere" can escape the demonic gates of Hell.[13] This is truly what separates human beings from demons. So in the end I dare not cover over what common custom calls unseemly and descend into a den of demons. If our friend Geng understood my intentions, he would absolutely refuse to paint over and cover up my faults to this extent.

What our friend Geng says in the middle of his letter about "Zen tricks" is completely wrong. When students first started coming from all four directions, and a Zen master had as yet no way to distinguish the depth or shallowness of their understanding, he would simply address them in isolated

---

10. See also "On the Childlike Mind," pp. 111–13.
11. This is an oblique reference to the second chapter of *Zhuangzi*, which criticizes those whose thought is hampered by excessive concern with facts and definitions.
12. "The superior man must be watchful over himself when he is alone" (*Great Learning*, ch. 6; Legge, *The Chinese Classics*, 1:366).
13. The diction in this passage borrows heavily from the *Great Learning*.

words or clipped phrases. To test their abilities he would sometimes smack them with a board or recite a *gāthā*.[14] This is called "using a rod to probe the depth of the water." If the students failed to comprehend, if they clung fast to the rod itself, unwilling to let go of his words, he would immediately dismiss them with one whack of the board. If they exhibited any understanding, he would show them the shadow of the whip, and they would learn to distinguish between appearance and substance. It's laughable enough that later scholars, failing to understand, called these methods "Zen paradoxes." But as for me, I do what I do in all seriousness, with no pretension of "Zen"; it brings me enjoyment; it's not a "trick."

In the spring of the year *bingxu* [1586] I was suffering from a disease of the spleen that lasted for over a year. It nearly turned me into an old cripple. I tried a hundred remedies, but all to no avail. Since my family had already returned home [to Quanzhou] and I was living alone in Chu,[15] I often roamed freely, going wherever I wished. It was then that my lethargy dissipated all by itself. I did not have to take hawthorn to aid my digestion. My persistent bile subsided without the use of ginseng or other restoratives. It took less than half a year to bring me back to my old self. Then I came to understand that true healing requires no medicines; most illnesses come about because we oppose our own nature; we follow the multitude in everything, linking elbows and keeping time to their song. From now on I will do what suits *me*; ultimate bliss will be my guiding principle. Not even the slightest trace of the maladies of falsity or concealment will remain, and so any temporary affliction will simply heal of its own accord. Once I have cured this illness in myself, what need will I have of "Zen tricks"?

Since I am a sojourner here, I have no choice but to let disciples like you follow me.[16] For my sake you followed me, and in this way I gained someone on whom to rely. But why would someone like you leave his wife and children to follow me several thousand *li* from home? My heart truly goes out to you, and naturally I sympathize with you. What could this have to do with "Zen tricks"?

As for the widow, Elder Brother Geng has known about this situation all along. Ever since I came to this county and sent my family away, that woman has often presented gifts of tea and fruit to provide for us fleshy bodhisattvas [the monks]; she has exhibited extreme devotion. At first I did

---

14. A brief religious verse.
15. The diction is deliberately archaic. The ancient state of Chu encompassed both modern-day Hunan and Hubei, where Li Zhi resided. Elsewhere Li implies that his family returned to Quanzhou in 1587.
16. Li Zhi seems to be referring to the monks at the Vimalakirti Cloister.

not make inquiries since I treat all almsgivers as equal. Our interactions consisted only of my receiving offerings from her. I did not reciprocate. Later, because this matter became known in the county and rumors were flying, I too found fault with her. I scolded her and no longer accepted her offerings. All my friends in the county know this. But deep down inside I harbored doubts. I believed that since she had sworn not to remarry, she would abide by this vow even under compulsion [to break it]. She devoted herself to honoring the Buddha, hoping to be rewarded in the afterlife. How could rumors circulate about such a pious woman? For this reason, I once joined a large group of people visiting her. The widow, having no sons of her own, had adopted an heir who was over thirty years old. She asked him, as master of the house, to attend to us guests. As soon as we called on them, I learned from the host that the two of them were all alone and had no one to rely on. They had actually been threatened and defrauded. The woman was exceedingly advanced in years. This elderly widow of a Nanjing family had no relations to whom she could turn, having neither sons nor daughters. How must she have felt? Wise men pay no heed to rumors. So I believed even less in the rumors, and I simply pitied her. What has this got to do with studying the Dao?

Remember that it has been more than three years since I arrived in Macheng. Aside from the few people who have treated me affectionately, who has ever given me a leftover bushel or peck of grain? Since the widow treated me consistently from start to finish, since she never lacked respect or ritual correctness, I naturally felt grateful to her and repaid her kindness. I feel obligated to defend her against any unjust accusations made against her and to redress any grievances she incurred. This is the nature of my feelings; what have they to do with "Zen tricks" such that Geng Dingxiang would try to prove their impropriety by alluding to the story of Nanzi?

My basic constitution is the same as any ordinary person's. Even Confucius was a regular person just like any other. Anyone might meet a Nanzi; I too might meet a Nanzi. Where is the "Zen" and where is the "trick" in that? Of course, [Confucius's disciple] Zilu lacked common sense; small wonder he disapproved of Confucius's meeting Nanzi![17] Now, a thousand years later, [people of Zilu's type are] even more adamant. If it were permissible for everyone *except* Confucius to interact with women [such as Nanzi], this would constitute a limitation on Confucius. But Confucius brooked no

---

17. One of Confucius's disciples; see *Analects* 6.28.

limitations. So how could it have been improper for him to interact with Nanzi? Whether we speak of the situation in terms of "ritual propriety" or "Zen tricks," this sort of moralizing is reminiscent of Zilu and his ilk. It is not worthy of discussion.

As for Shannong's turning somersaults, my erudition is so meager that this is the first I've heard of it. If indeed he did behave in this way, then Shannong intuitively understood the true essence of innate knowledge and rolled around to express it. What does this have to do with anyone else, and why would Geng Dingxiang deem it a "Zen trick"? In this world, there are countless people who turn somersaults: night and day, without a pause, in great halls and before large audiences, they sycophantically wait upon the wealthy and powerful in order to garner a moment's attention. In dark rooms they perform servile deeds, hoping to enjoy an instant of glory. Everybody turns such somersaults all the time—and yet Shannong's one somersault made him a laughingstock! Geng Dingxiang is afraid that people may imitate Shannong, so day after day he keeps this story rolling. I maintain that even if Shannong did roll around once, we never hear of his rolling around after that. Not even Shannong was capable of turning somersaults for his whole life: so why should other people [be accused of performing analogous "somersaults" and capers their entire lives]? And considering that no one has been known to imitate Shannong's somersaulting, why worry that anyone would begin to copy his somersaults now? This is just a common case of excessive worrying, like the man of Qi who feared that the sky would fall.[18]

My only regret is that Shannong was *not* able to spend his whole life rolling around! While one is rolling, one's internal perception of oneself ceases, as does one's external perception of others. There is no "beauty" inside and no "unseemliness" outside. One "turns away and loses all consciousness of self, walks through a room seeing none of the people there."[19] Distinctions between internal and external are forgotten; body and mind are as one. How rare and difficult to achieve!

---

18. Allusion to *Liezi*, ch. 1. Li Zhi is here protesting that if Geng Dingxiang's sarcastic allusion to Shannong's somersaulting were taken seriously, Li's lack of deportment would not have been a momentary act like Shannong's but a choice reiterated over a whole lifetime. He goes on to observe that since very few people have imitated Shannong's behavior, it is unlikely that anyone will wish to follow Li's way of life. For an English translation of the relevant passage, see Graham, *The Book of Lieh-tzu*, 27–29.
19. *Classic of Changes*, hexagram 52, "Gen." On the esoteric interpretation of this hexagram among followers of Wang Yangming, see Liu Ts'un-yan, *Selected Papers*, 146, 164–71.

I don't know whether Shannong truly attained this state. I don't even know whether Shannong was actually capable of turning somersaults for his entire life. I fear that even he may not have been able to do so. But if he did attain this level, then he is my teacher. How could I doubt this man's accomplishments simply because other people laugh at him? To base my opinion of him not on my own investigation but on other people's ridicule would be a mistake. It would oppose the principles of empirical investigation, of learning for one's self. These were the very sources of Shannong's spontaneous intuition; it had absolutely nothing to do with "Zen tricks." Shannong attained the highest level of "studying for one's own sake." That is why he was able to behave in such a way. Had any fraction of his mind been diverted by the desire to impress other people, he would not have been able to succeed.

But acting on one's own behalf is identical to acting on behalf of others. Learning for one's own benefit is identical to learning for the sake of others. And learning to impress others is no different from learning for oneself. It was not Shannong's purpose to impress the multitude with "paradoxical displays"; he wanted each person to trust himself. Not to trust oneself would be a disaster!

There are indeed people with great insight who attain deep understanding without having to be instructed in words. Shannong remained in a state of perpetual bliss [by disregarding others' opinions of him]. How can I ascertain whether among my associates there is anyone as bright and likely to attain enlightenment as Shannong's disciple Luo Rufang, who would adopt such unseemly postures so as to appeal to Shannong?[20] There is no way to be sure. But if there is someone of Luo's caliber, then as soon as he sees a somersault, he will silently accept the Great Teaching from the West, the dharma. Should he care that others may mock him? Let the mockers mock. Let those who understand understand. Fortunately there are a few who understand! Let the mockers mock a thousand or even ten thousand times. Let them mock for a hundred years or even a thousand years. It won't matter to Shannong. And why not? The dharma is not spoken for the sake of ordinary people; it is not spoken for the sake of people who cannot understand lofty matters; and it will not be stopped by the fear of ridicule. Nowadays, we are so frantically fearful lest anyone mock us that

---

20. Luo Rufang was an influential member of the Taizhou school. See Li's "In Memoriam, Master Luo Jinxi," pp. 150–57.

we no longer rush to share a single person's joy in enlightenment. I do not know what to say about this. We are too influenced by external factors, too motivated by other people's expectations.

As for the assertion that I singled out Liu Luqiao as conspicuously "reverent and respectful," this statement is simply too absurd. I pity Geng for his coarse and superficial understanding. Nonetheless, I will endeavor to twist my tongue to explain the situation to him once again. How could "reverence and respect" be so easy to achieve? No sooner did the ancients exhibit sincere reverence than the whole world was at peace; no sooner did they esteem themselves than the way of kingship was rectified. Did Luqiao attain this level of reverence? Rather, I find fault with him for not being reverent enough! When have I ever implied that he suffered from an excess of reverence? No sooner did the ancients cultivate personal respect than peace reigned among the commoners. No sooner did they embody this respect than they were able to govern righteously. Did Luqiao attain this level of respect? I lament only that he was not respectful enough! When have I ever implied that he suffered from an excess of respect? Indeed, I am the one who suffers [to see the meaning of the word "respect" so misunderstood]! If you think that people like Luqiao exemplify "reverence and respect," then you must think that the dynasty's success and prosperity depend on those who attend the emperor in silence, standing stock-still like idols in a temple.

The "meal brought by the guards," the "daily hundredweight of documents": this is what real respect and zeal amount to.[21] What a pity that, over time, they have gradually been lost. Clearly, reverence and respect are not to be spoken of lightly. Not only are they not to be spoken of lightly, but it is no easy matter to *understand* reverence and respect. Those who understand *and* can speak of these qualities are sages. Those who do not understand but nonetheless speak of them and imitate them are like Zhao Kuo, who led the Zhao army to crashing defeat despite having read his father's books on military strategy;[22] they are like You Meng who flummoxed the king of Chu by

---

21. When the general Han Xin was concerned that by returning to camp for a meal he might miss a strategic opportunity to attack his enemies in the state of Zhao, he ordered his bodyguards to bring him a snack that he could consume on horseback; see Sima Qian, *Shiji*, ch. 92, "Biography of the Marquis of Huaiyin (Han Xin)," in Watson, *Records: Han Dynasty I*, 169. The First Emperor of Qin was so personally involved in governing his empire that "all affairs of the empire, large and small, [were] decided by [him]. He even [had] the documents weighed, making certain that each day and night produced a picul's weight of them" (Sima Qian, *Shiji*, ch. 6, "The Basic Annals of the First Emperor of the Qin," in Watson, *Records: Qin Dynasty*, 58).
22. *Shiji*, ch. 81, "Biographies of Lian Po and Lin Xiangru," in Nienhauser, *The Grand Scribe's Records*, 7:263–73.

dressing up as the deceased prime minister, Sun Shu'ao.[23] How could these actions be considered genuine? How could they be called anything other than false? It's truly laughable!

I am fully aware that you find my behavior troubling, and that Geng Dingxiang is concerned on my behalf. But in the end, I cannot adopt the common standard in order to please you and him. Such is the nature Heaven has given me.[24] Since Geng was willing to utter such words in an attempt to instruct me, how could I respond with silence, neither agreeing nor disagreeing? And how could I flatter you two by falsely mouthing the sycophantic phrases so common in the world today so as to curry a moment's favor?

TRANSLATED BY RIVI HANDLER-SPITZ

---

23. *Shi ji*, ch. 126, "Guji liezhuan" 滑稽列傳 [Biographies of wits and humorists].
24. Oblique allusion to the *Classic of Poetry*, Mao no. 260, "Sheng Min," in Waley, *The Book of Songs*, 275.

PART III
MISCELLANEOUS WRITINGS 雜書
SHORT ESSAYS AND DISCOURSES 小品與論說

"A SKETCH OF ZHUOWU: WRITTEN IN YUNNAN"
卓吾論略：滇中作
"ZHUOWU LUNLÜE: DIANZHONG ZUO"

This self-portrait[1] was written around 1578 when Li was serving as a prefect in Yao'an, Yunnan. Here Li Zhi masterfully reworks the traditional biographical literary form and cleverly plays off fact and fiction to express his larger philosophical views. (PCL)

Kong Ruogu[2] said, "I am old enough to have met the Recluse Zhuowu and I am able to provide some general comments about him. The Recluse is known by many names. 'Zhuowu' is simply one of them. The character 卓

---

1. *FS*, *j*. 3, in *LZQJZ* 1:233–42. For another quasi-autobiographical account, see "Reflections on My Life," pp. 185–89. The biography genre is first attested in Sima Qian's *Shi ji* [Records of the grand historian]. Parodic or semifictional biographies include Tao Yuanming's 陶淵明 "Wuliu xiansheng zhuan" 五柳先生傳 [Biography of Mr. Five Willows] (a veiled autobiography) and Han Yu's 韓愈 "Mao Ying zhuan" 毛穎傳 [Biography of Fur Point] (an allegorized description of a writing brush). On "A Sketch of Zhuowu" as a fictional invention, see Martin Huang, *Literati and Self-Re/Presentation*, 46, and Pei-yi Wu, *The Confucian's Progress*, 21; for interpretations that restore its factual status, see especially Suzuki, "Li Zhuowu nianpu," 47–143.
2. The main speaker of the dialogue is an invented person whose name combines Confucius's surname, Kong, with a compound (meaning "like a valley" or, by extension, "empty," "feminine") frequently occurring in the *Daodejing*.

is not pronounced in just one way.³ In everyday conversation the Recluse pronounces it according to the standard reading [i.e., "zhuo"]. When he is serving as an official, and his name is recorded in the official records, fellow officials pronounce it like the standard reading of the character 篤 [i.e., "du"].⁴ Even in his own birthplace in the countryside, some say 'Du' and others say 'Zhuo' without coming to any final agreement."

The Recluse said, "In my local dialect, 卓 and 篤 are pronounced the same. Country folk cannot make the distinction and so refer to me using either pronunciation."

I responded, "You can change this. Only it will cost you a fortune to have the block engraver down in Ironsmith Alley straighten it out."

The Recluse laughed and said, "You think so? You want me to exchange something useful for something that's useless?⁵ But, now without a doubt I am Zhuo. And I am also Du. But if you address me as 'Zhuo' [outstanding], right now I cannot measure up. And if you address me as 'Du' [serious], right now I don't measure up to that either. How would I go about changing one thing I don't measure up to for something else that I don't measure up to?"

Li Zhi is still addressed as both "Zhuo" and "Du." The Recluse was born on the thirtieth day of the tenth lunar month of the *dinghai* year in the Jiajing reign of the glorious Ming [1527].⁶ When he was young, his mother (*née* Xu) passed away and he was orphaned.⁷ Nobody knows who raised him. When he reached the age of seven years old, he studied under his father, Mr. Baizhai, and learned to read books, chant poetry, and practice ritual ceremony. When he was twelve, he wrote an essay titled "Discourse on the Old Farmer and the Old Gardener."⁸ The Recluse said, "At that age, I already understood the point of Fan Chi's asking about agriculture and why he was classed among those who wield carrying poles and baskets.⁹ The superior

---

3. The character 卓 can have the sense of "outstanding," "far," or "to be upright."
4. The word represented by the character 篤 can be translated roughly as "serious," in the two senses of genuineness (a serious person) and severity (a serious illness).
5. This line echoes the debates of Zhuangzi's fictional characters over which is superior, usefulness or uselessness.
6. November 23, 1527. He was the eldest son in the family. His father's name was Li Baizhai 李白齋.
7. Typically in Li Zhi's time, one was considered "orphaned" only when one's father had passed away even if one's mother was still alive. In 1532 when Li was six years old, his stepmother also passed away.
8. On the dating of this essay, see Rong, *Li Zhi nianpu*, 18–19.
9. In *Analects* 13.4 Fan Chi asks Confucius a question about growing grain and vegetables. When Fan Chi leaves, Confucius responds, "What a petty man! . . . If rulers love righteousness, then the state will be populous and the people will be happy. There will be no need to talk about growing grain." In *Analects* 14.14 and 18.7 it is the turn of such men to scoff at Confucius.

person, Confucius, could not bear to hear such views and so he said, 'What a petty man is Fan Chi.' Thanks to Fan Chi's question, we know at least this about Confucius."

When he completed his essay, his fellow students praised the work. The multitudes exclaimed, "What a fine son Mr. Baizhai has!"

The Recluse said, "Although I was quite young, I already had realized that my groundless opinions were not worthy of the compliments being paid to my father. Moreover, these compliments were much too vulgar and had nothing to do with the truth of the matter. Those people said I was clever with words and when I grew up I would perhaps be skilled at writing prose and poetry. Through such writing I would snatch the wealth and honors of this world and save us from poverty and low estate. They did not know my father did not think this way and was not like this at all. What sort of person was my father? His height reached to seven feet, his eyes did not wander carelessly about. Although extremely poor, from time to time he would suddenly pawn my stepmother's earrings in order to help a friend advance the time of his nuptials. My stepmother never stopped him. My father being such a man, could one really offer him compliments in terms valued by the vulgar world?"

When Zhuowu was a bit older, he often found himself confused and unsettled. He studied the commentaries and annotations but did not critically examine himself. He was unable to carve the teachings of Master Zhu[10] deeply upon his heart. He blamed himself and wished to abandon his studies. But with a great deal of time on his hands and nothing for him to do to pass the days, he sighed and said, "All this is nothing but playacting. My studies are no more than plagiarizing and superficial reading. Not even the examiners understand each and every detail of Confucius's teachings!"

And so he sought out the most popular and widely read eight-legged essays[11] of his time, and he recited several of these each day. By the time of the examinations he had memorized nearly five hundred essays. When the examination topic was given, he merely copied, transcribed, and recorded what he had memorized. He received high middle honors.[12]

The Recluse said, "I had unbelievably good luck, just at the time when my father was getting on in years and my younger brothers and sisters had reached the age of marriage." And so by accepting an official's salary, he

---

10. The great neo-Confucian thinker Zhu Xi (1130–1200), considered the founder of the School of Principle.
11. Essays for the civil service examinations.
12. At twenty-six the historical Li Zhi earned the title of *juren* in Fujian.

was able to take care of his father and to see to the marriages of each of his younger brothers and sisters.[13]

The Recluse said, "Upon first requesting an official position, I set my hopes on a convenient place like wealthy and populous southeastern China. I hardly intended to travel ten thousand *li* to Gongcheng and leave my father to worry about me. Even so, Gongcheng was where the Song-period official Li Zhicai spent his days, and the master Shao Yong called his house there an 'Abode of Peace and Happiness.'[14] Shao, residing in Luoyang, traveled as far as a thousand *li* to study the Dao with Zhicai. Now that, through me, my father and son have 'heard the Dao,' even a separation of ten thousand *li* will be tolerable. I've also heard that Master Shao threw himself into his studies and only late in life attained understanding. At forty, he returned to Luoyang and began to arrange for his marriage. Had he not heard the Dao, he never would have married.

"I am twenty-nine years old and already have mourned the death of my eldest son [in 1555], a grievous loss. I have not immersed myself in the Dao but instead have only wallowed in feelings of grief. When I observe the ways of Shao Yong, I am deeply ashamed!"

The Abode of Peace and Happiness is located up above Hundred Springs on Mount Sumen. The Recluse was born in Quanzhou [the "District of Springs"], a city known for having welcomed the Chan Buddhist master of Wenling [Warm Springs].[15]

The Recluse said, "Being a follower of Master Warm Springs, I should adopt the style 'The Recluse of Warm Springs.'"

One day when wandering above Hundred Springs, he said, "I was born in the District of Springs and have served as an official at the Hundred Springs. Spring waters and I are destined to be together!"

And so he refers to himself as "The Man of Hundred Springs" and also styles himself "The Recluse of Hundred Springs." During his five years in Hundred Springs [1555–1560], he languished and never did hear the Dao.

---

13. In 1556 Li was appointed director of education in Gongcheng, located in Hui prefecture, Henan province.
14. Shao Yong 邵雍 (1011–1077) was a reclusive philosopher of the Song period. Li Zhicai 李之才 (d. 1045) is commonly considered Shao Yong's most important teacher. Shao was connected with a circle of thinkers who aimed to disprove any relation between Confucianism and schools such as Daoism and Buddhism. Included in this circle were thinkers such as the Cheng 程 brothers, Zhang Zai 張載, and Zhou Dunyi 周敦頤, though Shao differed in his views from the other members. For Li Zhi's biographies of Li Zhicai and Shao Yong, see *CS*, in *LZQJZ* 6:492–99. On Shao Yong, see Birdwhistell, *Transition to Neo-Confucianism*, and Wyatt, *The Recluse of Loyang*.
15. A Buddhist monk of the twelfth century who authored a commentary on *The Lotus Sutra*.

In the end [i.e., in 1560], he was appointed as an erudite to the Academy in Nanjing and departed.

Some months later, he received news that his father, Mr. Baizhai, had died. He observed the traditional rituals of mourning and traveled east, returning to his birthplace. At that time, the Wokou pirates[16] were plundering the coasts of Fujian, and the oceans were all in flames. The Recluse had to travel at night and hide during the day. It was more than six months before he arrived at his birthplace. Even so, because of the unrest, he was still not able to devote himself to the business of a filial son. Though in mourning garb, day and night he led his younger brothers and nephews in mounting the parapets and sounding the watchman's clappers to prepare the guards. At the foot of the city wall it rained arrows and stones. No amount of money could purchase rice or corn.[17] The Recluse's family members numbered about thirty, and they were barely able to survive. [In 1563,] after the three-year mourning period was complete, he brought his entire family to the capital, since he desired to avoid the difficulties in Quanzhou.

He lived in official accommodations in the capital [Beijing] for over ten months but never obtained any official position. His bags by then were emptied of provisions, but he was able to pay for his accommodations by taking in pupils. After more than ten months, he finally received an official appointment [in 1564]. He was honored as an erudite of the Imperial Academy, a position formally of the same rank he had held in Nanjing. Soon afterward, an announcement arrived notifying Li of the death of his paternal grandfather, Zhuxuan. On this same day, the Recluse's second eldest son also fell ill and died in the official accommodations.

I heard this news, and with a sigh I said, "Alas! Is life not bitter? Whoever said that official rank brings happiness? Didn't the Recluse suffer even greater bitterness as a result of his service as an official?" I grieved for his losses.

When I entered the house to offer my condolences, I found there was nothing unusual about the Recluse's expression.

He said to me, "I have something in mind that I would like to talk with you about. My great-grandparents passed away more than fifty years ago. I was not able to give them a suitable burial because I was impoverished and had no means to obtain a plot. This is a great violation of custom. I fear that I will be picked out by Heaven as one who is outrageously lacking

---

16. These so-called Japanese pirates were most often local smugglers in the overseas trade.
17. Quanzhou was plagued not only by pirate attacks but also by a famine in 1560.

in filial piety. A filial son or grandson must find his parents a final place of rest. I never have heard of anyone who was considered filial because he chose first to protect himself from wind and rain. I fear that Heaven and the spirits above will never be willing to leave an auspicious burial plot for one as lacking in filial piety as I. Nothing can atone for my crime. This time, when I return to my natal home, I must find a resting place for all three generations. I would like to leave my family in Henan province and divide the money I've set aside for funeral expenses. I intend to use half this amount to purchase a field so that my family can till the land to grow food to eat. I will take the other half and return to my natal home. Then I will have done my duty. There is one thing, though. I am simply afraid my wife will not go along with my plans. If, when I walk in to talk with her, she does not go along with my wishes, I ask you to work at persuading her!"

The Recluse then went home and, pacing back and forth, spoke his mind.

His wife responded, "It's not that what you say is untrue, but my mother is elderly. She is widowed and lives for me. Now I am willing to remain here, but she weeps for me day and night, to the point that she is blinded in both eyes. If she sees that I have not returned, she will certainly die."

Before she had finished speaking, her tears came down like rain, but the Recluse remained unmoved. She knew that in the end she would not be able to change his mind.

She held back her remaining tears, changed her expression, and admitting her faults, said, "All right. All right. First, though, when you see my mother, tell her I am as well as ever and in good health. There is nothing to worry about. She will see me another time. I will work hard and help out with matters. I will not return to my parents' house, and I dare not complain."

He then packed up his bags and asked a family member to arrange to buy land and plant seeds according to his wishes.

At this time, a powerful but corrupt official was in office. When money wasn't coming into his hands, he would shake down the wealthy families. Subordinating everything else to canal-digging projects, he used up all the water from the springs to feed the canals and did not permit even half a drop to be diverted. The Recluse went to meet with this individual. Although the Recluse ardently pleaded on behalf of the local inhabitants, his requests were not granted. But because the Recluse himself had only a few acres, the official said he could have water diverted just to his fields.

The Recluse replied, "Alas! Heavens! How could I bear to sit and see the entire city and ten thousand acres of land dry up, and only my few fields irrigated and flourishing! I cannot accept this at all. I beg you to heed my request!"

He then returned to his natal home.

That year's harvest was extremely meager. The plot of land acquired by the Recluse barely yielded a few bushels of weeds. His eldest daughter had long endured difficult times. She ate the weeds as if she were eating grain. His second and third daughters were unable to gulp down the weeds and soon both, so young, had fallen ill and died.

An old woman came forward with an announcement, declaring, "The people are starving. The officials plan to distribute grain. I hear that the official who will be in charge is the judge Deng Shiyang.[18] He has known the Recluse for a long time. You can ask him to intercede for us."

Zhuowu's wife responded, "A wife's business is not outside the home. I cannot ask him. And moreover, if he really is an old friend of my husband's, why would he wait for me to ask him!"

Judge Deng indeed did send along a portion of his own salary as a vice commissioner. He also immediately wrote and had delivered a letter to a colleague seeking further assistance. In each of these two matters, he took great care and attended to every detail. Zhuowu's wife took half the money he sent and bought grain. With the other half she bought cotton thread and wove cloth. For three years there was no deficiency in food or clothing, and this was due to the efforts of Judge Deng.

The Recluse said, "My mourning period had then passed. My family's burial matters were completed, putting the seal on three generations of good fortune, and I was now free of any of the concerns of an official. I turned my head toward the horizon, and nothing was in my mind but thoughts of my wife and children who were ten thousand *li* away. I then returned to Gongcheng. When I walked through the doorway and saw my family, I was deeply joyful. I asked about my two younger daughters and only then discovered that both had died a few months earlier before I had even begun my journey back to my birthplace."

At this time, the tears were already at the tips of Zhuowu's wife's eyelashes. When she saw the Recluse's expression alter, she acted according to custom and asked about the burial matters and her mother's well-being.

---

18. See "In Response to Deng Shiyang," pp. 7–9.

The Recluse recounts, "That evening my wife and I sat across from each other the entire night; it was truly like a dream. I knew that my wife's memories were vivid and her feelings were genuine. And so I corralled my feelings and controlled them. Still today I feel about that night as if one of the teeth on the bottom of my platform clogs had broken off!"[19]

Once he reached the capital, he took up an official position in the Ministry of Rites. A person remarked to the Recluse, "The poverty endured by a civil servant is even greater than the poverty endured in the Imperial Academy. Although you are able to bear it, are you the only one who has not heard the saying 'Wherever can one go without coming upon poverty?'"

He felt ridiculed; the man did not know when to stop.

The Recluse responded, "What I refer to as poverty is not the poverty of this world. As for poverty, there is nobody who is more impoverished than one who has not heard the Dao. As for joy, there is nobody who is as happy as one who knows where to rest. For more than ten years I have been hastily traveling from north to south, all for the sake of family matters. I completely forgot the thoughts of peace and joy that I had set my heart on while in Wenling and Baiquan. I hear that the teachers in the capital are excellent. I shall find one and study under him."

The person responded, "Your nature is too narrow. You often examine your own faults and also frequently examine the faults of others. If you hear the Dao, you will certainly become broader in your outlook."

The Recluse responded, "That is so. I am surely too narrow in my nature."

Consequently, he began to refer to himself as "Father of Vastness" and "The Recluse the Father of Vastness."

During the five springs of the Recluse's official service,[20] he plunged his heart and mind into the mysteries of the Dao. He regretted he was not able to bring Mr. Baizhai back from the land of the dead and longed for him often and deeply. And so he referred to himself also as "The Recluse Longing for Zhai."

One day he told me, "You have known me for a long time. When I die, could you please write an inscription for me? If I die in the hands of friends, then do as my friends instruct. If I die on the road, then definitely throw me

---

19. See *Jinshu* 晉書, ch. 49, "Xie An zhuan" 謝安傳 [Biography of Xie An]: at one point Xie An (320–385) is so happy he does not realize the platform of his shoe has fallen off.
20. Li accepted a position in the Ministry of Rites in 1566. It was at this time that he met Xu Yongjian (1528–1611) and through him was introduced to the writings of Wang Yangming and Wang Ji.

in the waters or cremate me.[21] Under no circumstances should you leave my bones for others to take care of. There is no need to write an inscription in the second case. If you could write a short biography, that would be fine."

I responded, "How can I claim to understand you fully? At some time in the future, a gifted portraitist, someone like Gu Kaizhi,[22] will come along and make a true record of you."

Consequently, I have written this essay offering a general sketch of his life. Afterward, I traveled far and wide and did not see the Recluse for a long time. And so from his time in Nanjing onward, I have not recorded anything at all. Some say the Recluse died in Nanjing. Others say he is still in southern Yunnan and has not yet died.[23]

TRANSLATED BY PAULINE C. LEE

---

21. See *Analects* 9.12: "Rather than dying in the hands of retainers, isn't it better that I die in the hands of you, my disciples? And although I may not be entitled to a grand funeral, it's not as though I were dying by the roadside, is it?" (Watson, *The Analects of Confucius*, 62).
22. The renowned painter Gu Kaizhi 顧愷之 (341–402), a free-spirited painter, writer, calligrapher, poet, and buffoon, also figures in the Six Dynasties anecdote collection *Shishuo xinyu* 世説新語 [A new account of the tales of the world].
23. From 1577 to 1580 Li served as prefect of Yao'an in the remote western province of Yunnan.

"ON HE XINYIN"
何心隱論
"HE XINYIN LUN"

Li Zhi's biography of He Xinyin[1] is partly conjectural, not to say imaginary: an exemplary life, already in the course of transformation from fact into legend. He Xinyin (1517–1579) took from the Taizhou school of Wang Yangming's neo-Confucianism the idea that all people were potentially sages. He abandoned the official path for a career akin to both knight-errantry and community organizing, calling lineage and local groups to band together and resist predatory tax collectors. Over the years he made many enemies, reputedly including the prime minister Zhang Juzheng. Arrested on charges of banditry, he died in prison after repeated beatings.[2]

Li never met He Xinyin. He studied with other thinkers of the Taizhou school. Li's close associates the Geng brothers knew him well, however, and it was their tacit assent to He's arrest and death (possibly motivated by a fear of having their association used against them) that eventually turned Li against his friends and former patrons. This biography depicts He Xinyin as a fearless champion of the Way—an identity Li Zhi would have longed to embrace. (HS)

The man who called himself He Xinyin was originally named Liang Ruyuan 梁汝元. I never knew He Xinyin, so how could I have known Liang Ruyuan? So I will simply speak of Xinyin here.

Some praise Xinyin, others belittle him. Those who praise him do so for three sorts of reasons; those who belittle him have three reasons likewise. Some who exalt him say,

---

1. FS, j. 3, in LZQJZ 1:245–51.
2. For the ascertainable facts of He's life, see DMB, 1:513–15, and MRXA 32:1a–4b, in Huang Tsung-hsi, Ming Scholars, 166–69.

There is no one who does not cherish his own life; he alone did not make much of his existence. He came from a family of great wealth but disdained such concerns, wishing only to live among the wise and virtuous of his age wherever they might be found; in this sense, his way of cherishing his life was unparalleled.[3] There is no one who does not fear death; he alone was not afraid, wishing only to brave death and leave behind a glorious name. As he saw it, all men are fated to die, burdened by numberless cares, bent down by worry, suffering in every part of their bodies, calling for death and not finding it. What is the difference between being slaughtered by one's fellow men or by demons? Is it better to die beheaded or to succumb gradually to one's ills? Between a poison compounded of a hundred kinds of venom and a single dose of a strong poison, what is the difference? To die gloriously or to die obscurely: which is more honorable? Having reflected deeply on all this, he quite properly no longer feared death.

Another group exalts him, saying,

He was an admirer and follower of Confucius. Ordinarily, those who follow Confucius imitate him only in the respects that are easily imitated. The challenge of the Way of Confucius is this: to take the world for one's home and to forgo a home of one's own, to take responsibility for leading virtuous men and to put aside responsibility for one's own house and fields. So Confucius was able to depart from the ordinary, to be "the one that rises above the rest,"[4] in the end becoming the greatest scholar in the state of Lu, indeed the greatest scholar in the history of the world. Only He Xinyin took on this challenge: thereby he rose above the rest, and thereby he incurred others' resentment. How then could he be spared! Confucius himself had to leave Wei abruptly, was narrowly missed by a falling tree, was nearly starved at Chen, and in fear for his life at Kuang; only by good fortune did he escape these brushes with death.[5] If he was fortunate enough not to be killed then, one assumes, he was sure to meet a dignified death; but had he had the misfortune to die then, would anyone have refused him the title of "a good and brave man who gave his life for the sake of benevolence"?[6] When death came, He Xinyin did not demur.

---

3. At the age of forty-three, He Xinyin left home and thereafter traveled the length and breadth of the empire, teaching and learning. See *LZQJZ* 1:247.
4. *Classic of Changes*, "Qian."
5. These perils of the Sage are recounted in the *Analects*.
6. *Analects* 15.9.

Did he not fear death? It is not that he had no fear of death, but he took it on without further ado. Now since he lived in this way, how could he fail to die in the same manner? Those who say that he sought death in order to make a name for himself are wrong; if he had to die, he had to die; what could fame offer him that would make death desirable?

And finally, some who exalt him say,

He "came and went as he pleased"[7] heedless of precedent. Now Confucius was a Sage, and those who emulate him only make themselves ridiculous; He Xinyin thought they were like ugly women attempting to prance like slender maidens. He reflected that "if people hear what I am trying to do, they are sure to object and persecute me to death, not knowing that Confucius in his day did no differently from me. I should then take Confucius as my exemplar; no one will then turn my words against me." But while good people suspected him, the bad worked to destroy him, at the end his friends deserted him, and He Xinyin finally had the misfortune to die for the sake of the Way. Loyalty, filiality, purity, justice: for such well-known principles as these, people are wont to give their lives—what is called "dying a death that has more weight than Mount Tai"[8]; but never has anyone been known to give up his life for the Way. For the Way is "without a name"[9]; and how could anyone die for the sake of something without a name? Now that He Xinyin is dead, I fear that the memory of his one death will sink without a trace. If you ask the tens of thousands of people who live in Wuchang, you will not find a one who knew him, yet everyone knows his death was an injustice. When they paraded the notice board through the streets to notify the population of his crimes, the people who stood by watching denounced it as a slander, snorting with indignation until they had to turn away; such was the feeling at the time. From Qimen to Jiangxi, and again from Jiangxi to Nan'an and to Huguang, along a circuit of over three thousand *li*, if people did not know He Xinyin personally, they knew his aims—this was true throughout the three-thousand-*li* circuit. It was not only those who had offended against Prime Minister Zhang [Juzheng] or who had some cause to resent him who felt this way; even those who sincerely considered Zhang the savior of the

---

7. From *Zhuangzi*, "Zai yu" (*Zhuangzi jishi*, 394); slightly misquoted.
8. From Sima Qian's "Letter to Ren An"; Watson, *Records: Qin Dynasty*, 233.
9. Quoting the *Daodejing*, sec. 1.

dynasty were particularly outraged by this act of injustice on his part, and those who had He Xinyin executed in order to please Prime Minister Zhang were condemned by all as the lowest kind of people. For as to this Way being inherent in the human heart, it is truly like the sun, the moon, and the stars: impossible to cloak with darkness. Although He Xinyin died a nameless death, the feelings of the people were with him: this was surely the doing of the Way—who can suppress it? Moreover, can it be true that He Xinyin had no fear of death? In a time with no Zhang Zifang, who was there to save the life of a Xiang Bo? In a time with no Zhu Jia of Lu, who could rescue a Ji Bu?[10] After reflecting on He's fate, I incline to think that those who preach the Way are liars. Looking on the matter from the present day, I notice that the plain people who still breathe outrage at this wrong never knew He Xinyin personally, but He Xinyin's intimates and fellow students calmly observed his death as if they were throwing stones down a well. It appears that ordinary people cannot be false but must give way to the sincerity of their thoughts, whereas the moralizers lack honesty and think only to cut down whoever surpasses them. In an age without real moralists, it was inevitable that He Xinyin had to die and "this refinement of his"[11] be lost forever. Was He Xinyin's death not a weighty one? Can it not be considered weightier than Mount Tai?

These three types of responses come from people who are worthies and gentlemen of the age, and it is appropriate that they should join with the ordinary people in sincerity to exalt He Xinyin.

Those who belittle He Xinyin say,

There are five types of human relationships,[12] and He Xinyin broke with four of them to live his life among friends, teachers, and other worthy

---

10. Zhang Liang (Zifang) was a brave swordsman from Hán who swore revenge on the Qin royal house after they obliterated the state of Hán; he later served the following dynasty. Xiang Bo was saved by Zhang Liang after committing a murder (see Sima Qian, *Shi ji*, ch. 55, "The Hereditary House of the Marquis of Lu," in Watson, *Records: Han Dynasty I*, 100–103). For the exploits of Zhu Jia, a swordsman of Lu, see Watson, *Records: Han Dynasty II*, 412–13. Ji Bu, a general of the defeated Xiang Yu (rival of the founder of the Han dynasty in the wars of succession following the collapse of the Qin), was spared under the Han thanks to Zhu Jia's intercession (see Watson, *Records: Han Dynasty I*, 247–51).
11. Quoting *Analects* 9.5.
12. The Five Relationships codified in official Confucian ethics included four of superior and inferior (ruler and subject, husband and wife, father and child, elder brother and younger brother) and only one of equality (that between friends). By taking to the road in search of fellow moral enthusiasts, He Xinyin neglected the first four.

people; his behavior was exaggerated, perverse, and cannot be taken as an example. It is the way of the pliant snake to know how to flatter one's superiors and intimidate one's inferiors, but He Xinyin displayed nothing but bold words and bold behavior, which piled up blame and trouble for him. He may have been learned, but not in the art of self-preservation. And anyway, the Way is rooted in human nature and the main thing in study is to make it approachable. Judging people by one's own overly strict standards will only drive them away; haranguing the ambitious will only cause those on top to be uneasy; using one's wealth to make friends[13] only brings out the greed and competitiveness in people. His own choices led him to his death!

These last three types of blame are typical of exactly the kind of scholar who disgusted He Xinyin.

I find such people unspeakable. They are just the vulgar type of man of the present age, concerned only with feeding, clothes, and sleep, occupied with their bodies and their mouths, with no idea at all about what the Way might be or why a person should study, and if they dare to curse and scold, it is tedious even to argue with them. Only those who exalt He Xinyin seem to have any understanding of him at all, and even they mistake him. I never had the chance to cast my eyes upon him or hear him in discussion and have taken only a cursory glance at the detail of his thought, so that I feel that to blurt something out might be wrong, but to repress it is wrong as well. What if I express my personal thoughts about him, hoping one day to hear from someone who knew him? I take He Xinyin to have been a dragon in plain sight,[14] manifesting himself with no ability to hide away. His whole attitude was lofty, whence his fate. But loftiness belongs to dragons; no other thing compares to them. If the dragon lacks loftiness, the yang line at the top of the hexagram will be vacant. This place, however, must not be vacant. The dragon cannot be confined to a less than lofty rank. He Xinyin alone matches this graph; he is the "great man" predicted by the top yang line of "Qian."[15] That is what I have to say about He Xinyin.

TRANSLATED BY HAUN SAUSSY

---

13. Reflecting the accusation that He Xinyin was surrounded by spongers and hangers-on.
14. Paraphrasing the *Classic of Changes*, hexagram 1, "Qian": "a dragon hidden in the field."
15. Ibid.: "There will be advantage in meeting a great man."

"ON THE WARRING STATES"
戰國論
"ZHANGUO LUN"

This essay[1] was initially composed as "The Biography of Liu Xiang" and intended for publication in *A Book to Keep (Hidden)*. Throughout that work, Li Zhi frequently reverses traditional evaluations of historical personages and events. Here he overturns the widely held view that the political chaos of the Warring States period (ca. 475 B.C.E.–221 B.C.E.) constituted a departure from the Dao. He adopts instead a position of historical relativism and claims that "The Dao changes in accord with the vicissitudes of each generation." The implication is that the violence and lawlessness of the Warring States period need not be considered as a deviation from the Dao but can be viewed as an instantiation of it. These ideas oppose those of the influential Return to Antiquity Movement. While members of that conservative group advocated reverence for and imitation of the past, Li proposes that each historical moment must develop strategies suitable for coping with the unique challenges it faces. (RHS)

From reading the *Strategies of the Warring States*, I learned that Liu Xiang was a superficial thinker.[2] After the Spring and Autumn period came the Warring States period.[3] Since it was a time of warring states, naturally it gave

---

1. *FS, j.* 3, in *LZQJZ* 1: 262–65.
2. Liu Xiang 劉向 (77 B.C.E.–6 B.C.E.) was the Han dynasty's chief librarian and is credited with having compiled many works from earlier materials, among them the *Strategies of the Warring States* (*Zhanguo ce* 戰國策).
3. In traditional historiography, the Western Zhou (approximately 1025 B.C.E.–770 B.C.E.) was a period of dynastic unity; the first half of the Eastern Zhou, known as the Spring and Autumn period (771 B.C.E.–476 B.C.E.), saw the beginnings of rivalry among the states composing the Chinese culture sphere; and the Warring States period was a time of virtually uninterrupted wars of conquest, up to the founding of the Qin dynasty in 221 B.C.E.

rise to the strategies appropriate for interstate warfare. The Dao changes in accord with the vicissitudes of each generation. This being the case, [China] could no longer be ruled by the methods of the Spring and Autumn period—much less the methods of the Three Kings![4]

[Domination by] the Five Hegemons was an artifact of the Spring and Autumn period.[5] But why was it that the Five Hegemons ruled only during the Spring and Autumn period? Probably it is because the Zhou dynasty was already weak and the Son of Heaven was no longer able to exert his power over rites and music or over military expeditions to maintain control over the feudal lords. Thus inasmuch as some feudal lords did not obey orders, the regional earls formed a common front and led other feudal lords in attacking them. Together, those who revered the Son of Heaven formed an alliance, reuniting all under heaven.

It was just as when parents fall ill and are unable to manage their own affairs: the children quarrel among themselves and no one is able to stop them. But if among them there is a worthy son who acts as supervisor, he rises to the challenge and takes upon himself the responsibility of a parent. Thus in name he is a brother, but in fact he is a parent. Although he may seem to have usurped the parents' authority, in fact his parents rely on him for security, his brothers rely on him for maintaining peace, and his servants, retainers, and others rely on him for stability. Thus he brings great benefit to his family.

Guan Zhong was prime minister to Duke Huan of Qi.[6] He has been deemed the first person to act in this way. From then on, the Five Hegemons rose and fell, one more valiant than the next. They propped up the monarchy and shielded the Zhou. That the Zhou dynasty, like "the centipede with its hundred legs," was able to hold out for more than 240 years is due entirely to Guan Zhong's meritorious service and the Five Hegemons' strength.[7] The

---

4. The three ancient kings Yu, Tang, and Wen are proverbial for having created order in the human realm by founding their respective dynasties. But a period of disorder, says Li, cannot be administered by following their precedents.
5. The Five Hegemons were feudal lords during the Spring and Autumn period who were able to exert unparalleled military and diplomatic strength over the other feudal states. Their dominance reflects the dwindling power of the "Son of Heaven," or Zhou monarch, their nominal superior.
6. Guan Zhong (ca. 720 B.C.E.–645 B.C.E.) assisted Duke Huan of Qi (d. 643 B.C.E.) in rising to become one of the Five Hegemons.
7. This is the first half of a popular saying: "The centipede with its hundred legs dies but does not topple over." The phrase, which appears in the *Huainanzi*, is used metaphorically to describe the way in which a powerful household or dynasty is often able to keep up appearances long after it has ceased to function internally. See *LZQJZ* 1:264n23.

feudal lords were incapable of accomplishing what the Five Hegemons had, so some feudal lords conceived the ambition to swallow up Zhou: in their minds they plotted about how to bring all of China under their control as King Xuan of Qi had wanted to do.[8] The Jin split apart into three states, and Lü was overtaken by Tian.[9] None of the feudal lords was able to set things right, so the situation inevitably degenerated into one of states at war for thousands of miles in every direction, each with its scheming ministers and strategizing officials. Under these circumstances, the fighting could not stop until the country was unified.

[Five hundred years later] Liu Xiang, at the end of the Western Han, sensed that his own dynasty was about to fall. He could only admire the flourishing era of the Three Kings; he could not fathom what was appropriate for the Warring States. His opinions were always wide of the mark. Bao Biao and Wu Shidao[10] were born in the Song and Yuan dynasties, respectively. Their minds were crammed with secondhand opinions and their ears filled with teachings concerning "benevolence" and "righteousness." Their weak attempts to judge the value of the *Strategies of the Warring States* are not even worth discussing. Now Zeng Gong was rather conceited; he claimed that all his essays were rooted in the Six Classics. He mocked Liu Xiang for not forming his own opinions,[11] charged that Liu ought to have corrected the biased accounts he gathered, and implied that Liu didn't even know what the Six Classics were but merely filched a few lines of praise and blame, which he then established as an ethical standard. In the end, Zeng Gong's commentary is to those of Bao and Wu as the state of Lu was to the state of Wei: identical in import.[12]

TRANSLATED BY RIVI HANDLER-SPITZ

---

8. King Xuan, who ruled the feudal state of Qi from 319 B.C.E. to 301 B.C.E., attempted to enlarge his territory and bring China under his control.
9. In 403 B.C.E. the state of Jin split into three smaller states: Han, Zhao, and Wei, and in 379 B.C.E., Lü, the ruling house of Qi, was overtaken by the Tian clan.
10. Bao Biao 鮑彪 and Wu Shidao 吳師道 both wrote commentaries on the *Strategies of the Warring States*.
11. Zeng Gong 曾鞏 (1019–1083), one of the Eight Prose Masters of the Tang and Song, wrote in his preface to the *Strategies of the Warring States* that Liu Xiang had been unduly influenced by the common perception that the strategists and advisers of Warring States kings lacked any moral compass and so destroyed the world order of their time.
12. This line alludes to *Analects* 13.7, in which Confucius says, "The governments of the states of Lu and Wei are like brothers." Li Zhi is saying that Zeng Gong's opinion is just as worthless as Bao Biao's or Wu Shidao's comments on the *Strategies of the Warring States*.

"ON WEAPONS AND FOOD"
兵食論
"BING SHI LUN"

Originally published in *A Book to Keep (Hidden)* in 1588, this essay[1] also appeared, with slight emendations and under a different title, in *Mr. Li's Discussion of Books*. The essay is a subversive commentary on a famous dialogue about political authority from the *Analects*:

> Zigong asked about government. The Master said, "[What is needed is] sufficient food, sufficient weaponry, and the trust of the people, that is all." Zigong then asked, "If you had no choice but to discard one of the three, which would be the first to go?" "Let weapons be discarded." "If you had no choice but to discard one or the other of the remaining two, which would go?" He said, "Let food be discarded. From ancient times to now, everyone has had to face death, but without the trust of the people, none can stand."[2]

Since before the formation of the first imperial dynasty, the Qin (221 B.C.E.–206 B.C.E.), political theorists had debated whether the perfect ruler was one who enlightened the people, motivating them to perform actions for the common defense and weal, or one who created conditions that indirectly influenced the people to act in a way that benefited the state, without knowing why they did so. Confucius, as represented in the *Analects* passage, became the figurehead of the first position, Laozi the figurehead of the second. In this essay Li Zhi, embracing an argument for which the examination elite to which he belonged traditionally had little sympathy, argues that Laozi's way of treating the populace like a mindless beast or like a self-organizing natural system is the more effective and therefore the correct one, and that the Way of the Confucians, dominant in

---

1. *FS, j.* 3, in *LZQJZ* 1:265–72.
2. *Analects* 12.7; translation mine. Compare Watson, *The Analects of Confucius*, 81.

Chinese society since the time of the Duke of Zhou (eleventh century B.C.E.), is an aberration. Li's favorable portrayal of rule by seduction and indirection (a theme prominent in the *Daodejing*) thus constitutes a subtle jab at the utopian Confucian ideal of transforming the people through education. (HS; RHS)

At the dawn of the human race, people were like wild beasts, living in caves and dwelling in the wilderness. We subsisted on the fruits we gathered from shrubs and trees. But having no claws or sharp teeth to help us grab or bite, no feathers or fur with which to cover ourselves, we were easy prey for wild animals. Since Heaven gave rise to human beings, we must be more precious than beasts. Yet abandoning people to be eaten would have been worse than not creating them in the first place. So circumstances required that, in order to survive, human beings borrow from and use objects in the natural world. This is how bows, arrows, halberds, spears, armor, swords, and shields came into being. Where there is life, there must be a means of sustaining this life—namely, food; and where there is a body, there must be a means of protecting this body—namely, weapons. In response to the urgent need for producing food, the well-field land-distribution system was established.³ In response to the urgent need for protection, bows, arrows, armor, and helmets sprang into being. Taking the place of claws, sharp teeth, fur, and feathers, these weapons made tigers, leopards, rhinoceroses, and elephants run for their lives and keep a safe distance from human habitation. Isn't this how human beings came to live in peace and quiet?

Confucius said, "When food and weapons are in ample supply, the people will trust the ruler." If the ruler provides the people with sufficient food and weapons, who could doubt that the people will trust and support him?⁴ In situations in which the ruler "has no choice" but to discard either food or weapons, and yet the people would rather die than relinquish their trust in him, this loyalty may be accounted for by the fact that the ruler previously

---

3. The well-field system's name derives from the character for "well," 井, the shape of which is used to represent the distribution of land: nine plots of land, of which those on the periphery were cultivated by families of serfs, and the produce of the central one was given to the feudal lord as tax. *Mencius* 3A3 praises this system.
4. Li slightly distorts the *Analects* passage to make it say that food and weapons are the only means by which the ruler secures the people's trust.

provided them with ample weapons and food.⁵ When Confucius said "Let food be discarded" and "Let weapons be discarded," he did not think these things *really ought* to be discarded; he [was simply answering the question of what a ruler should do if he] "has no other choice." When a ruler "has no other choice," the common people will not lose faith in him since, after all, he "has no other choice."

Yet Confucians reverse this logic and claim that trust is more important than weapons and food. They say such things because they do not understand the essence of the Sage's teaching. Is it really a matter of choosing between weapons and food? It is said that without weapons, it would be quite impossible to obtain food. But weapons belong to the "ground of death."⁶ The very word "weapons" is ugly. Yet without weapons we would have no means to protect ourselves. So in fact weapons are beautiful. [It's just that] their beauty is difficult to perceive. And since the word "weapons" is ugly, we do not want to hear it spoken. Since commoners do not wish to hear this word, rulers dare not let it pass their lips, much less command the populace time and again to employ these implements. For this reason, if in peacetime we teach the commoners military arts, they say, "But there's no conflict now. Why is the ruler bothering us with military drills?" Who would say, "Use my services; I won't complain no matter how hard you work me"?⁷

But if we mobilize the army [only] when there *is* trouble, then people say, "These are dangerous times; how can I avoid being killed?" Would anyone say, "Kill me for the sake of the life-sustaining Dao; even if I die, I will not complain of the ruler who sent me"?⁸

Words of this kind are misleading, and rulers merely seek to use them in order to throw a deceptive gloss over their arts of rulership. But don't they know that the ruler "uses the Dao to remold the people"? How can [a ruler]

---

5. In this sentence Li Zhi is paraphrasing Zhu Xi's commentary on the *Analects*: "A people without food must die, moreover death necessarily comes to every person. Without trust, even if life goes on, one cannot establish [a state]; in this case death is a better guarantee of order. So if [the ruler] is determined to die rather than lose the people's trust, the people will also rather die than lose [the ruler's] trust" (Zhu Xi, *Sishu zhangju jizhu*, 135).
6. This expression recalls the opening line of Sunzi's *Art of War*: "Military action is important to the nation; it is the ground of life and death" (Sun Tzu, *Art of War*, 59; *LZQJZ*, 1:268n19).
7. Alluding to *Mencius* 7A12: "If the services of the common people were used with a view to sparing them hardship, they would not complain even when hard driven" (Lau, *Mencius*, 184).
8. Further allusion to *Mencius* 7A12: "If the common people were put to death in pursuance of a policy to keep them alive, they would die bearing no ill-will towards the man who put them to death" (Lau, *Mencius*, 184).

go against the Dao, even if by doing so he wins the praise of the populace? What is needed is the wisdom to enlighten the people so that they conform to his purposes: they act rightly without waiting for a reward and spontaneously accomplish the same ends without grumbling,[9] although they do not understand why. This is the consummate achievement of sages who are reverent yet reserved.

The rulership of the Three Kings was grounded in that of the Five Emperors, of whom Xuan Yuan was the greatest.[10] Xuan Yuan was a ruler who fought seventy battles to gain control of all under heaven. Though he killed Chi You in the wilderness of Zhuolu and fought the Yan Emperor in the plains of Banquan,[11] he took pains to protect the lives of his people and poured out his heart to sustain them. Xuan Yuan thought that since the people were exceedingly gullible, he could appeal to their sense of self-interest; and since he, as ruler, was shrouded in mystery, they could not admonish him.

So he plotted the land into fields shaped like the character 井 and distributed eight parts [out of nine] so as to ensure that the people all understood that the ruler was providing for them. Then, if the spring hunting ritual were not performed, would not harm befall their tender crops? [Lacking game], how could they sacrifice to the God of Agriculture to pray for a good harvest [the following year]? Thus, as long as the people labored in the fields in all four seasons, there were sacrifices in all four seasons, and as long as there were sacrifices in all four seasons, there was hunting in all four seasons. This hunting, in fact, was undertaken for the sake of [ensuring the productivity of] the fields; that is why we speak of "hunting in the fields."[12] For the same reason, the state never incurred the expense of raising an army, yet every family enjoyed a portion of game. The rulers never officially enforced military training, yet everyone was a hunter skilled at cornering prey.[13] The people did not wait for the ruler to supply them with

---

9. Allusion to the "Appended Phrases" (Xici 繫辭) in the *Classic of Changes*.
10. The Three Kings refers to Kings Yu, Tang, and Wen. The Five Emperors are even earlier, legendary sage-rulers of China: the usual list includes the Yellow Emperor, Zhuang Xu, Di Ku, Tang Yao, and Yu Shun. Xuan Yuan refers to the Yellow Emperor, the legendary founder of Chinese civilization. See *LZQJZ* 1:269n5.
11. See Sima Qian, *Shi ji*, ch. 1, "The Five Emperors, Basic Annals, 1," in Nienhauser, *The Grand Scribe's Records*, 1:1–19.
12. This phrase appears in the Mao commentary to the poem "Huan" in the *Classic of Poetry*, Mao no. 97.
13. Literally, "hemming it in on three sides." In ancient China it was considered inappropriate to surround a hunted animal on all sides; compassion required providing an escape route. See *LZQJZ* 1:269n49.

aggressive implements like halberds and spears or defensive ones like helmets or suits of armor. They did not wait for the emperor to teach them but [of their own accord] became nimble on their feet and skilled with their hands, adept at long-range shooting with lances and arrows. They did not wait for the ruler to train them; children and white-haired men alike practiced the skills of mortal combat. They regarded catching ferocious beasts as no different from snagging a rabbit in a field. So what difficulty could they have had in battle? At home they treated one another amicably, and away from home they called out to one another. In illness, they looked after one another, and in trouble they took care of one another. They did not wait for the ruler to "teach the people human relationships."[14] When turning a corner, their formation was as regular as a T square, and when rounding a bend, it was as constant as a compass.[15] Whether encamped or on the move, advancing or retreating, they always performed each action flawlessly. They did not wait for the ruler to instruct them in ritual propriety. They feasted merrily, beating drums and dancing late into the night. They did not need the sovereign to recognize their prowess by bestowing upon them yak-tail flags and bronze drums, nor did they need to present the captives of war along with the severed left ears [of the slain enemy soldiers] before they rejoiced in their hearts.

The people were divided into eight administrative units and deployed according to eight battalions. In the midst was the central command.[16] There were eight vanguards and eight rear guards, whose powers corresponded to one another. They did not wait for these principles of organization to be set down in diverse forms of writing or to be established through precise calculations before they understood. These skills are associated with the Six Arts;[17] they are the means by which the ruler protects the people's lives. But in the beginning no sages instructed the people in the Six Arts: literary matters and military preparations arose together without anyone's waiting for a local school to be established or for filiality to be expounded—such elaborate provisions for educating the populace as we find in the *Mencius* are just a case of "improving the drawing of the snake by

---

14. See *Mencius* 3A4; Lau, *Mencius*, 102.
15. Alludes to the *Li ji* [Records of ritual], ch. 13.
16. In ancient China, armies consisted of "left," "right," and "central" divisions, also known as upper, lower, and central units. Commands were issued by the general, stationed in the central unit. See *LZQJZ* 1:270n66.
17. According to the *Rites of Zhou* (*Zhou li*), the Six Arts are ritual practice, music, archery, charioteering, calligraphy, and mathematics. See *LZQJZ* 1:270n70.

giving it legs" [i.e., they are superfluous additions].[18] Before the age of fifteen, [the ancients], on the other hand, were experienced and adept in the skills [of war], but they were perfectly unaware that their training had been orchestrated by the ruler; they assumed that the ruler's task was to provide for them. Families willingly went to war and people became soldiers simply as needed. [Among them], rituals and music shone forth, and human relationships flourished. Even now, several thousands of years later, people are still unaware of this. How much less did people back then understand it!

Superb! The sages had the skill of making ten thousand people dance to a drum beat. Since they could "make the people obey," they made them share the 井-shaped fields. And since they "could not make them understand," they did not disclose the essence of the Six Arts or the practices of filiality and loyalty.[19] Confucians have not investigated this; they erroneously believe that the sages took advantage of gaps in the agricultural calendar to instruct the people in military affairs. But hunting and planting take place in the fields in all four seasons. What gaps could there be? Moreover, since these activities are concerned with subsistence, how could they ever have been labeled as "military"? How could anyone have referred to them as "military affairs"? Fan Zhongyan said, "Ever since Confucians established the doctrine of classifying by means of names [i.e., moral philosophy], who has had any dealings with weapons?"[20] Consequently, no one recognized the importance of weapons. Zhang Zai[21] wanted to buy a parcel of land and call it a well-field plot. But he did not even know what the well-field system was; he only used this term because he admired antiquity. How utterly absurd! Lord Shang,[22] who understood the importance of weapons,

---

18. *Mencius* 1A7 prescribes that kings should organize agriculture, building village schools for the dissemination of virtue and the like in order to promote peace and social order. Against this top-down ideal, Li Zhi contends that communities can organize themselves on the basis of need.
19. *Analects* 8.9: "The people may be made to follow a path of action, but they may not be made to understand it" (Legge, *The Chinese Classics*, 1:211).
20. Fan Zhongyan 范仲淹 (989–1052) was a Song-dynasty neo-Confucian literatus and military strategist. According to the "Hengqu xue'an" 橫渠學案 [Scholarly record of Hengqu] in the *Songyuan xue'an* 宋元學案 [Records of Song- and Yuan-dynasty scholars], Fan made this remark to Zhang Zai, who is mentioned two sentences later. See *LZQJZ* 1:271.
21. Zhang Zai 張載 (1020–1077) was a philosopher of the Northern Song dynasty who believed that the well-field land-distribution system was the key to ensuring equality for all commoners, and for this reason he advocated reinstituting it in his own day.
22. Lord Shang refers to Shang Yang 商鞅 (ca. 390 B.C.E.–338 B.C.E.), a Legalist statesman from the state of Wei who served as prime minister of Qin and helped put in place the harsh policies for which that dynasty was known. He met a nasty end: accused of plotting sedition, he fled to the mountains, but when he arrived at a guesthouse, the owner demanded his papers, citing the law that Lord Shang himself had made—namely, that no travelers would

passionately pleaded for permission to advance: he concentrated on winning battles and divvying up the spoils to "reward the good and punish the bad."[23] To be sure, he swiftly strengthened the state of Qin, but when he was drawn and quartered, the people of Qin did not mourn him. Lord Shang's error was that he desired to make the people understand what they should not understand. Hence the saying, "The Way of the sage lies not in enlightening the people, but in hoodwinking them."[24] And further, "The fish must not be allowed to leave the deep; the instruments of power in a state must not be revealed to anyone."[25] How extremely profound! For generations this teaching has been treasured. Grand Duke Wang practiced it,[26] Guan Zhong cultivated it,[27] and the Archivist[28] made it manifest. But ever since Ji Dan,[29] Confucian teachings have occupied the mainstream. Confucians have strived by every means possible to indoctrinate the people with their trifling and petty arguments, through oaths and protestations. Meanwhile, Xuan Yuan's governance falls into decay.

TRANSLATED BY RIVI HANDLER-SPITZ

---

be allowed shelter unless they could document their identity. Turned away, he eventually died in battle, whereupon the Qin emperor had his body drawn and quartered as an example for anyone who would betray the state. See Sima Qian, *Shi ji*, ch. 68, "Biography of Lord Shang," in Watson, *Records: Qin Dynasty*, 89–99.

23. Li Zhi is quoting the Legalist text *Han Feizi* 韓非子, ch. 34.
24. See *Daodejing*, ch. 65: "Of old, those who excelled in the pursuit of the way did not use it to enlighten the people but to hoodwink them" (Lau, *Lao Tzu*, 127).
25. *Daodejing*, ch. 36; Lau, *Lao Tzu*, 95.
26. Refers to Jiang Shang 姜尚, a legendary military strategist who helped the Zhou dynasty establish itself and overthrow the brutal and oppressive Shang dynasty in the eleventh century B.C.E.
27. Guan Zhong 管仲 (ca. 720 B.C.E.–645 B.C.E.) assisted Duke Huan of Qi (d. 643 B.C.E.) in rising to become one of the Five Hegemons.
28. The Chinese term translated here as "Archivist" refers to Laozi 老子, who, according to legend, served as state archivist under the Zhou dynasty.
29. Ji Dan 姬旦 is better known as the Duke of Zhou (ca. 1100 B.C.E.), whose benevolent regency was characterized by the promotion of the well-field agricultural system, as well as state ritual and culture.

"DISCUSSION ON HUSBAND AND WIFE: REFLECTIONS AFTER LONG CONTEMPLATION"
夫婦論：蓄有感
"FUFU LUN: XU YOU GAN"

One of Li Zhi's most striking essays[1] on the subject of metaphysics, this essay opens with Li's accepting central Confucian concepts. He then reorganizes the ideas to support a bold vision of a social world and cosmos celebrating abundance and embodied reality. Li begins with the Five Relationships (*wulun* 五倫): ruler and minister, father and son, husband and wife, elder and younger brother, and friend and friend. He then challenges the traditional ranking, making the spousal relationship primary. (In other writings, and perhaps by implication in this one, he identifies the friend-friend relationship as central. See "On Friendship," pp. 207–8, and "Mr. Li's Ten Kinds of Association," pp. 135–37.) Li's adversaries are the adherents of the School of Principle, the Cheng-Zhu school of Confucianism, the pedantic "gentlemen of the Way," who see the world as founded upon a pure and undefiled One or a barren "nothingness of Nothingness." This essay was written in 1588 in Macheng. (PCL)

Husband and wife are the origin of humankind. Only on the basis of husband and wife can there be father and son; only on the basis of father and son can there be elder and younger brother; only on the basis of elder and younger brother can there be superior and subordinate. If the relations between husband and wife are properly established, then among the myriad things, nothing will fail to find its proper state. This is how husband and wife are the origin of all things.

To begin with the most fundamental, Heaven and Earth are husband and wife. That is, Heaven and Earth had to exist before the myriad things.

---

1. *FS*, *j*. 3, in *LZQJZ* 1:251–54.

So we can see that all things under Heaven are born from Two, and not from One.[2] Still, there are those who say that One can give birth to Two,[3] that "Principle" [*li* 理] can give birth to "substance" [*qi* 氣], that the "Supreme Ultimate" [*taiji* 太極] can give birth to Yin [陰] and Yang [陽].[4] How could that be?

When humans first came into existence, there were simply two forces— Yin and Yang—and two destinies, male and female; in the beginning there was no so-called One or Principle; certainly there did not exist a Supreme Ultimate! Looking at the matter today, as for this so-called One, indeed, what is this thing? And what is referred to as Principle: where does it reside? And what we call Supreme Ultimate: what does it refer to? If Two come from One, then where does One come from? A one and another one make two. Principle and *qi* are two; Yin-Yang and the Supreme Ultimate are two; the Supreme Ultimate and the Ultimateless [*wuji* 無極] are two. No matter how many times you look at the matter, there is nothing that arises without its paired term. Yet some who have never seen this so-called One nonetheless hastily and rashly speak of it!

So I have investigated the origin of things and see that husband and wife are their very beginning [*zaoduan* 造端].[5] For this reason I speak only of the two: husband and wife. That's all. I surely do not speak of One; I also don't talk about Principle. As I do not speak of One, I certainly do not speak of Nothingness.[6] Since I do not speak of Nothingness, I certainly do not speak of the nothingness of Nothingness.

---

2. To give Heaven (and, correlatively, the male or the sovereign) priority over all other things in the generation of the cosmos was one strategy of the School of Principle represented by Zhu Xi: Heaven is the source of "principle" and of the "mandate" that makes things what they are. See, for example, Zhu Xi, *Zhongyong zhangju* 中庸章句 [Chapter and verses of the *Doctrine of the Mean*]; English translation in Gardner, *The Four Books*, 107–30. Li Zhi contends that the cosmos arises from the conjuncture of two unlike things, thus inscribing diversity into the very nature of nature.
3. See *Daodejing*, ch. 42. Zhu Xi's use of the phrase to assign priority to Heaven is what Li Zhi opposes here.
4. The origin of things from Yin and Yang is described in the *Classic of Changes*, "The Great Commentary," 1:11, the passage from which the term *taiji*, or "Supreme Ultimate," is derived (*Zhou Yi zhengyi* 周易正義, "Xici" 繫辭, in Ruan, *Shisanjing zhu shu*, 7:28b–29a). Zhu Xi's version of neo-Confucianism gave priority to *li* (principle) over *qi* (substance), a thesis rejected here; Zhu Xi's prioritizing of principle would later be reversed by thinkers such as the seventeenth-century thinker Wang Fuzhi 王夫之.
5. For the term *zaoduan*, see the *Doctrine of the Mean*, ch. 12: "The Way of the gentleman has its very beginning in [ordinary] men and women."
6. See *Daodejing*, ch. 40: "All things under heaven sprang from being, and being sprang from nothingness."

Why? For fear of chaos and confusion in this world; "*too much talk leads to exhaustion*"[7] and even increasing bewilderment among the people. Better along with others to forget and together dwell where there are no words.[8] Then, with Heaven, Earth, humans, and the myriad things, find one's beginnings in the relation between a husband and a wife; once there, find nourishment and rest, and share in talk with others.

In the *Classic of Changes* it is said,

> Great is the great and originating power of *qian* [乾]; all things owe to it their beginning.
> Complete is the great and originating capacity of *kun* [坤]; all owe to it their birth.
> Providing origin and nurturing life, the changes of *kun* and *qian* know no limit.
>
> > Preserving in union the conditions of Supreme Harmony, all things in this world will find their own nature and purpose.[9]

The "nature and purpose" of things is to attain Supreme Harmony. The union of Supreme Harmony is found in the union of *qian* and *kun*. *Qian* is the husband, *kun* the wife. When each thing comes to find its own true nature and purpose, then nothing that exists will be out of place. Now, what indeed must the relation between husband and wife be like? What indeed?

TRANSLATED BY PAULINE C. LEE

---

7. See *Daodejing*, ch. 5.
8. See *Zhuangzi*, ch. 6.
9. Li here stitches together phrases from the *Classic of Changes* and phrases with a Daoistic resonance. See *Zhou Yi zhengyi*, "Qian," in Ruan, *Shisanjing zhu shu*, 1:6a, 22a; Legge, *The Yi King*, 213. "Qian," the symbol of the male, of firmness, and of Heaven, is the first hexagram of the *Classic of Changes*. "Kun," a symbol of the female, of submission, and of the Earth, is the second hexagram.

"ON MISCELLANEOUS MATTERS"
雜説
"ZA SHUO"

Written in 1592, this essay[1] has exerted a profound influence on Chinese views of literature and art from the late Ming to the present. Throughout we find Li insisting that truly great art is unrepressed self-expression flowing from an original childlike heart-mind. (PCL)

Bowing to the Moon[2] and *The Story of the Western Wing*[3] are works of Nature [化工]. *The Lute*[4] is a work of an artisan [畫工].[5] Artisans think they can seize heaven and earth's creative powers, but who among them understands that heaven and earth have no skill or technique? People see and delight in what heaven gives life to, what earth nurtures, and the varieties of vegetation found everywhere. But when they search for heaven's skill, no matter how they search, they cannot find a trace of it. Could it be that they lack the wisdom to discern Nature's workmanship?

One should know this: the Creator[6] is without technique. Even people who embody a sagelike spirit[7] are unable to discern where Nature's skill

---

1. *FS*, j. 3, in *LZQJZ* 1:272–76. For an alternative English translation, see Fei, *Chinese Theories*, 50–53. For a French translation, see Billeter, *Li Zhi*, 258–62. For an annotated Japanese translation, see Mizoguchi, "Funsho," 343–46.
2. *Bowing to the Moon* (*Bai yue ting* 拜月亭) is a late-Yuan drama attributed to Shi Hui (fl. 1295). A commentary on it attributed to Li Zhi is titled "Li Zhuowu xiansheng piping *Yougui ji*" 李卓吾先生批評幽閨記 [Mr. Li Zhuowu's critique of *Tales from the Hidden Women's Quarters*].
3. *The Story of the Western Wing* is a Yuan drama authored by Wang Shifu (fl. 1295–1307) and Guan Hanqing (ca. 1220–1300). For Li's commentary on this work, see "Li Zhuowu xiansheng pidian *Xixiang ji* zhenben" 李卓吾先生批點西廂記真本 [Mr. Li Zhuowu's annotations on the authentic edition of *The Story of the Western Wing*], in *LZQJZ* 20:591–682. For an English translation of the play, see West and Idema, *Moon and Zither*.
4. *The Lute* (*Pipa ji* 琵琶記), written by the Ming dramatist Gao Ming 高明 (ca. 1305–1368), is widely considered to be one of the great achievements in Chinese drama. For an English translation, see Mulligan, *The Lute*.
5. Throughout this essay, Li Zhi puns on the homophonous terms "work of nature" 化工 and "work of art" 畫工 (both *huàgōng*).
6. For this term, see *Zhuangzi*, ch. 6; Watson, *Chuang Tzu*, 77.
7. See *Zhuangzi*, ch. 13; Watson, *Chuang Tzu*, 150.

resides, so what ordinary person could understand it? Having considered our topic at some length, we can say: although artisanship may be clever, it has already sunk into the state of being secondhand.[8] Throughout the ages, the work of writing emerges from the pain within a writer's heart, alas![9]

I have heard it said: If you seek a horse whose hooves fly like the wind, a horse that chases after lightning, you will not find it by looking specifically for a yellow or black coat, a stallion or mare;[10] a sage whose voice genuinely responds and whose *qi* immediately attracts others[11] will not be found among pedantic scholars counting the number of lines written and measuring the ounces of ink used; writing so effortless that it moves like wind over water[12] does not depend on the use of this or that word or outstanding phrase. If a work possesses a tight structure, if the couplets are perfectly aligned, if the writing is grounded in solid logic and is in harmony with established models, if the beginning and end echo each other, and the abstract and concrete elements are in balance—all these various illusory criteria[13] are used to discuss literature. But such criteria cannot be used to discuss the most exquisite literature under heaven.

Variety plays[14] such as *The Story of the Western Wing* and *Bowing to the Moon* are first-class. But where in these can we find evidence of techniques? Now, no work is as skillfully executed as *The Lute*. Indeed, this scholar Gao [Ming] exerted all his efforts in exhibiting his skillfulness and reached the very height of his talent. Because he spared no pains to achieve the utmost of cleverness and skill, when his words come to an end, their meaning and flavor likewise dissipate and vanish. In the past I have picked up *The Lute* and

---

8. The term *er yi* 二義 ("secondhand" or "second order") derives from Buddhist teachings, meaning once removed from what is genuine.
9. Li Zhi is alluding to a poem by the Tang poet Du Fu, "Ou ti" 偶題 [Occasional composition]: "In literary matters throughout the ages, / The human heart is the gauge of success and failure."
10. Li combines a list of horse types from the *Classic of Poetry*, Mao no. 297, "Jiong," and a story from *Liezi*, ch. 8, in which the good judge of horses is perfectly indifferent to their appearance.
11. This plays on a passage in the *Classic of Changes*, "Wenyan" 文言 [Commentaries on words and texts], for the hexagram "Qian" 乾.
12. This sentence reworks a comment of Su Xun's 蘇洵 (1009–1066) comparing the unforced natural beauty of wind moving across water to "the utmost patterning [*zhiwen* 至文] under heaven." Li, however, here playfully takes *zhiwen* in the sense of "perfect writing." See Su Xun, "Zhongxiong zi Wenfu shuo" 仲兄字文甫説 [An elucidation of my brother Wenfu's name], in *Jiayou ji* 嘉祐集, *j*. 15; Fuller, *The Road to East Slope*, 82–83.
13. Literally, "meditation maladies" (*chan bing* 禪病), a Buddhist term referring to wandering thoughts and illusions that interfere with true insight.
14. *Zaju* 雜劇, a genre mixing high and low registers, from the Yuan period.

plucked its tunes: one strum and I sighed, a second and I was moved, a third strum and I found I no longer felt anything.[15] What is the reason for this? Could it be that the play seems genuine but is not, and so its tunes fail to impress themselves deeply upon the human heart? Even though the cleverness of the techniques is sublime, its power is sufficient only to penetrate no further than *between* the skin and the bone marrow.[16] Is it any wonder, then, that its ability to move people is nothing more than this?

The Story of the Western Wing and *Bowing to the Moon* are not like this. When I think that within the vast universe there exist such delightful people, the skill and cleverness that went into making them appears simply unfathomable, like the marvels of Creation itself. Among the truly great writers of the world, none begins with the intention to create literature. Their bosoms are filled with such and such indescribable and wondrous events. In their throats are such and such things that they desire to spit out but dare not. On the tip of their tongues, time and time again, they have countless things they wish to say but no one to whom to express them. They store up these feelings to the bursting point until, after a long time, their force cannot be stopped.

As soon as such a writer sees a scene that arouses his feelings or encounters something that catches his eye and sets him sighing, he snatches away another's wine cup and drowns his accumulated burdens. He pours out the grievances in his heart, and for thousands of years after, people are moved by his ill fortune. After spewing out jade, spitting pearls, illuminating the Milky Way, and creating the most heavenly writings, he listens to no one but himself, goes crazy and howls loudly, sheds tears and moans with sorrow, and is unable to stop. He would rather cause his readers and listeners to react passionately—to gnash and grind their teeth with the desire to slice him up—than hide his writings in a famous mountain[17] or consign them to destruction by fire or water.

When I read such a work I can begin to imagine what sort of person the author was. In his time, he must have harbored great aspirations that were

---

15. This passage contrasts with one in Liu Xie, *Wenxin diaolong* 文心雕龍 [The literary mind and the carving of dragons], in which the experience of writing is compared to that of rowing a boat: "When you stop your brush at the end of a work, it is like raising the oars when we ride in a boat." The momentum of the text should carry the meaning beyond the words. See Owen, *Readings*, 271.
16. Paraphrase of Bodhidharma's last conversation with his disciples: there it is said that the first two disciples' lesser understanding penetrated Bodhidharma's skin and bones, and the enlightened disciple's penetrated to the very bone marrow. For an English translation, see Dumoulin, *Zen Buddhism*, 93.
17. Alluding to Sima Qian's prophecy about the fate of his writings in "Letter to Ren An"; see Watson, *Records: Qin Dynasty*, 236.

frustrated by rulers, subjects, and friends; and so this writer expressed his feelings indirectly by using the device of the fated meetings and partings between a husband and a wife. In his script he rejoices over women of great beauty, commends Student Zhang for his remarkable encounter with Yingying,[18] and compares human society to the sudden changes of clouds and rain, inasmuch as people today value friendship no more highly than dirt.[19] Some may think it most laughable that a slight tale of romance should include comparisons—and favorable ones at that!—to the great works of Zhang Xu, Zhang Dian, Wang Xizhi, and Wang Xianzhi.[20]

Shao Yong said, "For the sage-king Yao, ceding the throne to Shun was no greater a matter than offering three cups of wine; and for Tang and Wu, conquering a dynasty was little more than a game of chess."[21] Now conquering a dynasty and ceding the throne are serious matters; but if one regards them merely as situations involving a single cup of wine or a single round of chess, how very trivial they are!

Indeed! Heroes past and present all tend to be of this sort. In the midst of what seems small, they see the vast, and in the midst of the vast, they miss no tiny detail. By lifting the tip of a feather they can erect a Buddhist temple; from atop the smallest mote of dust, they can turn the great dharma wheel of the universe. This is a universal truth and not just a comment on play scripts. If you doubt this, sit in the middle of a courtyard under the moonlight when in the stillness of autumn the leaves are falling, or alone in your study with not a soul to rely upon; try picking up the "Heart of the Lute" [Qin xin 琴心] section of *The Story of the Western Wing*.[22] Pluck it, then strum it. The inexhaustible treasures it contains are beyond the understanding, although the author's skill and craft are within the understanding.

Ah! Will I ever meet an author of this sort!

TRANSLATED BY PAULINE C. LEE

---

18. *The Story of the Western Wing* features Yingying as the "woman of great beauty" and Student Zhang as the leading man.
19. The phrase regarding the value of friendship is from Du Fu, "Pin jiao xing" 貧交行 [Song of friends in hard times].
20. In *The Story of the Western Wing*, act 5, scene 2, Student Zhang favorably compares the writing of his true love, Yingying, to the styles of these great and eccentric calligraphers.
21. This quotation comes from Shao Yong's poem "Shouwei yin" 首尾吟 [Ode with matching beginning and ending], representing a style of poetry inaugurated by Yong where the first and last lines of the poem are identical. Tang 湯 and Wu 武 were the military founders of the Shang and Zhou periods, respectively.
22. This aria appears in act 2, scene 5 of *The Story of the Western Wing*. The term *qin xin* dates back to the "Biography of Sima Xiangru" in Sima Qian, *Shi ji*, ch. 117, wherein the widowed Zhuo Wenjun hears Sima Xiangru play the lute and is thereby drawn to the stirrings of Sima Xiangru's heart. See Watson, *Records: Han Dynasty II*, 260–61.

"EXPLANATION OF THE CHILDLIKE HEART-MIND"
童心說
"TONGXIN SHUO"

Closely related to "On Miscellaneous Matters," this is Li Zhi's most famous essay, written around 1592.¹ "Explanation of the Childlike Heart-Mind" is at the same time an aesthetic and an ethics, centered on the idea of genuineness. Taking the opposite tack from the sophistication sought by most of his contemporaries, Li praises what is unpremeditated, simple, and authentic and thereby sets a cardinal value for writers and critics of the following century. Pushing on, as always, from paradox to provocation, he asks, "What need do I have of the Six Classics, Confucius and Mencius?" and closes with a paraphrase of the Daoist philosopher Zhuangzi, seeking to have a word with the kind of person who has forgotten all words. We offer two translations: one more meticulously annotated, one (the next chapter) in a freer style. (HS)

In the concluding remarks to his preface for *The Story of the Western Wing*,² the Mountain Farmer of Dragon Cave stated, "It is acceptable that those who know may not say that I still possess a childlike heart-mind."³

---

1. *FS, j.* 3, in *LZQJZ* 1:276–79. For published translations of Li's essay, see Owen, *Anthology*, 808–11; Ye, *Vignettes*, 26–28; Billeter, *Li Zhi*, 250–58; and Mizoguchi, "Funsho," 341–43. The locus classicus for the term "childlike heart-mind" (童心 *tongxin*) is the *Zuozhuan*. Speaking of the nineteen-year-old Zhao, presumptive heir to the throne, the narrator laments, "He still had a childlike heart-mind, and from this the gentlemen knew he would not come to a good end" (Xian, year 31; translation adapted from Legge, *The Chinese Classics*, 5:564).
2. The thirteenth-century Yuan drama *The Story of the Western Wing* was widely performed and read in the sixteenth century. In this drama a scholar and maiden overcome traditional obstacles as their passion and illicit romance transform into a celebrated marriage. The play differs from the source text, "Yingying's Story," by Yuan Zhen, in which the illicit romance turns to tragedy as the man abandons the maiden.
3. According to Zhang Jianye, the Mountain Farmer of Dragon Cave refers to Li Zhi's close friend Jiao Hong, who in his own writings cites a 1582 anonymous commentary on *The Story of the Western Wing* and adds the signature "Mountain Farmer of Dragon Cave." The

The childlike heart-mind is the genuine heart-mind. If one considers the childlike heart-mind unacceptable, then he considers the genuine heart-mind unacceptable. As for the childlike heart-mind, free from all falsehood and entirely genuine, it is the original mind[4] at the very beginning of the first thought. If one loses one's childlike heart-mind, one loses the genuine heart-mind. Losing the genuine mind is losing the genuine self. A person who is not genuine will never regain that with which he began.

A child is the beginning of a person; the childlike heart-mind is the beginning of the mind. How can the beginning of the mind be lost? But then, how can the childlike heart-mind suddenly be lost? From the beginning, sounds and sights enter through our ears and eyes. When one allows them to dominate what is within oneself, then the childlike heart-mind is lost. As one grows older, one hears and sees the "Principles of the Way" [i.e., moral teachings]. When one allows these to dominate what is within oneself, then the childlike heart-mind is lost. As one grows older, the "Principles of the Way" that one hears and sees increase day by day; what one knows and senses thus also increases daily. In time one comes to believe it is desirable to covet a good reputation and one endeavors to enhance one's reputation; one's childlike heart-mind is then lost. One believes that a bad reputation is to be disdained and endeavors to conceal such a reputation; one's childlike heart-mind is then lost.

The "Principles of the Way" that one hears and sees all come from extensive study of books and familiarity with moral principles. Could it be that the sages of antiquity did not study books? But even if they did not study books, their childlike heart-mind was secure and at ease; when they did study extensively, they simply protected their childlike heart-minds from being lost. They are unlike those scholars of today for whom the *more* they read books and become familiar with moral principles, the *more* they obstruct their childlike heart-mind. Now, if by reading extensively and familiarizing themselves with moral principles scholars in fact block their childlike heart-minds, why would the sages have written books and established teachings that would hinder these scholars? Once the childlike heart-mind

---

preface to the 1582 commentary concludes, "Having leisure in my humble home, I casually punctuate *The Story of the Western Wing*.... Alone, I hold the text and chant its verses on windy and rainy days or beautiful moonlit nights. I while away the time and break the strains of poverty and sadness. It is acceptable that those who know may not say that I still possess a childlike heart-mind." The translation is adapted from Cheang, "Li Chih," 272. For a reproduction of the preface, see Mizoguchi, "Min matsu," 189.

4. The locus classicus for "original mind" (*benxin* 本心) is *Mencius* 6A10. Mencius is known for his view that human nature tends toward good.

has been obstructed, one loses the ability to put into words one's innermost feelings, one's efforts to participate in government prove unsuccessful, and one's written compositions fail to express the truth. When beauty does not emanate from within and when brightness is not born from true sincerity,[5] any attempt at uttering words that express virtue will fail.[6] Why should this be so? Because when the childlike heart-mind is obstructed, then the Principles of the Way, which come from outside the self, *become* one's heart and mind.

Since the heart-mind is made up of what one sees and hears and Principles of the Way, what is spoken then are words that derive entirely from what one has seen and heard and from the Principles of the Way; one's words do not flow directly from the childlike heart-mind. Though these words may be artful, what do they have to do with oneself? How could such a situation lead to anything other than phony people speaking phony words, performing phony actions, and producing phony writings? Once a person is a phony, everything he does is phony. As a consequence, if one speaks phony words to a phony person, the phony person is pleased; if one talks about phony matters with a phony person, the phony person is pleased; if one discusses phony literature with a phony person, the phony person is pleased. When everything is phony, everyone is pleased. And when the entire theater is filled with phonies, how can a short person in the audience discriminate between real and fake?[7]

So even the most exquisite writing in the world can be buried by phony people and never even seen by later generations. Is this all that rare? Why does this happen? All the most exquisite literature in the world flows directly from the childlike heart-mind. As long as the childlike heart-mind is preserved, the Principles of the Way will not be endlessly perpetuated, what one hears and sees will have no authority, no period will lack great literature, no person will lack literary talent, and not a single pattern, genre, or word will fail to be genuine! Why must verse necessarily conform to aesthetic standards from antiquity or from the *Selections of Refined Literature*?[8] Why must prose necessarily resemble models written

---

5. See *Mencius* 7B25.
6. See *Analects* 14.5.
7. See *Zhuzi yulei* 朱子語類 [The classified conversations of Master Zhu], *j*. 27, for reference to a short person in the theater who cannot see the stage and instead of judging for himself takes his cues to laugh when others around him do so.
8. *Wenxuan* 文選 [Selections of refined literature], compiled by Crown Prince Xiao Tong 蕭統 (501–531), of the Liang dynasty, is one of the most influential literary anthologies in Chinese history. With the rise of new verse forms in the seventh century, it began to appear archaic.

in the pre-Qin period? Writing evolved through the ages; it developed into the literature of the Six Dynasties, then changed and became the new regulated verse of the Tang, then transformed into fantastic tales[9] and play scripts,[10] which developed into Yuan comedies, and those in turn evolved into *The Story of the Western Wing* and *The Water Margin*;[11] now they have become the eight-legged essays[12] of today: in each case, the transformation produced the most sublime writings of the age, which can never be understood through a discussion of historical contexts, precedents, or influences. And so, I am moved all the more by writings that immediately flow from the childlike heart-mind. Why speak of the Six Classics? Why speak of the *Analects* or the *Mencius*?

As for the Six Classics, the *Analects*, and the *Mencius*, if they are not words of overdone reverence from official historians, they are phrases of bloated praise from loyal subjects. If not one or the other, then they are what misguided followers and dim-witted disciples wrote down of what they *recalled* their teacher had said. What they wrote had a beginning but was missing an ending; or the followers remembered the conclusion but forgot the introduction. These disciples put down in writing whatever they happened to see. Later scholars did not scrutinize these writings. They simply declared that these words came directly from the mouths of sages and decided to establish them as great classics. Who knows whether more than half these writings are *not* words from the mouths of sages?

Even *if* these words are those of the sages, still, they were uttered in response to a specific situation. This is much like the case of prescribing a medication for a particular illness, applying a specific remedy depending on the circumstances in order to cure this dim-witted disciple or that misguided follower. The medicine prescribed depends on the illness; surely there is no fixed and unchanging prescription. Given this, how could we hastily accept these writings as the perfected doctrine for endless generations? And so, the Six Classics, the *Analects*, and the *Mencius* have become nothing more than a crib sheet for those belonging to the School

---

9. The genre known as fantastic tales (*chuanqi* 傳奇) emerged in the late Tang period.
10. The genre known as theater scripts (*yuanben* 院本) emerged during the early Yuan period.
11. *Shuihu zhuan* 水滸傳 (translated variously as *The Water Margin, Outlaws of the Marsh*, and *All Men Are Brothers*) is an anonymous novel from the Ming period, generally considered one of the four masterpieces of Chinese fiction. A famous commentary to this work is attributed to Li Zhi. For Li's views on the novel, see pp. 125–28.
12. The highly structured eight-legged essay form was prescribed as the standard for examination answers from the mid-fifteenth to the beginning of the twentieth century.

of Principle, a fountainhead for phonies. It would be utterly impossible to describe such writings with the label of "childlike heart-mind."

Oh! Wherever can I find a genuine great sage who has not yet lost his childlike heart-mind and have a word with him about writing?[13]

TRANSLATED BY PAULINE C. LEE
AND RIVI HANDLER-SPITZ

---

13. Li Zhi plays on a sentence from *Zhuangzi*, ch. 26; Watson, *Chuang Tzu*, 302.

"ON THE CHILDLIKE MIND"
童心說
"TONGXIN SHUO"

As an experiment and an invitation to imagine a different way of translating Li Zhi, we offer a second, freer-style version of "Tongxin shuo." (HS)

"... and, despite the freshness and simplicity of the work itself, I hope that the reader will not suspect the editor of simple-mindedness."—that's how the Denizen of Dragon Cave closes his preface to *The Story of the Western Wing*.

But simplicity is nothing other than authenticity. Someone who is afraid of being taken for a simpleton is afraid of truthfulness. A simple mind is pure of artifice; it is the mind of our first thought. When simplicity goes, authenticity goes; when the mind has lost its authenticity, the authentic person vanishes with it. When we lose our authenticity, nothing is left to set us straight again.

We begin as children, in simplicity. The child's mind is the beginning mind, the mind everyone has necessarily shared. But somehow this mind is lost: how indeed? It must be that impressions and sensations, crowding in through the ears and eyes, come to dominate the inner life and suppress the original mind. Then words and ideas learned from without come to dominate, suppressing the original mind. These external influences multiply with time. Eventually we become aware of the beauty of a good name and desire to acquire it; the ugliness of bad repute, likewise, we strive to avoid, and the simple mind is lost.

And then through reading we take in more words, ideas, impressions, and sensations. Can it be that the sages of old refused to read books [and thus preserved their simplicity of action]? But whether or not they were reading books, they maintained their childlike simplicity and did not let it stray. In this they were unlike the scholars of today who pile up terms and concepts from books in an effort to quash the original mind. Given their use of book learning and verbiage to subdue the original mind, what sage can hope to use writing or speech to suppress these scholars' misguided action? Once the original mind has been vanquished, its expression in language can only be indirect and superficial; its action in governing will be without deep roots, its writing style will be weak. You will see none of that "strength and clarity," the "flashes of genius," the "weighty word craft" [that the ancients prized]. So what then? Once the original mind has been lost, only impressions, words, and concepts are available to fill the gap.

Once impressions, words, and concepts replace the missing mind, speech will be drawn from these impressions, words and concepts alone—nothing like the simple mind uttering its direct speech. Sophisticated words, perhaps, but what do they offer us? What will result but artificial language and artificial deeds, artificial speech spoken by artificial people? When the person has become artificial, everything else is artificial too. Then make artificial speeches for artificial people; these artificial people will find everything to their taste. Perform artificial deeds for artificial people; they will be delighted. Write artificial essays for artificial audiences; they will applaud you. Nothing but artifice, and nothing but approval; but can anyone see beyond the false stage set? Even if somewhere someone writes a masterpiece that goes straight to the point of things, it will be buried in artifice and denied to posterity—is this not a pity? What then? For every masterpiece of writing flows from simplicity of mind. Where the childlike mind prevails, no ideas or words can have currency, no outer impressions can take its place; with the childlike mind, no time and no individual will be devoid of artistry, indeed no type or style of writing will be unartistic. Poetry need not be sought in the ancient *Classic of Poetry* and *Anthology*; prose need not be modeled on the age before the empire arose. The artistic mind broke out in the Six Dynasties to create recent-style verse form; it broke out again in Tang tales of the fantastic; again in the Yuan to make libretti and *zaju* opera; again in our time to make *The Story of the Western Wing* and *Outlaws of the Marsh* and the masters of the essay form. What I respond to is the direct expression of those who have retained the childlike mind. What need do I have of the Six Classics, Confucius, and Mencius?

As for the Six Classics, Confucius, and Mencius, where they are not exaggeration, they are flattery, or the inaccurate notes of muddleheaded students who tried to set down in books what they could not remember themselves. Subsequent scholars, purblind, mistook them for the actual words of the sages and elevated them to the rank of classics, despite their ramshackle composition. Or where the actual words of a sage are recorded, how are we to know whether the words refer only to some specific occasion or are addressed to the failings of this or that ignorant disciple, like a medicine prescribed for one disease but useless to cure another? Such occasional prescriptions can hardly be handed down as the timeless wisdom of the ages. And yet the philosophers of our time talk of nothing but the Six Classics, Confucius, and Mencius, that limitless resource of hypocrites. Nothing could be farther from the direct language of the childlike original mind, you see! Oh, where can I find a genuine sage who has not lost his childlike mind, so that I can exchange a word with him?

TRANSLATED BY HAUN SAUSSY

"THE HUB OF *THE HEART SUTRA*"
心經提綱
"*XIN JING TIGANG*"

The Heart Sutra is unique among Buddhist sutras in its brevity and multivalence.[1] Before leaving Yunnan in 1581, Li wrote this sutra out for a friend,[2] appending to the manuscript his own thoughts in the form of the commentary translated here. The word *tigang* (hub) in the title of Li's commentary refers literally to the point on a net where all the strands meet and are bound together, but the term is also lexicalized in Chinese as "outline" or "summary"—a short piece of writing intended to communicate the heart of a matter.

The Heart Sutra is itself designed to communicate the heart of a matter: it distills the essence of the teaching—and indeed the literature—of Prajñāpāramitā, or Perfect Wisdom.[3] "Perfect Wisdom" refers to the wisdom required to attain buddhahood, a wisdom that rejects the independent reality of subjects (or agents), objects, or actions. It is concerned with mastery of the doctrine of emptiness (*kong* 空, Skt. śūnyatā), which holds that all dharmas—all things perceived, all organs of perception, and indeed all means of perception—are empty of self-nature and have no independent existence.[4] Although the sutra presents core doctrinal ideas, its form is unique, its text compact, and it closes with a mantra. Some have argued that it is not even properly a sutra: it functions also as an incantation

---

1. *FS, j.* 3, in *LZQJZ* 1:280–84. *The Heart Sutra*, or *The Heart of Perfect Wisdom Sutra* (*Bore boluomiduo xinjing* 般若波羅蜜多心經, Skt. *Prajñāpāramitā-hṛdaya-sūtra*), exists in several recensions, although Li Zhi's commentary seems to have been made in reference to a version of the short recension. For an introduction to *The Heart Sutra* and two translations by Stephen Teiser and Stephen West, see the chapter "Heart Sūtra (Xin jing)," in Yu et al., *Ways with Words*. West translates the sutra, on pp. 121–29, as Li Zhi may have read it.
2. See "Notes on 'The Hub,'" pp. 119–20. "The Hub of *The Heart Sutra*" was subsequently published in *A Book to Burn*.
3. Jean Nattier has shown that *The Heart Sutra* appears to have been constructed in China by appending an introduction and conclusion to an extract of the Kumārajīva translation of *The Large Sutra*; see Nattier, "The Heart Sūtra."
4. Buswell and Lopez, *Princeton Dictionary*, 656–57.

(*dhāraṇī*), and indeed the text has played diverse roles in Buddhist practice.[5]

Li's commentarial essay is but one of many works aiming to elucidate *The Heart Sutra*; it is his summary of a summary, distilling what he sees as the heart of the heart of Perfect Wisdom. Not only is this piece a response to a text at the heart of Chinese Buddhism, it is to Li Zhi also most deeply concerned with the heart's function as the seat of consciousness (*xin* 心, often translated as "heart-mind," is rendered below simply as "the mind"). Li's emphasis on the potential of all individuals to achieve buddhahood by using this mind—by making use of their own unique capabilities of contemplation—is an individualistic twist both on the Chan notion that all human beings can achieve buddhahood and on the Taizhou school's conviction that sagehood is within reach of even commoners. Also of note is that Li ties the Buddhist nonduality of subject and object to the original nonduality of existence and nonexistence. This colors his interpretation with a style of apophasis distinctly reminiscent of Zhuangzi—a feature not obvious in *The Heart Sutra*.[6] (DL)

The Heart Sutra is the shortest way to what the Buddha said about the mind. The mind is fundamentally nonexistent, and yet people blindly take it for an existent thing. It is also *not* nonexistent, yet scholars insist it is nonexistent. When existence and nonexistence divide, subject and object take root.[7] Consequently, [one encounters] snagging and hindrance, fear and distress, inversion and reversal.[8] How can one achieve self-realization? Is it just that we don't reflect on our Self-Realized Bodhisattva?[9] "Coursing

---

5. See McRae, "Ch'an Commentaries." McRae cites Fukui Fumimasa's argument that the term translated as "heart" (*xin* 心, Skt. *hṛdaya*) in the title was originally understood to express the centrality of the *dhāraṇī* to Buddhist practice (89–90).
6. See Watson, *Chuang Tzu*, 43.
7. To perceive the independent existence of a subject (*neng* 能) from an object (*suo* 所) is delusive, according to Buddhist doctrine. Subject and object arise dependently during the cognitive act.
8. These are conventional Buddhist terms for delusive views and obstacles to enlightenment: "snagging and hindrance" (*gua ai* 掛礙, Skt. *āvaraṇa*); "fear and distress" (*kongbu* 恐怖, Skt. *bhaya-bhairava*); "inversion and reversal," literally, "[being] turned upside down" (*diandao* 顛倒, Skt. *viparyāsa*).
9. The bodhisattva referred to here is Guanzizai, also known as Guanyin, and identified as Avalokiteśvara in Sanskrit.

deeply in the wisdom" [of Perfect Wisdom], he arrived at the other bank of self-realization. At this time, his insight revealed of itself that the five aggregates—form, feeling, perception, volition, and consciousness—are all empty.[10] There is fundamentally no life or death to be had, therefore one can escape the Bitter Sea of [Cyclic] Life and Death,[11] traversing it and there casting off all suffering and distress. This is the main point of the whole sutra. The lines that follow, shattering [illusion] over and over, all make this clear. And so [the Bodhisattva] then called out to him, saying,[12]

> Śāriputra![13] Don't think that when I speak of "emptiness" I'm just attaching to [some reified] emptiness! When we say "form does not differ from emptiness," or when we say "emptiness does not differ from form," these are just to say that the two things are no different. Still, we have these two things in opposition, and even if we could merge them as one, we'd still have the one thing. In fact, whenever we speak of "form," we are speaking precisely of "emptiness"; there's no emptiness beyond form! Whenever we speak of "emptiness," we are speaking precisely of "form"; there's no form beyond emptiness! Not only is there no form, there is also no emptiness: this is True Emptiness.[14]

So then [the Bodhisattva] again called out to him, saying,

> "Śāriputra! These are all marks of the emptiness of dharmas."[15] And since there is no emptiness to be named, how much less are there arising or extinguishing, defiling or purifying, increasing or decreasing, names or appearances?

---

10. The five aggregates, or *skandas*, are five categories of mind and matter. The first, form (*se* 色, Skt. *rūpa*), is material and the rest are aspects of perception and mind: feeling (*shou* 受, Skt. *vedanā*); perception (*xiang* 相, Skt. *saṃjñā*); volition (*xing* 行, Skt. *saṃskāra*); consciousness (*shi* 識, Skt. *vijñāna*). "Empty" here means that the aggregates are devoid of self-nature or independent existence.
11. I.e., the bitter sea of *saṃsāra*, the realm of rebirth.
12. Save for a few phrases quoted verbatim, the following two "quotations" of Guanyin are not present in the text of *The Heart Sutra*; rather, they illustrate how, in Li Zhi's imagination, the dialogue may have unfolded.
13. Disciple to the Buddha.
14. "True Emptiness" (*zhen kong* 真空) evokes both the concepts of emptiness (*kong*, Skt. *śūnyatā*) and thusness (*zhenru* 真如, Skt. *tathatā*). "Emptiness" here is vacuity with regard to self-nature (*zixing* 自性), or independent existence. "Thusness" is reality established as empty in this sense.
15. "Marks of emptiness" (*kong xiang* 空相), or empty attributes, refer to elements of experience that have no independent, lasting existence and are thus regarded as empty.

Therefore, form fundamentally doesn't arise;[16] emptiness fundamentally isn't extinguished. To speak of form is not impure; to speak of emptiness is not pure. In form there is no increasing; in emptiness there is no decreasing. There's no imagining it: in emptiness there is fundamentally no "it" [to reify]!

Therefore the Five Aggregates are all empty: there are no forms, feelings, perceptions, volition, or consciousness. The Six Sense Roots are all empty: there are no eyes, ears, nose, tongue, body, or mind.[17] The Six Dusty Sense Fields are all empty: there are no sights, sounds, smells, tastes, sensations, or mental elements.[18] The Eighteen Realms are all empty: there is nothing from the realm of sight on up through the realm of consciousness.[19] The same is even true of birth and old age, sickness and death, knowledge and ignorance, the Four Noble Truths, wisdom and actualization, and all the like—there is nothing to be attained.

This is the Self-Realized Bodhisattva, through wisdom and reflective illumination, reaching the shore of nothing-to-be-attained. In this way, since what is to be attained is nothing, it follows naturally that there can be now neither snagging nor hindrance, neither fear nor distress, nor any inverted dreamlike thoughts. The cycle of life and death [is revealed], and one completes nirvana.

How could this be [achievable] only for the Bodhisattva? Although the buddhas of the Three Ages, past, present and future, all reach the other shore by this wisdom, and all together attain Unsurpassed Perfect Enlightenment, there are assuredly no sentient beings on the Great Earth that are *not* buddhas. And moreover, know that this Sublime Wisdom of True Emptiness, with

> This great spiritual incantation,
> This great illuminating incantation,
> This unsurpassed incantation,
> This unequalled incantation,

---

16. The word *se* 色 is the accepted translation of the Sanskrit term *rūpa*, which generally denotes materiality or matter. Here it is rendered as "form"; in other contexts it can mean "the passions" or even "lust."
17. "The Six Sense Roots" (*liu gen* 六根, Skt. *ṣaḍ indriyāṇi*) refer to the six sensory organs or faculties of sense.
18. "The Six Dusty Sense Fields" are these six objects of the sense organs.
19. "The Eighteen Realms" are the Six Sense Roots plus the Six Dusty Sense Fields and the Six Modalities of sight, audition, olfaction, taste, touch, and awareness that represent the interaction between the sense organs and their sense objects.

enables one to escape the Bitter Sea of [Cyclic] Life and Death, traversing it and "casting off all suffering and distress."

It is real and not vacuous.

And yet it has long been difficult to explain "emptiness." Those who grasp at form are mired in it; those who explain emptiness are obstructed by it, and they arrive at the conclusion that the two don't depend on anything. This is also to reject the doctrine of cause and effect for all things, and to disbelieve the truth so clearly praised by the sutra:

"Emptiness is form"—what emptiness is there really?
"Form is emptiness"—what form is there after all?

There is no emptiness and no form, so how can there be anything having existence or having nonexistence to snag or hinder our attaining self-realization?

And so you who are reflective need only persist in using your own unique wisdom in reflective illumination, and the other shore will be reached of itself. Why should the Bodhisattva be someone other than you?! It just takes a single flash of insight to reach it—that's all! All people are the Bodhisattva, yet they do not themselves realize it. So as to [being] the Bodhisattva, all men are as one—there are no sages or simpletons. As to the Buddhas of the Three Ages, ancient and modern are as one—there's no first or last. What can be done about the fact that so many people can be made to follow but not to understand?[20] Those who can be made to understand become the Bodhisattva; those who can't become common men, birds and beasts, rocks and trees, in the end expiring and returning to the turbulent depths.

TRANSLATED BY DAVID LEBOVITZ

---

20. Alludes to *Analects* 8.9.

"NOTES ON 'THE HUB'"
提綱説
"TIGANG SHUO"

In the year 1581, while Li Zhi was in Huang'an, he wrote "Notes on 'The Hub,'"[1] a short piece that reveals the circumstances under which he composed "The Hub of *The Heart Sutra*." The "Notes" warn of the inherent unreliability of language and the dangers in placing too much faith in the core texts and exegetical writings of canonical traditions: without the right guiding intellect, sutras, scriptures, canons, or classics—all referred to by the single term *jing*—are only imperfect guides to the Way; explanation of these core texts is likewise liable to lead one astray. And so Li Zhi's "Notes on 'The Hub'" not only serve to explain his explanation of *The Heart Sutra* but also address the problems inherent in all explanation.

Apparently as a foil to his own exegetical choices, Li Zhi chose to publish this piece alongside his *Laozi Explained*, a commentary on the *Daodejing*. (DL)

The Way is fundamentally great, but since the Way [is presumed to] rely on scriptures, one cannot clearly make it out. [Moreover], when seeking to clarify the Way by clarifying the scriptures, one can't discern the Way because of [the attached scriptural] explanations. Thus scriptures are robbers of the Way and explanations are barriers to the scriptures. So what use are they?

Despite all this, good scholars penetrate the scriptures while bad ones are stuck clinging to them. Explanations enlighten the capable and mislead the incapable. And so it is that [scriptures and explanations] *should* serve as robbers and barriers. So when our forebears lectured on the scriptures and

---

1. The *Li Wenling ji*, *j*. 9, collects this piece immediately following "The Hub of *The Heart Sutra*," although the two works were originally published separately. See also *LZQJZ* 24:504.

those who followed explained them, even the ones who weren't especially capable just traversed that same path; the incapable, [however], can't be given the Way.[2]

While I was in central Yunnan, a friend asked me to copy out *The Heart Sutra*, and when I had finished writing it, I inscribed a few words at the end, calling them "The Hub." Although I didn't call it an "explanation," how could it be anything else!

The Huang'an magistrate has already had "The Hub" printed. Let's append this to my notes on the *Book of the Way and Virtue* [*Daodejing*] and print the two together. When we reflect on its heart, have I penetrated the scripture? Have I avoided clinging obstinately to it? Do my explanations not mislead? I write it out in order to see.

TRANSLATED BY DAVID LEBOVITZ

---

2. The text here may contain an error or omission; the meaning of this sentence is unclear.

"ON LOFTINESS AND CLEANLINESS"
高潔説
"GAO JIE SHUO"

This essay,[1] written in Macheng in 1589, reads like a companion piece to "Self-Appraisal" (pp. 138–39), written the previous year. Both essays function as ethical self-portraits in which the author feigns to present himself in an extremely unflattering manner. Yet this brusque, unattractive exterior is shown to encase—or even mask—a sterling character.

The present essay opens with the assertion that Li loves loftiness. But almost immediately the author begins heaping disapproval on himself: he describes himself as arrogant, short-tempered, intolerant, and unyielding. Gradually, however, the essay reveals that these critical remarks do not in fact represent Li's true self-assessment. He is merely repeating the aspersions cast on him by others. Because Li fled officialdom, took up residence in a remote monastery, and refused to admit visitors, his behavior earned him the reputation of a misanthrope. Li repeats these accusations but indicates no contrition. Instead, he decries his accusers for failing to understand that he was driven into solitude against his will by the hypocrisy of contemporaries who cared only for wealth and power. The essay concludes by praising two visiting monks from Huang'an, whose insight, Li feels certain, will enable them to empathize with him in his solitary struggles. (RHS)

By nature I love loftiness. Since I love loftiness, I am arrogant and incapable of accommodating other people. Or more precisely: I will not accommodate the type of people who cozy up to wealth. If people have a speck of goodness in them, even if they are base and servile, I'll readily honor them.

---

1. *FS, j.* 3, in *LZQJZ* 1:294–97.

By nature I love cleanliness.[2] Or more precisely: I am short-tempered and intolerant. But the only people I can't tolerate are the type who flock around the powerful and flatter the rich. If someone possesses a speck of goodness, even if I were a prince or duke, I'd readily treat him with reverence.

Accommodating others is a sign of humility. People who are humble are receptive to a wide array of influences; and drawing widely from diverse sources is a mark of even greater loftiness. So the people in this world who are capable of accommodating others are precisely those who most love loftiness. Am I, then, not right to love loftiness?

In recruiting [officials, the ruler] must take care not to exclude people. When no one is excluded, everyone has a chance. And when everyone has a chance, there are no dirty dealings. So the people in this world who know how to include others are precisely those who most love cleanliness. Am I, then, not right to love cleanliness?

These days, the unwashed all think I am short-tempered and intolerant, arrogant and unwilling to give others a chance. They say I went of my own accord to Huang'an, where I've locked the door all day and made quite a laughingstock of Fang Danshan for [saying that I] seek friends everywhere.[3] [People say that] ever since I moved to Dragon Lake, I've turned guests away even when I have not locked the door, or, [that] even if I've greeted them, I've not adhered to proper ritual. [They claim that] although I may have received one or two people with respect, I soon cast them off in disgust. This is the customary way in which people speak of me.

But what they don't realize is that although I keep the door closed all day, I will yearn, to the very last of my days, to meet someone whose heart's aspirations surpass my own. For a full year I have sat alone, and for a full year I have endured the sorrow of not meeting a soul friend. It is difficult for me to talk with people who make such accusations. Even the people with whom I thought I could converse took me for a man with no eyes, incapable of understanding other people, so in the end I was deceived. They thought I was biased and unfair, so in the end I was unable to maintain relations with anyone. They claimed that they had "brushed apart the fur to see the skin beneath" and "blown aside the hairs to see the pores below,"[4] and indeed

---

2. The concept of cleanliness refers not only to physical cleanliness, which Li Zhi prized highly, but also to political cleanliness—i.e., freedom from corruption.
3. Refers to Fang Yifeng (dates unknown).
4. In other words, they claimed that they had seen through Li Zhi's pretended virtues.

they had. But in fact the differences between them and the unwashed were negligible—a matter of nothing more than "fifty paces."[5] How could such people merit discussion?

Hearing footsteps in a deserted valley or even seeing a face that looks as if it might belong to a countryman inspires delight.[6] Yet they say that I do not wish to see anyone. How could this be? I just regret that so far no one resembling a human being has stopped by. Even if a shadow slightly resembling that of a human being paid a call, I would immediately greet it with respect, giving no heed to whether the person was of lowly status. I would run toward him, giving no heed to whether the person was of noble rank. In every case, I would perceive his strengths and overlook his shortcomings. Not only would I overlook his shortcomings, but I would also, with the utmost respect, honor him as my teacher. All the more so if I am "biased" in favor of such people!

Why would I behave this way? Because good friends are hard to come by. If I did not treat such a person with the greatest reverence and sincerely honor him as my teacher, how could an intelligent and worthy gentleman be willing to consider me his friend? If I wish to have him as my friend, I have no choice but to treat him with extreme respect. But in this world, very few people possess genuine talent and intelligence. Time and again I exert myself to the utmost serving them with sincere respect, but in the end those "men of intelligence" and "men of talent" prove false. In these situations, I have no choice but to separate myself from them. If they are not only insincere but also treacherous, I have no choice but to distance myself from them day by day. For this reason, the multitude says that I lack eyes. But if I truly had no eyes, I would certainly not be able to distance myself from them permanently. If I truly were biased and unfair, I would certainly shield them from their shortcomings and remain friendly with them for life. Thus the accusations that I am biased and have no eyes may seem compelling, but they are false.

---

5. Allusion to *Mencius* 1A3. On the battlefield, when soldiers abandon their weapons and flee, those who flee fifty paces are not more courageous than those who flee one hundred paces. Li Zhi uses this analogy to show that whereas he may have been able to converse with some people better than others, no one truly understands him.
6. From the Daoist classic *Zhuangzi*, ch. 24. Zhuangzi tells of men exiled to the far southern region of Yue: "A few days after they have left their homelands, they are delighted if they come across an old acquaintance. When a few weeks or a month have passed, they are delighted if they come across someone they had known by sight when they were at home. By the time a year has passed, they are delighted if they come across someone who even looks as though he might be a countryman" (Watson, *Chuang Tzu*, 262).

Now that the two monks of Huang'an have arrived,[7] people will certainly say I am biased. The two monks have a lifelong commitment to me; they surely will not allow me to endure [the insult of] being labeled a person with no eyes. The two monks truly understand the bitterness I suffer inside; they truly understand that words cannot express my loneliness; they truly understand that I yearn to form relationships with others more keenly than others desire to associate with me. I do not prize the two monks on account of their talent but truly on account of their virtue; not on account of their intelligence but truly on account of their sincerity. The virtuous are sincere and the sincere virtuous: what need have I to worry about the two monks? The two monks are disciples of Li Tao'an.[8] Tao'an is a disciple of Deng Huoqu's. Deng Huoqu is as resolute in his aspirations as a diamond; his courage is as vast as the heavens; in his studies he follows his mind to enlightenment, and his wisdom surpasses that of his teacher.[9] For this reason his students resemble him, and his students' students resemble his students. Because of this, I predict that the two monks will be quite capable of expressing their indignation on my behalf. Thus it is for them that I have composed this treatise on loving loftiness and cleanliness.

TRANSLATED BY RIVI HANDLER-SPITZ

---

7. Refers to Ruowu and Zeng Jiquan. See "Three Essays for Two Monks of Huang'an," pp. 21–28.
8. A monk in Huang'an.
9. Zhao Zhenji (1508–1575).

"PREFACE TO *THE LOYAL AND RIGHTEOUS OUTLAWS OF THE MARSH*"
忠義水滸傳序
"ZHONGYI SHUIHUZHUAN XU"

Outlaws of the Marsh, also known in English as *All Men Are Brothers* and *The Water Margin*, is a vernacular novel about a group of 108 bravos driven to banditry.[1] The main cause of their lawbreaking is the feckless policy of the Northern Song government, which allowed China to be invaded and conquered and left the ordinary people at the mercy of rapacious officials. Gathered at Liangshan Marsh, the outlaws form a sizable resistance army. In the end they are granted amnesty by Emperor Huizong and sent on campaigns to resist foreign invaders and suppress rebel forces. The novel went through many editions, and its authorship is debated. Li Zhi's preface refers to a hundred-chapter edition dating from the mid-sixteenth century, attributed to two authors, Shi Nai'an 施耐庵 and Luo Guanzhong 羅貫中. Li composed this essay in 1592 while residing in Wuchang. (HYC)

The Grand Historian says, "'The Difficulty of Persuasion' and 'The Loner's Indignation' are works of wise men and sages that were written to express their indignation."[2] From this we can see that if the ancient wise men and sages weren't indignant, then they simply didn't write. Writing when you aren't indignant is like shivering when you're not cold, groaning and moaning when you aren't sick. Although you could write *something*, would it really be worth reading?

---

1. *FS, j.* 3, in *LZQJZ* 1:301–4.
2. A citation of Sima Qian's preface ("Taishigong zixu" 太史公自序) to his *Records of the Grand Historian* (*Shi ji*, ch. 130); the two essays mentioned are both by the Legalist thinker Han Feizi (ca. 280 B.C.E.–233 B.C.E.).

Outlaws of the Marsh is a work written to express indignation. Once the Song royal house lost its strength, the world went topsy-turvy: the most worthy men were in the lowest positions, and the least worthy in the highest positions; things even got to the point where the barbarians were on top and the Chinese were subservient to them.

At that time, the emperor and ministers were like birds building nests inside a burning building without even noticing the blaze. The Song government paid tribute and made itself a vassal to barbarians, willingly bowing before dogs and goats.

Shi [Nai'an] and Luo [Guanzhong], the two authors of *Outlaws of the Marsh*, lived in the Yuan dynasty, but their hearts were in the Song. Though born in the Yuan, they still felt indignant about events that had occurred during the Song. They were indignant about the two Song emperors being held captive in the north by the Jin, so in order to express their indignation, they wrote [in chapters 83–89 of their novel] about [the bandit leader Song Gongming] defeating the Liao to the north.[3] They felt indignant that the Song emperor [Gaozong] had retreated to the south in search of peace [and begun there the dynasty of the Southern Song], so they wrote [in chapters 90–99 of their novel] about [the outlaw army] quelling the Fang La rebellion. They wrote all this in order to vent their indignation.

And through whom do they vent this indignation? It's through the outlaws who sent out the call to gather at the Water Margin. You couldn't call them anything but loyal and righteous. That's why Shi and Luo wrote their story, and that's why they named it *Loyalty and Righteousness at the Water Margin*.

Why do the loyal and the just gather at the Water Margin? The reason is obvious. And how is it that each and every one of the many who are at the Water Margin is loyal and just? It's equally obvious how this came to be. The proper principle is that "princes of little virtue are submissive to those of great, and those of little worth to those of great." If those of little worth rule over those of great worth, will the more worthy ones willingly consent to being ruled without feeling ashamed? It's as if the weak tried to push the strong around—would the strong take that lying down? Such a situation drives the empire's strongest and most worthy to its edges—to the Water Margin. That's how it came to be that those whom we call the

---

3. In 1126, the Jurchen army seized the capital of the Northern Song and took Emperor Huizong and Emperor Qinzong captive.

"Outlaws of the Marsh" are all the strongest and the most worthy, the loyal and the righteous.

Yet there's never been anyone as loyal and righteous as Song Jiang, the hero of *The Water Margin*. Now, taking a look at the 108 outlaws, they share the spoils in victory and the blame in defeat, they live and die as one—but even their loyalty and righteousness couldn't possibly compare to Song Jiang's. Song Jiang is the only one of those living at the Water Margin who still cares about the dynasty. He wholeheartedly wishes to be enlisted; he single-mindedly seeks to serve his country. Finally, [when the emperor sends him and his outlaws on campaigns against rebels and invaders,] Song Jiang and his outlaws meet with great disaster and great success, after which he drinks poison and the others hang themselves—dying together and not daring to part.

Such an intense sense of loyalty and justice is truly enough to earn the obedience of the 108 outlaws; and that's why he is able to become the leader of all 108, binding them together into a sworn brotherhood at Mount Liang. In the end, he leads them south to put down the rebels of Fang La, where over half of his 108 men die in battle. However, [not all are so loyal]: [in chapter 99] Lu Zhishen leaves for the Pagoda of the Six Harmonies, where he dies; Yan Qing weeps and runs away from his leader; and the two Tong brothers plot with [the pirate] Li Jun and stay behind [instead of serving the government with Song Jiang].

It's not that Song Jiang doesn't know about such plans and schemes. He simply sees them as weak attempts at self-preservation made by small-minded, opportunistic men—definitely nothing worthy of someone who is loyal to his leaders and faithful to his friends. That is Song Jiang. That is loyalty. How could his story *not* have been written? How could his story *not* be read?

That's why the one who runs the country can't afford *not* to read it. If only he'd read it once, then the loyal and righteous wouldn't be out at the Water Margin anymore—instead they'd be right back beside the ruler. The wise prime ministers can't afford not to read it. If only they'd read it, then the loyal and righteous wouldn't be out at the Water Margin anymore—instead they'd be right back at court. The chiefs of staff and the field commanders, they can't afford not to read it either. If only they'd read it someday, then the loyal and righteous wouldn't be out at the Water Margin anymore—instead they'd be back in the cities to serve and protect the homeland. However, if it isn't read, then the loyal and righteous won't be beside the ruler, or at court, or in our cities. Where will they be? At the Water Margin. This is the indignation expressed by the *Water Margin*.

If meddlesome people use this book as mere material for conversation, and people who command troops only borrow tactics from the book, then everyone's just taking what he can put to his advantage—and then no one will be able to see the loyalty and righteousness that this book contains!

TRANSLATED BY HUIYING CHEN AND DREW DIXON

"PREFACE TO SU CHE'S *EXPLICATION OF LAOZI*"
子由解老序
"ZIYOU *JIE LAO XU*"

Su Che 蘇轍 (1039–1112), whose sobriquet was Ziyou 子由, is perhaps best known as brother to the great poet Su Shi 蘇軾 (1037–1101).[1] Both were among the Eight Masters of the Tang (618–906) and Song (960–1279) periods. Su Che wrote a commentary on the Daoist classic *Daodejing*, attributed to the mythical Laozi. Li's preface, composed in 1574 in Nanjing, exhibits a perspective that both finds its source in Su Che's commentary and resonates with trends in late-Ming thought. The preface begins with the analogy of the Dao to food: one nourishes the body, the other the spirit. And just as physical nutrition can be derived from a variety of foodstuffs, so can spiritual edification come in diverse philosophical forms. Developing this line of reasoning, Li advocates the functional equivalence of Daoism and Confucianism, a relativistic stance concordant with late-Ming religious syncretism. Moreover, the earthiness of the analogy of the Dao to food, along with the casual, anecdotal style of the preface as a whole, evinces Li's debt to Wang Yangming's Taizhou school followers, who believed that teachings on the Dao must be presented in language that is simple and easy to grasp. The preface was published in Jiao Hong's *Commentaries on the Laozi* as well as in Li's *A Book to Burn*. (RHS)

All foods are alike if they fill the belly. Southerners like to eat rice, while northerners like to eat millet. Northerners and southerners have never envied one another on this account. And yet if a northerner and a southerner were to switch places and each were to taste the other's food, they

---

1. *FS, j.* 3, in *LZQJZ* 1:305–7.

would not go so far as to reject [the unfamiliar fare]. The presence of the Dao in the teachings of Confucius and Laozi is like rice in the south and millet in the north. When there is enough of *this*, even if one doesn't covet *that*, could one actually reject it? Why not? Because each is satisfactory for filling the belly. And when one is truly starving, one does not distinguish between them.

Once I was studying in the north and ate as a guest in somebody's home. The weather was cold, and it rained and snowed heavily for three days. I had not eaten any grain for seven days. I was so cold and hungry I could no longer stand up. I gazed yearningly toward my host. He pitied me and cooked me some millet. I gulped it down in big mouthfuls to my heart's content, lacking the leisure to distinguish what I was eating. Pushing aside the utensils, I asked, "Could that have been rice? How could it have tasted so delicious?" My host laughed and said, "That was millet. It's just as good as rice. Moreover, the millet you ate today is no different from the millet you've eaten in the past. It's only because you were especially hungry that it tasted especially good; and only because it tasted especially good did you feel especially full. From now on think no more of 'millet' and 'rice.'"

When I heard this, I sighed with emotion. If my eagerness to study the Dao resembled my yearning for food on that day, would I be at leisure to choose whether to study Confucius or Laozi? Ever since then, I have concentrated on studying the *Laozi*, and at all times benefited from reading Su Che's *Explication of Laozi*. Many people have interpreted the *Laozi*, but Su Che is the best. Su Che cites the *Doctrine of the Mean*: "When pleasure, anger, sorrow, and joy have not yet been aroused, we call this equilibrium."[2] This "state when emotions have not yet been aroused" is "the inner sanctum of the myriad things."[3] Song-dynasty Confucians from Cheng Hao onward[4] transmitted this teaching from one to the next and frequently reminded their disciples to evaluate their own bearing by it. But Su Che alone grasped the import of the subtle phrases scattered throughout brief and incomplete chapters. This is why he was able to bring out the hidden message of the *Laozi* and make the meaning of its five thousand characters gleam as

---

2. For more on this phrase, see "Record of Master Geng Dingli," pp. 166–71.
3. The first part of the sentence alludes to the *Doctrine of the Mean*; the second invokes the *Daodejing*, ch. 62. My translation of the latter phrase borrows from Ivanhoe, *The Daodejing of Laozi*, 65.
4. Cheng Hao (1032–1085), his younger brother Cheng Yi (1033–1107), and Zhu Xi were among the most influential pioneers of neo-Confucianism. See Graham, *Two Chinese Philosophers*, and Wong, "Single-Rootedness."

brightly as the sun.[5] Scholars must absolutely not allow this book to leave their hands for a single day.

When the *Explication* was complete, Su Che showed it to Daoquan,[6] and Daoquan approved of it. He then sent it to Su Shi, and he too approved. Now more than five hundred years have passed since the time of Su Che.[7] I doubt that there will ever be another interpretation as outstanding as his. Alas! Only when one truly *hungers* for understanding is one able to attain it.

TRANSLATED BY RIVI HANDLER-SPITZ

---

5. The *Daodejing* is slightly longer than five thousand characters.
6. Daoquan 道全 (dates unknown) was a Buddhist monk and friend of Su Che's.
7. Mencius (7B38) suggests that roughly every five hundred years a sage arises. Li Zhi may be suggesting that *he* is the sage who can understand Su Che. I am grateful to Zhu Jinghua for sharing this observation with me.

"POSTFACE TO *THE PROSE OF OUR TIME*"
時文後序
"*SHIWEN* HOUXU"

In this essay,[1] Li Zhi defends "the prose of [his] time"—the eight-legged essay. Citing a well-known passage in the *Zuozhuan* that establishes "patterned refinement" as the criterion for judging literature and enabling it to "travel far" in both space and time, Li argues that the eight-legged essay, the formulaic genre used for selecting examination candidates in Ming China, met these aesthetic criteria.

Li's defense of the eight-legged essay seems somewhat out of place, for many leading intellectuals in the following generation attacked this genre for its stifling rigidity. Both formally and ideologically, the essays were indeed highly regulated: each section or "leg" was required to set forth a thesis that was then challenged in a counterargument. This tightly balanced, antithetical structure, repeated within individual "legs" and amplified on the level of the essay as a whole, encouraged students to make predictable, well-rehearsed arguments that regurgitated orthodox interpretations. Individual interpretation was strongly discouraged.[2]

Given the conventions of the genre, one wonders why a staunch individualist like Li Zhi would endorse it. One possible answer has to do with Li Zhi's historical relativism, his belief that in each era new genres and styles develop to address the particular concerns of the day. Unlike adherents of the powerful Return to Antiquity Movement, who advocated writing in imitation of ancient models, Li championed a theory of literature characterized by constant innovation. He therefore lent his support to the eight-legged essay and maintained that this form, a creation of the Ming, did indeed have the power to "travel far." (RHS)

---

1. *FS, j.* 3, in *LZQJZ* 1:324–25.
2. For more on the eight-legged essay, see Elman, *Cultural History*, 383. See also Gong, *Mingdai baguwenshi tan*, and Plaks, "Prose."

The prose of our time, the eight-legged essay, is the literary form used in official examinations in our time. It is not an ancient form. When we consider the ancient from the standpoint of the present, the ancient is surely not the present. But when we consider the present from the perspective of the future, the present will indeed become ancient. It is said that the superiority or inferiority of literature depends upon the times. Assessing superiority or inferiority is called judging. Once a standard of judgment becomes established in a period, its luminous essence is passed down to later generations. How could it be otherwise?

From ancient times to now, ethical values are unchanged, [the purpose of] writing is unchanged; what differs is nothing more than the style of each period. Thus in the heyday of pentasyllabic poetry, quadrisyllabic poetry was considered ancient. In the heyday of Tang regulated verse, pentasyllabic poetry was in turn considered ancient. Just as, according to the standard of contemporary "recent-style poetry," Tang poetry is considered ancient, [so too] ten thousand generations hence will our contemporary poetry be considered as ancient as that of the Tang. All the more so the eight-legged essays we use to select our scholars!

Those who say that the prose of our time—the eight-legged essay—can be used in examinations but will never "travel far" not only fail to understand literature, they also fail to understand history.³ For there has never been a form of literature that could be used for selection but had no wider relevance. Scholars of national repute do meritorious deeds and compose writings that manifest their integrity; these works shine forth to this day. Are such authors not selected for office on the basis of their eight-legged essays? Compositions issuing from three days spent in the thorny examination halls determine these men's lives. If their writings cannot travel far, it must be because their words lack pattern and refinement, and therefore

---

3. In this passage, Li Zhi is playing with the noun and adjective meanings of the word *wen* 文. As a noun, this word refers to literature, and more broadly to the cultural values conveyed through writing. As an adjective, it refers to "pattern" or "refinement." The phrase "travel far" (*xing yuan* 行遠) signifies the dissemination of literary works across both space and time. It calls to mind the dictum from the *Zuozhuan*, "The Master said, 'If a person does not use words, who will know what is on his mind? And if the words lack pattern and refinement, they will not travel far [in persuading others]'" (Xiang, year 25; cited in Nylan, *The Five "Confucian" Classics*, 93).

the authors do not deserve to be selected for office. But the eight-legged essays selected by Censor-in-Chief Li[4] will travel far. I hope that scholars will examine them closely.

TRANSLATED BY RIVI HANDLER-SPITZ

---

4. Zhang Jianye suggests that this may refer to Li Yuanyang 李元陽 (1497–1580, *jinshi* 1526). See *LZQJZ* 1:325.

"MR. LI'S TEN KINDS OF ASSOCIATION"
李生十交文
"LI SHENG SHI JIAO WEN"

This essay[1] constitutes one of Li Zhi's several contributions to the flourishing late-Ming discourse on friendship. Framed as a letter to an unidentified recipient, the essay rebuts the claim that Li withdrew from all social relations after he resigned his post as prefect of Yao'an. Writing from Huang'an in 1583, Li lays claim to a wide network of associations, which he arrays before the reader and ranks according to quality. The theme of ranking characterizes many Ming-dynasty essays, yet here the criteria by which Li classifies his companions strike readers as quirky and eccentric. Lurking just below the surface lies a criticism of the superficial basis on which many of his contemporaries formed associations. The essay thus demonstrates Li's unconventional and highly critical perspective on a subject heatedly debated among his peers. (RHS)

Someone said to Mr. Li, "You are fond of friends. But for roughly the past two years [since you resigned your post in Yunnan] I haven't seen you associating with anyone. Why is that?"

Li said, "You simply do not understand. I associate with all sorts of people. I daresay if you compared me with anyone in the world, no one would have as broad a range of associates as I. My associations with others are of ten kinds, and these ten exhaust all possible associations.

"What are these ten? The most important is the association between friends who eat and drink together. Next is the association between friends of the marketplace. In his exchanges with people, Mr. Hè is fair and levelheaded. Mr. Min does not vary the price of oil based on the customer to whom he is selling. You associate with them. I too associate with them.

---

1. *FS, j.* 3, in *LZQJZ* 1:354–56.

Although you may not be aware of it, they have gradually become part of your daily life. The third kind of association is between friends who go on outings together. And next is the association among friends who engage in idle chatter. When we go on outings, if we're going far, we take a boat, and if we're staying nearby, we just talk and laugh. We 'chaff and joke' but are 'never rude.'[2] And when we guess what's on one another's minds, we're 'often right.'[3] Although as people, these outing companions need not be remarkable, I can still enjoy myself with them so thoroughly that we forget when it's time to go home. And when we part, we miss one another.

"If you wish to associate with men of skill, there are master lute players, archers, chess players, painters, and others. Or, if you prefer technicians, there are prognosticators, geomancers, astrologists, fortune-tellers, and such. Yet among such people you cannot easily find an accomplished or brilliant scholar. But since these men's arts are refined, their spirits thrive. They are certainly of a level that limited, vulgar, or lowly people cannot reach. So taking an excursion with these outing companions makes one's spirit soar. Isn't this a more worthy pursuit than poring over old books, discussing ethics, or debating benevolence and righteousness?

"Then come literary associations—associations between friends as intimate as one's own flesh and blood, friends whose hearts beat together as one, friends who would live and die for one another. One associate is not enough. How could anyone say that I have no associates! And how could anyone simply look at one of my associates and hope, from him, to gain insight into the others!

"As for the kind of associate to whom I could sincerely entrust my life and death, I have roamed the world for more than twenty years and not yet encountered such a person. If we're talking about someone I trust with all my heart, I think only Zhou Youshan of Guting fits that description. As for someone I consider as intimate as my own flesh and blood and expect never to abandon me, this is how I feel toward my friend in life and death, Li Weiming.[4]

---

2. This line alludes to the *Classic of Poetry*, Mao no. 55, "Qi yu": "How cleverly he chaffed and joked, / And yet was never rude" (Waley, *The Book of Songs*, 47).
3. This line alludes to *Analects* 11.19, which states that Confucius's disciple Zigong was "often right in his conjectures."
4. Li Weiming refers to Li Zhi's friend Li Fengyang 李逢陽 (1529–1572). See *LZQJZ* 1:293.

"In the field of poetry there is Master Li; and in calligraphy there is Master Wen,[5] and that is all. But must we necessarily attain their level of mastery? If we can amuse our minds with brush and ink and become known in literary circles, if we can let ourselves roam freely like unbridled horses that will not tread the beaten track, then we can entertain ourselves together till old age overtakes us. When there is someone at hand with whom to drink and eat, I associate with him. And when there is not, I don't. But he must love virtue and delight in guests; if poor, he must be dignified; if rich, he must be clean.[6] Only if he meets these criteria will I associate with him. Delighting in guests is most important; appreciating virtue is next; after these come dignity and cleanliness. Wine and food are the most basic elements of life. Only wine and food are essential to me; I consider banqueting an indulgence. This sort of associate is bound to me by food and drink, not by any other means. So if he delights in guests, if he loves them for their qualities, if he is dignified and clean, I'm willing to associate with him. There's no one I'm not willing to associate with! And therefore there's no one I'm not willing to befriend. And how much more joy do I take in associating with close friends with whom no medium is even necessary—[when we are together] even water tastes rich. Enough!

"Today I have spoken plainly of matters of drinking and eating so that you may understand what I take to be the most important kind of association. Other people scorn those who drink and eat together. I would very much like to associate with you. I hope you will not cast me aside."

TRANSLATED BY RIVI HANDLER-SPITZ

---

5. The referents are unclear, but according to Zhang Jianye, Li likely refers to Li Panlong 李攀龍 (1514–1570), a towering figure in late-Ming literary theory and one of the Later Seven Masters of the Return to Antiquity Movement. Wen may refer to the renowned painter and calligrapher Wen Zhengming 文徵明 (1470–1559). See LZQJZ 1:356.
6. Here and throughout Li's writings, the word "clean" (jie 潔) carries a moral valence closely allied with integrity.

"SELF-APPRAISAL"
自贊
"ZI ZAN"

Written in Macheng in 1588, likely in response to Geng Dingxiang's stinging criticism of Li earlier that year, this arresting essay[1] exudes irony as if from every pore. From the outset, Li poses as a thoroughly objectionable individual, an arrogant, vulgar hypocrite. Pouring invective on himself, he bolsters this image with a series of recondite classical allusions. Yet these scholarly allusions effectively undercut his claim to boorishness. The repeated use of paradox throughout the essay unsettles readers and prompts them to question the sincerity of Li's self-appraisal. The essay's inconclusive ending illustrates Li's skeptical stance and his simultaneous embrace of incongruous identities. (RHS)

He was by nature narrow-minded and he appeared arrogant. His words were vulgar, and his mind was wild. His behavior was impulsive, his friends few, and his countenance ingratiating. When interacting with people, he took pleasure in seeking out their faults; he did not delight in their strengths. When he disliked people, he cut them off and sought to harm them for the rest of his life. His ambition was to keep warm and well fed, but he professed to resemble Bo Yi and Shu Qi.[2] Fundamentally deceptive like the man of Qi,[3]

---

1. *FS, j.* 3, in *LZQJZ* 1:356–58.
2. Bo Yi and Shu Qi, ancient paragons of virtue, preferred to die of starvation rather than eat the grain grown in a land ruled by a wicked king. See Sima Qian, *Shi ji*, ch. 61, "Biography of Bo Yi and Shu Qi," in Watson, *Records of the Historian*, 11–15.
3. Mencius tells the story of a poor man from the state of Qi who tricked his wife and his concubine by bringing them luxury foods and telling them that these tasty morsels had been offered to him as gifts from government officers. In fact he had stolen the food from grave sites, where they had been ritually offered to the dead and were therefore taboo to eat. Eventually the wife and concubine figured out the man's deception and cried bitterly about having been tricked (*Mencius* 4B33).

he claimed that his belly was filled with the Dao and virtue. Not the type to give anything away lightly, he nonetheless praised himself as another Yi Yin.[4] He would not even pluck a single hair from his head, but he cursed Yang Zhu for harming the practice of benevolence.[5] His actions deviated from social norms, and the words he spoke conflicted with the feelings in his heart. This is the sort of person he was. The people in the village all hated him. In ancient times Zigong asked Confucius, "What if all the people in the village hate a person?"[6] The master said, "One cannot judge him yet." As far as this reclusive scholar, Li Zhi, is concerned, perhaps one can!

TRANSLATED BY RIVI HANDLER-SPITZ

---

4. Mencius describes Yi Yin 伊尹 in the following words: "If it was not righteous, if it was not the Way, even if you gave him the whole world as his salary, he would not consider it. Even if you gave him a thousand teams of horses, he would not glance at it. If it was not righteous, if it was not the Way, he would not give or accept from others so much as a twig" (*Mencius* 5A7; Van Norden, *Mengzi*, 126–27).
5. According to *Mencius* 7A26, Yang Zhu was so selfish that he would not pluck a single hair from his head, even if by doing so he could benefit the entire world.
6. Zigong, a disciple of Confucius's, asked, "When the people in the village all like a person, how's that?" The Master said, "That is not sufficient." "When the people in the village all hate a person, how's that?" "That is not sufficient. It would be better that the good villagers like him and the bad dislike him" (*Analects* 13.24; my translation).

"AN APPRAISAL OF LIU XIE"
贊劉諧
"ZAN LIU XIE"

This satirical essay,[1] which blends fact with fiction, narrates an encounter between the mandarin Liu Xie (courtesy name Hongyuan 宏源, fl. 1570) and a pretentious young man posing as an orthodox Confucian gentleman. In their humorous exchange, Liu, an official from Macheng who was known for his unconventional bearing and fondness for banter, as well as for his unsurpassed intelligence and extraordinary literary skill, uses sarcasm to expose the affected gentleman's phoniness and superficiality. The exact date of composition is unknown, but this essay was likely written in the late 1580s and exemplifies a theme central to Li's work—unrelenting mockery of the pedantic, conventional, unimaginative, hypocritical scholar-officials of his day. (RHS; PCL)

There once was a gentleman from the School of Principle who wore dignified platform shoes and walked with large strides. He dressed in a generously long-sleeved robe with a wide sash. Wearing the obligations of morality as his cap and the principles of human relations as his garments, he sprinkled his writings with one or two phrases picked up from the classics, and on his lips he always had several passages from orthodox texts. On this basis he claimed that he was a true disciple of Confucius. One day this gentleman came across Liu Xie. Liu Xie was a clever man. He saw the gentleman from the School of Principle and said with a wry smile, "This man does not know that I am Confucius's older brother."

The other suddenly changed color, rose up, and said, "If Heaven had not given birth to Confucius, then the ancient period would have been like one

---

1. *FS, j.* 3, in *LZQJZ* 1:358–59.

long night. What kind of person are you that you dare to declare yourself Confucius's older brother?"

Liu Xie replied, "No wonder, then, that ever since the primordial time of Fu Xi and the Yellow Emperor, sages have walked around all day lighting candlewicks!"

The other was speechless and came to a halt. But how could he truly understand the supreme wit of Liu Xie's words?

Mr. Li heard of this and praised Liu Xie, saying, "Those words are simple and yet fitting, terse and yet rich—words that can break through the web of uncertainty and light up the sky. From words like this, we can comprehend the man who uttered them. In my opinion, although his words were spoken in jest, the ultimate truths they contain will endure for generations upon generations."

TRANSLATED BY PAULINE C. LEE

"ON A SCROLL PAINTING OF SQUARE BAMBOO"
方竹圖卷文
"FANG ZHU TU JUAN WEN"

This short essay,[1] composed in Macheng in 1589, takes as its central conceit the animating force of friendship, whether between humans or between humans and things. Punning on "square shaped" (*fang* 方) as a descriptor for the physical attributes of the bamboo and as a metaphor for the forthright virtues of a gentleman, Li playfully envisions a scene where humans assume the qualities of things and things come to embody the highest ideals of human behavior. Behind the wordplay, however, Li reflects on the ways in which one's persona is ultimately predicated on recognition and acceptance from an "other."

The essay interlaces two sets of themes. The first is how to judge character and recognize "spirit" (*shen* 神), a concern that can be traced to the collection of anecdotes and character sketches from the Wei-Jin period *A New Account of Tales of the World* (*Shishuo xinyu* 世說新語), compiled and edited by Liu Yiqing 劉義慶 (403–444). The essay begins by citing from the *New Account* the story of a scholar who treated bamboo plants as equals and companions, yet Li Zhi gives the tale a new twist: whereas in the *New Account* Wang reveals his obsessive love for bamboo, Li argues that the bamboo recognized Wang's worth and fell in love with him first.

Like many intellectuals of the late Ming, Li Zhi was an avid reader and ardent advocate of the *New Account*. He wrote a commentary to the *Supplement to "A New Account of Tales of the World"* (*Shishuo xinyu bu* 世說新語補), compiled by He Liangjun 何良俊 (1506–1573), and reworked by Wang Shizhen 王世貞 (1526–1590). Li's own *Upon Arrival at the Lake* (*Chutan ji* 初潭集) extracts episodes from the *New Account* and from Jiao Hong's 焦竑 (1540–1620) *Jiao's Forest of Anecdotes* (*Jiaoshi leilin* 焦氏類林). Li's *Upon Arrival* was widely popular in the

---

1. *FS, j.* 3, in *LZQJZ* 1:359–62.

late Ming, and its influence can be seen in many of the prominent *Shishuo xinyu* imitations from the period.

Li's essay is also a work of ekphrasis, eulogizing a painting of bamboo by his friend and patron Deng Shiyang 鄧石陽. In this respect, Li Zhi draws on the vocabulary of a series of earlier colophons and poems dating back to the Song-dynasty poet Su Shi 蘇軾, who praised literati painters for their ability to invest their paintings of bamboo with elements of their own personality. As the essay progresses, Li's focus shifts from Wang's vaunted friendship with his bamboo to Deng Shiyang's relation to his painted subject matter, and finally to Li's personal friendship with Deng as Deng takes leave of Macheng for Sichuan. (TK)

There was a fellow of ancient times who loved bamboo plants[2] and referred to them as "gentlemen" on account of this affection. It was not so much because they resembled refined men that he treated them as gentlemen; it was rather that he felt depressed and there was no one for him to converse with. He was thus of the opinion that the only ones he could take for company were the bamboo, and it was for precisely this reason that he struck up close ties with them and addressed them in such a manner. He himself was unaware that it had reached this point.

Someone said, Wang spoke of the bamboos as "gentlemen," and so it must also have been the case that the bamboo regarded Wang as a "gentleman." Just as those gentlemen are squarely built and pliant, that gentleman also held a foursquare stance and yet was flexible. It is not uncommon for one to have a pliant disposition, but those who can sustain their rectitude are rare. Because they differed from the common and uncommon, they regarded one another as gentlemen. Being of the same breed, and therefore equals, they treated one another as close associates.

And yet it was not that Wang loved the bamboos. The bamboos themselves loved Wang. For when a man such as Wang gazes upon mountains

---

2. The story in *Shishuo xinyu* 23.46 reads, "Wang Huizhi was once temporarily lodging in another man's vacant house and ordered bamboos planted there. Someone asked, 'Since you're only living here temporarily, why bother?' Wang whistled and chanted poems a good while; then abruptly pointing to the bamboos, replied, 'How could I live a single day without these gentlemen?'" (Richard Mather's translation, Liu I-ch'ing, *Shih-shuo Hsin-yü*, 388).

and rivers, or earth and rocks, they all spontaneously start to radiate their charms. How much more would this have been the case with these "gentlemen"!

Moreover, all things between heaven and earth possess a spirit, so how could anyone suppose that these looming, empty-hearted gentlemen lacked an inner core?[3] There is a saying: "For a true soul mate, a squire will exert himself; for an admirer, a lady will adorn herself."[4] These gentlemen were much the same. As soon as they encountered Wang, their lofty bearing and marvelous aspect would naturally have exuded a distinct aura, and their intractable stance, firm amid ice and frost, would have drifted away with the fluty ballads of phoenixes. All this was born of their desire to adorn themselves for the one who truly loved them. For how could they have stood isolated, year upon year softly swooshing with the wind, harboring their regrets at not having met a soul mate?

If we look at the matter from this perspective, then we see that the white crane soared on high because of Wang Zijin,[5] and the gleaming violet *Ganoderma* grew in order to satisfy the hunger of the Four Hoary Heads of Shang Mountain.[6] No wonder, this: after all, the dragon horse bore the Yellow River Chart on its back;[7] the Luo turtle revealed an auspicious omen;[8] the phoenix pranced before Shun[9] and sang to King Wen;[10] and the unicorn presented itself to be captured by Lu.[11] All these events occurred because of a thing's love for a person. From antiquity it has been like this, and who can gainsay it?

---

3. As the essay has already noted, bamboo is "upright" and "pliant"; it is also hollow.
4. Taken from Sima Qian's "Letter to Ren An"; see Watson, *Records: Qin Dynasty*, 227–37.
5. Wang Ziqiao 王子喬, or Crown Prince Ji Jin (ca. 565 B.C.E.–549 B.C.E.), was the son of King Ling of Zhou. The *Liexian zhuan* 列仙傳 [Biographies of immortals], dating from the late Han, records that he ascended to immortality on the back of a white crane.
6. The Four Hoary Heads of Shang Mountain were four legendary hermits who left their positions as scholars at the Qin court and withdrew to the hills, where, according to an ancient song, they fed on purple mushrooms.
7. A *longma* (dragon horse) was said to have revealed the "Yellow River Chart" (*hetu* 河圖), an ancient magic square arrangement of the eight trigrams and five phases, to the culture heroes Fu Xi or Shun.
8. Often paired with the "Yellow River Chart," the "Luo Writing" (*Luo shu* 洛書), a three-column magic square, was revealed to the legendary sage-king Yu on the back of a mystical turtle.
9. After a performance of ritual music for sage-king Shun, a phoenix arrived and displayed itself before him.
10. A phoenix visited King Wen of Zhou on Mount Qi and called to him.
11. The last event recorded in the *Gongyang Commentary* to the *Spring and Autumn Annals* is the capture of a mythical *qilin* on a hunt in the west of Lu, which Confucius took as an omen indicating that his "Way is used up"; *Gongyang zhuan* (Ai, year 14); see also Sima Qian, *Shi ji*, ch. 47, "Kongzi shijia" 孔子世家 [The hereditary house of Confucius], partially translated in Csikszentmihalyi, *Readings*, 89–93.

As for the bamboo lovers of today, well, I am a little confused by them. They are certainly of a different breed from Master Wang. Their haughty attitude and disdain are detestable, and the affection they have only resembles a love *for* bamboo. Although they might be fond of bamboo, the bamboos certainly show no love for them in return. How can they love bamboo when the bamboos care nothing for them? It is precisely because of this state of affairs that I can't stand this sort of person's purported affection for bamboo. Why? Because they are only imitators and do not belong to the same class as Wang. Shiyang's love for bamboos, however, is on a par with Wang's, and the bamboos truly admire that gentleman. Shiyang went to study sutras on Lushan, a mountain resplendent with square and upstanding bamboos. He came to love them and sketched and painted them; he felt that such square, upright bamboos were seldom seen in the whole world. When Shiyang was about to return home and he and I were parting, he brought [his paintings] to me and asked what he should do with them. I said that "these gentlemen" were surely already accompanying him back to Shu. How could they ever be separated?

TRANSLATED BY THOMAS KELLY

"IN MEMORIAM, MASTER WANG LONGXI"
王龍溪先生告文
"WANG LONGXI XIANSHENG GAOWEN"

This essay,[1] written in 1583 in Macheng, pays tribute to Wang Ji 王畿 (1498–1583), whose sobriquet was Longxi. One of the most renowned and controversial students of the influential mid-Ming thinker Wang Yangming, Wang Longxi was wary of cleaving too rigidly to any doctrine. Instead, he endorsed flexible practices that varied "in accordance with the times" and allowed for individual difference. However, these methods garnered criticism from Qian Dehong 錢德洪 (1496–1574), a more conservative disciple of Wang Yangming's, who charged that by daring to deviate from the master's way, Wang Longxi was actually harming the legacy of Wang Yangming.

Li Zhi heaped praise on this figure, who he believed embodied many of his own values. Indeed, throughout this tribute, Li Zhi treats Wang Longxi as more than an individual whose death deserves to be mourned. Wang comes to symbolize the depth and sincerity of scholarship and self-cultivation Li finds lacking among his colleagues, whose only concern, Li maintains, is the superficial quest for profit and reputation.

In this tribute, as well as in a biographical essay Li dedicated to Wang Longxi in *Another Book to Keep (Hidden)*,[2] Li applauds Wang Longxi's commitment to principled action. As Li implies, throughout his long life Wang Longxi lived according to ethical principles, and in so doing he exemplified Wang Yangming's ideal of "unifying words and action." Li's only regret is that many who came in contact with this master failed to understand him and mistook his words for the essence of his philosophy. Li's insistence that words alone are

---

1. *FS, j.* 3, in *LZQJZ* 1:335–38. Wang Longxi's biography is included in *MRXA*, ch. 13.
2. "Bureau Director Wang" [Langzhong Wang gong 郎中王公], in *XCS, j.* 22, in *LZQJZ* 11:112.

PART III: MISCELLANEOUS WRITINGS 雜述   147

mere husks of meaning resonates with the Chan doctrine of "not establishing words" as well as with Daoist ideas about the unreliability of language. Moreover, his criticism of contemporaries' inability to appreciate lived experience echoes opinions he expresses in "On the Childlike Mind" (see pp. 111–13). The essay concludes with Li's implicitly contrasting himself with those unskilled interpreters and expressing the hope that Wang Longxi would have recognized Li as a man of insight. (RHS)

This leading Confucian of our great dynasty possessed the compassionate vision of a bodhisattva, which extended to both the celestial and terrestrial realms. He was like a flawless piece of translucent jade, like gold refined a hundred times. But now he is dead. To whom can his followers turn? I have heard that in his youth the master studied under Master Wang Yangming, and later, owing to his extraordinary achievements, he ascended to the master's seat just as [the faithful disciple] Zixia carried on for Confucius; to the end of their days, these students never abandoned their masters' teachings. In sum, Wang Longxi "delighted in friends visiting from afar and was unperturbed when others failed to recognize his abilities."[3] He truly grasped the essence of Confucius's praise of Yan Hui that he never "transferred his anger or made the same mistake twice."[4] Indeed, he desired to make people believe the sages' teachings based on their own understanding and was not lenient toward those who had not yet attained this understanding. He truly conformed to the Confucian principle of "studying tirelessly and teaching indefatigably."[5] He practiced self-cultivation and lived in accord with the Dao until he was nearly ninety years old; and for sixty years he sprinkled his teachings like rain wherever he went. For this reason, throughout China there are old people who still hold fast to classical texts, and nearer the capital many carry on his work.

Thus he exposed the deep mysteries of innate knowledge and caused them to be clearly manifest as if in broad daylight. He made the Zhu and Si Rivers, sources of Confucian learning, resemble the mighty waters of the Yangzi and Yellow Rivers overflowing their banks as they rushed toward

---

3. Quoting *Analects* 1.1.
4. *Analects* 6.3.
5. *Analects* 7.2.

the four oceans.⁶ Because of him, not only will "this culture of ours"⁷ not die out; it will flourish because his actions truly exemplified the great enlightenment of our Dao. This was the gentleman's most outstanding accomplishment.

I remember that Wang Gen's disciples used to cover the entire earth.⁸ How they thrived! They were without rival. But now I observe that what issues from Wang Longxi's source flows even farther and lasts even longer. How could anything match it? And yet I regret that people who study the Dao suffer from the malady of loving themselves more than they love the Dao. Because of this, they do not comprehend the value of the wisdom entrusted to them by the ancients. Instead, they scheme only for their own profit and interest. Their sickness is that they respect reputation but do not respect themselves, and so they disregard the painful fact that their sons and grandsons are sinking into moral decline. Instead, they consider it their chief responsibility to steer clear of suspicion and slander. Alas! Establishing their hearts and minds in such a manner diminishes the Dao, it does not transmit it. Through such actions they forfeit their true selves; they do not actualize themselves. How could Wang Longxi have tolerated this? Alas for him! His greatest concern was the deafness and blindness of the present generation. For this reason, even if he had been able to "present the Dao without stirring from his seat,"⁹ he would not have condescended to explain his thoughts to those who ridiculed them. Always concerned lest his disciples fall into danger, Wang Longxi behaved like the natives of Wu and Yue, who, when a storm blew up while they were traveling together by boat, thought nothing of risking their own lives to rescue one another.¹⁰ This is how strong Wang Longxi's sense of mission was: there was no stopping it. And this is why I, his junior, immediately acknowledged him as an extraordinary person.¹¹

---

6. The Zhu and Si rivers are located in what was the state of Lu (modern-day Shandong province), where Confucius taught. Because of the Master's proximity to these rivers, they are used to stand for the sources of Confucian learning. See *LZQJZ* 1:337.
7. *Analects* 9.5.
8. On Wang Gen, see the introduction, pp. xxi–xxii; "Three Essays for Two Monks of Huang'an," 23n6.
9. "He who presents the Dao without stirring from his seat is preferable to one who offers gifts of jade followed by teams of four horses" (*Daodejing*, ch. 62; Ivanhoe, *The Daodejing of Laozi*, 65).
10. Allusion to Sunzi, *Sunzi bingfa* [Art of war], 11.4.
11. Li Zhi first encountered Wang Longxi in Nanjing in 1573.

Although I was born long after him and lived far away from him, his actions left me transfixed, my spirit captivated, my heart inclined to listen to his teachings in awe. Now the master is dead. To whom can I now turn?

Alas! "Accomplishing deeds while remaining silent and being trusted without speaking are intrinsic to virtuous conduct."[12] The master expressed his teachings in language, but whenever scholars recited his words, they mistook these words for the master's essence and did not realize that words were merely the dregs of his philosophy.[13] They were of no value to him. Through his actions he exhibited his beliefs. But scholars continually regarded his actions with suspicion and surprise and deemed them inessential. They did not realize that his spirit was in his actions; they were what Wang Longxi esteemed. As I think back on the ancients, none of them really compares to the master. So when I heard the news of his death, my thoughts circled again and again back to him alone. The master's spirit now roams through the Eight Directions; his Dao crowns the ages; he makes no distinction between the newborn and the centenarian; life and death are all one to him.[14] Although Wang Longxi has died, I know that something of him remains. He surely must consider me someone "skilled in interpretation"![15] He surely must regard me as someone who understood him!

TRANSLATED BY RIVI HANDLER-SPITZ

---

12. Slightly misquoted from the "Commentary on the Appended Phrases" in the *Classic of Changes*; see Lynn, *The Classic of Changes*, 68.
13. Allusion to *Zhuangzi*, ch. 13.
14. Alluding to *Mencius* 7A1: "For a man to give full realization to his heart is for him to understand his own nature, and a man who knows his own nature will know heaven. . . . Whether he is going to die young or live to a ripe old age makes no difference to his steadfastness of purpose" (Lau, *Mencius*, 187).
15. The phrase "skilled in interpretation" echoes the wording of *Mencius* 2A2.

"IN MEMORIAM, MASTER LUO JINXI"
羅近谿先生告文
"LUO JINXI XIANSHENG GAOWEN"

This intensely personal testimony[1] commemorates the life and thought of one of the most influential members of the Taizhou school, the itinerant teacher Luo Rufang 羅汝芳 (1515–1588). Luo, who went by the sobriquet Jinxi, exuded an air of simplicity and directness and welcomed students from all social classes and walks of life. Li admired Luo's egalitarian spirit and, although the two met only once, regarded this elder teacher with the utmost respect. In the present essay, written in Macheng in 1589, Li expresses his intense grief upon learning of the master's death.

The essay opens with Li's narrating the shock he experienced upon receiving the news of Luo's death. Stunned, he could find no words to express his sorrow. Li's uncharacteristic silence puzzled the monks with whom he was residing. The abbot, Wunian, questioned him closely as to the reason for this silence and remonstrated with Li by recollecting how, in times past, Li had frequently praised Luo's teachings. Chided by these recollections, Li set about composing a biographical sketch of the master next to whom Li hoped to reside. Li's esteem for Luo is everywhere apparent, as is his desire to preserve and transmit the master's teachings. Among the salient themes in this essay are the intimate bond between masters and disciples and the fear—which Li both raises and repeatedly attempts to quell—that Luo may have died without an intellectual heir. (RHS)

---

1. *FS, j.* 3, in *LZQJZ* 1:338–46. A biography of Luo Jinxi, titled "Canzheng Luo gong" 參政羅公 [On Vice-Grand-Councilor Luo], can be found in *XFS, j.* 22, in *LZQJZ* 11:131–36.

PART III: MISCELLANEOUS WRITINGS 雜述   151

On the twenty-fourth day of the eleventh month of the year *wuzi* [1588], word of the death of Master Luo of Nancheng arrived. But the gentleman's death had actually occurred on the second day of the ninth month. Only a small river separates us from Nancheng. It never takes a traveler more than ten days to get here from there. Yet the news of the master's death took more than eighty days to arrive! How very slow! Could the delay have been caused by the fact that Dragon Lake is located in a remote place and few people come here? Or perhaps, although many people come here, only a few knew the master? But I have heard that the master had at least as many students as Confucius—if not more. I think his students outnumbered half the population of Lu!² So it makes sense that many people knew the master. But what are we to make of people "intensely devoted to studying," who, even after becoming his disciples, still failed to grasp their connection to the universe and all under heaven? If they tarried in transmitting the news of the master's death, the reason must be that they did not hold him in high regard. Since [they cared so little], I bitterly regret the master's death and strongly believe that he ought not to have died.

The person who informed me of this death said, "On the first day of the ninth month, the master was about to take leave of the world and 'roam afar.' To this end, he imparted words of farewell to his many students. The students were overwrought, unable to bear the master's departure. So the master remained in this world for one more day, conversing with them. When they had finished conversing, he died. Now the master is gone, and nothing can be done about it. The students wiped away their tears and choked back their grief. Together, they printed the master's parting words to show them to the scholars of the world. In the matter of 'attaining rectitude in death,' our teacher was in no way inferior to Zeng Shen.³ Leaning on a staff, he wandered free and easy; if compared with Confucius, our master would have nothing to be ashamed of.⁴ Not only did he not begrudge death;

---

2. Confucius's home state. The phrase "his students outnumbered half the population of Lu" is borrowed from *Zhuangzi*, ch. 5.
3. See p. 60n77.
4. One morning Confucius awoke and ambled about in his garden, singing. Seeing this, his disciple Zigong had a premonition of the Master's death. Soon after, Confucius did indeed die. The story illustrates the equanimity with which Confucius is believed to have regarded his own death; see *Liji* 3.49; Legge, *The Li Ki*, 138.

he was skilled in the art of dying. This is how truly accomplished the master was! Because his students were so happy for him, they wanted to print his words so that they would be passed on."

Alas! Our teacher lived to the advanced age of seventy-four, an age that even Confucius did not live to see. Since antiquity it has been rare for people to live to the age of seventy. Even a commoner who lived to such an age would not begrudge death; how then could anyone say that the master begrudged death? And how could his students have rejoiced in his not begrudging death? The commoners of the marketplace work industriously their whole lives and earn nothing more than a few strings of cash or paper money. Even so, when death approaches, they recoil from it; they revive themselves and reopen their eyes, fearful that they will have no one to whom they can entrust their meager earnings. Had they such a person, they would gladly close their eyes.

What about the master's life? How could he have looked at his robes and alms bowls—his teachings to be passed on to future generations—and not have wondered who would inherit them? Why did he remain in this world for that one additional day? Perhaps he, too, feared that he had not found anyone to whom he could entrust his teachings. Had he found such a person, he would have fared well even if he had not been skilled in the art of dying. Lacking such a person, he would not have fared well even if he *had* been skilled in the art of dying. So how could anyone praise the master on account of his skill in dying?

I say that when the master was on the verge of death, just as he wanted to cry out but dared not, he conceived the desire to persevere one more day in the hope of finding [an intellectual heir]. But in the end, he couldn't find such a person. A thousand years hence, when people hear this story, they will still cry their hearts out over it. When they look back on his death, they will still shed tears over the unendurable pain the master suffered. How could anyone say that the master was ungrudging in his attitude toward death? Indeed, no one begrudged death more than the master did! I am afraid that the master begrudged death even more than his many students begrudged his passing.

Why? "Since Heaven has abandoned me, I abandon Heaven!"[5] When the father dies, one looks to the orphaned son. When the son dies, all hope is

---

5. When Confucius's outstanding student, Yan Hui, died, the master feared that he no longer had anyone to whom he could pass on his teachings (*Analects* 11.9). The *Gongyang Commentary* (Ai, year 14) transmits these words of lament.

lost. The pain and despair of such loss are the same for all. If what has just been said is true, then the spiritual heritage of a thousand sages is really not equal even to a commoner's string of cash. Commoners in the marketplace can't abide dying without an heir. But this is what the master did. What a master he was!

When I heard the announcement of the master's death, the monk Wunian Shenyou was at my side and praised him, saying, "You should immediately make an altar tablet to honor the master's spirit." At that time I was silent and made no reply. Eventually, the twelfth month came and the year ended. Then it was the new year, Wanli *yichou* [1589]. The first and second months came and went, and soon the vernal equinox was upon us. Shenyou said, "I have been studying with you for nine years. The name Master Wang Longxi is always on your lips, followed by that of Master Luo Rufang. In the winter of the year *kuimo* [1583], news of Master Wang's death arrived. You immediately wrote an essay memorializing him and embellished it in accordance with ritual etiquette.[6] You did not wait for an official edict. I remember that you told me, 'In Nanjing I had the opportunity to meet Master Wang twice and Master Luo once.[7] After I moved to Yunnan province, I got the chance to see Master Luo again in Longli.' But those events all took place before the year *dingchou* [1577]. Ever since then, not a year has passed when you have not read books by these two masters, and never have you opened your mouth without speaking of their teachings. When I heard you speak of them, I found their teachings intimate and arresting, clear and compelling. If, during one of these discourses, someone skilled at writing had picked up a brush and taken dictation at your side, he would surely have sprained his wrist and shrieked in pain. For you would not have been able to limit your praise to ten or a hundred pages; even a thousand pages would not have sufficed! Why now, for the first time, are you silent?

"In spring of the year *bingxu* [1586], I traveled to Nanjing begging for alms with my metal staff. Again you instructed me that I must urgently go up the Xu River to visit Master Luo. At that time Wang Longxi had already died. In the summer of the year *wuzi* [1588], I returned here from Nanjing to inform you that Master Luo had written a letter expressing his desire to go to Nanjing. The letter said, 'Let's take advantage of the fact that there is an imperial examination this autumn. Scholars from all over the empire

---

6. See "In Memoriam, Master Wang Longxi," pp. 146–49.
7. While serving in the Bureau of Punishments in Nanjing, Li Zhi met Luo in 1572 and Wang Longxi in 1573. See *LZQJZ* 1:343.

will convene in the capital. As soon as they arrive, let's plan to gather our friends together.' You immediately wrote a letter to Jiao Hong saying, 'When Master Luo comes this time, let's be careful not to miss the opportunity to see him! I fear he is getting on in years; it may be difficult to meet with him in the future.' Later, on several occasions, you sought out people who lived near the Xu River, and they periodically mentioned Master Luo's illness. When they spoke of his illness, you became somewhat concerned. You told me, 'If Master Luo is indeed unwell, he will not be able to travel south. But I do not think Master Luo is actually severely ill. I have observed that his bones are strong and his life force is in harmony; his spirit is undiminished and his intentions firm. In these ways, he resembles Master Wang. Master Wang enjoyed eighty-six years of life. Even if Master Luo does not live to one hundred, he'll certainly live to ninety!'

"But I secretly scrutinized you, and it seemed to me as if—even if you didn't say so—you suspected that Master Luo might die after all. I tried to ask you about this matter several times, but all you would say was, 'The master will not die. He absolutely will not die!' Now Master Luo is indeed dead. Why are you so silent?"

Alas! I was silent and did not reply. I did not know how to respond. Ever since I heard the news of the master's death, I have felt as if I'd been passing my days in a dream. Only now do I understand that the phrase "True grieving expresses no grief; true weeping sheds no tears" is not just empty words. I now struggle to calm my anguished thoughts. Looking back on the past, how ridiculous it seems! Could anyone say I did not think about the master? Indeed I did think of him. Could anyone say I did not understand him? Indeed I did understand him, deeply. Could anyone say I was incapable of speaking about the master? Indeed no one was more capable of speaking about him than I! And yet my lips were sealed, my mind a blank; I was paralyzed, unable to lift my brush. Even I do not understand the reason why. Is this really the moment to call out, "Heaven has abandoned me, I give up on Heaven"? "Fatherless, on whom can I rely?"[8] Am I really in the position of a son or orphan to him?

Now I, too, am old. Although I never formally studied with the master, I hoped to buy a field, build a hut, and live beside the master. This intention was constantly on my mind, but now that the master is dead, what am I to do? Since I never formally studied with the master, I could not befriend all

---

8. Quoting the *Classic of Poetry*, Mao no. 202, "Lu'e."

the master's disciples or find out who was the most outstanding student. I almost hope there is no such person, since I would be disappointed not to have met him. They say that as soon as the master was of an age to go to school, he threw himself wholly into his studies, and when he sat for his examination at the Ministry of Rites, his name circulated in the examiners' halls. But for a long time he desired to leave the world and become a recluse. This thought consumed him. He set his sights on the Dao but feared isolation from teachers and friends. So he journeyed in all directions, entered into discussions with people of all sorts, and, having consulted them extensively, followed them on the path of rectitude. He was content to drink from rivers and return home empty-handed.[9] He spent ten years in this manner, and then in the year *guichou* [1553] he appeared at the imperial court [to receive his *jinshi* degree], shedding the clothes of a commoner to don those of an official. While he was in charge, lawsuits were scarce and tranquil joy abundant; civilized discourse replaced implements of torture, and people spoke their minds without contention. He was on familiar terms with subordinates like clerks and runners. Even after becoming an official, he continued to study, and his studies—not his official title—were the basis of his greatness.[10] If he acted this way at court, we can infer how he must have acted in daily life. He behaved in this manner both as an official and in private life: outside the hall, drums were beaten and songs sung; young and old thronged together, and friends sat side by side.[11] This was how the master spent his seventy-four years of life.

Traveling to Buddhist temples and scenic spots both south of the Yangzi River and north of the Yellow River, he joined hands with his fellow travelers, and crowds formed wherever he went. The master's writings spread even to the remotest regions of the south: Dong Ou, Luo Shi, Gui Guo, Nan Yue, Min Yue, Dian Yue, and Teng Yue—places where only birdcalls are heard[12] and where human footsteps rarely go. He took his students from among shepherd boys and woodcutters, old fishermen, street urchins from the marketplace, officials from the yamen, peddlers and retailers, weaver women and plowmen, reputable Confucians who might "steal grass

---

9. Allusion to *Zhuangzi*, ch. 1.
10. Allusion to *Analects* 15.7.
11. This sentence contains allusions to the *Classic of Poetry*, Mao no. 18, "Gaoyang," the *Classic of Changes*, hexagram 26 ("Da chu"), and *Zuozhuan* (Xiang, year 26).
12. I.e., the languages of non-Chinese tribes, considered as incomprehensible as birdcalls. The list of place-names refers to regions in modern-day Zhejiang, Guangdong, Guangxi, and Yunnan provinces in southern and southwestern China.

sandals," and great bandits wearing caps and robes. If only they "had the right mind-set," the master did not inquire into their origins.[13] He cared not at all whether his followers were poor scholars wearing threadbare clothes, hermits who lodged by streams and cliffs, pale-skinned young students, *xiucai* degree holders[14] wearing green-collared robes, Daoists wearing yellow robes and feathery accoutrements, Buddhist clergy wearing black garments, or Confucian officials wearing the red silk girdles and vermilion slippers of office and holding ivory tablets. For this reason, wherever his cart went, people came running out to greet him. Clapping his hands, the master would sit down to chat and laugh with them. Commoners looked up to the master on account of his elegant bearing, and scholars delighted in his down-to-earth manner. They loosened their robes and let the eight winds [of his teachings] waft over them. The master was as magnanimous as Liu Xiahui, but I've never heard of his lacking dignity;[15] and he was as kind as a Buddha, but I've never heard of his acting inappropriately. Although he mingled with people from all walks of life, he harbored "great aspirations," and his accomplishments were "visible for all to see."[16] Like a skilled salesman, he hid his wares, [awaiting the right buyer]. While readily approached, he was difficult to know.[17] Although on easy terms with everyone, he was no "gossipmonger."[18] He embodied the true spirit of equality: his love and toleration extended to people of all kinds. He possessed both the strength and the skill to hit the mark.[19] None could match him. And his wisdom and

---

13. When Mencius stayed at a hostel in Teng, a pair of grass sandals mysteriously went missing. The proprietor accused Mencius's disciples of having stolen the shoes. Mencius neither affirmed nor denied the charge. He merely stated that as a teacher, he turned no one away: "So long as he comes with the right mindset, I accept him. That is all" (*Mencius* 7B30; translation altered slightly from Lau, *Mencius*, 200).
14. The *xiucai* was the degree granted after students had passed the prefectural examination. Successful candidates could then sit for examinations on the provincial level and ultimately the national level.
15. According to Mencius, Liu Xiahui was considered magnanimous because he was "not ashamed of a corrupt lord, and did not consider a petty office unworthy.... When he was discharged, he was not bitter. In difficult and impoverished circumstances...[he even said] 'Even if you are stark naked beside me, how can you defile me?'" However, Mencius also criticized Liu for lacking dignity (*Mencius* 2A9; Van Norden, *Mengzi*, 49).
16. Quotation from *Analects* 5:22.
17. Allusion to Sima Qian, *Shi ji*, ch. 63, "Biographies of Laozi and Han Feizi," where Laozi rebukes Confucius for his pride and meddlesomeness, saying, "I have heard that an able merchant has the deepest storerooms, yet they look empty; a gentleman has the fullest virtue, but he appears foolish." The phrase "difficult to know" derives from the historian's concluding judgment on Laozi. See Nienhauser, *The Grand Scribe's Records*, 7:21–32.
18. The word is borrowed from *Analects* 17.13, where Confucius derides gossipmongers as "outcasts of virtue" who violate moral principles.
19. *Mencius* 5B1 compares wisdom to skill and sageliness to strength: hitting the target requires both.

teachings were both marvelous and transformative. Who could have comprehended them fully? It seems that the master brought deliverance to both himself and others through these means. For more than seventy years he traveled north, south, east, and west but never went anywhere in vain. He weathered wintry nights and summer mornings, but never lived a day in vain. His acquaintances included worthies and fools, young and old people, poor invalids and wealthy nobles, but he never interacted with anyone in vain. His teachings were so focused and enduring that I doubt any student who came to his door could have left without understanding. Fortunately, the master had this satisfaction.

Although I am old, I am still able to exert myself on his behalf. For the master's sake, I must not hesitate to trek high and low searching for someone among his disciples who truly possesses understanding and scholarly accomplishment. When I find this person, I will commemorate the master by burning incense, and I will utter words intended to reassure his soul: "From now on, I will know that you died without regret [as one who has 'heard the Way']; now you need not begrudge death [for you have someone to carry on your teachings]. It is truly not hypocritical praise to say that you 'had a good death.'" Then will I finally be released from the deep regret I have been feeling over the master's death. What Confucius said to the lord of Lu [about Yan Hui], I apply here: "Now that he is dead, I have yet to hear of anyone who is truly fond of learning."[20] Those who leave no sons behind have nothing more to hope for; but the master was not one of these.

TRANSLATED BY RIVI HANDLER-SPITZ

---

20. *Analects* 6.2; Legge, *The Chinese Classics*, 1:185.

"AFTERWORD TO *JOURNEYING WITH COMPANIONS*"
征途與共後語
"ZHENG TU YU GONG HOU YU"

In the winter of 1595, when this essay[1] was written, Li Zhi's son-in-law, Zhuang Chunfu, was living in Macheng with Li Zhi. The two men engaged in regular study sessions with the prefect of Ningzhou, Fang Ziji 方子及 (courtesy name Hang 沆, 1542–1608), who was visiting from neighboring Jiangxi province. In the notebook in which the three men recorded their studies, Li Zhi jotted down this short essay, which is addressed to another friend, Jiao Hong. It seems Li Zhi may have felt that Fang Ziji had been unduly influenced by views expressed in Jiao Hong's preface to a printed edition of the collected works of the eleventh-century poet Su Shi. In that preface Jiao Hong argues that great art cannot be produced by raw talent alone; formal training is also required. Li Zhi, on the other hand, maintains that training may impede the creative process, and that great art arises from unmediated "chance encounters" with nature.[2]

    Both Li Zhi and Jiao Hong cite the legend of the ancient zither player Bo Ya, who studied for three years under the tutelage of Master Cheng Lian. Although the disciple attained technical proficiency, he was not adept at expressing his feelings. Cognizant of this deficiency in his student, Cheng Lian invited Bo Ya to accompany him to Penglai Mountain to see his own master, Fang Zichun, whose zither playing conveyed deep emotion. When they arrived, Cheng Lian left Bo Ya alone in the wilderness to practice and told him that the teacher would join him shortly. Bo Ya waited patiently for ten days, but Cheng Lian did not return, nor did the teacher arrive. Frightened and alone, Bo Ya craned his neck in every direction, searching for some sign of the teacher, but he could hear nothing but the

---

1. *FS, j.* 4, in *LZQJZ* 2:11–13. It appears that the text *Journeying with Companions* is now lost.
2. See also "Explanation of the Childlike Heart-Mind," pp. 106–10.

PART III: MISCELLANEOUS WRITINGS 雜述   159

crashing of the waves and the sad cries of birds. Gazing up at the sky, he called out, "Master Cheng Lian has no teacher! He left me here because he wanted to stir my emotions!" Thereupon, plucking his zither, Bo Ya composed his most moving piece, "The Melody of Water Immortals."[3]

Jiao Hong interprets this story to mean that without formal education, Bo Ya would not have been able to produce such extraordinary music. He writes,

> [If someone is to produce outstanding music,] he must revere antiquity . . . follow the score closely, and receive instruction from a great master: just as in the case of Cheng Lian and Bo Ya, the disciple needed to travel to that remote shore, [to dwell in] those deep mountain forests, and [to experience] those hollows from which the seawater rushes forth. [Only once he had had these experiences did he] suddenly grasp the emotive power of the zither and express the landscape in music of surpassing beauty.
>
> But if an ignoramus were by chance to encounter a zither, strum it, and think to himself, "This is music," such a situation would be akin to asserting that one could dispense with studying the ancients, do away with drawing inspiration from one's own heart, and instead defiantly do whatever one pleased. How absurd!

Yet Li Zhi endorses just such chance encounters. For this reason he concludes the present essay by hinting that companions in study should help one another to avoid excessive reliance on book learning and should instead encourage one another to engage in direct experience of the world. (RHS)

Jiao Hong, it seems to me that your preface was written for people who *claimed* to understand but who had not yet fully understood. Someone like Fang Ziji is still in the stage of advancing his knowledge; how could your advice have been appropriate for him? And yet I have heard that a great many scholars claim to understand before they truly understand, so it

---

3. Zhu Changwen, *Qin shi*, 2:12.

makes sense that your counsel would be suitable for them. In this world, people easily become mired in reputation and riches. I am old and may die any day; yet I still cannot avoid the burden of notoriety. This is especially so when, in a bustling arena where people conceal their faces behind cosmetics in order to please others, *I* endeavor to concentrate my mind on matters of life and death, to regard the world's excesses of pleasure as extremes of sorrow, and to prevent them from increasing my bodily cares. How could I find in this world what I am seeking? And it seems to me that as long as thoughts of life and death are not sprouting in the minds of gentlemen who practice Zen or study the Dao, they, too, are unable to progress beyond this point. How strange, then, that they should turn up their noses conceitedly. Yet I hope that you will not reproach them too harshly. Let's drop that subject for the time being. Instead, I propose to select some passages from your preface to discuss with you.

You said that the Dao of music is comparable to Zen. This seems plausible. You cited the story of Bo Ya as evidence and said that dispensing with the study of the ancients and the instruction of a master, and instead defiantly doing whatever one pleased, was laughable. But I disagree.

We could say that in Cheng Lian, Bo Ya found a master who taught him systematically; his teaching combined a score with a method; it unified past and present. How could Bo Ya have failed to benefit? But if Cheng Lian had felt that scores and teachers were *all* that was necessary, he should have spent his days and nights teaching melodies to Bo Ya. Why would he have sent him to a deserted shore, a lonely uninhabited place? And if Bo Ya's talent had been no greater than that of a "blind ignoramus," what good would Master Cheng Lian's instruction have done? What would this Dao have to do with the sea, and why would Bo Ya have attained it only by going to the shore? How extremely odd this all is! It seems that Cheng Lian had Cheng Lian's distinctive sound; not even Cheng Lian could transmit it to a disciple. And Bo Ya had Bo Ya's distinctive sound; not even Bo Ya could learn it from Cheng Lian. What we call "sound" is the sort of thing that one encounters by chance and instantly grasps; one cannot obtain it through study or imitation.[4]

"Blind ignoramuses," having received no training, resonate immediately upon such a chance encounter. Bo Ya, having been trained, was able to

---

4. The notion that an art cannot be transmitted from master to disciple is reminiscent of the parable of Wheelwright Bian in *Zhuangzi*, ch. 13; see Watson, *Chuang Tzu*, 152–53.

produce marvelous sounds only after he had shed this training. If Bo Ya had not gone to the ocean, or if he had gone to the ocean but Master Cheng Lian had remained by his side, then Bo Ya would never have attained true understanding. It was only because Bo Ya went to a remote seashore, to a wilderness of hollow caves, a place distant from any human trace, that the ancient scores ceased to exist for him and that there no longer was anything to be passed on nor any teacher to be found; in short, when none of the things he had formerly studied were available to him, he attained understanding *by himself*. Now this Dao transcended the zither's strings and paulownia-wood body, it went beyond any formal instruction; and yet could Bo Ya have attained it without the instruction of Master Cheng Lian? Those who study the Dao are capable of understanding this. Even by daylight, some forms elude our vision; we recognize them by the shadows they cast. And there are sounds we cannot hear: the striking of bamboo gives rise to a *gāthā*.[5] This is a general rule—how could it apply only to "ignoramuses" and Bo Ya?

I hope that Fang Ziji will be like an "ignoramus" [who intuitively grasps the Dao], and that you will resemble the person on the shore [and cast aside book learning]. For this reason, I am respectfully writing this afterword for you two. It is titled "Journeying with Companions." The phrase "with companions" means "with *study* companions." Esteeming Chunfu as his companion, Fang Ziji undertook a journey so that the two men would be able to study together every day. If they can *truly* study together, I hope that Fang Ziji will share this essay with Chunfu.

TRANSLATED BY RIVI HANDLER-SPITZ

---

5. The Tang-dynasty Chan monk Xiangyan Zhixian 香嚴智閑 received his enlightenment from the chance striking of a brick against a bamboo stalk and instantly wrote a *gāthā* declaring this insight (see Sasaki, *The Record of Linji*, 92–93).

"READING A LETTER FROM RUOWU'S MOTHER"
讀若無母寄書
"DU RUOWU MU JI SHU"

When Li Zhi was living in Macheng, he made the acquaintance of two young men studying Buddhism, Wang Shiben 王世本, who took the Buddhist name Ruowu, and Zeng Jiquan.[1] When in 1596 Ruowu made known his intention to become a monk, his mother, greatly distressed, wrote a letter attempting to dissuade him. In the letter, which Li Zhi quotes at length, Ruowu's mother pits her son's Confucian duty to take care of his family against his Buddhist asceticism and urges him to "seek tranquility in his own mind."

Li Zhi found the mother's letter both moving and philosophically compelling, for it voiced syncretic ideals he shared. The letter maintains that fulfilling one's familial obligations accords with the practice of Buddhism; these two duties need not come into conflict.[2] The essay ends with Li's praising the power of Ruowu's mother's prose. But his admiration is tinged with self-reproach, for he recognizes that she has expressed their shared view more eloquently and more effectively than he. (RHS)

Ruowu's mother's letter said, "With each passing year, I grow older. Ever since you were eight years old I raised you myself. If you had simply abandoned me to leave home and become a monk, I could have tolerated that. But now [in addition to becoming a monk] you want to go far away! Your teacher waited until after his parents had passed away; only then did he

---

1. *FS, j.* 4, in *LZQJZ* 2:19–21. For another published translation of this essay, see Yu, "Letter to Ruowu." On Zeng Jiquan, see "To Zeng Jiquan," p. 255.
2. Geng Dingxiang also read and responded to Ruowu's mother's letter. See "Du Li Zhuowu yu Wang Seng Ruowu shu" 讀李卓吾與王僧若無書 [On reading the correspondence between Li Zhuowu and the monk Wang Ruowu], in Geng, *Geng Tiantai xiansheng wenji, j.* 19; see also *LZQJZ* 2:20.

become a monk. If you must go far away, it won't be too late if you wait till I'm dead."

Ruowu replied, "When I lived near you I was never any help to you, Mother."

His mother answered, "I have a few aches and pains, but I manage by myself; of course I would not be a source of worry to you. Your mind is at ease and you are not a source of worry to me. Both our minds are at ease and we do not worry about each other. Wherever one feels at ease, one can attain tranquility. Why do you insist on going far away to seek tranquility? What's more, ever since Uncle Qin Su[3] endowed the monastery on your behalf, he has not treated you shabbily. While you are contemplating the Dao, I am thinking of worldly matters. And taking care of one's worldly needs is also a kind of Dao.

"Apart from the fact that you have obligations to me in my old age, you must also care for your two children. When your teacher left home to become a monk, he still looked after his sons in years of famine; surely he did not have the heart to do otherwise. A parent who does not look after his children and instead lets them sink into moral decline will become a laughingstock. Now, although you may seek tranquility, will you be able to prevent yourself from feeling troubled at heart? It is impossible that you would not feel troubled at heart. And if you do feel troubled at heart, you will spend your days agonizing silently, fearful lest people mock you. So which course of action is honest and which false, which commendable and which reprehensible? Not to trouble your heart caring for your children, or to trouble your heart caring for them now? If you care for them now, your actions may *seem* to issue from a troubled heart, but inside you will be serene, your heart untrammeled. On the other hand, if you do not take care of them, your actions will seem to issue from an untrammeled heart, but inside you will experience pangs of anxiety and your heart will be troubled indeed! Examine your heart closely: there is no other good than the Eternally Abiding One, the Adamantine.[4]

"So why listen only to what other people say? Simply to heed their words, without examining your own heart, is to allow your perspective to be distorted by your surroundings. And if your perspective is distorted by your surroundings, you will not attain tranquility of mind. But already you

---

3. Qin Su, presumably a relative of Ruowu's, is otherwise unknown, as is the situation that prompted this remark.
4. I.e., the Buddha. "Adamantine" refers to the unbreakable solidity of a diamond.

don't dwell in your own mind; you go seeking a place to live in the external world. I suspect that you will find Dragon Lake insufficiently tranquil[5] and will want to dwell in a place of Adamantine Resolution.[6] But what if you find the place of Adamantine Resolution insufficiently tranquil? Where will you dwell then?

"All day long you want to discuss the Dao; here and now I'm talking with you about the heart and mind. If you don't believe me, go ask your teacher; he will confirm what I say. If attaining tranquility depends upon your surroundings, you ought to reside in the place of Adamantine Resolution. But if attaining tranquility depends on your own state of mind, you need not travel far. When one's mind is not at ease, then even journeying beyond the oceans—to say nothing of dwelling in a place of Adamantine Resolution—only further unsettles one's heart and mind."

Reading this letter, I was overcome with emotion and said, "How fortunate that in this family there is a wise mother, a true Buddha. Day and night she is guided by her heart and mind. Her voice is as steady as the sound of waves at the ocean, her instructions issue from the marrow of her bones; their strength is irresistible. When I consider what ordinary people of our generation say, I see how unreasonable and ineffective their words are: they speak as if they were trying to scratch their feet without taking off their boots, or attempting to feed someone simply by *talking* about food. How could words satisfy hunger? Such behavior would attract jeering onlookers. Yet the people of our generation know no shame.

"When I think back on the many letters I've written you [Ruowu], I realize that they were all bluff and bluster meant to intimidate a fool; they had nothing to do with my genuine emotions and true intentions. I entreat you: please destroy them immediately by fire or water. Do not let your sage mother see them, lest she say that I have spent my whole life harming people by babbling about the Dao! Also, please hang a copy of your mother's instructions on the wall so that all people who recite the name of the Buddha or study the Dao may have them constantly before their eyes, and so that, seeing how to worship true Buddhas, they will not dare worship false Buddhas. Whoever has the ability to recite the name of a true Buddha is himself an Amitābha. Even if he has never once pronounced the word 'Amitābha,' Amitābha will certainly see to his salvation. Why?

---

5. The Cloister of the Flourishing Buddha, where Li resided.
6. Ruowu's mother may be contrasting the somewhat unconventional Cloister of the Flourishing Buddha with stricter Buddhist establishments.

Because Buddhists must engage in self-cultivation, the most important practice of which is filial piety. To recite the name of the Buddha but fail to act in a filial manner is tantamount to asserting that Amitābha is a Buddha deficient in filial piety. Could such a thing be? Surely it defies reason! If I seek Amitābha by worshipping false Buddhas, then which Buddha did Amitābha worship so as to become Amitābha? He could only have modeled himself on an ordinary person who exhibits filial piety.

"Your mother's words express her profound sincerity: they cut to the quick, causing those who hear them to sob with emotion. You must agree with me: no one could possibly hear a mother utter such words without weeping!"

TRANSLATED BY RIVI HANDLER-SPITZ

"RECORD OF MASTER GENG DINGLI"
耿楚倥先生傳
"GENG CHUKONG XIANSHENG ZHUAN"

This testimonial essay[1] poignantly sketches the contours of Li's friendship with Geng Dingli (1534–1584; *jinshi* 1570) and charts the tumultuous relationship that ensued between Li and Dingli's older brother, the successful statesman Geng Dingxiang. Li explains that his acquaintance with Dingli began when Dingli presented Li with an ethical question regarding the balance between self-confidence and arrogance. Li's startling answer set Dingli thinking, and the two men soon developed a friendship so deep that in 1581, after Li resigned his post as prefect of Yao'an, he moved into the Geng family residence in Huang'an in order to enjoy the daily company of his soul friend.

However, during the several years Li spent at the Geng home, differences of opinion surfaced among Dingli, Li Zhi, and Dingxiang. Although all three men were proponents of the Taizhou school, Dingxiang held that the essence of Confucian teachings could be expressed in a single phrase from the *Mencius*; Dingli, on the other hand, emphasized a passage in the *Doctrine of the Mean*. Li Zhi's preference for Dingli's interpretation had serious implications.

After Dingli's untimely death in 1584, the philosophical differences between Li Zhi and Geng Dingxiang mushroomed into an acrimonious controversy.[2] The two men flung insults at each other, and Li published a series of open letters publicly excoriating Dingxiang for hypocrisy. (See "Li Zhi and Geng Dingxiang: Correspondence," pp. 34–62). However, by 1595, when this testimonial was written, the two men seem to have reconciled their differences, for the essay ends on a note of genuine contrition. (RHS)

---

1. *FS, j.* 4, in *LZQJZ* 2:21–26.
2. For more on the quarrel between Li Zhi and Geng Dingxiang, see Jiang, "Heresy and Persecution." See also *MRXA*, ch. 35.

PART III: MISCELLANEOUS WRITINGS 雜述   167

The gentleman's given name was Dingli [定理], his courtesy name Ziyong [子庸], and his sobriquet Chukong [楚倥]. Scholars nicknamed him "Mr. Eight" [Ba xiansheng 八先生].[3] All scholars knew of this Mr. Eight except for Dingli himself, who at first was not aware of his reputation. So why am I calling this essay a "Record of Master Geng Dingli"? Well, *records* serve to *record*. And although at first Dingli did not expect anyone to record his life, yet here I am recording it. Why should I do this? It's precisely because he did not at first expect anyone to record it that I truly cannot bear *not* to record it. I noticed that the gentleman possessed virtue but did not draw attention to it because he did not want to flaunt his virtue. He possessed talent but did not take office because he did not want to restrict his talent to official matters. Not to draw attention to one's virtue is to attain great virtue; not to engage one's talent deserves to be called true talent.[4] How could such a life go unrecorded?

Moreover, the gentleman made studying the Dao his life's work. Although he studied the Dao, this fact was not outwardly perceptible; for days on end he scarcely spoke of the Dao. But those who observed him could discern that the Dao resided within him. As the saying goes, "He was permeated by the Dao but not dripping with it."[5]

Zhuang Chunfu[6] once reported to me that Mr. Eight had said, "I started out as a disciple of Fang Yilin's [方一麟],[7] but Yilin did not understand how to study; he enjoyed a hollow reputation for scholarship, so I left him. Ultimately I obtained the essence of all practical wisdom from Deng Huoqu[8] and learned to direct my sight and hearing inward.[9] From He Xinyin, I learned that the mind is opaque and self-contained.[10] Only then did I begin

---

3. By way of a flattering comparison to the Eight Masters of Tang and Song Dynasty Prose, whose works had been collected by Zhu Youcai 朱右采 in a widely circulated Ming anthology, *Ba xiansheng wenji* 八先生文集 [The collected works of eight masters].
4. These paradoxical statements echo *Daodejing*, ch. 38.
5. The expression derives from the "Jingce wen" 警策文 [Warning-stick essay] of the Tang-dynasty Zen monk Lingyou 靈祐, recorded in *Quan Tang wen, j.* 919.
6. Li Zhi's son-in-law.
7. Fang Yilin hailed from Huangpi district in modern-day Hubei province, not far from Macheng county. Along with He Xinyin and Deng Huoqu, he is listed as one of "three eccentrics in the district" in Geng Dingxiang's essay by that title. See "Lizhong san yi zhuan" 里中三異傳, in Geng, *Geng Tiantai xiansheng wenji, j.* 16; see also *LZQJZ* 2:23.
8. On Deng Huoqu, see "Three Essays for Two Monks of Huang'an," pp. 21–28.
9. Allusion to Lu Ji, "Wen fu" 文賦 [Rhapsody on literature].
10. See "On He Xinyin," pp. 84–88.

to experience complete self-content, to feel deep faith, and to doubt no more. But I could not articulate these insights to ordinary people, so to the end of my days I never spoke of them; I discussed them only with my older brother, Master Geng Dingxiang, in the privacy of our home. Thus I came to regard Dingxiang as my teacher, and he himself averred: 'Although I have attained a certain level of understanding in my studies, I rely heavily on the strength of Dingli.'"

Dingli once asked Dingxiang, "The *Great Learning*, the *Doctrine of the Mean*, the *Analects*, and the *Mencius* are all similar in that they deal with study, but I have yet to determine which phrase best encapsulates the meaning of these writings." Dingxiang said, "The single phrase 'The sages embody the perfect attainment of human relationships' is the best."[11] Dingli replied, "But in the end that phrase is not as good as 'a state of equilibrium, before any emotion has stirred.'"[12]

When I heard this, I found their exchange revealing. For "the perfect attainment of human relationships" is precisely "a state of equilibrium, before any emotion has stirred." How could one who has not experienced this state of equilibrium attain perfection in human relationships? Perfection is attained when the Dao achieves equilibrium. Hence it is said "equilibrium is the perfection of virtue," and it is also said "[the operations of Heaven] are perfect, having neither sound nor smell."[13]

In the year *renshen* [1572], Dingli traveled to Nanjing. At that time, I was quite ignorant, though I took delight in intellectual discussion. A man of few words, Dingli simply asked me the following question: "In study, it is important to trust oneself. [This is illustrated in the *Analects*, which] states, [when Confucius instructed his disciple Qi Dan to take office, Qi Dan replied,] 'I do not yet trust myself with this responsibility.'[14] At the same time, we must beware of self-confidence, for it is also said that 'it is not possible to embark upon the path [Dao] of Yao and Shun with an arrogant person.'[15] How would

---

11. From *Mencius* 4A2. Compare Lau, *Mencius*, 137: "The compasses and the carpenter's square are the culmination of squares and circles; the sage is the culmination of humanity."
12. "While there are no stirrings of pleasure, anger, sorrow, or joy, the mind may be said to be in the state of Equilibrium [or the Mean]": *Doctrine of the Mean*, ch. 1; Legge, *The Chinese Classics*, 1:384.
13. Quoting the *Doctrine of the Mean*, ch. 3 and ch. 33, the latter quoting the *Classic of Poetry*, Mao no. 235, "Wen Wang."
14. *Analects* 5.6. Confucius was pleased with this answer. The anecdote implies that had Qi Dan possessed the requisite self-confidence, he would have been capable of taking office.
15. *Mencius* 7B37. Here Mencius criticizes the "village worthy," who, although he exhibits every outward sign of virtue, is in fact devoid of righteousness. The translation of this passage is slightly altered from Lau, *Mencius*, 203.

you venture to characterize the difference between trust in oneself and arrogance?"

Without hesitation, I replied, "With an arrogant person, 'one cannot enter upon the path of Yao and Shun;' but with a person who lacks arrogance, 'one cannot enter upon the path of Yao and Shun' either." Dingli burst out laughing and departed. He probably took profound pleasure in recognizing that I might eventually enter upon the path myself. After this, I could not stop thinking about Dingli and missing him. I also regretted not having met Dingxiang.

In the year *dingchou* [1577], I went to Yunnan,[16] and my route took me through Tuanfeng.[17] There I left my boat, climbed ashore, and as soon as I reached Huang'an, met with Dingli, saw Dingxiang, and conceived the intention to forfeit my official post and take up residence with the Geng brothers. Dingli observed that I barely had enough to live on, so he urged me to return to officialdom. Heeding his advice, I left my daughter and my son-in-law, Zhuang Chunfu, in Huang'an, and because I had made an agreement with Dingli, I said, "Wait three years for me. When I attain the salary of a fourth-level official,[18] I will return and provide for my own living expenses. Then together you and I can climb to the other shore."[19] Geng Dingli held fast to my words and rigorously instructed Chunfu in the study of the Dao. In every respect, Dingxiang, too, treated my daughter and son-in-law as if they were his own.

Alas! How dare I forget Dingxiang's kindness for even a single day? After three years, I returned [to the Geng residence] as planned. But sadly, just a few years after this gathering, Dingxiang was summoned away [to assume high office in the capital].[20] And abruptly, Dingli's days came to an end. I felt sorrowful and mirthless. Dingxiang, for his part, tenaciously set his heart on the phrase "The sages embody the perfect attainment of human relationships." He constantly feared that, in relinquishing worldly affairs,

---

16. Li Zhi had been appointed prefect of Yao'an prefecture, Yunnan, and was traveling south to take up the position.
17. In present-day Hubei province.
18. For purposes of remuneration and prestige, official positions in premodern China were classified according to nine ranks, with first being the most prestigious and ninth the least.
19. This line calls to mind the Buddhist idea of leaving the world of samsara and climbing ashore to nirvana or enlightenment. Li Zhi made good on his promise. In 1580, he resigned his position as prefect of Yao'an and in 1581 took up residence at the Geng family household in Huang'an. See "A Sketch of Zhuowu: Written in Yunnan," pp. 75–83.
20. In 1584 Geng Dingxiang was summoned to the capital to assume the position of senior vice-censor-in-chief of the Censorate. See *LZQJZ* 2:25.

I had committed an error. For my part, I tenaciously insisted on the phrase "a state of equilibrium, before any emotion has stirred" and feared that perhaps he had failed to perceive the origin of things or to investigate the source of their principles. We debated back and forth, never pausing, and our debate turned into a quarrel that continues even to the present day.[21]

Thankfully, heaven has led me by the heart and induced me to abandon the phrase "a state of equilibrium, before any emotion has stirred," and Dingxiang has also forgotten all about the phrase "The sages embody the perfect attainment of human relationships." In this way, we have come to understand the Dao of study: when each person relinquishes his own position, he learns from following the other; when each person insists upon his own position, he finds fault in the other: this is how things inevitably turn out. But when each person relinquishes his own position, he forgets about any differences separating him from the other. These differences having been forgotten, the two parties join together as one, and there the matter ends.

Thus, inhibited neither by my advanced age nor by the cold weather, I went directly to Huang'an to meet Dingxiang in the mountains. When Dingxiang heard I was coming, he went wild with joy, [since he understood that] it was by no mere coincidence that we cherished the same aspirations and shared a common path; [rather, this reconciliation had come about through sustained effort]. If Master Dingli had still been alive, a few words from him would have decided the matter; a single phrase from him would have possessed the providential power to turn us from our dispute. Then this conflict would not have cost me more than ten years of misery, during which time neither Dingxiang nor I would budge, until at last we became aware of our errors.[22] What if I had died suddenly during that ten-year period? Would I have missed the chance to reform? Would I have forfeited the opportunity to reconcile with Dingxiang?

With these thoughts in mind, on the very next day, I went with Dingli's [eldest] son Runian 汝念 to pay my respects at his [Dingli's] grave. The trees by the grave were already bowed with age. Deeply pained that he could not return from the underworld, I decided to compose this record of his

---

21. This line explicitly contradicts the end of the letter, in which Li narrates his reconciliation with Geng. The discrepancy may have arisen if during the process of editing and printing *A Book to Burn* two letters were spliced together, or if Li began the letter before the conflict was resolved and added to it later.
22. The word translated here as "budge" (*hua* 化) has the connotation of transformation, education, moral reformation. I translate it as "reform" below.

life and copied it out three times as an offering. The first copy I submitted to Dingxiang to signify the joy I took in our friendship. The second copy I gave to Runian and [Dingli's second son] Rusi 汝思 so that they could recite it and burn it at the gentleman's grave site; this copy represents my regret over Dingli's death. The third copy I sent to Dinglih[23] in the capital; it signifies both my joy and my regret, my regret and my joy. Dinglih extended to me his love for his older brother, and this love knows no bounds. So I have written this record to record my feelings and to console him.

TRANSLATED BY RIVI HANDLER-SPITZ

---

23. Geng Dinglih 定力 (b. 1541), younger brother of Geng Dingli and Geng Dingxiang.

"A PETITION OF WORSHIP AND RECITATION TO THE MEDICINE BUDDHA"
禮誦藥師告文
"LISONG YAOSHI GAOWEN"

In *A Book to Burn*, Li Zhi included seven petitions, a genre of prayerful supplications beseeching help from various buddhas or gods. Three of these are addressed to the Medicine Master Lapis Lazuli Radiance King Buddha (hereafter "Medicine Buddha"). The 1593 supplication[1] translated here intermittently beseeches, cajoles, and attempts to reason with the Medicine Buddha in hopes that the 120-day ritual program of recitation and penitential offerings organized at the Cloister of the Flourishing Buddha will move this buddha to cure Li's breathing ailment. This ritual began in the tenth lunar month not long after the end of the monastic "rains retreat," a period ideally dedicated to intense meditation and study.

That Li would reach out to the Medicine Buddha is not in the least unusual and follows a long ritual tradition of religious reliance on the power of a buddha's vows. When still a bodhisattva, this buddha took twelve vows, including vows to heal physical deformities and cure the illnesses of those who hear his name. Ritual procedures developed to entreat the Medicine Buddha to exercise his healing powers often include recitation of *The Medicine Buddha Sutra*, a practice adopted by Li and the monks at his monastery. (JE)

These past two years I have suffered greatly from illness.[2] In the calculation of allotted life spans, others my age have already reached their time of death. Since my time of death is upon me, to allow me to die would be in

---

1. *FS, j.* 4, in *LZQJZ* 2:38–39.
2. In 1592, Li suffered from a bout of dysentery, and in 1593 he experienced the breathing ailment discussed in this petition and the next one.

accordance with correct principle. How is it that I am not granted death but, to the contrary, illness is visited upon me? The reason given for bestowing the pain of illness is that my number is not yet up and for the time being there is a desire to keep me in this world. For this reason, I am tormented by illness, making it difficult to spend my days in carefree happiness. As for me, I deserve to die: I have lived to an age "rarely seen since antiquity;"[3] this is the first reason I can die. I am of no benefit in this world; this is the second reason I can die. Among the living, perhaps there are some who have not yet accomplished what they need to do here. As for me, I absolutely have nothing left to do; this is the third reason I can die. For these three reasons I can die. Yet death does not come; instead, I am greatly tormented by illness. Why is this?

Having heard that in the east resides the Medicine Master Lapis Lazuli Radiance King Buddha who took a great vow to save sentient beings suffering from disease and cause their sickness to lead to nirvana, Monk Zhuowu publicly notified the great assembly to avail themselves of this 120-day ritual of sutra recitation and penitential offerings at this monastery.[4] The ritual will begin on the fifteenth day of the tenth month and commence by reciting *The Medicine Buddha Sutra* in a cycle of forty-nine repetitions for the sake of entreating [the buddha] to offer relief from my illness.

I think your vows are vast and deep and absolutely without fabrication. Given the power of your vows, if I do not beseech you, I am at fault. If when I beseech you, you were to ignore me, then you would lack compassion. If I beseech you but you are unaware of this, then you would lack intelligence: you would be no buddha. I know this is absolutely not the case. I hope for my sake that the great assembly will sincerely recite. Each month, on the first and fifteenth days, they will recite this sutra. This will result in a total of nine intervals, during which the sutra cycle will have been recited nine times. Indeed! Reciting the sutra cycle nine times will be nothing less than

---

3. Li Zhi was only sixty-seven years of age in 1593. The phrase "rarely seen since antiquity" refers to an oft-quoted line from a poem by the famous Tang poet Du Fu 杜甫, "Qujiang shi zhi er" 曲江詩之二 [Qu River poems, no. 2]: "Since antiquity, people have rarely lived to the age of seventy."
4. Li's use of the term "nirvana" here is somewhat unusual given that this is a Mahayana text. However, it likely refers to the promise made in the seventh vow, which claims that this buddha not only eliminates all disease but will also cause those who call on him to achieve unsurpassable awakening. See *Yaoshi liuli guang rulai benyuan gongde jing* 藥師琉璃光如來本願功德經 [Sutra on the merits of the fundamental vows of the Medicine Master Tathāgata of Lapis Lazuli Radiance], T450:14.405.b4. Furthermore, although he refers to himself as a "monk" (*heshang* 和尚), Li follows it with the secular name Zhuowu.

exhaustive. The great assembly's attentiveness will be nothing less than devout. After all this, it is inconceivable that there would be no response. I am willing to die, but I cannot bear to be sick. I earnestly beseech you a million times over and hope that you, [Medicine] Buddha, hear me!

TRANSLATED BY JENNIFER EICHMAN

"A PETITION UPON COMPLETION OF WORSHIPFUL RECITATION OF *THE MEDICINE BUDDHA SUTRA*"
禮誦藥師經畢告文
"LISONG *YAOSHI JING* BI GAOWEN"

At the end of the 120-day ritual period discussed in the preceding essay, Li must have been elated to find himself cured. The 1594 petition[1] translated here mentions that during the 120-day ritual, Li adopted a meatless diet, a practice that became part of the recovery process. How long he adhered to this dietary choice after the conclusion of the ritual is unclear. In a surprising turn, Li not only praises the Medicine Buddha for help in his own recovery but also petitions this buddha on behalf of a monk at his monastery, Changtong 常通, who was suffering from a painful ulcer.[2] Unfortunately, the ritual supplication presented here did not produce the desired result.

In 1594 Li wrote yet another petition on Changtong's behalf. The second petition (not translated here) describes in vivid detail this monk's physical suffering. Doctor consultations, medicines, and Buddhist rituals all failed to alleviate his symptoms. Li came to the conclusion that the ulcer was caused by malevolent forces or past karma and that this monk's less-than-stellar adherence to monastic precepts, a topic already raised in this essay, may have deterred the Medicine Buddha from exercising his healing powers. (JE)

---

1. *FS*, *j*. 4, in *LZQJZ* 2:41–42.
2. Changtong was a longtime resident monk at the Cloister of the Flourishing Buddha. He is mentioned in several of Li's essays and appears to have had some monastic responsibilities. We do not know why Li and not Changtong wrote this particular petition. However, the Medicine Buddha had already responded to Li's supplication by healing his illness. This put him in the rather prestigious position of someone this Buddha deemed worthy of an audience, perhaps allowing him to vouch for others.

I have had the good fortune to have recovered from my respiratory illness and at the completion of this recitation express gratitude for the Buddha's help. I note that today is the fifteenth day of the first month: as of today, the nine intervals are finished; as of today, the nine sessions of recitation have been completed. After just two sessions of reciting the sutra, my breathing illness was almost entirely cured. In continuing to recite, having not yet finished the fourth cycle, I exercised some dietary restraint and was able to maintain a vegetarian diet. After I adhered for some time to this diet, my breathing sickness nearly disappeared. After the breathing sickness was cured, I found the vegetarian diet even more pleasing. Were it not for the Buddha's power, how could I have recovered? Although the assembled monks were reverently devout beyond compare, the cure was due to the Medicine King Bodhisattva's profound compassion. I cannot offer enough worshipful gratitude and prayerful thanks.

I further offer the following supplication: There is a novice monk, Changtong, who, having witnessed that the Medicine-Master Tathāgata cured my illness, promptly strengthened his resolve. He approached the altar and continued reciting in prayerful hope for the speedy healing of his ulcer. He bowed respectfully [to you] and exhibited extraordinary sincerity. On the sixteenth day of this month, he asked the great assembly to recite one cycle of this sutra.

Indeed! The Buddha is none other than the great father of the three realms. How is it possible that he would deem this monk useless and abandon him? What's more, how could a true disciple of the Buddha, like myself, bear to think that you would ignore him despite my entreaties! I hope you will see that this monk, despite his lack of superior conduct in the monastic community, still has not committed any great transgression. When he strikes the bells and chimes, the sound rises uniformly; when he strikes the drum and bowl, the sound rings forth;[3] his sutra-recitation voice is bright

---

3. In a 1596 text on monastery rules, Li claimed that the clear sound emitted from striking the drum was a direct result of a monk's adherence to precepts and dismissed the idea that a newly arrived novice could assume this role. In this petition, Li implies that because Changtong is allowed to strike these ritual instruments and does it well, he is of sound moral character. See "Rules Agreed Upon in Advance" (Yuyue 豫約), in *FS*, *j.* 4, in *LZQJZ* 2:102.

and clear. By means of your power swiftly grant this supplication. These past two years his ulcer has not healed. Medicine King, quickly offer your protection. What good fortune could compare with this? In this matter, on his behalf, I beseech you in utmost reverence!

TRANSLATED BY JENNIFER EICHMAN

"A BRIEF INTRODUCTION TO *RESOLVING DOUBTS ABOUT THE PURE LAND*"
淨土決前引
"JINGTU JUE QIANYIN"

Late-Ming Buddhists often argued about which was the correct path to spiritual liberation, Pure Land or Chan. Some Pure Land practitioners envisioned that after death one would literally be reborn in a distant land presided over by Amitābha Buddha. In contrast, some Chan practitioners were committed to the ideal of an ultimate awakening in this lifetime. In an effort to demonstrate the compatibility of these two contrasting visions, Li compiled *Resolving Doubts About the Pure Land*. He undertook to reconcile the differences between the paths by asserting that both lead to purification of the mind and are simply different conceptualizations of the same ultimate goal.

"A Brief Introduction to *Resolving Doubts About the Pure Land*"[1] opens with a famous citation from the *Vimalakīrti-nirdeśa-sūtra*: "When the mind is pure, the buddha land will be pure."[2] Li uses this claim to argue that Pure Land and Chan practitioners were neither reborn in separate pure lands nor required to wait until after death to achieve rebirth in Amitābha Buddha's Land of Supreme Bliss. The emphasis on achieving immediate results without having to "wait" (*dai* 待) draws equally on developments in Yangming Confucian thought. The second-generation Wang Yangming disciple Wang Longxi and his lineage descendants argued that self-cultivation and its realization were simultaneous occurrences. This use of *dai* (wait) is unique to Li's interpretive gloss; it does not appear in any of the textual excerpts that make up *Resolving Doubts About the Pure Land*.

Resolving Doubts About the Pure Land consists of twelve excerpts interspersed with the occasional interlinear note. The excerpts are far more nuanced in their doctrinal exposition than one might con-

---

1. *Xinbian wanxu zangjing* 新編卍續藏經, vol. 108, 357.a1–a17.
2. *Vimalakīrti-nirdeśa-sūtra* (*Weimojie suoshuo jing* 維摩詰所説經) (T475); see Watson, *The Vimalakirti Sutra*.

clude from simply reading this short preface. They are often drawn from the work of monks who supported the joint practice of Chan and Pure Land. (JE)

Li Zhuowu of Wenling said, "The bodhisattva Vimalakīrti said, 'When the mind is pure, the buddha land[3] will be pure.'[4] As to Amitābha Buddha's Land of Supreme Bliss, the land is pure. When practitioners contemplate [*nian* 念] Amitābha Buddha's Land of Supreme Bliss, their minds are pure. Those who contemplate Amitābha Buddha's Land of Supreme Bliss are reborn in Amitābha Buddha's Land of Supreme Bliss. When the mind is pure, the buddha land will be pure. This being so, those who recollect the name [*nianfo* 念佛] recollect this Pure Land.[5] Those who investigate Chan investigate this Pure Land. How could the results differ? Consequently, those who recite the name [*nianfo*] will certainly be reborn in the Pure Land. How could those who investigate Chan reject this Pure Land and find another place of rebirth? If there is another place of rebirth, then there are two lands. This is impure. Amitābha Buddha's Land of Supreme Bliss cannot be conceived of in this way.

As for those who investigate Chan, of course they need not wait to be reborn. As for those who recite the name, how could it be that they wait to go and only later are reborn there? If one must wait for rebirth and only later be reborn, then this is to say that those here recite the name to be born there, and those there "recite their own name" and are reborn here.[6] This coming and going also creates two lands. This is impure. Amitābha

---

3. A *buddha-kṣetra* (literally, "buddha field") represents the power of a buddha and his field of influence, a world sphere. The *Vimalakīrti-nirdeśa-sūtra* depicts a cosmological landscape filled with infinite numbers of Buddhas who each inhabit their own buddha field. It is for this reason that Li quickly moves from the cited passage, which does not specify a particular field or buddha, to his chosen subject of Amitābha Buddha and his Pure Land of Supreme Bliss. For an extended description of the Pure Land of Amitābha Buddha and buddha fields, see Gómez, *The Land of Bliss*.
4. Li misattributes this line of text to Vimalakīrti. In fact, it is Śākyamuni Buddha who makes the claim in a long exchange between himself and the bodhisattva Jeweled Accumulation (*Baoji pusa* 寶積菩薩) in the first section of the sutra.
5. By the late Ming, *nianfo* usually meant repeated recitation of the name Amitābha Buddha. However, this expression never entirely lost its original meaning: to recollect or keep the name or to contemplate or visualize a buddha. See Harrison, "Commemoration and Identification in *Buddhānusmṛti*."
6. Li adds the outrageous claim that one would recite one's own name (*nianwo* 念我) to drive home the point that it would be ridiculous to conceive of the Pure Land of Amitābha as external to one's own mind.

Buddha's Land of Supreme Bliss cannot be conceived of in this way. For this reason, one should know that Amitābha Buddha's Pure Land is none other than the Pure Land of one's own mind. Whether one recites the name or investigates Chan, one does so for the purpose of purifying one's own mind. I have advised various scholars that they should neither revere Chan guests[7] nor disdain the Pure Land. For this reason, I have collected the words of various great Buddhist sages who advised people to cultivate Pure Land practices, and I have combined them to create *Resolving Doubts About the Pure Land*.

TRANSLATED BY JENNIFER EICHMAN

---

7. A Chan guest (*chanke* 禪客) could be either a monk or a layperson.

"DISCIPLINING THE SANGHA"
戒眾僧
"JIE ZHONGSENG"

In this prescriptive essay,[1] Li Zhi demonstrates his familiarity with monastic life and with regulations or precepts (*jie* 戒) governing monk behavior. Li first lays out an age-old normative view of the relationship between precepts, meditation, and wisdom, stressing that precepts are the foundation for all other practices. Just as Confucians might invoke Confucius to bolster their stance, Li bolsters his authority by invoking the exemplary behavior of Śākyamuni Buddha, the so-called progenitor of the Buddhist tradition. Yet it is clear that Li is conceiving of the tradition in Mahayana terms. This is evident in his introduction of the Six Perfections, a cornerstone of Mahayana practice.

After leaving the Geng household in 1585, Li took up residence first at the Vimalakīrti Monastery in Macheng and then, from 1588, at the Cloister of the Flourishing Buddha beside Dragon Lake. Though it is not clear whether he vowed to follow the precepts of a fully ordained monk, he devoted this essay to their promotion.[2] Li rallies rank-and-file monks at the cloister to expend their utmost energies adhering not only to the 250 precepts[3] of a fully ordained monk but also to the 3,000 deportments and 80,000 minor adjustments, a tall order indeed! Li reminds monks that all material donations come with a spiritual responsibility. Rather than naively thinking that monks eat for free and enjoy a livelihood funded by others, newly arrived novices need to develop a mature ethic of gratitude

---

1. *FS, j.* 4, in *LZQJZ* 2:73–75.
2. The scholarly literature has often noted the monk Zhuhong's 袾宏 (1535–1615) criticism of Li's behavior but has failed to note Zhuhong's praise of Li for his exhortations to his disciples, most notably to remain in the monastery and cultivate ascetic practices. See Zhuhong, "Li Zhuowu er" 李卓吾二 [Li Zhuowu, second essay], in *Zhuchuang sanbi* 竹窗三筆 [Jottings by a bamboo window, third volume], 24–25; reprinted in Zhuhong, *Lianchi dashi quanji*, 3958–59.
3. The first five precepts are to abstain from killing, stealing, engaging in sexual activity, lying, and using intoxicants.

and spiritual repayment through diligence in their individual practice of the precepts, fulfillment of monastic responsibilities, and the performance of Buddhist rituals for others. Failure to do so results in an animal rebirth. Through a colorful array of metaphors Li draws an irrevocable link between personal behavior and karmic results.

In 1566 the Jiajing emperor closed the officially sponsored ordination platform, and it was rarely reopened during the Wanli reign (1573–1620).[4] Among the monks at the Cloister of the Flourishing Buddha, Wunian Shenyou was fully ordained, yet many of his disciples and their disciples were likely to have received the full precepts under unofficial circumstances only and did not possess ordination certificates. Some scholars have suggested that the closing of the ordination platform had a detrimental effect on the sangha.[5] While this was true on a number of levels, Li's essay presumes continued adherence to the strictest preceptual standards. Li attributes lack of discipline to individual shortcomings, not to the practical impossibility of receiving full ordination. (JE)

The Buddha discoursed on the perfections.[6] There are six perfections, of which keeping the precepts is primary. The Buddha explained precepts, meditation, and wisdom. Of these three, precepts precede the others. The word "precepts" is truly difficult to explain. Precepts give rise to meditation, meditation gives rise to wisdom. Wisdom further gives rise to precepts; there is no wisdom outside precepts. Wisdom is derived from precepts; it does not eliminate the need for precepts. This being so, meditation and wisdom are the foundation of Buddhahood. Precepts are the foundation of meditation and wisdom. Before our venerable Śākyamuni Buddha became a Buddha, he cultivated ascetic practices for twelve years. He adhered to the precepts, as formulated here, as you all know. After our venerable Śākyamuni Buddha attained Buddhahood, he preached the dharma for forty-nine years, and he continued to cultivate the precepts, as you all know.

---

4. Jiang Wu, *Enlightenment in Dispute*, 28–30.
5. See, for example, Chu, "Bodhisattva Precepts."
6. The Six Perfections (*pāramitā*) are virtues or qualities cultivated by Mahayana Buddhists, especially bodhisattvas. They are giving, morality, patience, vigor, concentration, and wisdom. See also Li's 1578 essay "Liu du jie" 六度解 [Explanation of the Six Perfections], in *FS*, *j*. 4, in *LZQJZ*, 2:75–76.

If one were to say that a Buddha is free from precepts or that precepts are a hindrance to Buddhahood or that once one has already realized Buddhahood, there is no harm in breaking the precepts, then this would be to abandon the monastery and return to the emperor's palace. What strictures would there be? How could anyone [under those circumstances] continue to wear a monk's robes and go on begging rounds? You should know that the "milk debt" owed to one's parents is difficult to repay. You must diligently work at repaying it. To say that "when one son achieves the Way, nine relatives are reborn in heaven"[7] is not reckless talk! [The debt of gratitude owed for] grain donations received from the ten directions is difficult to repay. One must vigorously work to eliminate this debt. As for the saying, "One becomes an animal with fur or horns in order to repay sincere donors,"[8] how could this be a lie!

In this respect, the word "precepts" is the "gateway to myriad mysteries." The locution "breaking the precepts" is the origin of myriad disasters. The word "precepts" [conjures up a sensation] as if, upon encountering military troops, one immediately ceded all discipline, incurred losses, and fled. It makes one feel as if upon entering a deep valley, in a split second of inattention one may lose one's footing and die. Thus, you should know that the 3,000 deportments[9] are weightier than towering mountains; the 80,000 minor adjustments[10] are dense like the hairs of an ox. All affairs demand vigorous adherence to regulations.

Do not say, "No one will see me" and conclude that it is fine for me to live a quiet life indulging my passions. As soon as one violates the precepts, others immediately know. One's lack of restraint will be witnessed not only by a single pair of eyes or ten pairs but by millions of pairs that will all see this transgression. Do not say, "No one will point a finger at me" and conclude that I can deceive myself like the man in the adage who "covered his ears to steal a bell."[11] If for a split second you violate the precepts, ghosts

---

7. Li has either misremembered this citation or changed it. The canonical Buddhist saying is "When one son leaves home to become a monk, nine family members are reborn in heaven."
8. A number of Buddhist texts use this same language to warn monks that if they do not repay their spiritual debts, they risk rebirth as animals.
9. Deportment, or, literally, "movement" (weiyi 威儀, Skt. īryāpatha). The 3,000 deportments consist of monastic regulations that govern the four postures of sitting, standing, walking, and lying down.
10. The "minor adjustments" are a further enhancement of the 3,000 deportments and include other affective and behavioral categories to which the original 250 precepts can be applied.
11. Li is referring to a common Chinese adage with origins in the Lü shi chunqiu 呂氏春秋 [Annals of Lü Buwei].

will punish you. And bystanders angered by your deception will point their fingers at you. Not one finger or ten fingers but millions of fingers will point out your transgression.

Strictness upon strictness, precepts upon precepts, from today onward create this image: To sit and receive communal meals is like swallowing hot iron pills. If I am not consumed by fear, what distinguishes me from dogs and pigs? To practice the precepts and seek out the precept jewel is like entering a refreshingly cool pavilion. If I am again frightened out of my wits, then what distinguishes me from a common beggar? Only when one is attentive in this way can one be called a monk.

As the current moves a boat, wind and waves cause it to capsize. As a cart travels along a road, an inclined slope causes it to overturn. Who creates the wind and waves? The capsizing is of your own making. Who creates the inclined slope? The overturning of the cart is your own doing! Our great assembly, be cautious in this! In addition to senior monks who have practiced for a long time and have no need for such superfluous instruction, we also have in our midst new monks who do not yet know shame. I have no choice but to explain this to them once again. Within this great assembly, I hope each of you will spur yourselves on so that the Cloister of the Flourishing Buddha may receive praise. By rallying our spirits, we can together create the great assembly at Dragon Lake.

TRANSLATED BY JENNIFER EICHMAN

"REFLECTIONS ON MY LIFE"
感慨平生
"GANKAI PINGSHENG"

"Reflections on My Life"[1] is the last section of the "Rules Agreed Upon in Advance" (Yuyue 預約), a collection of notes Li Zhi wrote in 1596 presumably for his disciples and followers in his temple. However, while the first four sections are mostly about rules, the last two sections are quite different, the fifth being his "will" and the sixth his reflections on his life. Elsewhere, Li Zhi suggests that this section could be read as his biography.[2] In "Reflections on My Life," he explains in detail the reasons behind his decision to take the Buddhist tonsure and talks about his deep frustrations in his official career and the heavy price he had to pay for trying to maintain his independence. "Reflections on My Life" provides us with a unique opportunity to have a direct look into the mind of this eccentric thinker, who cherished his independence above all else.[3] (MH)

You tend to believe that the moment you "leave home" [join the Buddhist sangha], you achieve Buddhahood and become far superior to those lay Buddhist believers. Now that I have left home and taken the tonsure, could I be said to be superior to others? I took the tonsure because I had no alternatives. I did not leave home because I believed that leaving home was a good thing or that I could cultivate my Buddhahood only after I had left home. Why cannot one pursue the Way at home? In fact, throughout my life I have never liked the idea of having to take orders from another person. Once born,

---

1. FS, j. 4, in LZQJZ 2:108–20.
2. See "To Zhou Youshan," pp. 249–52.
3. The beginning paragraph is omitted in the translation here because it contains information on two of Li Zhi's female students that does not contribute directly to the central concerns of this essay—reflections on his own life; also omitted here is the somewhat extraneous last portion of the original essay.

one is immediately subjected to the control of others. I do not need to mention that young children and those studying with tutors have to obey their superiors. As soon as one reaches school age, one has to follow instructions from his teacher and various education officials; once an official, one has to take orders from one's superiors; after retiring and returning home, one is under the supervision of the officials of the local county and prefecture; one has to attend all the social functions, contribute to funds for birthday gifts for these officials, and entertain them with banquets; one really must be very careful. If any of these officials is displeased, disaster will immediately ensue. Even after one is dead and buried, one is still not liberated from these constraints—in fact, they may become worse. For this reason I would rather roam the world than return home. Although I have always been eager to meet friends and seek soul mates, I realize that I have found very few true soul mates. I left officialdom and decided not to return home only because I really didn't want to be controlled by anyone. This is my real intention, but few are willing to believe it. This is why I do not like to mention this. Even if I travel around, I could still face the possibility of having to take orders from the local officials wherever I happen to stop.

When Deng Dingshi was the magistrate of Macheng,[4] I did not dare to enter his yamen casually. However, when he sent me an invitation, how could I fail to send my name card to him in return! It would not have been appropriate for me to sign the card as "student at service" because this would have been too presumptuous [and would have suggested that we were equals in status], but I could not have presented myself as "a student to be trained" because that would have made me feel too constricted.[5] After careful consideration, I decided to sign the card as "a sojourner-traveler," which was more appropriate.[6]

---

4. Dingshi 鼎石, given name Deng Yingqi 鄧應祁, was the son of Li Zhi's friend Deng Shiyang 石陽. Deng Shiyang was serving as a judge in Hui county, Henan province, where Li Zhi left his family in 1564 after returning to his hometown for the burial of his grandfather. During Li Zhi's absence, Deng Shiyang aided Li's wife and daughters when famine was ravaging the area.
5. "Student at service" (*sisheng* 侍生) was the term a junior official would use to present himself to a senior official. It was also used by officials of equal status or by a member of the local gentry when presenting himself to an official. "A student to be trained" (*zhisheng* 治生) is a term that an official would use to present himself to his superior or that an official stationed elsewhere would use to present himself to a higher official stationed in his hometown. The term Li uses for "sojourner-traveler" is *liuyu kezi* 流寓客子.
6. As the following paragraphs make clear, by designating himself a "traveler" rather than specifying his administrative rank or educational attainments, Li Zhi was announcing his refusal to perform his social roles in the way expected of him. Taking on the identity of sojourner and adopting the tonsure of a monk were, in the eyes of the more conservative among his contemporaries, rebellious and escapist acts.

PART III: MISCELLANEOUS WRITINGS 雜述 187

There have been many sojourners throughout history. In a local gazetteer, following the section devoted to famous officials, there is always a section titled "sojourners." "Famous officials" refers to virtuous local officials; "sojourners" refers to famous virtuous recluses. Where the local official is known to be good, virtuous recluses will be sure to come and dwell. Being listed in the "sojourners" section, one is automatically considered virtuous just as is an official mentioned in the "famous officials" section. An official must have a good reputation in order to be listed in the local gazetteer, and this is why the relevant section is titled "famous officials;" as for those listed in the "sojourners" section, they are considered virtuous in and of themselves. This is why the section is called simply "sojourners," since there have been very few people who could live away from their homes as sojourners without possessing outstanding virtues. Zhu Xi was from Wuyuan but later spent time in Yanping, Fujian, as a sojourner; Su Shi and his brother, Su Che, were both from Meizhou, Sichuan, but one was buried in Xiaxian and the other in Xuzhou, Henan. There were many more such cases: Shao Yong was from Fanyang, Hebei, and Sima Guang hailed from Xiaxian, Shanxi, but both sojourned in Luoyang almost all their lives; the same is also true of Bai Juyi, who was originally from Taiyuan, Shanxi, but who eventually sojourned in Luoyang. No one would believe someone could leave his home and live as a sojourner wherever he traveled if he was not a man of great virtue.

Why would I sign the card as both a sojourner and a traveler? Isn't that redundant? Not necessarily so: if one lives in some place other than his hometown, unless one is able to build a house and do farming there, it will be virtually impossible to avoid taking orders from others. I presented myself as a "traveler" so as to imply that I was not a resident who had already settled down there, just as in the cases of Sima Guang and Shao Yong. Not sure whether I would leave or how long I would remain there, the magistrate was not in a position to issue orders to me in his capacity as a local official. If he could not issue orders to me as a local official, how could he boss me around even if he was supposed to be a figure of authority in that area? This was why I signed the card the way I did—to make it clear that as a traveler I was not supposed to be controlled by the local officials.

However, the above option is not as good as becoming a monk by shaving one's head. After taking the tonsure, even a resident of Macheng, let alone a monk from another area, does not have to take orders from the local magistrate. But one might ask, "If this is indeed the case, why did you have to choose to shave your head in Macheng instead of doing it in your hometown?" Shaving my head in Macheng was something I had contemplated for a long time before I actually went ahead with it. Deng Dingshi was very sad when he found out that I had shaved my head. He quoted his mother's words as follows: "Tell [Li Zhi] that when I heard of his decision to shave his head I could not eat for an entire day and that I still cannot swallow even the food in my mouth! Maybe then Uncle Li will keep his hair. If you can persuade him to grow back his hair, then I will regard you as a filial son and as a first-rate official." Alas! The decision to shave my head was by no means an easy one! My decision rested entirely upon my desire to be free from the control of others. How could this have been easy? Writing about this, I am in tears. Do not think that taking the Buddhist tonsure is a good thing and do not casually accept others' alms.

Despite my dislike for taking orders from others, I have nevertheless encountered many tribulations. Precisely because I don't like to be controlled by others, I have suffered so much in my life that even if the entire earth could be turned into ink, there would not be enough of it to record these sufferings. When I was the director of a district school, I had conflicts with the district magistrate and superintendent; when I was an erudite at the Imperial Academy, I had conflicts with the academy's chancellor and the directors, including Zou [Leiming], Chen [Yiqing], Pan [Sheng], and Lü [Tiaoyang]; when I was serving as the manager of the General Services Office in the Ministry of Rites, I had conflicts with Minister Gao Yi, Minister Yin Shidan, Vice-Minister Wang Xilie, and Vice-Minister Wan Shihe. Later both Gao and Yin served in the imperial cabinet, and so did Pan, Chen, and Lü. Gao had fired numerous young officials with *jinshi* degrees. Yet I was not let go even though I had once upset him. Because of this, Gao can be considered a person of outstanding moral character. What was most frustrating was that I could not gain the trust of Minister Xie Dengzhi or of Dong Chuance and Wang Zong, the two chief ministers of the Court of Judicial Review, when I was serving as the vice-bureau-director in the Ministry of Justice. Though Xie Dengzhi is hardly worth mentioning, Wang and Dong were both upright persons with whom I ought not to have had any conflict. However, both of them were so anxious about their own career advancement that they felt they should be far superior to others ethically even though their moral character was not necessarily purer than that of others. How could I manage to avoid having conflicts with them? Another very frustrating experience was dealing with Minister Zhao Jin, who was a renowned Confucian of the School of Principle. Who could have expected that the greater his reputation was, the more intense my conflict with him would be? Finally, when I was serving as the prefect of Yao'an, I had conflicts with the grand coordinator Wang Yi and circuit intendant Luo Wenli. Wang Yi possesses a lowly moral character and does not deserve mention here. Luo and I understood each other quite well. He was both talented and morally upright, learned, and skilled at dealing with practical matters. However, eventually I could not avoid arguing with him. Why? This was because he was too strict and harsh. Initially, he treated me with respect because I was a poor official with integrity, but later he considered me incompetent and deliberately made things difficult for me. He was quite conceited and did not consider others' opinions. Throughout history, the so-called gentlemen of great virtue have all been like him. I remember I once pleaded with him, "With so many different types of savages living in this border area, it is difficult to enforce the laws to the fullest. If the soldiers are able to live peacefully day by day alongside these wild people, that should be considered quite an accomplishment. Those who come without families have found it difficult to reside here; those who bring along their families must traverse great distances to get here and must undergo equal hardships to return home. We must treat them with compassion. If an official has any ability, he should be treated with respect. How could one fault him for not being perfect? So long as one has not been reported for wrongdoing, we should not try to find fault with him. Why must we scrutinize every minute detail? Being scrupulous and bravely insisting on utter integrity are behavioral standards one should apply only to oneself, not to others. If one insists on judging others by these standards, then one cannot be considered to exemplify perfect integrity. Moreover, one should apply one's standards consistently." Alas, how could anyone have expected that I would quarrel with Luo over this! Despite our quarrel, if I were to be asked to recommend a talented official, Luo would still top my list. The above is a summary of my life.

TRANSLATED BY MARTIN HUANG

"THE PAVILION FOR WORSHIPPING THE MOON"
拜月
"BAI YUE"

This short essay[1] comments on *The Pavilion for Worshipping the Moon*, a play believed to have been written by Hui Shi 惠施 (1296-1371) and adapted from a work by Guan Hanqing 關漢卿 (ca. 1234-1320). The play narrates a romance between a scholar, Jiang Shilong, and an official's daughter, Wang Ruilan. Fleeing a war, they meet and secretly marry. Wang Ruilan's father, however, looks down on Jiang Shilong and separates the couple. Continuing to flee, Jiang Shilong later encounters a man named Xingfu, who turns out to be Wang Ruilan's brother. Jiang Shilong and Xingfu become sworn brothers and together triumphantly pass the imperial examination in the capital. The work concludes with Wang Ruilan's reunion with Jiang Shilong and Xingfu's marriage to Jiang Shilong's sister. Writing in Wuchang around 1592, Li Zhi praises the plot of the play and the rebellious spirit of the couple. He compares Wang Ruilan with Cui Yingying, the heroine of the well-known play *The Story of the Western Wing*. In another essay, "On Miscellaneous Matters" (102–5), Li Zhi declares that *The Pavilion for Worshipping the Moon* and *The Story of the Western Wing* are as beautiful as nature itself. (HYC)

In this play, the plot is excellent, and the dialogue is good. The songs are also good. It truly exemplifies Yuan-dynasty writing. At the beginning, it seems disjointed, but by the finale it achieves marvelous singularity. Put it next to *The Story of the Western Wing*, and it will give the more famous play a run for its money. This play should endure as long as heaven and earth do. As long as this world exists, we cannot do without this marvelous play. Would you

---

1. *FS, j.* 4, in *LZQJZ* 2:132–33. *Bai yue* is short for *Bai yue ting ji* 拜月亭記 or *Bai yue ji* 拜月記.

not agree with me? Even if you disagree, I think the matter is self-evident. Just try to give it a careful reading. It should awaken in your mind thoughts of righteous relationships between brothers, sisters, husbands, and wives.

Lan[2] values her good name more than Cui[3] does, but Lan is more elegant and refined. When Lan has no choice but to part from her new husband, Shilong, she vows to Heaven that she will never betray him. Her oath is the acme of chastity and rectitude. Though Xingfu, the second protagonist of the story, flees into the woods and becomes a bandit, he is grateful for Shilong's help and repays him when he is in need. This action accords with common sense. The play ends by tying the plot together with happy unions: Shilong is reunited with Lan and allows his sister to marry Xingfu. Shilong and Xingfu, who were previously sworn brothers, become brothers-in-law. No virtue goes unrewarded and no gratitude is unreciprocated. How exquisitely these unexpected outcomes reflect the ways in which Heaven rewards good people!

TRANSLATED BY HUIYING CHEN

---

2. Wang Ruilan, the heroine of *The Pavilion for Worshipping the Moon*.
3. Cui Yingying, the heroine of *The Story of the Western Wing*.

"RED DUSTER"
紅拂
"HONG FU"

This concise essay[1] comments on Zhang Fengyi's 張風翼 (1527–1613) play *The Story of Red Duster*, which mixes elements of Du Guangting's 杜光庭 (850–933) Tang-dynasty "Tale of the Curly-Bearded Stranger" with plot details derived from the "Story of Princess Lechang" included in Meng Qi's 孟棨 *Poems and Their Anecdotes* (*Ben shi shi* 本事詩).[2] The play centers on the romance between a singing girl, Red Duster, and a future military commander, Li Jing. Having eloped, the lovers meet a curly-bearded stranger who bestows all his wealth on them and becomes Red Duster's sworn brother.

Li Zhi wrote this commentary in 1592 in Wuchang. He cites Confucius's comments on the function of poetry and claims that contemporary entertainment such as vernacular drama can be evaluated by the same standards as classical poetry. (HYC)

In this play, the plot is good, the songs are good, the dialogue is good, and the action is good. Princess Lechang, having broken a mirror, reunites the halves when she reencounters her husband. The singing girl Red Duster shows peerless insight [by choosing to run away with Li Jing immediately after meeting him]; the curly-bearded stranger abandons his fortune [to Red Duster and Li Jing] and goes abroad [with his wife]; the Duke of Yue[3] simultaneously frees Red Duster and Princess Lechang [from their servitude]. These actions are all worthy of emulation. They deserve respect

---

1. *FS, j.* 4, in *LZQJZ* 2:133–34.
2. According to *Poems and Their Anecdotes*, Princess Lechang, the younger sister of the last emperor of the Southern Dynasties, had to separate from her husband in the turmoil of the dynasty's fall. She broke a mirror and gave half to her husband. After years of fleeing, they were finally reunited and reassembled the broken mirror.
3. Yang Su, duke of Yue (544–606), frees the two singing girls Red Duster and Princess Lechang after hearing their stories.

and admiration. Who says that *chuanqi* do not possess the ability to "stir" people, to inspire them to "make observations," to "join together," and to "express grievances"?[4] Amid eating and drinking, banquets and entertainments, we are often moved by feelings of righteousness. Contemporary entertainments are just like those of antiquity; I hope we may regard them no differently!

TRANSLATED BY HUIYING CHEN

---

4. Quoting Confucius on the *Classic of Poetry* in *Analects* 17.9. *Chuanqi* 傳奇 fiction "transmits marvels," as its name indicates. Popular plays mixing comic, suspenseful, and supernatural elements were also called *chuanqi*.

PART IV
READINGS OF HISTORY 讀史

"ON THE LETTER TERMINATING RELATIONS"
絕交書
"JUE JIAO SHU"

This essay[1] (date unknown) comments on a text by Ji Kang 嵇康 (224–263) titled "Terminating Relations with Shan Juyuan." Ji Kang and Shan Tao 山濤 (205–283) were two of the reclusive Seven Masters of the Bamboo Grove.[2] However, when Shan's relative Sima Yi 司馬懿 (179–251) became a powerful general in the state of Wei, Shan came out of reclusion and rose to high office. While serving as the attendant to the general in chief, he attempted to recommend his friend Ji Kang to succeed him in this post. A year later, Shan Tao received a scornful letter from Ji Kang, terminating their friendship. In this letter Ji Kang grandiosely compares himself to Zhuangzi and intimates that stooping to take office would defile his perfect virtue, something he would never consider doing. Scholars had for centuries praised Ji Kang for his lofty ideals and untarnished virtue, but Li Zhi took delight in criticizing Ji Kang's actions and attitude. (RHS)

---

1. *FS*, *j*. 5, in *LZQJZ* 2:164–66.
2. For Li Zhi's biographies of these men, see *CS*, *j*. 10 and *j*. 31.

If the letter had been written by a close friend on Ji Kang's behalf, that would have been all right; but for Kang to write the letter himself, I fear, was not the same thing at all. Shan Tao recommended Kang for office because he knew him intimately, and Kang's talent genuinely corresponded to Tao's praise.

Kang averred that his own character was not suited to taking office, and that if he took office, he would surely bring disaster upon himself. That much was correct. But to say that Tao did not appreciate Kang, or that Tao deliberately sought to bring disaster on him, was not right. And for Kang to liken himself to the *yuanju* bird and to compare Tao to the [owl feasting on a] rotten rat carcass, that also was not right.[3] To think that the person who has recommended one fails to appreciate one's talents, and for this reason to terminate relations with him, and to portray oneself as indifferent to official rank and the other as lusting after it—this is the behavior of one who thinks highly of himself but despises others; moreover, since the facts were otherwise, it is especially wrong.

Alas! If Kang's native talent had been augmented with a little learning, who could have matched him? How dare he emulate the language of the ancients in writing these false and evasive words? The haughtiness of his letter is truly frightful: even at a distance of a thousand years, he seems to rise up right before our eyes. The above censure of Kang is not mine alone; the same opinions have already been expressed by people of impeccable virtue and wisdom.

TRANSLATED BY RIVI HANDLER-SPITZ

---

3. Zhuangzi recounts that when Hui Shi was prime minister in the state of Liang, he learned that Zhuangzi was coming to visit. Immediately he began to worry that Zhuangzi might supplant him in his post. To allay Hui Shi's fears, Zhuangzi told a parable: There is a bird, the *yuanju*, so pure that it alights on no tree other than the *wutong* and drinks only water from the clearest streams. One day the *yuanju* soared high above a place where a greedy owl was feasting on a rotten rat carcass. The owl became afraid that the *yuanju* might steal part of his dinner, so he quickly shooed the bird away. Comparing himself to the *yuanju* and Hui Shi to the rat-eating owl, Zhuangzi ended the parable by asking Hui Shi, "Now that you have this Liang state of yours, are you trying to shoo me away?" (*Zhuangzi*, ch. 17; Watson, *Chuang Tzu*, 188). Ji Kang's letter to Shan Tao cites this story.

"DRAGONFLY DITTY"
蜻蛉謠
"QINGLING YAO"

The title of this brief essay[1] refers to a lyric poem written by the sixteenth-century scholar Yang Shen 楊慎 (1488–1559). Dragonfly county was an alternative name for Dayao county in Yunnan province, where Yang resided for many years after having been banished from the capital. This remote region of southwestern China, where Li would later serve as prefect of Yao'an county from 1577 to 1580, was home to many indigenous peoples. In the poem to which Li's title refers, as well as in an essay titled "How the Military Strategist Jiang Long Did Away with Deliberation" (*Binglüe Jiang Long qu si ji* 兵略姜龍去思記), Yang praises Jiang Long for effectively and humanely quelling tribal rebellions. According to Yang, Jiang believed that pacifying the natives was preferable to overwhelming them with brute force.

Li fully endorsed this view. As prefect of Yao'an, he opposed the suppression of native culture and strove to promote toleration. As he himself wrote, during his tenure in Yao'an, he governed by "maintaining simplicity in all things, following the natural course of events, and considering it his responsibility to educate the [native] people by means of virtue."[2] Although the present essay was written in 1596, many years after Li retired from his post in Yunnan, it expresses Li's profound admiration for Jiang's humane policies toward indigenous populations. (RHS)

Though human nature is constant and the way of the world unchanging, I have never yet, despite a lifelong study of the matter, encountered anyone whose way of thinking is similar to my own. So I am perpetually astonished,

---

1. *FS, j.* 5, in *LZQJZ* 2:177–79.
2. *FS, j.* 2, "You shu shi Tongzhou hou" 又書使通州後 [Afterword to another letter to the commissioner of Tongzhou].

and I wonder how Heaven could have made me so unlucky. If "human nature does not vary much"³ but I alone am unlike others, is that not unlucky?

When I began my official career, I personally experienced the havoc wrought by Japanese pirates in the south and by the Jurchens in the north. Ultimately, I moved to Yunnan, but there I often heard about rebellions by indigenous leaders and people of the Yao and Tong tribes. I suspect that scholars who live on official salaries all share similar views. Since my opinions cast doubt on theirs, they either regard me as crazy or think I should be killed. But when I recently read Master Yang's collected works, I made a note of the part about Master Jiang. Master Jiang was of precisely the same mind that I am, and Master Yang praised him for it. From this I can tell that although Master Yang held no official post, if he *had* held a post, he would have seen things as Master Jiang did. Of this there is no doubt.

Although I was born later, my outlook corresponds to that of these old-time sages; so my birth was not unlucky after all. I have recorded this with delight.

TRANSLATED BY RIVI HANDLER-SPITZ

---

3. From "Jia Yi zhuan" 賈誼傳 [The biography of Jia Yi], in *Han shu* 漢書, *j.* 18.

"BIOGRAPHY OF BO YI"
伯夷傳
"BO YI ZHUAN"

This essay,¹ written in Macheng in 1596, addresses the age-old questions of loyalty and dissent and whether righteous action is ever rewarded—questions traditionally associated with the story of two brothers, Bo Yi and Shu Qi, whose virtuous character was such that each yielded his hereditary position to the other. They left their own country and went to the kingdom of Zhou in search of good governance but found King Wu of Zhou about to launch an expedition against the ruling imperial dynasty, the Shang. In protest, Bo Yi and Shu Qi composed a song denouncing King Wu's violence and, refusing henceforth to taste any grain produced in the state of Zhou, ate ferns instead and died of starvation. From Confucius onward, opinions about the brothers have been divided: were they righteous or merely self-righteous? In this short essay, Li Zhi draws on several interpretations, pitting them against one another, reserving the position of judge for himself. (HS)

Zhen Dexiu 真德秀² said, "[Sima Qian's] biography [of Bo Yi and Shu Qi] must be evaluated for its literary qualities."³

Yang Shen⁴ said, "That is entirely beside the point! If the message of the work is incorrect, the work cannot be established as writing: how could anyone consider the literary quality of a work separately from its message?

---

1. *FS, j.* 5, in *LZQJZ* 2:185–87.
2. Zhen Dexiu (1178–1235) was a Southern Song adherent of the School of Principle and a proponent of Zhu Xi's philosophy.
3. Zhen Dexiu is responding to Zhu Xi's commentary on Sima Qian's "Bo Yi Shu Qi liezhuan" (*Shi ji*, ch. 61). For a translation of the latter text, see Burton Watson, "Biography of Po Yi and Shu Ch'i," in *Records of the Historian*, 11–15.
4. On Yang Shen, see also "Xunzi, Li Si, and Master Wu," pp. 204–5.

This remark amply demonstrates that Zhen Dexiu knew nothing about writing. More recently, some authors have rounded out 'The Biography of Bo Yi' with revisions and additions. How odd!"[5]

Yang Shen also contended, "Zhu Xi declared that although Confucius said Bo Yi 'sought benevolence and attained benevolence. What cause did he have for resentment?,'[6] yet when the Grand Historian[7] wrote 'The Biography of Bo Yi,' he gave vent to a 'bellyful of resentment.'[8] Zhu's words were exceptionally unfair."

Master Zhuowu comments, "'What cause did he have for resentment?' was Confucius's interpretation. That [Bo Yi and Shu Qi] acted out of resentment was Sima Qian's interpretation. To translate a lack of resentment into resentment, a piece of writing must be extremely marvelous and subtle.

"What did Bo Yi resent? He resented the fact that 'violence was met with violence'; he resented the fact that the way of Kings Yu and Xia no longer prevailed; he resented not knowing where to turn; he resented the fact that he could not even eat the ferns growing on the territory of Zhou.[9] But then he swallowed his resentment, starved, and died. How could anyone minimize such resentment? Our problem today is that scholars dare not express their resentment. That's why they accomplish nothing."

TRANSLATED BY RIVI HANDLER-SPITZ

---

5. Yang Shen is referring specifically to Fang Xiaoru 方孝孺 (1357–1402), whose essay on Bo Yi and Shu Qi criticizes these two men for having taken their loyalty to the Shang state too far. See LZQJZ 2:186.
6. Analects 7.15.
7. Referring to Sima Qian.
8. Li Zhi's account of Yang Shen's opinion is based on Zhen Dexiu's comments at the end of Sima Qian's biography of Bo Yi. See LZQJZ 2:186.
9. Li Zhi's language borrows from Sima Qian's narrative, according to which, before starving to death, Bo Yi and Shu Qi sang as follows: "We climb this western hill and pick its ferns;/replacing violence with violence, he will not see his own fault./Shen Nong, Yu and Xia, great men gone so long ago—/whom shall we turn to now? Ah—let us be off, for our fate has run out" (Shi ji, ch. 61; translation slightly altered from Watson, Records of the Historian, 13).

"ADORNED WITH EVERY MARK OF DIGNITY"
無所不佩
"WU SUO BU PEI"

Written in Macheng in 1596, this essay[1] addresses the relationship between internal virtues and external adornments and, by extension, the crisis of representation taking place in late-Ming society. Li begins by quoting the Han-dynasty scholar Wang Yi's 王逸 (89–158) idealistic commentary on the ancient poetry collection *Songs of the South* (*Chu ci* 楚辭), to which he offers a pessimistic response.[2]

Wang conjures up the image of an ideal society in which inner virtues are manifested by outward ornamentation. In "Encountering Sorrow" (*Li sao* 離騷), the centerpiece of the *Songs of the South*, the speaker and putative author, Qu Yuan 屈原 (339 B.C.E.–278 B.C.E.), repeatedly depicts himself "adorning" his body with flowers and herbs to represent his many virtues. Linking these images of bodily adornment to a line from the *Analects* that reports that "once a period of mourning was complete, [Confucius] placed no restrictions on the kind of ornament he wore,"[3] Wang praises Confucius's expansive virtue and bolsters the claim that physical adornments correspond to internal ethical qualities.

Li's remarks begin from a similar premise: he concurs that in ancient times external adornments corresponded neatly to the internal virtues they signified. But he observes that in his own day this correspondence has been disrupted. A degree of arbitrariness has seeped in, and external signs no longer serve as reliable indicators

---

1. *FS, j.* 5, in *LZQJZ* 2:208–9. Li Zhi borrows the topic of this and the following two essays from the prominent mid-Ming intellectual Yang Shen (courtesy name Sheng'an 升庵). See Yang Shen, *Sheng'an jing shuo* 升庵經說 [Sheng'an's explication of the classics], *j.* 13.
2. Wang Yi, a scholar in the Han imperial library, is thought to have compiled the *Songs of the South*, an anthology of poetry centered on the legend of Qu Yuan. Although the exact nature of Wang's editorial role is a matter of debate, he undoubtedly commented on many of the poems in the collection and even added some poems of his own. See Hawkes, *Ch'u Tz'u*, 2.
3. Translation modified from Lau, *Confucius*, 102.

of internal virtues. The rhetorical questions with which the essay closes lend the piece an air of resignation and nostalgia. (RHS)

Wang Yi said, "People whose conduct is pure and clean are adorned with fragrant grasses. Those whose virtue is bright and radiant are adorned with jade. People who can untangle difficulties are adorned with a *xi* hook made of bone, and those who can resolve doubts are adorned with a *jue* disk made of jade.[4] And so [as long as Confucius was not in mourning,] he adorned himself with every mark of dignity."

Li Zhuowu says, "Those who study the Way have traced the origins of this emphasis on external ornamentation: since antiquity it has always been thus. Why would we suppose the Sage to have been any different?

"In ancient times, when a man went out walking, he did not part from his sword or his ornaments. When he traveled abroad, he did not part from his bow and arrow. Day or night, he did not part from his *xi* or his *jue*. Jade talismans were objects worn directly on the body and used for serving one's parents;[5] indeed, insofar as they kept people alert to danger and warded off evil,[6] they accomplished the ends of both civil and military arts; no less than the well-field system and [the custom of] lodging soldiers, they exhibited the Way that the many could follow, if not understand.[7] The meaning [of these objects] is not in the patterned adornments themselves;[8] it was human beings who gave them their names [and endowed them with meaning].

---

4. In ancient times it was customary for people to wear different types of jade ornaments marking their profession or status in society. A *xi* 觿 is a carved, ornamental hook made of horn or bone. The sharp end could be used for untying knots. A *jue* 玦 is a flat doughnut-shaped jade disk, often with a narrow slit in the top. The round shape may have symbolized the resolution of doubt. See *Li ji* [Records of ritual], ch. 12, "Neize" 內則 [Pattern of the family].
5. The *Records of Ritual* list jade ornaments among the articles that well-born children should wear when "serving their parents"; see Legge, *The Li Ki*, 449.
6. Li Zhi quotes from the "Jiqi" 既濟 chapter of the *Classic of Changes*, where the thought of danger is said to prevent disaster.
7. Allusion to *Analects* 8.9: "The people may be made to follow a path of action, but they may not be made to understand it"; see Legge, *The Chinese Classics*, 1:211. For further discussion of this passage, as well as Li's views on the well-field system, see "On Weapons and Food," pp. 92–98.
8. Li is playing with the word *wen* 文, which means both "pattern" and "literature" and refers to "civil" as opposed to "military" pursuits. Similar wordplay is evident in "Postface to *The Prose of Our Time*," pp. 132–34.

"People of later generations lost sight of the substance of these talismans; they saw in them nothing more than beautiful adornments to be cherished. Those who value internal qualities were displeased and said, 'You just want to attract notice on account of your lavish adornments. What benefit could there be in that?' Since then, the custom of using these talismans began to fall into disuse, and their ornamental and protective functions became disassociated. It's not merely that civil officials do not know how to use a weapon; even military men at home or visiting friends imitate the attire of civil officials, wearing loose garments and wide belts. How refined and proper they appear! But as soon as there is danger, not only are civil officials at a loss, but even military men—what use are they?"

TRANSLATED BY RIVI HANDLER-SPITZ

"XUNZI, LI SI, AND MASTER WU"
荀卿, 李斯, 吳公
"XUN QING, LI SI, WU GONG"

Written in 1596, this essay[1] (and that following) is dense with historical allusions and examines a relationship of central importance to the Confucian tradition—that between teachers and students. Being both a teacher and a student himself, Li Zhi took a lively interest in the ethical dimensions of the master-disciple relationship. The first essay takes the form of a brief imaginary exchange between Li Zhi and his predecessor, Yang Shen.[2] The essay opens with Yang's description of a perplexing phenomenon: three generations of scholars who consistently rejected the teachings of their masters. These two essays examine who is to blame when students betray their teachers' values.

Li Si (ca. 280 B.C.E.–208 B.C.E.), prime minister to the despotic First Emperor of Qin, renounced the teachings of his teacher, Xunzi (312 B.C.E.–230 B.C.E.). While Xunzi had been a leading interpreter of Confucian texts,[3] Li Si discarded Confucian thought and espoused instead the philosophy of Legalism, associated with another of Xunzi's acclaimed students, Han Feizi. Among Li Si's most infamous schemes was his plan to root out political dissent by burning

---

1. *FS, j.* 5, in *LZQJZ* 2:209–10. Li Zhi borrows the topic of this essay from Yang Shen. See *Sheng'an ji* 升庵集 [Sheng'an's collected writings], *j.* 51.
2. As tutor to the Jiajing emperor, Yang Shen took a strong stand against breaches in ritual propriety. For his remonstrations, he was imprisoned, beaten, bastinadoed, and ultimately banished to Yunnan province to serve as a common foot soldier. During his thirty-five years in exile, Yang published copiously on a wide range of subjects. Both on account of his acclaimed writings and on account of the unjust treatment he suffered, he attracted a devoted following that included prominent thinkers such as Wang Shizhen and Jiao Hong. According to one report, Yang was so beloved that he was paraded through the streets adorned with flowers and surrounded by students. After the death of the Jiajing emperor, Yang was formally rehabilitated and received the posthumous title of vice-minister of the Court of Imperial Entertainment. See *DMB*, 2:1531–35.
3. Although in many respects Xunzi's views accord with those of Confucius, some scholars view him as an eclectic on account of the pragmatic, rationalist strain running through his thought.

PART IV: READINGS OF HISTORY 讀史 205

the books of the Hundred Schools of Thought, including the Confucian classics. Li Si further suggested burying alive any scholars who would dare continue to teach the forbidden books. Both proposals were implemented by the tyrannical first emperor. However, despite Li Si's ruthlessness, his student Master Wu, also known as Wu the Chamberlain, managed to earn a reputation for righteousness. From these stories Yang adduces that virtue rests irreducibly in each individual and that masters hold little sway over the moral formation of their students. Li Zhi's nuanced response to Yang's statement both corroborates and criticizes this claim. (RHS)

Yang Shen said, "Although Xunzi was a great follower of Confucius, one of his disciples, Li Si, [framed the policy of the Qin dynasty that] burned the Confucian classics and buried scholars alive. Among those who regarded Li Si as their teacher was Master Wu, who accomplished great feats in governance.⁴ Whether people are virtuous or not depends on their standing on their own two feet; it has nothing to do with teachers or friends."

Li Zhuowu says, "In order for people to be able to stand on their own two feet, they must have bones. With bones, a person can walk or stand. But if one has no bones, even if a hundred teachers and friends supported him and propped him up left and right, what good would that do? The moment [these supporters] leave his side, the person would lose his footing. But one who can already walk or stand can run to seek a teacher for himself. This is how Yan Hui and Zeng Shen⁵ sought out Confucius. [Yet] to say that their success had nothing to do with their teachers and friends also is not correct."

TRANSLATED BY RIVI HANDLER-SPITZ

---

4. Master Wu mentored the great Confucian statesman and critic of Qin-dynasty tyranny Jia Yi. See Sima Qian, *Shiji*, ch. 84, "Qu Yuan, Jia sheng liezhuan" 屈原賈生列傳 [Biographies of Qu Yuan and Master Jia]; Watson, *Records: Han Dynasty I*, 443–52.
5. Legend has it that Confucius had seventy-two students; these two were among his most outstanding. Yan Hui, Confucius's most promising student, tragically died young. Zeng Shen was known for his filial piety. See also "People of the Song Dynasty Disparaged Xunzi," p. 206.

"PEOPLE OF THE SONG DYNASTY DISPARAGED XUNZI"
宋人譏荀卿
"SONG REN JI XUN QING"

People of the Song dynasty said that Xunzi's teachings were flawed[1] and that as soon as they were passed down to Li Si 李斯, the misfortunes of the "burning of the books" and the "burying of the Confucian scholars" ensued.[2] Is it reasonable, when disciples behave wickedly, to blame the teacher? If Li Si's misdeeds can implicate Xunzi, then Wu Qi's 吳起 misdeeds can likewise implicate Zeng Shen 曾參.[3] The *Discourses on Salt and Iron* (*Yantie lun* 鹽鐵論) say, "Li Si and Bao Qiuzi 苞丘子 both served Xunzi as their teacher, but Bao Qiuzi cultivated the Dao in a simple hut."[4]

Master Zhuowu says,[5] "If Li Si could implicate Xunzi, for Bao Qiuzi's sake Xunzi deserves a title."

TRANSLATED BY RIVI HANDLER-SPITZ

---

1. This essay can be found in *FS, j.* 5, in *LZQJZ* 2:210–12. Li Zhi borrows its title from Yang Shen. See *Sheng'an ji* 升庵集 [Sheng'an's collected writings], *j.* 46. On Xunzi, see "Xunzi, Li Si, and Master Wu," pp. 204–5.
2. The words "as soon as they were passed down" refer to a comment made by the Song literatus Su Shi 蘇軾 in an essay titled "Xun Qing lun" 荀卿論 [On Xunzi]. Su blames Li Si's excesses on the "preposterous positions" advocated by his teacher, Xunzi. Su's comment is transmitted in the essay by Yang Shen, to which the present essay responds. See *LZQJZ* 2:211.
3. Zeng Shen's student Wu Qi (d. 381 B.C.E.) placed his career above his family obligations and did not return home even when his own mother died. On learning of this egregious breach of filiality, Zeng Shen cut off all ties with his former student. See Sima Qian, *Shi ji*, ch. 65, "Biographies of Sunzi and Wu Qi," in Nienhauser, *The Grand Scribe's Records*, 7:42.
4. The *Discourses on Salt and Iron* record a debate on governance that took place in 81 B.C.E. after the death of Emperor Wu of Han. Xunzi's student Bao Qiuzi is also known as Fu Qiubo.
5. By reserving his assessment until the end of the essay and employing the locution "Master Zhuowu says," Li mimics the style of the Grand Historian, Sima Qian.

"ON FRIENDSHIP"
朋友篇
"PENGYOU PIAN"

This essay[1] constitutes one of Li Zhi's several contributions to the flourishing late-Ming discourse on friendship (see also "Mr. Li's Ten Kinds of Association," 135–37). Written in 1595, the essay opens with a reference to the *Compilation from the Dark Studio* (*Anrantang leizuan* 闇然堂類纂) by Li's contemporary Pan Shizao 潘士藻. Pan was a well-connected man of letters and a personal acquaintance of both Li Zhi and the Yuan brothers, founders of the Gong'an school. Admiring Pan's compilation, Li composed both a preface for that work and also an *Epitome of the Compilation from the Dark Studio* (*Anran lu zui* 闇然錄最), which contains another version of this essay.[2] The translation here is based on *A Book to Burn*. (RHS)

Pan Shizao's devotion to friendship was extremely sincere. Therefore the first essay in his *Compilation* addresses sincere friendship. In this world true friendship has been lost for a long time. Why should this be so? The whole world is fond of profit; no one is fond of righteousness. People who love righteousness view death as no different from life.[3] To this sort of person one could entrust a child or an orphan; one could even entrust one's family or one's own life—how could a righteous friend decline? But those who are fond of profit lead lives no different from death; they reach out their arms to snatch food away from others, and if they see a person in difficulty, they rain stones upon him to stop up his mouth—these are the kinds of acts of which they're capable.

---

1. *FS*, *j*. 5, in *LZQJZ* 2:227–28.
2. The preface can be found in *FS*, *j*. 5; it is not translated in this volume. On the Gong'an school, see Chang and Owen, *Cambridge History*, 85–90. On Ming ideas about partnership, equality, and mutual appreciation, see Ricci, *On Friendship*.
3. I.e., they would be willing to sacrifice their lives for the sake of righteousness.

All the people who pass for friends today lead lives no different from death. The only reason for this is that they are fond of profit, not friendship. In this day and age, is there anyone fond of the righteousness between friends? Since there have never been any friends fond of righteousness, it is fair to say that friendship has never existed. If we were to serve our ruler in the same [false] manner [in which we treat our friends], on whom could the ruler rely?

TRANSLATED BY RIVI HANDLER-SPITZ

PART V
POETRY 詩

INTRODUCTION TO LI ZHI'S POETRY

Li Zhi's poetry is just what you would expect from his character: simple, frank, emotional, slightly irregular, and highly personal. He was capable of writing the exquisite parallel couplets that were the pride of "recent-style poetry" (*jinti shi* 近體詩) (see "Watching the Rain with Dazhi"), but he was not fastidious about metrical rules, and only twenty of his three hundred or so extant poems were composed in the strictest classical form, the eight-line, sonnetlike heptasyllabic regulated verse (*lüshi* 律詩). (See the following five examples: "Drifting on East Lake with Li Jiantian," "The Glazed Temple," "Encountering Troops Marching East . . . ," and the two Paradise Temple poems; and see, in pentasyllabics, "To Matteo Ricci of the Far West"). By typical Chinese literary standards, Li Zhi's poetry is more valuable for its biographical content than its literary merit (see "Eight Quatrains from Prison"), but we may question the hierarchy and sureness of that distinction, and most readers will probably find at least some of Li's poetry genuinely moving. It is strikingly forthright at times, especially in the idiom of modern translation, but even by late-Ming standards: "If you have something to say, / just spit it out" (*you hua bufang ren jin tu* 有話不妨人盡吐) ("Spring Night"). This may not be exquisite verse, but it has a grab-you-by-the-collar quality that is startling in its own way, just as Du Fu's highly crafted lines were startling in theirs (see "On Reading Du Fu").

About one-fifth of his poems have to do with Buddhism directly or indirectly, and some may have been intended to resemble *gāthā* verses in their simplicity (see "Lantern Festival" and "Monastic Seclusion"). A tone of melancholy pervades much of Li's poetry—unsurprising, considering the circumstances of his life—but among the scenes of dispirited loneliness ("Evening Rain," "After the Snow," "A Sudden Chill"), there are moments of blissful solitude ("Sitting Alone in Meditation") and quiet camaraderie ("Watching the Rain with Dazhi"). He wrote half a dozen poems to his closest friend, the famous scholar Jiao Hong, but in these as well as those to other friends, we find the true spirit of friendship without any hint of the sort of competition or literary debate that was typical of the period. Indeed, he rarely wrote "courtesy" poetry for the maintaining of connections, or poetry on political topics unassociated with personal relationships (but see "Watching the Army at the East Gate of the City"). Li's "The Pleasure of Reading" seems to express both his ars poetica and raison d'être at the same time, from its iconoclastic preface to its quick tetrameters and jaunty rhymes: the verses are disarmingly silly and self-deprecating at first, then transform into lines of breathtakingly genuine seriousness and candor. The preface is particularly notable for Li's claim that he had a special gift that allowed him to visualize a person's whole being as if that person were present by merely reading that person's writing. The notion is not at all a commonplace of Ming literature, and he repeats the idea elsewhere (see "My Feelings Upon Ascending . . ."). If this was indeed Li Zhi's ideal of literary communion across time and space, in his poetry he left us the means by which to attempt it ourselves. (TB; YZN)

"'THE PLEASURE OF READING,' WITH A PROLOGUE"
讀書樂並引
"'DU SHU LE' BING YIN"

As Duke Cao once said, "Count up everyone who is old and still capable of studying, and you will have only myself and Yuan Boye."[1] Indeed, even when the country was splintered into factions and pikes and halberds raged across the land, the general could still be found with a book in his hands. So think how much easier studying is for an old man like me, withdrawn from the world without a care, living in peace and tranquility. Nevertheless, studying is not something that one can do by sheer force of will. For my part, I have certain heavenly blessings.

My eyes are a blessing, for even though I am a septuagenarian, I can still read the small print of commentaries. My hands are a blessing, for even though I am a septuagenarian, I can still write commentaries in small print—although that may turn out to be not such a blessing after all.

My disposition is a blessing, for I have never enjoyed the company of ordinary people, and so from my early days to my old age, I have avoided the constant nuisance of social interactions with relatives and visitors and have devoted myself single-mindedly to reading.

My feelings are a blessing, for I have never enjoyed intimacy with family members, and so, spending my final days at Dragon Lake, I have blessedly escaped the hardships of being forced to support my family, and so, once again, I have devoted myself single-mindedly to reading—although that may turn out to be not such a blessing after all.

The power of my mind's eye is a blessing, for when I look into a book, I can see the person who wrote it, and moreover I can see the state of that person's whole being. Of course, a great many writers since antiquity have read books and commented on the affairs of the world. Some of them see the visage;

---

1. Composed in 1596 when Li Zhi was seventy years old, this poem is placed at the head of the poetry section in *A Book to Burn*; *FS, j.* 6, in *LZQJZ* 2:240–43. "Duke Cao" is a reference to the legendary general of the Three Kingdoms period, Cao Cao (155–220); Boye was the style name of Yuan Yi (d. 192).

some of them see the body covered with skin; some of them see the blood vessels; and some of them see the muscles and bones. But the bones are as far as anyone ever goes. And although some of these scholars claim to have burrowed into the internal organs, in fact they have not even penetrated the bones. This is what I consider to be the foremost of my blessings.

My audacity is a blessing, for those who were envied and admired in earlier ages so much that they are regarded as worthies, I myself have mostly regarded as fakes. I have mostly regarded them as old-fashioned, worthless, and useless. Yet those who have been despised, abandoned, reviled, and spit upon, I truly believe could be entrusted with our country, our families, and our individual selves. My sense of what is right and wrong, as in this instance, gravely transgresses what people in earlier ages used to think—so what could I do without audacity? This is the next most important of what I call my blessings from heaven.

I love studying in my old age because of these last two blessings, so I amused myself by composing "The Pleasure of Reading."

THE PLEASURE OF READING

Heaven gave birth to Dragon Lake
To wait for old man Zhuowu's sake;
Zhuowu was born, for heaven's sake,
Right where you find the Dragon Lake.

At Dragon Lake, Zhuowu resides.
His happiness is in his looks.
He spends the seasons reading books.
He doesn't know much else besides.

So, how does all my reading go?
In fact, I understand a lot.
And when a thing makes sense to me,
I laugh aloud and sing, you know.

When singing songs is not enough,
I then begin to sigh and shout.
I weep with passion, sigh, and shout!
And streams of tears come pouring out.

My singing has an explanation,
For in each book there is a person.
And when I truly see that person,
My heart is seized with admiration.

My weeping has an explanation,
For on the lake, there's no one at all.
And when I see there's no one at all.
My heart is filled with sad vexation.

Now stop this reading! Empty your shelf!
Pack all your books away for safe keeping!
Refresh your spirit! Enjoy yourself!
Silence the songs, and banish weeping!

Why waste your life in reading texts,
Insisting happiness come next?
I hear such comments quite a lot,
As if I were a pitiable sot.

But if I pack up the books on my shelf,
Where will I find my happiness?
Refreshing my spirit, enjoying myself,
For me lies precisely in nothing but this.

The great big world is rather small,
And slender books are broad and wide,
With countless sages crammed inside.
So how could you despise them all?

My body has no family.
My head's as bald as any stone.
What dies is but the bodily.
What rots away is but the bones.

And these alone will never fade.
I long to end my days with these,
To shout in the woods, to lean on trees,
And thunder my voice to the hawks in the glade.

My songs and tears are friends to me;
My joy so boundless, no one knows.
My precious little time will flee.
How dare I waste it in repose!

TRANSLATED BY TIMOTHY BILLINGS AND YAN ZINAN

BALLAD OF THE NORTH WIND
朔風謠
SHUO FENG YAO

They come from the south, they head to the north:[1]
Is there ever an end to it all?
They go seeking profit, they go seeking fame:
There is never an end to it all.
The ones seeking profit, the ones seeking fame
Already fill the world.
They come from the south, they head to the north:
It's just as it should be.

The winds in the north in the early spring
Make any coat feel thin;
And travelers along the border
Can hardly bear the cold.
But those who live in the peace of the mountains
Can only smile and laugh
At those who freeze in the wind on the borders
For no good reason at all.

If some say I travel seeking profit,
They do not know me at all.
If some say, "He travels seeking fame,"
How could they possibly know?
Yet if my affairs have nothing to do
With either profit or fame,
Then wherefore do I rush about
On every path and highway?

---

1. *FS, j.* 6, in *LZQJZ* 2:249–50. Probably composed sometime in 1596 or 1597 while Li Zhi was traveling in Shanxi province in the north.

Ask the old man his true intentions,
And he will surely say,
"My wish is but to join the rest
Who travel for profit and fame
In singing together the emperor's praise,
Rejoicing in our great ways."

TRANSLATED BY TIMOTHY BILLINGS AND YAN ZINAN

CHRYSANTHEMUM REGRETS
恨菊
HEN JU

It is not that the gentleman[1]
preferred chrysanthemums:
In the clear frost only
chrysanthemums were blooming.

The color of autumn fills my courtyard
with no one else to see it.
Do I dare hope for someone in white
to come bearing wine?

TRANSLATED BY TIMOTHY BILLINGS AND YAN ZINAN

---

1. *FS, j.* 6, in *LZQJZ* 2:286. This poem alludes to a story about the famous Six Dynasties poet Tao Yuanming, who received a gift of wine from the prefectural governor, Wang Hong. In the story, the impoverished poet is without wine on the Double Ninth Festival, but just as he finishes picking some chrysanthemum flowers (which were traditionally placed in wine cups), he spots a figure in white approaching (i.e., in the color worn by common people, servants, or unranked officers), who turns out to be a servant bearing wine from the governor in a gesture of friendship.

MONASTIC SECLUSION
閉關
BI GUAN

Seclusion is, indeed, intended for meditation.[1]
I allow the host to leave me here alone.

But the mind's fixation on the world remains uncured:
Like everyone else, I go out to celebrate the new year.

TRANSLATED BY TIMOTHY BILLINGS AND YAN ZINAN

---

1. *FS, j.* 6, in *LZQJZ* 2:289–90. Probably composed in 1598 while Li Zhi was lodging at the Temple of Bliss in Beijing.

LANTERN FESTIVAL
元宵
YUANXIAO

The night of the Lantern Festival is truly a lovely night.[1]
I sit alone at a single lamp
surrounded by emptiness and silence.

If not for the discipline of this monastic seclusion,
The anger that poisons the mind[2]
would be aroused by the snow and wind.

TRANSLATED BY TIMOTHY BILLINGS AND YAN ZINAN

---

1. *FS, j.* 6, in *LZQJZ* 2:290. The Lantern Festival is held on the fifteenth night of the first lunar month—roughly in February but varying by several weeks from year to year—in order to celebrate the arrival of spring. This poem was composed in 1598 while Li Zhi was living on West Mountain in the suburbs of Beijing.
2. "The anger that poisons the mind" translates the term *chenxin* 嗔心 (angry mind, anger, hatred), which refers to one of the "three poisons" that impede progress to enlightenment, according to Buddhist thought, along with "desire" (*tan* 貪) and "ignorance" (*chi* 痴).

RED AND WHITE PLUM BLOSSOMS FLOURISHING AT THE LAKE—AN AMUSEMENT
湖上紅白梅盛開戲題
HUSHANG HONG BAI MEI SHENGKAI XI TI

I now understand that thoughts of spring[1]
come to the idle person:
Red and white flourishing together
keep coming into sight.

By the time the blossoms finally come,
you're already much older:
The one who comes to gaze at flowers
is not the one who sows the seeds.

TRANSLATED BY TIMOTHY BILLINGS AND YAN ZINAN

---

1. *FS, j.* 6, in *LZQJZ* 2:305. This playful and somewhat cryptic poem has the feel of a parable, with a final line like a moral to the story. It may suggest that someone's hard work and accomplishments can be enjoyed only by leisured latecomers; but it may also be a comment on the vanity of pleasures, which are available only to those who cannot really enjoy them, such as old men like Li Zhi.

AT A BANQUET ON A SPRING EVENING, I RECEIVE THE WORD "LACK"
春宵燕集得空字
CHUNXIAO YANJI DE KONG ZI

Lanterns fill the high hall in the evening.[1]
With good wine, there is no lack of inspiration.

An old friend arrived yesterday—
A spring wind blowing a thousand miles.

Shadows of bamboo fall into the cool pond.
Echoes of song rise into the fine rain.

How beautiful this new season is—
Except that it comes to a weak old man.

TRANSLATED BY TIMOTHY BILLINGS AND YAN ZINAN

---

1. *FS, j.* 6, in *LZQJZ* 2:308. Composed in 1582 in Macheng. The title refers to the traditional literary amusement of extemporizing poetry using a given rhyme word. Li Zhi ends up with *kong* 空 (empty, lacking, in vain), which he uses in the second line. It is also a crucial term in Buddhism corresponding to the Sanskrit *śūnyatā* (emptiness) and is associated with enlightenment and buddha-nature.

SENDING OFF ZHENG ZIXUAN, ALSO FOR JIAO HONG
送鄭子玄兼寄弱侯
SONG ZHENG ZIXUAN JIAN JI RUOHOU

I myself have no place to return to—[1]
But why must you go so far from home?

In times of disappointment, weep your grief.
In times of complacency, do not linger long.

The temples of the wanderer will meet frosty days;
His saddlebag of poetry will bear rainy autumns.

If ever it feels cold and lonely in Beijing,
Remember that Jiao Hong is also there somewhere.

TRANSLATED BY TIMOTHY BILLINGS AND YAN ZINAN

---

1. *FS*, *j.* 6, in *LZQJZ* 2:311–12. Composed in 1589. Zheng Zixuan was a like-minded skeptic and friend whom Li Zhi knew in Macheng but about whom little is known. Ruohou is the courtesy name of Jiao Hong. *Pace* Zhang Jianye, this poem appears to us to be addressed primarily to Zheng Zixuan, not to Jiao Hong.

TO MATTEO RICCI OF THE FAR WEST
贈利西泰
ZENG LI XITAI

The Italian Jesuit missionary Matteo Ricci[1] (1552–1610) was one of Li Zhi's many acquaintances. In "A Letter to a Friend" (pp. 256–57), Li Zhi wondered what the foreigner's purpose was in coming to China. Here, addressing Ricci, he asks more or less the same question, though in the allusive and indirect language of classical poetry. Ricci's diaries proudly register this homage among the many *sonetti* dedicated to him by Chinese scholars and officials. (HS)

Descending in *xiao-yao* fashion through the northern darkness,[2]
Through long and twisted wanderings marching toward the south:
Like the Kshatriya, you announce your [new] clan and personal names,[3]
And like a visitor from the Immortals' island, you record the watery stages.[4]
Behind you is a hundred-thousand-*li* voyage,

---

1. *FS, j.* 6, in *LZQJZ* 2:319–20. "Xitai" was Ricci's Chinese sobriquet. It suggests both "the farthest west," his place of origin, and "western peace," a pun on Guotai 國泰, or Cathay.
2. The term *xiao-yao* 逍遙, left untranslated here, derives from the first chapter of *Zhuangzi*, "Free and Easy Wandering" (*xiaoyao you* 逍遙遊). It tells of an immense bird, the Peng, that flies ninety thousand *li* from one end of the world to the opposite.
3. The Chinese surname adopted by Ricci, Li 利, coincides with the second half of the term *chali* 刹利, the Chinese rendering of "Kshatriya," the warrior caste of India. The royal families of several small Buddhist kingdoms far to the south of China all bore the clan name Kshatriya (Chali). In Ming times they sent tribute to the Chinese emperor and accepted Chinese advisers.
4. The Island of the Immortals, Xianshan or Penglai, was supposed to be out in the Pacific Ocean (it was at times identified with Japan) but invisible to most travelers. One of Ricci's most famous productions was his world map depicting several new continents and dozens of strange-sounding place-names. Li Zhi may be evoking the effect of this representation on his visitors.

And now you raise your eyes upon the nine-walled capital.[5]
Have you seen the glory of our country yet, or not?[6]
From the middle of heaven the sun shines directly down.[7]

TRANSLATED BY HAUN SAUSSY

---

5. Namely, the capital in Beijing, Ricci's goal during his first decade and more in China.
6. "The glory of the country" is a phrase from the *Classic of Changes*. Under the hexagram "Guan" 觀, the oracle interpretation says, "Observe the country's glory. It will be advantageous to become the guest of a king." Wang Bi's first-century commentary, expanded on by Kong Yingda, paraphrases this as, "By staying in the intimacy [of the court], one may obtain an appropriate position; one becomes familiar with the rituals of the country. Therefore it says: there is advantage in being the guest of a royal court" (*Zhou Yi zhengyi*, in Ruan, *Shisanjing zhu shu*, 3:10a–b).
7. The sun in the sky, being unique, is a traditional symbol of the monarch and, by extension, of the Chinese realm.

ENCOUNTERING TROOPS MARCHING EAST DURING A MORNING WALK, I SEND A POEM TO VICE-CENSOR-IN-CHIEF MEI
曉行逢征東將士卻寄梅中丞
XIAOXING FENG ZHENG DONG JIANG SHI QUE JI MEI ZHONGCHENG

Beacon fires to the west of the city—[1]
a garrison of a hundred generals—
Cold smoke from the cookstoves at dawn—
a village of ten thousand encampments.

These heroes of ours on the frontiers
dote on their horses' tackle;
And the brave generals in their fortresses
shut their gates before dusk.

On the shores facing out to sea,
will we ever see the waves grow quiet?
Those who mount the platform of promotion[2]
give empty thanks for imperial favor.

---

1. *FS, j.* 6, in *LZQJZ* 2:327–28. Composed in 1597 while traveling from Datong to Beijing and dedicated to General Mei Guozhen 梅國楨 (1542–1605), member of a prominent Macheng lineage and father of Li's female student Mei Danran. Li Zhi evidently witnessed the troops heading out to defend the Korean Peninsula against the second major Japanese invasion of the decade.
2. According to tradition, the promotion of a field general should take place on a high platform built for the occasion in full view of the army so that the emperor's appointment can be witnessed and accepted by the troops.

Even now, in Yunzhong,
there awaits a true Po and Mu—[3]
How can he not have been promoted yet
to appear before His Majesty?

TRANSLATED BY TIMOTHY BILLINGS AND YAN ZINAN

---

3. Both Lian Po (fl. 260 B.C.E.) and Li Mu (d. 229 B.C.E.) were great generals of the state of Zhao during the Warring States period. Comparing Mei Guozhen to these generals is particularly apt since the area designated by the Yunzhong Commandery is roughly the same as that of the historical state of Zhao.

COMPOSED WITH JOY UPON ARRIVING AT THE TEMPLE OF BLISS ON THE DOUBLE NINTH FESTIVAL AND LEARNING THAT YUAN HONGDAO WOULD SOON BE HERE
九日至極樂寺聞袁中郎且至因喜而賦
JIU RI ZHI JILESI WEN YUAN ZHONGLANG QIE ZHI YIN XI ER FU

It has never been the wisdom of the world[1]
to be alone in life;
For hundreds of years, we disciples
have been together here.

When the day of the Double Ninth arrives,
even the flowers should get drunk!
And when a bosom friend arrives,
even my illness abates.

Deep in the branches of an ancient juniper,
the evening magpies chatter;
In the courtyard, the west wind blows at sunset
as the shade tree sheds its leaves.

From the Golden Terrace, my thoughts go out
hundreds and hundreds of miles
To meet you on the road and say,
"Hongdao, quicken your pace!"

TRANSLATED BY TIMOTHY BILLINGS AND YAN ZINAN

---

1. *FS, j.* 6, in *LZQJZ* 2:329–30. Composed in either 1597 or 1601. Zhonglang is the style name of Yuan Hongdao (1568–1610), the second of the three Yuan brothers of the Gong'an school.

HEAVY RAIN AND SNOW AT THE TEMPLE OF BLISS ON NEW YEAR'S DAY
元日極樂寺大雨雪
YUAN RI JILE SI DA YUXUE

When all the officials under heaven[1]
gather for the great renewal,
I alone, free and at ease,
dwell in the temple's spring.

Who else even notices this day of cheering
"Long live the emperor!"
Is also a paradise at dawn
when snow petals float around you?

A monk returns in perfect silence
to a temple on the edge of the clouds.
The moon shines down with perfect brilliance
on the denizens of the borderlands.

For years now I have let my hair
fall to the shaving razor;
I tried to escape the cares of this world
but have only attracted more.

TRANSLATED BY TIMOTHY BILLINGS AND YAN ZINAN

---

1. *FS, j.* 6, in *LZQJZ* 2:330–31. Composed in 1598. The poem's first line translates literally as "The robes and caps of ten thousand states." The line alludes to a couplet from a poem by Wang Wei 王維 (ca. 701–761): "The nine heavenly gates open to the palace court, / The robes and caps of ten thousand states bow to the imperial crown and tassel." See "He Jia Zhi sheren zaochao daminggong zhi zuo" 和賈至舍人早朝大明宮之作 [Rhyming with Palace Secretary Jia Zhi's poem "The Morning Audience at the Palace of Great Brilliance"]. Adapted from Wagner, *Wang Wei*, 66–67.

THE GLAZED TEMPLE
琉璃寺
LIULI SI

On the shining road to the Glazed Temple[1]
the sun comes out of the west.
The autumn wind circles my horse.
Trees by the thousands look tiny.

The monk's lodging is never closed—
guests may arrive at will.
The neighboring farmer has plenty of wine—
with whom else could he share it?

Yellow chrysanthemums along the fence
flourish in the drizzle.
Stars on the mountain ridges dazzle.
A rooster heralds dawn.

With Wunian[2]
as my guide and companion,
Let's laugh
and cross another stream.

TRANSLATED BY TIMOTHY BILLINGS AND YAN ZINAN

---

1. *FS, j.* 6, in *LZQJZ* 2:337. Composed in Huang'an in modern-day Hubei province in 1584.
2. On Wunian (Xiong Shenyou), see p. 20n5.

SELECTIONS FROM *ANOTHER BOOK TO BURN* (*XU FENSHU* 續焚書)

PART I
PREFACES 序引

"PREFACE TO MASTER LI'S *ANOTHER BOOK TO BURN*—BY JIAO HONG"
李氏續焚書序
"LI SHI *XU FENSHU XU*"

The following three prefaces, by Jiao Hong 焦竑, Zhang Nai 張鼐, and Wang Benke 汪本鈳, aim to establish the authenticity of *Another Book to Burn*, a text first published in Xin'an, Anhui, in 1618, sixteen years after Li Zhi's suicide.[1] As all three preface writers confirm, during the intervening years a great number of texts had been spuriously attributed to Li Zhi: printers eager to capitalize on Li Zhi's scandalous reputation slapped his name on texts bearing little or no connection to the author. All three preface writers decry this practice and display keen interest in transmitting Li's ideas intact. Zhang Nai exhibits the greatest concern; he worries that readers may be unable to distinguish between true and false editions and that they may therefore misunderstand Li's thought. Like Jiao Hong, Li's close friend and the author of the first preface, Zhang credits

---

1. Jiao Hong's preface is in *LZQJZ* 3:419. Jiao Hong was a prominent intellectual of the late Ming period, a friend and major supporter of Li Zhi's, as well as a disciple of Li Zhi's rival, Geng Dingxiang. In 1589, after over twenty-five years of sitting for imperial examinations, Jiao Hong passed the palace examination as the top graduate. Thereupon, he served in several governmental positions, including member of the Hanlin Academy and coexaminer for the metropolitan examination. Numerous letters from Li Zhi to Jiao Hong are preserved in *A Book to Burn* and *Another Book to Burn*.

Wang Benke, the author of the third preface, with having meticulously gathered and sifted through Li's writings and published an admirably authoritative edition. Wang, too, devotes a large portion of his preface to shoring up his own credibility as an editor. It is no accident that these three preface writers all address an issue central to his thought—the problem of differentiating between authenticity and phoniness. (RHS)

Wang Benke of Xin'an[2] followed Li Zhuowu for ten years. He gathered together Li Zhi's scattered writings, leaving none behind. Although Li Zhi's letters are already widely available, there are many inauthentic editions. People of understanding consider these editions faulty. Benke published Li Zhi's *On Speaking Righteously*, *Another Book to Burn*, and *On the Four Books* so that the world would know that the late gentleman spoke about reason, and so that those who published false editions might no longer be able to do so. Benke has truly benefited Li Zhi.

TRANSLATED BY RIVI HANDLER-SPITZ

---

2. Wang Benke moved to Macheng in 1594 to study with Li Zhi and played a major role in the posthumous publication of Li's writings.

UPON READING OLD ZHUOWU'S WRITINGS—ZHANG NAI
讀卓吾老子書述－張鼐
DU ZHUOWU LAOZI SHU SHU—ZHANG NAI

Even though Zhuowu has died, his books are important.[1] Because Zhuowu's books are important, both real editions and fake editions circulate in the world. In this world, few people have eyes. For this reason, they are not able to discover the intention behind the real editions; and when they read the fake editions, they are misled. For people know that Zhuowu wrote books for later generations, but they do not know that in doing so he created his own likeness. Zhuowu's person can no longer be seen, but what people ten thousand generations from now will still be able to see are his books.

Zhuowu hated Confucians of recent times who study to impress others, who borrow principles of righteousness to erect walls. With every kind of written explanation they chase after what they perceive with their eyes and ears, yet they do not understand the source of life. Because he deviated from established models and went off the beaten path, and because he exposed people's tendency to put on a show and wear a false face, his deeds may be condemned, but his mind was pure; his actions may have been peculiar, but he had a warm heart. Moreover, he put no stock in whether the world thought ill or well of him. Worries over life and death did not burden his breast. His brush could slice through matters of right and wrong, whether they happened a thousand years ago or a thousand years hence; no one could [gainsay][2] his judgments. In brief, he wanted people to cut completely through the branches and vines and to see straight through to the original heart [beneath];[3] if they were ministers, to die for the sake of loyalty; if sons, to die for the sake of filial piety; if friends, to die for the sake of camaraderie; and if military men, to die in battle. But only people of the highest caliber can truly accept this message. In this world afflicted with

---

1. Zhang Nai, *jinshi* 1604. The preface is in *LZQZJ* 3:420.
2. A word is missing from the text here.
3. The word Li Zhi uses here for "original heart" (*benxin* 本心) links closely to Wang Yangming's theory of "innate knowledge" (*liangzhi* 良知).

the "five types of degeneration,"⁴ where could I find a hero who might excel at reading Zhuowu's books and differentiate between right and wrong?

Today commoners surpass Li Zhi's outrageousness and indulge in wanton acts; they take pleasure in behaving like petty, unscrupulous men. At the slightest provocation, they pick up their brushes and throw into confusion the writings Li Zhi left behind, and they claim that *their* works are his lost manuscripts. For instance, if reading an ancient book, someone with a solid foundation [in learning] might investigate the evidence and establish a definitive edition. By doing so, he would "dot the eyes of the painted dragon."⁵ But people who lack this foundation comment at random; they are only "marking the gunwale to show where the oar sank."⁶ Alas! How can I find a person with eyes to read Zhuowu's book?

Someone might say that Zhuowu's shaving his head was strange, growing his beard was strange, being bald but having a beard was strange, reciting sutras while eating meat was strange, and not fearing death was strangest of all! But as for me, I do not think this was the real Zhuowu. Even if Zhuowu had not grown his beard, eaten meat, or slit his throat, he would still have been strange. Because of this, Zhuowu's books are even more difficult to read. Now the books that are counterfeited and muddled focus on the fact that he grew his beard, ate meat, and died by the blade. How exceedingly misleading! It's true! Zhuowu's genuine books are important. His genuine books are important, but fakes are not worthy of discussion!⁷

Wang Benke showed me *Another Book to Burn* and *On the Four Books* and also requested that I write a preface to *On the Three Teachings*. I said if Benke is to repay Zhuowu's kindness, he must establish definitive copies of his real books, provide them with a table of contents, and transmit them to people throughout China. Although he has done this so that Zhuowu's merit may

---

4. The "five types of degeneration" (*wu zhuo* 五濁) refer to degeneration of life span, degeneration of views, degeneration of afflictions, degeneration of sentient beings, and degeneration of age. See Buswell and Lopez, *Princeton Dictionary*, 2615.
5. The line "dot the eyes of the painted dragon," meaning add the crucial touch that would bring the authentic work to life, refers to a story involving the monk Zhang Sengyou 張僧繇 of the Liang dynasty (sixth century). Upon the wall of Anle Temple in Jinling, he painted a dragon. As soon as he painted in the pupils of the dragon's eyes, the dragon flew away, soaring into the sky. This story is recounted in the Tang-dynasty collection by Zhang Yanyuan 張彥遠, *Lidai minghua ji* 歷代名畫記 [Famous paintings throughout history], *j.* 7.
6. This common adage, referring to fruitless and illogical methods, derives from an anecdote told in the *Annals of Lü Buwei*: When paddling a boat, a dim-witted man from the state of Chu accidentally dropped his oar into the water. Oblivious to the fact that his boat was moving, he made a notch in the gunwale, saying, "This is to mark the spot where the oar sank."
7. The text appears to be corrupt at this point. An almost identical phrase appears in "On Loftiness and Cleanliness" (pp. 121–24) and is adopted here.

now extend to ten thousand generations, and although Benke has prevented the authoritative editions from rotting away, how could these deeds repay even a little bit of Zhuowu's kindness? I did not have the opportunity of meeting Zhuowu, but I have had the pleasure of reading his books, and so I've written these words and included them here.

TRANSLATED BY RIVI HANDLER-SPITZ

PREFACE TO THE SECOND PRINTING OF LI ZHI'S WRITINGS
續刻李氏書序—汪本鈳
XU KE LI SHI SHU XU—WANG BENKE

I, Ke, followed the late gentleman [Li Zhi] on his travels for nine years.[1] Day and night I kept him company and never left his side for even a moment. No one served him for as long as I did, and no one was in a better position to know his true nature than I. But on what grounds can I claim to know Li Zhi? On the grounds that he knew himself, and he shared his true self with all people under heaven for thousands of generations to come.

Throughout his life, there was no subject the gentleman did not study, nor any heartfelt emotion he did not express. He approached his reading voraciously, in the same way in which a starved or parched person approaches food and drink; he would not stop until he was sated. In disgorging his emotions he was like a man who chokes and cannot keep his food down; he did not stop until he had vomited it up completely. For this reason, simply by pointing his finger he leveled criticism powerful enough to guide the judgment of ten thousand generations; indeed, his every grunt bore a connection to the ethical teachings of ten thousand generations. Whether conveying derisive laughter or angry rebukes, each work of his was a masterpiece. His language was exceedingly truthful, and his diction astonished the heavens and shook the earth; it could make the deaf hear, the blind see, the dreaming wake, the drunk sober, the sick arise, the dead revive, the fidgety calm, and the noisy settle down; it could make those with icy innards hot and those with inflamed organs cold; it could make those who were "hemmed in by pickets and pegs"[2] tear out those "pickets and pegs," and make those who were stubbornly unyielding bow their heads in admiration and respect. How spiritual and peculiar a feeling his writings produced in anyone who came in contact with them! But in the end, on account of his writings, he could not escape [misfortune] and even went so far as to kill himself, though this is something I dare not [profess to] understand.

---

1. This preface is in *LZQJZ* 3:421–22.
2. Refers to *Zhuangzi*, ch. 12; see Watson, *Chuang Tzu*, 141.

Alas! Who is exempt from death? It is just that we do not all die an appropriate death. As soon as Li Zhi died, his writings began to circulate even more broadly, and his fame increased. He himself once said, "Whatever stick deals me my final blow will be famous for all eternity." Since being beaten to death is just as much a death as killing oneself, [some people assumed] he must have died for the sake of [increasing his] fame. But now sixteen years have passed since his death. The doubts have been dispelled, the hostility has been smoothed over, and the anger has subsided. The doubts have not only been dispelled, but trust has been established; the hostility has not only been smoothed over but transformed into delight. The anger has not only subsided but has sparked acts of virtue. Within our four seas there is no one who does not read Li Zhi's writings, no one who does not aspire to read all of them. They read them without stopping, and even read forgeries.

Those who counterfeit Li Zhi's works, imitate his style, and forge his commentaries want to deceive people. But they cannot deceive people incapable of being deceived. The world does not lack people of insight; undoubtedly *they* can tell the difference [between authentic and spurious editions]. Yet down to the present day, every play, lewd joke, and fiction commentary that you see in bookstores is marked with the words "By Master Zhuowu." People gullible enough to believe whatever they hear[3] are enthralled by these editions, which inflict considerable damage on people's hearts and minds. Li Zhi's spirit must be in deep anguish. This is what I greatly fear.

As for Li Zhi's writings that have not yet been printed, there are so many of them that they cannot be counted. Even I have not been able to read them all. In recent years, I've been eking out a living taking care of my mother and haven't had the leisure to read. Now, unfortunately, my mother has passed away. Overcome with hardship and grief, I have not been able to read Li Zhi's writings even though I've wanted to. What a shame! Yet to let these manuscripts rot away and become food for bookworms would have been like ordering the sun and moon not to shine, but instead seeking light from an extinguished lamp. Could anything have been more absurd? It would have been a crime [to allow these books to remain unpublished]. So I collected the unpublished manuscripts of *A Book to Burn* and *On the Four Books* and collated them with my brother Bolun.

A Book to Burn contains much discussion of karmic causality as well as many angry and provocative sentiments, not familiar clichés. The author

---

3. Literally, "to eat through their ears." Allusion to "Liu guo nianbiao" 六國年表 (Chronological tables of the Six States) in Sima Qian, *Shi ji*, ch. 15.

himself already explained this [in his introduction]. He himself said that one-fifth of *On the Four Books* had been printed at Dragon Lake. Four-fifths of the book remained to be printed. I had two of those sections printed first, and I shall gradually have the rest printed.

Written by the disciple Wang Benke of Xin'an at the Studio of Rainbow Jade in midsummer of the *wuwu* year of the Wanli reign [1618].

TRANSLATED BY RIVI HANDLER-SPITZ

PART II
LETTERS 書答

"TO MA LISHAN"
與馬歷山
"YU MA LISHAN"

This letter[1] was written in 1601, after Li Zhi had fled from Macheng and was residing near Beijing, in Tongzhou, on the property of Ma Jinglun 馬經綸, son of Ma Lishan. Here we find Li Zhi working within the tradition. He begins with the Confucian classic the *Great Learning*,[2] annotating it phrase by phrase, and reads the text to support his philosophical view that all humans are born with a distinctive childlike heart and within it an instinctive sense of right and wrong. (PCL)

Yesterday I was edified by your letter on the *Great Learning*. Because I had guests staying with me, I have not replied to your letter until now.

I venture to say that the *Great Learning* is a teaching for adults.[3] Once a person has reached eight years of age, he learns in primary school to obey

---

1. *XFS, j.* 1, in *LZQJZ* 3:11–14.
2. For an English translation of the classic, see Gardner, *The Four Books*, 3–8.
3. Li here echoes the gloss of Zhu Xi. The title of the *Great Learning* "means the learning of adults," i.e., "great" persons as opposed to children, according to Zhu Xi, *Sishu zhangju jizhu*, 3; see Legge, *The Chinese Classics*, 1:355. Wang Yangming declared that the "great person" assumed by the text is rather the sage who can communicate with heaven and earth; see *Daxue wen* 大學問 [Questions on the *Great Learning*]; Ivanhoe, *Readings*, 160–61.

his father, older brothers, teachers, and elders. These teachings consist in the rules of propriety, such as bowing and making way for one another, advancing and retiring, and the arts of performing rituals, music, archery, charioteering, calligraphy, and arithmetic. Even today, the wise sayings passed down from the sages of antiquity and their worthy disciples amount to nothing more than this; they were established for no other reason than to teach the younger generations.

At the age of fifteen, one becomes an adult and embarks upon adult studies. How could a person day in and day out willingly lap up the snot and spit of the adults as if one were still a child? Therefore, the first lines of the *Great Learning* state that it contains teachings for adults.

Wherein consists this Way of Great Learning? Each and every person possesses this Great Perfect Mirror Wisdom,[4] what we also call our "luminous virtue." As for this luminous virtue, it is identical to that in the heavens above, the earth below, and the countless sages and worthies in between. Nobody else possesses an excess, nor myself a deficiency of it. Since one can neither add to nor subtract from this source, even if one wished to decline to be a sage or worthy rather than taking the position, and instead to give up the opportunity to study as an adult and forsake learning for oneself, it would not be possible. If one does not pursue learning, one cannot know the luminous virtue residing within oneself. One unwittingly becomes a self-contented fool. Therefore the text says the Great Learning "resides in *illuminating* luminous virtue." Without doubt I desire to clearly know luminous virtue, but this virtue is something I definitely possessed all along. This is the most significant and most critical topic discussed in the *Great Learning*. Therefore, these are the very first words in the text.

Where does my luminous virtue really reside? I think that although one cannot see its substance, it truly flows and fills in all the spaces within one's family, one's country, and everywhere under Heaven. In our daily behavior we exercise this luminous virtue. It is utterly present and immediate: who could part from it?

---

4. According to the Yogācāra and Tantric schools of Buddhism, this is one of five types of wisdom exclusive to a buddha. It enables one to see the interconnection among all things as if they were all reflected in a great mirror. For Li Zhi's views on context-specific right and wrong, see also "To Yang Dingjian" (pp. 63-64) and "Introduction to the Table of Contents of the Historical Annals and Biographies in *A Book to Keep (Hidden)*," pp. 317-19.

If I can "draw close to the people"[5] so as to "illuminate my luminous virtue," then won't the essential brightness of my virtue come plainly into view? Therefore the *Great Learning* also says the Way "resides in drawing close to the people."

Now, the Way is One, and learning too is one. In our times it is said Great Learning "resides in illuminating luminous virtue." Also, Great Learning "resides in drawing close to the people." Clearly, these are two things. Things naturally have their roots and their branches. As for "drawing close to the people" in order to "illuminate my luminous virtue," even if I say it is a single matter, still, a single matter has its own beginning and end. Ten thousand affairs each have their own beginning and end. When the beginning and the end are distinguished from each other, then the root and the branch can be clearly distinguished. One sees there are two things. The Way can be two! Learning can be two!

So there must be a state of supreme goodness for us to attain. But it is not easy for people to realize they have arrived at this state of supreme goodness. If one comprehends this state of supreme goodness, then one will naturally attain "steadfastness," "serenity," "peace," and the "ability to reflect,"[6] and each person will rest content with himself.

Thus, if one comprehends this state, then "illuminating luminous virtue" is not a meaningless and ineffective task since one already embodies the Way of "illuminating luminous virtue" and "drawing close to the people." "Drawing close to the people" is not worthless, empty talk since the results of one's having "drawn close to the people" and "illuminated virtue" are readily apparent. If one does not know where to rest, then "illuminating virtue" becomes as vacuous as mere eclecticism, and "drawing close to the people" becomes as fragmented as vulgar teachings. Thus neither of the teachings is accomplished; so it would be better that one consider them two distinct things.

Consequently, the Way of the *Great Learning* ultimately is found in resting in supreme goodness and in recognizing that to know when to rest constitutes the utmost achievement. Attaining this state is indeed what is desired! But if one studies and still does not reach this state, the reason why is that one has not yet grasped it.

---

5. The relevant phrase from the *Great Learning* has been read in two ways: as "draw close to the people" or "renew the people."
6. These terms are the catchwords of successive paragraphs in the *Great Learning*.

Alas! Knowing when to rest is of the greatest importance. Extending one's knowledge is of great merit. The reason why adult studies are difficult lies in the difficulty of knowing when to rest. If teachers, friends, fathers, and elder brothers discuss and examine this topic together, then people will no longer delight in life or despair in death. Is this not what the countless sages and worthies sought?

TRANSLATED BY PAULINE C. LEE

"DISCUSSING LITERATURE WITH A FRIEND"
與友人論文
"YU YOUREN LUN WEN"

In 1594, Wang Benke, likely the friend to whom the title of this letter refers,[1] traveled to Macheng to study with Li Zhi. Together the two men pondered the mysteries of the *Classic of Changes*, and in 1600, four years after writing this letter, Li published a commentary on that work.[2]

The strategies of writing and interpretation that Li endorses here apply not only to the *Classic of Changes*; similar techniques are evident throughout his comments on history and philosophy. The militaristic metaphor with which the letter opens suggests that Li views the act of writing—and perhaps especially that of commenting on extant writings—as antagonistic: the reader treats the text before his eyes as an enemy to be conquered. Moreover, Li maintains, writings must manifest the author's genuine experience. This emphasis on authenticity resembles statements found in Li's "On the Childlike Mind" (pp. 106–13). (RHS)

When ordinary people write, they begin from the outside and fight their way in; when I write, I start from the middle and fight my way out. I go straight for the enemy's defenses and moat, eat his grain, and command his troops; then, when I level my attack, I leave him utterly shattered. In this way I do not expend so much as a whit of my own energy and naturally have powers to spare. This [strategy] applies to everything: why should writing be an isolated case?

---

1. *XFS, j.* 1, in *LZQJZ* 3:21.
2. The work (not translated in this volume) is called *Jiuzheng Yiyin* 九正易因 [Factors of the changes]; see *LZQJZ*, vol. 15.

But since everyone has his own concerns, the topics each person addresses will differ. When an individual addresses his chosen topic and simply rolls out his views on it, the result is always marvelous. For instance, people who are devoted to taking care of their parents should write on devotion to parents: because that topic is close to their hearts, what comes out will certainly be a satisfying piece of writing.

But whenever people cast aside the standard topics and seek to write on novel subjects, no one understands. Even discriminating readers dislike works of that sort.

How do these remarks compare with the commentaries on the *Classic of Changes*?[3]

TRANSLATED BY RIVI HANDLER-SPITZ

---

3. Li Zhi is referring to a line from the "Wenyan" 文言 [Commentaries on words and texts] on the hexagram "Qian" in the *Classic of Changes*, which states that "the noble man . . . keeps his task in hand by cultivating his words and establishing his sincerity": see Lynn, *The Classic of Changes*, 133. Li's intellectual forebear Wang Yangming develops this idea when he states that "one's writings must conform to one's experience; if one's words exceed these parameters, they do not constitute 'establishing sincerity'" (Chen Rongjie, *Wang Yangming Chuanxilu*, sec. 233, p. 308).

"A REPLY TO LI SHILONG"
復李士龍
"FU LI SHILONG"

The recipient of this letter[1] was one of Geng Dingxiang's most accomplished disciples, an elderly gentleman who had risen to prominence in the Ministry of Rites. Yet in this letter, composed in Nanjing in 1599, Li Zhi pokes fun at Li Shilong for failing to resist the lure of profit and reputation. The letter exemplifies Li Zhi's penchant for exposing and denouncing hypocrisy wherever he encountered it. (RHS)

There is no such thing as obtaining both profit and reputation.[2] The only people who have been able to move beyond the sphere of reputation and profit and to conceive of themselves in terms other than reputation and profit are the three great sages Confucius, Old Master Li, and the Śākyamuni Buddha.[3] Apart from them, everyone else is after either profit or reputation. Who could avoid this trap? But whether one shares their views or not, why doubt oneself? Since there is no way to obtain both, it is as foolish to seek profit while rushing after reputation as it is to seek reputation while rushing after profit. Can it be that you, who all your life have revered Confucius as the Master of the Dao,[4] have failed to understand this principle? A man who at seventy-three[5] instructs others not to pursue profit is just as foolish

---

1. *XFS, j.* 1, in *LZQJZ*, 3:44–45.
2. In *Mencius* 6A10 (echoed here), the choice is between life and righteousness rather than between reputation and profit.
3. The phrase "Old Master Li" refers to the mythical Daoist Laozi, who was surnamed Li. However, since Li Zhi shares this surname with the Daoist thinker, and since throughout his writings he often refers to himself as "Old Li," a layer of playful ambiguity is introduced.
4. Throughout his writings Li repeatedly spoofs pedantic "gentlemen of the Dao." See, for instance, "An Appraisal of Liu Xie," pp. 140–41.
5. Li Zhi's age at the time, in Chinese *sui*.

as a man who at seventy-six[6] pursues both profit and reputation. In either case it amounts to "toiling one's mind and daily becoming more oafish."[7] I hope you will consider this carefully, because you only get one choice.

TRANSLATED BY RIVI HANDLER-SPITZ

---

6. Li Shilong's age at the time.
7. The phrase comes from *The Book of Documents*, which states, "Let reverence and economy be [real] virtues with you, unaccompanied by hypocritical display. Practicing them as virtues will put your mind at ease, and you will daily become more admirable. Practicing them in hypocrisy will cause you to toil your mind, and you will daily become more oafish" (Legge, *The Chinese Classics*, 3:533, with modifications).

"TO ZHOU YOUSHAN"
與周友山
"YU ZHOU YOUSHAN"

In this letter,[1] written in 1596 and addressed to Li's soul friend Zhou Youshan, Li Zhi protests the threat of deportation. In 1588, Li Zhi took up residence at the Cloister of the Flourishing Buddha, located at Dragon Lake, over thirty *li* from the town of Macheng in Huguang province. From this solitary retreat, Li entered into correspondence with several gentry women, most notably the daughter of the high-ranking field official Mei Guozhen—a correspondence that later created a scandal. Along with her sisters, Mei Danran, a widow, took a keen interest in Buddhism and frequently wrote to Li Zhi seeking his guidance on Buddhist self-cultivation. Li Zhi recorded their correspondence in an essay titled "Questioning Guanyin" (*Guanyin wen* 觀音問), which he published in 1596. In the same year, he circulated his "Rules Agreed Upon in Advance" (*Yuyue* 豫約) to several friends, including Zhou Youshan, Pan Shizao, Fang Hang, Yuan Hongdao, and others. In this text, Li expresses deep admiration and respect for the women's piety.

Unsurprisingly, news of his peculiar and unorthodox interactions with women soon came to the authorities' attention. The provincial surveillance commissioner of Huguang, Shi Jingxian 史旌賢, happened to be a follower of Geng Dingxiang and a close friend of the Geng family. Upon learning of Li's correspondence with the widows, Shi threatened that in order to "rectify local customs" it might be necessary to deport Li to his hometown in Fujian province. (RHS)

---

1. *XFS*, *j*. 1, in *LZQJZ* 3:46–49. In addition to being Li Zhi's close friend, Zhou Youshan was also a disciple of Geng Dingxiang's. Along with his brother Zhou Liutang, they built the Cloister of the Flourishing Buddha, where Li resided as their guest; see *LZQJZ* 3:36 See also Rowe, *Crimson Rain*, 95.

The monks all fear that since I am old I will die soon and disaster will befall them. For this reason, I wrote "Rules Agreed Upon in Advance."[2] Without my even realizing it, that piece grew to over twenty pages. Although I wrote it merely for the monks' benefit, the last portion also touches on my life. If people of later generations wish to see what kind of person Li Zhuowu was, this last section can serve as a chronology of my life. Recently, my friends have wanted to have it printed. If it is printed, even if I lose my patrons,[3] I will be able to reside at Dragon Lake forever.

Since my words are extremely incisive and true, and my diction shakes heaven and earth, small wonder that people love this piece and pass it on to others. They grieve for me and pity me. Unfortunately, the manuscript is now in the hands of people who wish to print it, so if you would like to see it, you must seek it from them. Then you will understand the bitterness afflicting this old man's heart.

Living more than thirty *li* outside the city [of Macheng],[4] I have not had a single visitor for several years. I have heard that some have criticized me, saying I ought to be deported to my hometown. That seems entirely appropriate to me. They say, "If we don't deport this man, we will not be able to rectify the local customs in Macheng." I don't know how an old man alone and far from home, begging for food and sitting peacefully awaiting death, could harm local customs. It's the same people who *talk* of "rectifying local customs" who *actually* inflict great harm on local customs. Oh! Enough! I must speak no more of this. It has nothing to do with me. I am merely an old fellow who has left home to seek enlightenment; like other monks, when I have exhausted my interest in a place, I leave. Why wait for circumstances to become unfavorable? But now not only has the situation become unfavorable, people are jabbering about it. If under such circumstances I still do not depart, I must surely have no shame. But if I do leave, what need is there to deport me? And if I do not leave, still no one can

---

2. For a partial translation, see "Reflections on My Life," pp. 185–89.
3. The word Li Zhi uses here, *waihu* 外護, was used by Buddhists to describe laypersons who provided them with food and clothing.
4. The remoteness of the cloister, as well as the natural scenery there, was also noted by Li's friend Yuan Zongdao. Yuan describes the cloister as nestled among "ten thousand mountains and thunderous waterfalls." See his essay "Longhu" 龍湖 [Dragon Lake] in *Baisu zhai leiji* 白蘇齋類集 [Collection of the White Basil Studio], *j*. 14.

deport me. Why? I am old and ready to die. There is no need to leave. So why deport me?

What's more, I am by nature gentle and mild. I have learned the value of enduring humiliation. So if they want to kill me, I'll face the knife; if they want to beat me, I'll face their fists. If they want to curse me, I'll face their censure. I know only how to confront them head-on, not how to yield. Why would I wait around to be deported? Indeed, I have been practicing the method of enduring humiliation and exhibiting filial piety from the time I was seven or eight years old right up to my present age of seventy. I've used this method for years and I'm accustomed to it. Otherwise how could this old man of seventy, without half a cent on his person, nor even a trusted companion by his side, venture to go wandering and take up lodgings ten thousand *li* from home?[5]

I reckon that my mind harbors no evil thoughts, nor has my body committed any transgression; my physical form is untainted, and my shadow free from dust.[6] Therefore I truly embody what the ancients called "having no cause for shame or remorse."[7] Thus, the reason why I am undefeated when, confident in my own righteousness, I "array my battalions," "raise my battle flags,"[8] and daily join battle with the world is that the soldiers of right are on my side. Their discipline is strict and flawless. Who would dare to bring utter destruction upon himself by attacking the righteous and self-assured?

In the essay "Questioning Guanyin," there are two sections that address issues as yet unaddressed by Buddhists.[9] Printing them will benefit people of the younger generation. Among such people, Danran is indeed outstanding.[10] Shanyin, Mingyin, and the others are also exceptional.[11]

---

5. This number is geographically inaccurate but symbolically significant: living in his remote mountain retreat, he felt millions of miles away from his secular obligations.
6. This locution recalls the diction of *The Platform Sutra*.
7. *Mencius* 7A20 states that the gentleman is "neither ashamed to face heaven above nor remorseful to face earth below." However, taken out of context, the same words can be understood to imply that an individual is amoral, "shameless and remorseless." In this passage, Li Zhi may be exploiting the ambiguity of the language to poke fun at his deriders, who characterized him in similar terms.
8. Quoting *Sunzi bingfa*, ch. 7.
9. Zhang Jianye suggests that Li Zhi is referring to the second and fifth letters to Mei Zixin, a female relative of Mei Danran's. These letters, which appear in "Questioning Guanyin," address issues once hotly debated among Song neo-Confucians. See *LZQJZ* 3:49n20, *LZQJZ* 2:85–86n1.
10. Following the death of her husband, Mei Danran shaved her head and converted to Buddhism. During the years Li Zhi spent at Dragon Lake, Danran and Li Zhi carried on a lively correspondence on subjects relating to Buddhism.
11. Other women of the Mei household who also studied and practiced Buddhism.

They are stalwarts who have transcended this world.[12] As for the "exposure" of the fact that men and women have been mingling [here], whom will such reports deceive? Will they deceive Heaven?

From this situation we can perceive the bitterness of human life. It is perilous indeed to seek to transcend the human realm while still unable to free one's body from the cares of this life. The sages took compassion on widows, widowers, childless people, and orphans; nothing surpasses the cultural and ethical achievements of these wise men. Dwelling in the mountains or the wilderness brings delight to deer and boars. Why not people? If this place provides no refuge for me, then no place will. From this I understand that the true reason to study the dharma of transcending this world is that human beings inhabit a sea of sorrows. Bitterness upon bitterness. Ultimate bitterness. I can only take the Buddha as my vehicle.[13]

TRANSLATED BY RIVI HANDLER-SPITZ

---

12. Li Zhi's diction here is remarkable: although Danran and her sisters are female, Li Zhi uses the masculine-inflected word "stalwarts" (zhangfu 丈夫) to accentuate their steadfastness. For a discussion of Li Zhi's use of the term zhangfu with reference to women, see Ying Zhang, "Politics and Morality," 52. See also Grant, "Da Zhangfu."
13. Referring to Mahayana (Greater Vehicle) Buddhism.

"TO GENG KENIAN"
與耿克念
"YU GENG KENIAN"

In 1595, responding to complaints that Li Zhi's presence in Macheng was causing a disturbance, General Surveillance Commissioner Shi Jingxian threatened to deport Li from Macheng to his ancestral home in Fujian. The recipient of this letter,[1] Geng Runian, who went by the courtesy name of Kenian, in an attempt to prevent Li's deportation, invited him to flee to Huang'an. But Li staunchly refused. This letter registers Li's resistance to intimidation and his refusal to circumvent the law, even if doing so meant risking his own death. Li's stance may thus be compared to that of Socrates. Yet despite the gravity of his situation, Li still manages to strike a humorous tone and subject the general surveillance commissioner's threats to a reductio ad absurdum.

In addition to the recipient, Geng Kenian, who was the eldest son of Li's close friend Geng Dingli, the letter also mentions Dingli's two brothers, Kenian's uncles, Geng Dinglih and Geng Dingxiang. (RHS)

Your last letter was very clear. But since some people suspect [that my leaving Macheng and joining you in Huang'an would be tantamount to my fleeing the law], I dare not go. Even if it means opposing your respected command, I dare not leave. I hope you will ask Dinglih and Dingxiang to forgive me.

Personally, I say that if the general surveillance commissioner wishes to censure me under the law, that's fine. But if he wants to intimidate me and drive me out, that is not acceptable. When it comes to people who have committed crimes, who break the law and turn order into chaos, they

---

1. *XFS, j.* 1, in *LZQJZ* 3:78.

should be investigated according to the law. They may also be punished. But if I plead for mercy, I'll no longer be Old Li Zhuowu. If I leave under intimidation, then a person harmful to the law will have moved, spreading his poison to another region. That would be extremely unkind! How could I choose between the people of Macheng and those of a different locality? Thus, they can kill me but they cannot make me leave. They can chop off my head, but they cannot desecrate my body. This is my firm conviction. It is not difficult to understand.

TRANSLATED BY RIVI HANDLER-SPITZ

"TO ZENG JIQUAN"
與曾繼泉
"YU ZENG JIQUAN"

Upon hearing in 1588 that his student Zeng Jiquan was considering becoming a monk, Li Zhi dashed off two notes urging him not to act rashly. The longer note[1] pleads with Zeng Jiquan to uphold his familial obligations. In the briefer missive, translated here,[2] Li simply lays out his own rationale for "impulsively" taking the Buddhist tonsure. For related material, see "Reading a Letter from Ruowu's Mother" (pp. 162–65). (RHS)

The reason I shaved my head was that the members of my family were constantly expecting me to return home, and, time and again, "thinking nothing of a journey of one thousand *li*," they came to compel me and urge me to abide by lay customs.[3] So I cut my hair to show them that I would not return. As for lay customs, I am absolutely unwilling to be ruled by them. What's more, people of no insight mostly view me as a heretic. So I've *become* a heretic, the better to conform to this demeaning name. For these several reasons—and not because I planned to do so—I impulsively shaved off my hair.

TRANSLATED BY RIVI HANDLER-SPITZ

---

1. For a translation of the longer letter, see Yu, "To Zeng Jiquan," 259–60.
2. *XFS*, *j*. 1, in *LZQJZ* 3:149. Zeng Jiquan studied Buddhism with Li Zhi at the Cloister of the Flourishing Buddha at Dragon Lake. Along with Ruowu, he is one of the two monks referred to in Li Zhi's "Three Essays for Two Monks of Huang'an"; see *LZQJZ* 1:195n1.
3. Citing *Mencius* 1A1.

"LETTER TO A FRIEND"
與友人書
"YU YOUREN SHU"

This letter,[1] addressed to an unknown recipient in 1600, provides a remarkable firsthand account of the personal manner and physical appearance of the Jesuit missionary Matteo Ricci, to whom Li Zhi refers by his Chinese name.[2] Ricci and Li met on three occasions between 1599 and 1600. On each occasion, Ricci impressed Li with his extensive knowledge of Chinese language, history, and customs. Li also composed a poem for Ricci, included in this anthology (pp. 223–24). The most arresting portion of this essay comes in its final lines, where Li confesses he cannot comprehend what motivated Ricci to come to China. Was Li writing ironically, or was Ricci hesitant to disclose his purposes? Both might be true. (RHS)

Since you ask about Li of the Far West: he is a man of the Great Western Regions.[3] He has traveled over a hundred thousand *li* to come to China. He first came by ship across the ocean to southern India, where he first learned of the existence of Buddhism; by then he had already come more than forty thousand *li*. On arriving in Nanhai, near Guangzhou, he learned that the nationally acclaimed scholars of our great Ming dynasty were preceded by the sage-kings Yao and Shun, and later by the Duke of Zhou and Confucius. He lived in Nanhai and Zhaoqing[4] for more than twenty years.

There is scarcely a Chinese book he has not read. He asked scholars of the older generation to teach him the sounds and translations of Chinese

---

1. *XFS*, *j*. 1, in *LZQJZ* 3:109–10.
2. For another account of Ricci by Li's contemporary Yuan Zhongdao, see Ye, *Vignettes*, 60.
3. Ricci adopted the Chinese name Li Madou 利瑪竇. For Ricci's impressions of Li Zhi, see Gallagher, *China in the Sixteenth Century*, 400–401. For an annotated English translation of Ricci's treatise on friendship, originally written in Chinese, see Ricci, *On Friendship*.
4. In modern-day Guangdong province.

characters, and he invited those who possess insight into the Four Books and the doctrines of the School of Principle to explain to him their essential meanings. He also invited those versed in the Six Classics and the commentaries upon them to help him comprehend their interpretations. Now he is fully able to speak the language of our country, to write using our characters, and to practice our rituals.

He is an exquisite human being. His mind is sharp as can be, but his demeanor is simple and down-to-earth. In a crowd of several tens of people all talking at once, he responded to each person appropriately and did not lose his calm on account of their heckling. Of the people I have met, none can compare with him. Most people are either extremely arrogant or utterly obsequious; if they're not flaunting their intelligence, they're bumbling fools. None can compare with him.

But I don't understand why he came here. I've already met with him three times, and I just don't understand what he came here to do. I suspect he may want to replace the teachings of the Duke of Zhou and Confucius with his own knowledge. But that would be very foolish. I suspect that couldn't be his purpose!

TRANSLATED BY RIVI HANDLER-SPITZ

PART III
MISCELLANEOUS WRITINGS 雜書
SHORT ESSAYS AND DISCOURSES 小品與論說

"PREFACE TO SELECTIONS FROM 'A RECORD OF A CART FULL OF GHOSTS'"
選錄睽車志鈙
"XUANLU KUICHE ZHI XU"

The belief that all actions elicit a response has pervaded the Chinese religious landscape from early medieval times onward and cannot be conceived of as the sole domain of any one religious tradition.[1] Li's own serious engagement with this concept is readily apparent in his desire to republish *The Tract of the Most Exalted on Action and Response* (*Taishang ganying pian* 太上感應篇),[2] produce his own collection of tales under the Buddhist title *The Record of Karmic Consequences* (*Yinguo lu* 因果錄),[3] and issue an abridged version of Guo

---

1. This essay is in *XFS*, j. 2, in *LZQJZ* 3:188–90.
2. This text was first published ca. 1164. *Taishang* (the god most exalted) refers to Laozi. Despite the incorporation of this text along with commentaries in the Daoist canon, the text itself contains citations from Buddhist scripture. The text has a rich publication history, especially during the Ming and Qing, when it was reprinted numerous times. For instance, the famous late-Ming Buddhist monk Zhuhong paid to republish this work. For an overview of the text, see Brokaw, *Ledgers*, 36–43.
3. *The Record of Karmic Consequences* is a fairly obscure text. It was never as popular as *The Tract of the Most Exalted on Action and Response* and may have enjoyed rather limited circulation and a short afterlife. Li's text consists largely of excerpts from Buddhist works. Most notably, Li republished in toto Zhuhong's extremely popular *Fangsheng wen* 放生文 [On releasing life].

Tuan's 郭彖 twelfth-century *A Record of a Cart Full of Ghosts* (*Kuiche zhi* 睽車志),[4] a compilation of *zhiguai* stories.[5]

From the Buddhist perspective, karma is an impersonal, immutable law such that all actions (*yin* 因) generate karmic results (*guo* 果). In contrast, *The Tract of the Most Exalted on Action and Response* postulates a host of supernatural overseers who constantly record human action (*gan* 感), most notably transgressions, and respond (*ying* 應) appropriately. Confucian interpretations attribute such responses to "heaven" (*tian* 天). Tales of karmic retribution and *ganying* stories draw on some of the same literary tropes found in the genre of strange or grotesque tales (*zhiguai* 志怪), such as trips to hell or voyages to other realms. However, texts like the six-fascicle *A Record of a Cart Full of Ghosts*, with its 144 or so tales (depending on the recension), are not as programmatic in the degree to which they highlight the moral dimension of cause-effect relations, nor do they necessarily use the terms *ganying* or *yinguo*. In *A Record of a Cart Full of Ghosts*, clear causal relations are evident in some stories, while others simply regale an audience with strange tales that blur the line between human and ghostly realms. Li's 1598 redaction of the text to the two-fascicle work *Selections from 'A Record of a Cart Full of Ghosts,'* comprising only fourteen to fifteen of these tales, likely strengthened his assertion that these anecdotes fit the criteria set for karmic tales.

Despite Li's ability to find common ground among these disparate texts, his ritual response to the plight of creatures stuck in an undesirable realm of rebirth was far more parochial. He relied solely on Buddhist ritual technologies and did not incorporate Daoist or Confucian methods. In keeping with a journey by boat, Li organized a Buddhist recitation ritual for the purpose of liberating water gods and ghosts. Buddhist rituals for the propitiation of spirits generated merit, a form of "spiritual cash" that could be transferred to others through a written dedication of merit or by ceremonial means. In choosing to recite *The Rebirth Dhāraṇī* (*Wangsheng shenzhou*

---

4. Compiled ca. 1181, *A Record of a Cart Full of Ghosts* was reduced in Li's selection from its original six fascicles to two. Barend ter Haar translates the title in an article that gives some information on the publication and contents of this text. *Kui* refers to the thirty-eighth trigram in the *Classic of Changes*. See Haar, "Newly Recovered Anecdotes."
5. For a discussion of *zhiguai* literature in the Ming, see Zeitlin, *Historian of the Strange*. For early medieval references and an extensive bibliography, see Campany, "Tales of Anomalous Events."

往生神咒), Li presumably wanted to release these forlorn creatures from their present existence so that they could be reborn in the Pure Land of Amitābha Buddha. (JE)

When I was residing in Nanjing, Jiao Hong[6] and I published *The Tract of the Most Exalted on Action and Response*. Later retreating to my monastic quarters at Dragon Lake, I further compiled *The Record of Karmic Consequences*. Recently Jiao Hong was dismissed from his post as lecturer at the imperial academy, and I again traveled south with him by boat. In our leisurely travel, Jiao Hong showed me Guo Tuan's *A Record of a Cart Full of Ghosts*.

I selected the most cautionary and reliable stories. During the day I copied out several pages' worth in fine characters and gave them to the monastic community to reflect on. When evening arrived, I directed the monastic assembly to recite *The Lotus Sutra* and *The Rebirth Dhāraṇī* to liberate water gods and water ghosts. In this way, day and night I delved into affairs concerning ghosts.

In writing a formal dedication of merit[7] at the conclusion of the sutra recitations, I had to describe the impetus for this ritual. I thus honestly wrote that "Principal Graduate Jiao Hong[8] and I took a boat together" and so forth. Jiao Hong said, "There's no need to put in the title 'Principal Graduate'!" I argued, "If gods and ghosts recognize true worth, then not including your title would be all right. However, if they do not recognize true worth, then this title of yours might elicit their great respect, so what harm would come from including it?" Jiao Hong said, "If it's to frighten ghosts, then go ahead." I laughed, saying, "To claim that a title might elicit the respect of the gods is acceptable; to claim that it could frighten ghosts is impossible. If you were really able to frighten ghosts, then you would not be on this boat!"[9]

---

6. In 1589 Jiao Hong was assigned to the Hanlin Academy. However, by 1597, when serving as chief examiner of the metropolitan examinations in Shuntian, he had already fallen out of favor and been demoted to an assistant magistrate post in Fujian. His departure from Beijing likely followed this demotion.
7. *Huixiang* (回向, Skt. *pariṇāmanā*), or more commonly (*huixiang* 廻向), is a Buddhist technical term for the dedication or transfer of merit. For more on this idea, see Foulk, "Huixiang 廻向."
8. Jiao Hong achieved the top distinction in the civil service examinations of 1589.
9. Jiao Hong had just been demoted. This banter about gods and ghosts functions metaphorically as a way to laugh off an inability to "scare off" other officials and retain power.

Thereupon he laughed heartily. I thus recorded this anecdote to introduce *A Record of a Cart Full of Ghosts*.

A Record of a Cart Full of Ghosts is extensive. The stories I hand copied are not more than a tenth of the original collection. The ignorant read these tales out of a love for the strange. The discerning think they can be read alongside *The Record of Karmic Consequences* and *The Tract of the Most Exalted on Action and Response*. If this book can be read in conjunction with *The Tract of the Most Exalted on Action and Response*, then how could one claim it is a "cart full of ghosts"? This, of course, is the most exalted one's point.

TRANSLATED BY JENNIFER EICHMAN

"PREFACE TO THE ANTHOLOGY UNSTRINGING THE BOW"
説弧集敍
"SHUO HU JI XU"

In 1598 Li Zhi compiled yet another volume of ghost stories titled *Unstringing the Bow*. This text is no longer extant. However, the preface[1] indicates that Li's initial enthusiasm for *A Record of a Cart Full of Ghosts* had waned considerably. "Preface to *Selections from 'A Record of a Cart Full of Ghosts'*" framed the reading of ghost stories in terms of cause-effect relations and ritual propitiation but did not question the ontological status of ghosts. In contrast, *Unstringing the Bow* is made up of anecdotes that purportedly elide the distinction between the human and ghostly realms. This collection emphasizes their interconnectedness and argues against the notion, depicted in *A Record of a Cart Full of Ghosts*, that such beings inhabit two separate realms. The preface ends with a number of philosophical questions that were doubtless addressed in the text itself. The main thrust of this second volume is not to expand the repertoire of ghost stories but to interject a contrasting point of view as a philosophical corrective to the conceptual apparatus inherent in *A Record of a Cart Full of Ghosts*.

The difference between these two collections of ghost stories is most evident in Li's pithy contrastive summation of each text. The summation is drawn from a passage in the *Classic of Changes*: seeming to see "a carriage full of ghosts," a lone traveler "first bends his bow ... and afterwards unbends it, for he discovers that the other is not an assailant to injure, but a near relative."[2] Li uses this story to direct skepticism at skepticism itself. (JE)

---

1. *XFS, j.* 2, in *LZQJZ* 3:190–91.
2. The *Classic of Changes*, hexagram "Kui"; see Legge, *The Yi King*, 140. For a discussion of this story and the legend it draws on, see Gao, *Zhouyi*.

A Record of a Cart Full of Ghosts records ghost stories. In raising the question, who is a ghost, the text treats humans and ghosts as distinct. Consequently, it has the effect of "drawing the bow for the purpose of shooting [ghosts]." *Unstringing the Bow* is another anthology of ghost tales, but its purpose in bringing together anecdotes of ghosts is to show that humans and ghosts are the same. Consequently, it bears the name *Unstringing the Bow*—from "unbending the bow,"[3] with no intent of shooting.

When people reach the point at which in daylight they do not see humans and in the darkness they do not see ghosts, then "a single thread runs through"[4] darkness, daylight, people, and ghosts. What matters of birth and death are there left to comprehend then? What nirvana could one hope for? And as for those who contend that there are no ghosts, how can one be certain that *they* have not penetrated the mystery of life?

TRANSLATED BY JENNIFER EICHMAN

---

3. The passage from the *Classic of Changes* uses the character *shuo* 說, which in Wang Bi's commentary is glossed as *tuo* 脫; in archery this means to unstring or unbend a bow.
4. Playfully alluding to Confucius's statement that "a single thread runs through" his Way (*Analects* 4.15).

"A BRIEF INTRODUCTION TO A SELECTION OF DAOIST TEACHINGS"
道教鈔小引 |
"DAOJIAO CHAO XIAOYIN"

Li embraced a vision of Buddhist monastic education that incorporated training in Daoist texts. Although the compendium for which this brief introduction[1] was written never materialized, it would have consisted of selections from Daoist texts. The compendium likely incorporated all or part of Laozi's *Daodejing* and other writings on inner alchemy in line with the tenth-century *Book of Transformations* (*Huashu* 化書) and thirteenth-century *Authentic Scripture of Master Wenshi* (*Wenshi zhen jing* 文始真經), which are mentioned here. Li's claim that these two texts diverge not an iota from Śākyamuni's path to liberation suggests that he is thinking quite specifically about cultivation regimens and modes of inner spiritual transformation, not about Buddhism and Daoism writ large.

"A Brief Introduction to a Selection of Daoist Teachings" opens with a reference to a famous albeit fictional dialogue between Confucius and Laozi. The dialogue states only that Confucius asked about ritual but does not present a specific question. Laozi's response dismisses the notion that advancement in public office is within the control of individuals. Laozi further asserts that virtuous men appear to be fools and successful merchants appear to have nothing. He continues, "Dispense with your arrogant airs and many desires, your showy appearance, and your excessive ambitions. All of these are of no benefit to your body."[2] Li argues that the educated will take

---

1. *XFS, j.* 2, in *LZQJZ* 3:195–96.
2. See Sima Qian, *Shi ji*, ch. 63, "Biographies of Laozi and Han Feizi," partially translated in Csikszentmihalyi, *Readings*, 102–3.

Laozi's advice immediately to heart. He reflects on his own moral shortcomings in this regard. (JE)

Most monks are versed only in Buddhist teachings and are unfamiliar with Daoist teachings. In general, the Daoists consider their founder to be that Lord Lao[zi] whom Confucius once asked about ritual. When we reflect upon the few words Laozi offered our teacher, how could it be that myriad generations of scholars have failed to wear them on their bodies at all times and inscribe them on their hearts in every breath? Unless this teaching is inscribed on the heart with every breath, arrogant airs will arise, showy appearances will come to light, excessive ambitions will crop up, and disaster will soon follow.[3]

I am old and will die soon, yet time and time again I have suffered from these symptoms of illness [i.e., the moral shortcomings of arrogance, ambition, and thoughtlessness]. No wonder that so often I have been the victim of others' bullying and oppression. How could people like Yang Dingjian[4]—whose resolve surpasses mine yet whose knowledge and insight lag behind mine—not diligently carry with them [Laozi's words] throughout their lives!

Laozi's *Daodejing* sits on my desk every day. When I go out, I stash it up my sleeve so that it will be handy when I wish to recite it. Texts like the Keeper of the Pass's *Authentic Scripture of Master Wenshi*[5] and Tanzi's *Book of Transformations*[6] ought to accompany one's person. How could they differ by even a fraction from Śākyamuni's own path? For this reason, I have taken it upon myself to compile these excerpts to show to dedicated monks. I further most urgently wish to show them to Yang Dingjian.

TRANSLATED BY JENNIFER EICHMAN

---

3. Translation follows Csikszentmihalyi, *Readings*, 102–3.
4. On Yang Dingjian, see "To Yang Dingjian," pp. 10–11, 63–64.
5. Yin Xi (sixth century B.C.E.), known as the Keeper of the Pass, is more mythical figure than historical personage. The text that Li likely read was a three-fascicle textual reconstruction published in 1233 under the title *Authentic Scripture of Master Wenshi*. The work has a strong inner alchemical focus. See Kohn, "Yin Xi." For a translation, see Decaux, "True Classic."
6. This is a text on inner alchemy by Tan Qiao 譚峭 (ca. 860–940). It combines Buddhist, Confucian, and Daoist ideas and was often studied by neo-Confucians. See Didier, "Messrs. T'an," and Andersen, "*Huashu*."

"WRITTEN AT THE END OF YUAN ZHONGDAO'S HAND SCROLL"
書小修手卷後
"SHU XIAOXIU SHOUJUAN HOU"

This lighthearted essay,[1] composed in the form of a dialogue, addresses the serious ethical ramifications of eating meat. Presented as a casual conversation between the author and Yuan Zhongdao, who would later become an acclaimed man of letters, the essay positions Li as representing the Confucian outlook and Yuan the Buddhist stance. Playfully citing ancient authorities on both sides of the debate, the essay concludes with Li's ceding to his interlocutor and agreeing not to eat meat. Although Li allows himself to be persuaded, his choice to present himself initially as the voice of orthodox Confucianism raises questions. By the time this essay was composed in 1601 in Tongzhou, near Beijing, Li had long since voluntarily resigned his position in the bureaucracy and taken up residence in the Cloister of the Flourishing Buddha at Dragon Lake. Thus the decision to portray himself in Confucian guise indicates the many faces of Li's identity and his refusal to conform to a single standard. Partly because Li shifted so easily among diverse personas, he attracted national attention. The image in the penultimate paragraph, of "all eyes [being] fixed upon [him]; all fingers point[ing] toward [him]," illustrates the intense scrutiny to which his actions were subjected. The following year, Li was arrested and committed suicide in prison. (RHS)

---

1. *XFS, j.* 2, in *LZQJZ* 3:201–3. Yuan Zhongdao was the youngest of the three Yuan brothers and the author of a biographical sketch of Li Zhi (see pp. 325–33). For translations of poetry and essays by the Yuan brothers, see Chaves, *Pilgrim of the Clouds*, and Ye, *Vignettes*. For analysis of Gong'an aesthetic theory, see Chou, *Yüan Hung-tao and the Kung-an School*. See also Chaves, "The Panoply of Images," and Hung, *Romantic Vision*.

In the year *xinchou* [1601] at Ma Jinglun's[2] house in Luhe,[3] I once again met the youngest brother, Yuan Zhongdao. Although I didn't get a chance to see the eldest brother, the Hanlin Compiler [Yuan Zongdao], seeing Zhongdao was enough, especially since I got to see this scroll again!

Zhongdao urged me to stop eating meat. I asked him, "Why do you not want me to eat meat?"

He said, "I fear that Yama, king of the underworld,[4] may get angry and issue a special order that you not be reborn in the Pure Land."

I said, "King Yama is a meat eater himself! How dare he question Li Zhuowu? I only refrain from killing; I do not refrain from putting meat in my mouth. That should be enough to avoid incurring King Yama's wrath. Didn't Mencius say, 'A seventy-year-old man cannot be satiated unless he eats meat'?[5] I'm old, and what's more I'm a Confucian, and I have once again let my beard grow. It's *appropriate* that I should eat meat."

Zhongdao said, "Because sages offer ritual sacrifices, they 'stay away from the kitchen.'[6] This is also why they refrain from eating meat. When Mencius said a seventy-year-old man cannot be satiated unless he eats meat, he was only talking about old people in the villages. Could it be that he uttered such words for Old Li Zhuo? I wish you would not brush me off like this!"

I said, "All my life I have been fastidious about cleanliness. Worldly indulgences such as alcohol, sex, and wealth have not polluted me even one bit. Now I am seventy-five years old. If you were to question the ghosts and spirits about my customary deportment, they surely would not make a fuss about my [carnivorous ways] or ask hard questions about Old Li."

---

2. Ma Jinglun 馬經綸 (courtesy name Chengsuo 誠所, 1562–1605) was a student, close friend, and avid supporter of Li Zhi's and hosted Li at his home near the end of Li's life. When Li was arrested and clapped in prison, Ma advocated on Li's behalf, and after Li's death, Ma buried him. See "Master Li Zhuowu's Testament," pp. 291–93. Li addresses several pieces in *Another Book to Burn* to Jinglun's father, Ma Lishan; for example, "To Ma Lishan," pp. 241–44.
3. Luhe is another name for Tongzhou.
4. According to Buddhist mythology, Yama, king of the underworld, is in charge of punishing wrongdoing in hell.
5. Li Zhi cites *Mencius* 7A22: "If fifty-year-olds do not wear silk, they will not be comfortable. If seventy-year-olds do not eat meat, they will not feel full" (Van Norden, *Mengzi*, 177).
6. *Mencius* 1A7 recounts that King Xuan of Qi was unwilling to permit an ox he had seen alive to be ceremoniously sacrificed. Mencius explains to the king that his compassionate behavior toward the ox is a mark of his humanity: "Gentlemen cannot bear to see animals die if they have seen them living. If they hear their cries of suffering, they cannot bear to eat their flesh. Hence, gentlemen keep their distance from the kitchen" (Van Norden, *Mengzi*, 9).

Zhongdao said, "Few people in the world possess ambition. And fewer still love to study. Now luckily we live under the peaceful rule of the great Ming. Everyone has eyes, and we frankly think that to leave society and study in reclusion is indeed an important task. If you were to perch in the mountain groves, abandon the human world, and eat meat to your heart's content, that would be fine. But these days there is no way for you to conceal your deeds. Everyone knows that Old Man Zhuowu has abandoned his family to study the Dao, that you are a recluse and a hero. All eyes are fixed upon you; all fingers point toward you. If your behavior slackens for a moment, or even if in your heart you experience ambivalence, men of ambition will consider this deeply lamentable. For this reason, I hope that you, sir, will stop eating meat. Your self-denial will, in time, inspire bright and ambitious scholars. By enduring a period of gustatory privation, you can save a generation of scholars. What further scruples could you have?"

I flashed him a grin and replied, "If you can persuade me that they truly have their minds set on the Dao, I'll willingly chop off my own finger and swear never to eat meat again!"

TRANSLATED BY RIVI HANDLER-SPITZ

"ON *THE LOTUS SUTRA* CHAPTER ON EXPEDIENT DEVICES"
法華方便品説
"*FAHUA* FANGBIAN PIN SHUO"

In this short piece[1] written in 1592, Li Zhi draws attention to the position of the audience in the second chapter of *The Lotus Sutra*. A polemical work of scripture, *The Lotus Sutra* claims that all previous teachings of Śākyamuni Buddha were merely a form of *upāya*—provisional truths—used to teach those not yet ready to hear about the One Vehicle, a much higher path to spiritual liberation. The text is written in the form of a dialogue between Śākyamuni and his disciple Śāriputra, who plays the role of an interlocutor. Śāriputra asks the Buddha three times to preach this dharma, yet the Buddha is reluctant, declaring it most difficult to understand and beyond the capacities of previous disciples—such a teaching will bring doubt and fear. Once the Buddha finally agrees to preach, five thousand monks respectfully bow to the Buddha and retreat, declining to listen to this teaching. The third chapter of *The Lotus Sutra* opens with Śāriputra's rejoicing at having just heard the second chapter's teachings on *upāya* and the One Vehicle.

Li's commentary focuses on audience reaction both by emphasizing Śāriputra's joyful response to hearing this teaching and by musing on how he himself and his contemporaries might have responded. He wonders whether, if he had seen that other (new) shore, he would have reached for it or retreated from it. Li's attention to *The Lotus Sutra* further demonstrates that his broad interest in Buddhist scripture extended beyond the narrow confines of Chan texts and Pure Land polemics. Both he and his disciples recited *The Lotus Sutra*,

---

1. *XFS*, *j*. 2, in *LZQJZ* 3:212–14.

and this text appears in a number of other entries in *A Book to Burn* and *Another Book to Burn*.² (JE)

In this sutra chapter, those of overweening pride do not know of the Buddha's *upāya*³ and therefore confidently think they possess the Buddha's truth. Upon hearing this subtle dharma, how could they not be fearful? It is for this reason that the World-Honored One, Śākyamuni, thrice refused Śāriputra's request and did not respond; that five thousand monks subsequently withdrew and did not return.

The preaching of this subtle dharma is as rare as the appearance of the *udumbara* flower.⁴ The sages of the Three Vehicles could not immediately be taught this doctrine—how much less those who are arrogant! As for Śāriputra, although in the end he chose the path of a *śrāvaka*,⁵ for a very long time previous to that he had planted deep roots and immersed himself in the Buddha's teachings. That he rejoiced must be because he intuitively grasped the teaching's import without further explanation. What a pity he did not record in detail the subtle dharma that inspired his deep trust at the time.

As for what has been recorded, how can we know whether Master Zhuowu, if he were to read it, would not gaze toward that shore and also retreat?⁶ But

---

2. See, for example, *Gao fo yueshu ji* 告佛約束偈 [Presenting the *gāthā* on binding regulations to the Buddha], in *FS, j.* 4, in *LZQJZ* 2:48–50; "Preface to *Selections from 'A Record of a Cart Full of Ghosts*,'" pp. 259–62; "Yu you ren" 與友人 [Letter to a friend], in *XFS, j.* 1, in *LZQJZ* 3:118–21. For a translation of *The Lotus Sutra*, see Hurvitz, *Scripture of the Lotus*.
3. The Chinese equivalent for this Sanskrit term is *fangbian* 方便. It is an important Mahayana Buddhist technical term, often translated as "expedient device" or "expedient means." The "Expedient Devices" chapter of *The Lotus Sutra* argues that all previous teachings of the Buddha were merely provisional truths offered in accordance with the capacities and dispositions of those he wished to teach. Now the Buddha is about to offer a new, higher teaching. *Upāya* has remained a cornerstone of Mahayana doctrine and is often employed to explain how the tradition could absorb conflicting views. It also refers to determining the correct approach to teaching each disciple.
4. The *udumbara* is said to bloom perhaps once every thousand or three thousand years.
5. Literally, "voice hearers" (*shengwen* 聲聞). This term originally referred to disciples who personally heard instruction from the Buddha.
6. Though some readers will recognize the trope of "turning back from the other shore" commonly found in both Buddhist and Daoist texts, the exact wording Li Zhi employs here is repeated in a number of canonical Buddhist texts. Li may have been familiar with the Song monk Juefan Huihong's 覺範慧洪 (1071–1128) commentary to *The Lotus Sutra*, which uses this exact phrase in describing the retreat of the five thousand monks mentioned in the opening of Li's preface.

if there is a subtle dharma that can be recorded, even if Old Man Zhuowu desired not to retreat, he would be compelled to do so.

This sutra contains twenty-eight sections. Each section explains the subtle dharma of the lotus blossom. Even if one pursues to the utmost this subtle dharma of the lotus blossom, one still cannot grasp it. Alas! This is why it is called the *Subtle Dharma of the Lotus Blossom*!

TRANSLATED BY JENNIFER EICHMAN

"ON *THE DIAMOND SUTRA*"
金剛經說
"*JINGANG JING SHUO*"

Given the title of this short essay,[1] one might expect the topic to be Buddhist doctrine. However, Li is, in fact, defending Confucian ideas deriving from Wang Yangming about how the self-cultivated individual's mind ideally functions. In a letter to his disciple Lu Cheng 陸澄 (dates unknown; *jinshi* 1517), Wang Yangming wrote that the ceaseless application of utmost integrity is the sage's cultivation technique for extending innate knowing.[2] Innate knowing is an intuitive moral impulse that, when allowed to operate unencumbered by emotions or cognition, always leads one to respond appropriately. In his letter, Wang Yangming affirms the correctness of *The Diamond Sutra*'s imperative that "one should give rise to the mind of nonabiding." He suggests that the mind should function like a mirror and allow objects simply to be reflected in passing; one must not attempt to latch on to them.

Li extends the practical applications of this type of mental attitude to the cultivation and practice of good ethical behavior. To do this, he draws out several ideas from the *Great Learning* and *Doctrine of the Mean* that are central to Yangming Confucian discourse. He then proceeds to demonstrate how nonabiding can be used to realize the goals of setting the mind straight and developing the authentic practice of integrity.

Yangming Confucians not only rejected many of Zhu Xi's Confucian ideas, they also rejected his attacks on Buddhist ones. In this essay, Li neutralizes Zhu's criticism of *The Diamond Sutra* and would-be monks by making Zhu a critic of wrongheaded approaches to Buddhist cultivation, not of true Buddhist cultivation itself. Li then offers a pointed critique of Zhu in a short caricature of him as

---

1. *XFS, j.* 2, in *LZQJZ* 3:214–17.
2. This letter is translated in Wing-tsit Chan, *Instructions for Practical Living*, 148–49.

someone whose erudition is unsurpassed yet irrelevant to others' most pressing question: how does one set the mind straight? (JE)

The Diamond Sutra [Jingang jing 金剛經] is a section of the Sutra on Great Wisdom [Mahāprajñā-sūtra]. I have heard this said about the sutra, "Jin [metal] is the most indestructible [gang] substance.³ It can quell an army of demons and save all sentient beings. For this reason, the text is called diamond [jingang]." When human nature is sharp and unwavering, then nothing can destroy it.⁴ It, too, is like a diamond. For this reason, when the monk Hongren was explaining The Diamond Sutra to Huineng, as they reached the sentence "Only in nonabiding should one give rise to thoughts,"⁵ Huineng suddenly experienced a great awakening.⁶ This was none other than to "see one's nature and become a buddha." Isn't this extraordinary!

Those who explicate this scripture by saying that Master Zhu [Xi] disparaged its message assume that the sutra is an affront to the teachings of our Sage [Confucius]. They do not understand that Master Zhu had a reason for saying what he did. He saw people who grabbed on to the outward features of existence in their pursuit of buddhahood and who did not know that the mind *is* the buddha. In the end, they shaved their heads and changed robes, abandoned the kindness of rulers and family, and personally rebelled against [Confucian] teachings. This is why Zhu Xi offered these words. He never intended them for people who were completely loyal and filial and could fulfill the Way within relations established between rulers, ministers, fathers, and sons.

For those whose "integrity is intact," whose "hearts have been set straight," and whose relations with others are beyond reproach,⁷ even if they recite *The Diamond Sutra* daily, what affront could there be in this? Now consider that Master Zhu spent his entire life broadly studying a wide

---

3. Strictly speaking, *jingang* 金剛 is a translation of the Sanskrit term *vajra*, which means variously "adamant," "diamond," "indestructible," or "hard." English-language translations of the sutra's title and of this term are derived from the Sanskrit. However, Chinese readers did not grasp intuitively the relation between the Sanskrit meaning and the translated term *jingang*. For this reason, many Chinese commentaries open, as Li's does, with a parsing of the term *jingang*. This does make for a somewhat awkward English translation.
4. *Mencius* 2B1.
5. *The Diamond Sutra* (T235:8.749.c23).
6. See McRae, *Platform Sutra*, 34.
7. Phrases from the Confucian text *The Great Learning*.

variety of books. Even among the numerous schools of thought, no one possessed his level of erudition. This is readily apparent in Zhu's annotations to *The Seal of the Unity of the Three*.[8] Be that as it may, the only thing scholars need to worry about is the inability to set the mind straight.

The authentic realization of integrity resides in avoiding all self-deception.[9] Not setting the mind straight begins with indulging the emotions.[10] When emotions are indulged, there is abiding. When there is abiding, then one cannot set the mind straight and the mind cannot be free.[11] Thus [the *Great Learning*] says, "When the mind is inattentive, we look and do not see; we hear and do not understand," and thus our vital impulses cease. When there is no abiding, then the mind is vastly open. When open, it is broad and impartial. This is the state of being free from objects. Since there are no objects, how could they be destroyed? When there is no abiding, then the mind is luminous. When luminous, the mind responds to things as they come before it. It does so ceaselessly. Since it never ceases, how could it be exhausted? This is the principle of ceaselessness of the utmost integrity and the nature of the indestructible diamond. Both reside within each living person like this.

But the ignorant do not trust in it; the educated offer forced interpretations; the man from Song yanked up his shoots; and Gaozi tried to help it grow.[12] None of them possessed the true mind of nonabiding.[13] They recklessly established subject-object distinctions and thereby destroyed the ceaseless activity of the mysterious principle of life. This is self-deception. This is why the sutra reinforced the following meaning: "One should give rise to the mind of nonabiding." With this mind, one can carry on conversations with those disloyal, unfilial, head-shaving, strange robe-wearing monks in person!

TRANSLATED BY JENNIFER EICHMAN

---

8. *Cantong qi* 參同契, a work of Daoist internal alchemy. For a translation, see Pregadio, *Unity of the Three*. Zhu Xi discussed it in his *Zhouyi "Cantong qi" kaoyi* 周易參同契考異 [Critical investigation of the Zhouyi Cantong qi].
9. Li cites the *Great Learning* with one important modification, the addition of the word *shi* 實 (true, authentic).
10. Most of this passage is a paraphrase of another section of the *Great Learning*. For a discussion of its strategies of uniting Buddhist and Confucian ideas, see Eichman, "Intertextual Alliances."
11. *Zizai* 自在 (Skt. *aiśvarya*). The mind is free from attachment, dependence on external phenomena—i.e., free from the karmic fetters of this world.
12. Alluding to *Mencius* 4B26 and 2A2.
13. Li ends here with an idea he likely learned from Wang Ji. In response to a query about *The Diamond Sutra*, Wang Ji offered a succinct explanation of the impermanence of the three minds (*sanxin* 三心), none of which can be held on to or represents a fixed point in time. This he calls the true mind of nonabiding.

"ON RECLUSES"
隱者說
"YINZHE SHUO"

This essay,[1] likely composed in Macheng sometime before 1588, originally appeared in the "Biographies of Unemployed Ministers" (Waichen zhuan 外臣傳) chapter of *A Book to Keep (Hidden)*. In it, Li Zhi refutes the canonical understanding of reclusion. Confucius was said to have asserted that retreating from society is acceptable only when the Dao is lacking. Drawing a distinction between bodily and mental reclusion, Li contends that truly great recluses need not absent themselves from society at all. This view is consonant with his opinion that one need not seek the solitude of a monastery in order to devote oneself to Buddhist practice (see "Reading a Letter from Ruowu's Mother," pp. 162–65) and with his disregard for the rules of literary composition (see "On Miscellaneous Matters," pp. 102–5, and "Explanation of the Childlike Heart-Mind," pp. 106–10). (RHS)

Reclusion from the times means going into reclusion at the appropriate time. It's what is meant by "when the Dao does not prevail in the state, one goes into reclusion."[2] It comes about because people have the wisdom to protect themselves. Anyone with even the slightest will can do that; there's nothing hard about it.

Those who go into physical reclusion feel obliged to do so regardless of whether the times require it of them. It seems to me that recluses of this kind fall into several categories. Some aspire to dwell amid tall forests and lush grasses: they go into reclusion because they hate noise and love solitude. Others are lazy and undisciplined, incapable of putting themselves to a productive trade; they tend to have no recourse but to go into reclusion. If this is what is meant by reclusion, what is so special about recluses?

---

1. *XFS, j.* 2, in *LZQJZ* 3:220–22.
2. Allusion to *Analects* 8:13: "When the Way prevails in the world, [the principled scholar] appears; when the Way is lacking, he retires" (Watson, *The Analects of Confucius*, 55–56).

In a higher category, have there not been people like Tao Hongjing and his ilk, who aspired to become divine immortals and depart the human world?[3] Or others like Lu Lianzi, whose bodies roamed beyond the phenomenal world and whose hearts were intent on succoring humanity?[4] What about people like Zhuang Zhou, Yan Guang, Tao Yuanming, Shao Yong, and Chen Tuan, whose aspirations knew no bounds and who would submit to no one?[5] I hold that although [these men] went into seclusion physically, their minds certainly never went into reclusion. This type of recluse may be characterized as lofty, but not quite great. That [designation] applies only to a person of the caliber of Ruan Ji:[6] someone capable of taking both mind and body into reclusion, "leaving behind nothing for the common people to acclaim."[7]

Indeed! Great recluses may dwell in [bustling] cities and at court: Dongfang Shuo is an example.[8] Whereas Ruan was a great recluse, his reclusion was tainted by the fact that he deliberately fled reputation and never fully abandoned the outward signs of reclusion. I say that Ruan wanted, but failed, to accomplish what Dongfang and Feng Dao did.[9] Feng Dao was truly one of those for whom nothing is impermissible.

TRANSLATED BY RIVI HANDLER-SPITZ

3. Tao Hongjing 陶弘景 (456–536) lived in reclusion on Mount Juqu, where he conducted research on the medicinal properties of plants and refused several invitations to join the government. See *LZQJZ* 3:221.
4. The Warring States period recluse Lu Lianzi 魯連子 was unwilling to take office, yet he nonetheless traveled from state to state giving rulers strategic advice. See *LZQJZ* 3:221.
5. Zhuang Zhou 莊周 is the Daoist philosopher Zhuangzi; Yan Guang 嚴光 was a scholar of the Eastern Han dynasty who declined an invitation to serve as an adviser at court, preferring to live in reclusion on Mount Fuchun; Tao Yuanming 陶淵明 (365–427) was a poet during the Eastern Jin dynasty who several times abandoned minor governmental posts and lived out his days in reclusion; Shao Yong 邵雍 (1011–1077) was a neo-Confucian philosopher of the Northern Song dynasty who was deeply influenced by Daoism. He turned down offers to take office, preferring to study mysticism outside Luoyang. Chen Tuan 陳摶 (d. 989) was a Daoist sage who, having failed to pass the imperial examination, lived on Mounts Wudang and Hua. Biographies of all these figures appear in *A Book to Keep (Hidden)*; see *LZQJZ* 3:222.
6. Ruan Ji 阮籍 (210–263), to whom Li Zhi refers by his sobriquet, Sizong 嗣宗, was one of the Seven Sages of the Bamboo Grove; he absented himself from court so as to avoid becoming involved in intrigue and instead to focus on art, nature, and the enjoyment of wine.
7. See *Analects* 8:1 (Watson, *The Analects of Confucius*, 54).
8. Dongfang Shuo 東方朔 (154 B.C.E.–93 B.C.E.) was an entertainer in the court of Emperor Wu of Han. Even in his own lifetime his humorous and at times outrageous behavior earned him the reputation of someone who, paradoxically, cared nothing for his reputation. His biography is included in *A Book to Keep (Hidden)*.
9. Living in a period of disunity, Feng Dao 馮道 (882–954) served in prominent positions in the governments of several successive dynasties. Yet Li Zhi enrolls him among the recluses. Paradoxically, Li reasons, although many scorned Feng for his opportunism, the fact that Feng refused to pursue a reputation enabled him to embody most fully the spirit of reclusion. The memorial that the imperial censor Zhang Wenda submitted to the Wanli emperor impeaching Li Zhi cites Li's views on Feng Dao as an example of Li's outrageous and incendiary opinions. See pp. 334–37.

"HOW THE THREE TEACHINGS LEAD BACK TO CONFUCIANISM"
三教歸儒說
"SAN JIAO GUI RU SHUO"

Although this essay[1] is found in *Another Book to Burn*, it first appeared in *Chutan ji* (Upon arrival at the lake), a book Li began in Macheng and published in 1588. The essay grew from reflections and marginal notes on a collection of passages and anecdotes that Li compiled to engage each of the "three teachings"—Confucianism, Daoism, and Buddhism—separately. These three teachings were often seen as convergent in Li's time, and the Taizhou school recognized commonality of intent among them.[2] The essay seems inspired largely by Li's frustration with the fraudulent and careerist Confucianism of his day but also by the hopeful thought that the teachings—taken together—might reveal the uncorrupted spiritual pursuit that "authentic" Confucianism shared with Buddhism and Daoism.

In Li's view, the success of Confucianism as an orthodox political philosophy contributed to its undoing as a teaching that had originally sought to hear the Way. As Confucianism became a path to political influence and the emoluments of official life, and as its teachings were reinterpreted by "Confucians" who were concerned primarily with wealth and status, true Confucianism became corrupted, cut off, and lost—a degenerative process that Li identifies as starting with the death of Confucius's favorite disciple, Yan Hui. The essay therefore hinges on the distinction Li sees between the vital and sincere quest to hear the Dao (or the Way) that all three schools had originally pursued and the School of Principle (also known as the school of the Study of the Way [*daoxue* 道學]), which had come to refer in name only to what the three teachings had originally sought.

---

1. *XFS, j.* 2, in *LZQJZ* 3:223–24; cf. *Chutan ji, j.* 11, in *LZQJZ* 12:310–11.
2. For a more detailed introduction to this topic, see Brook, "Rethinking Syncretism."

Ultimately, Li finds that the Buddha was unique in seeing the true danger of wealth and status, and so he sees in Buddhism the only recourse to recovering the fundamental Way that Confucius also sought. The term "transcending the world" (*chu shi* 出世) refers to what Li sees as an essential means to attaining the Way: one must disentangle oneself from the traps of wealth and influence. In a Buddhist context, however, this same term also means "to enter monastic life," a role Li experimented with as he sought to recover Confucian truths. (DL)

Confucianism, Daoism, and Buddhism are one in that they all originally sought to hear the Way. Only after one hears the Way is one ready to die. Therefore [Confucius] said, "If one is able to hear the Way in the morning, one may die in the evening without regret."[3] If one has not heard the Way, then one *may not* yet die. Thus [when Confucius also said [to Yan Hui], "I thought you had died," [Yan replied, "While you were alive, how would I presume to die?"][4]

Since Confucius's intent lay in hearing the Way, he regarded wealth and status as mere "drifting clouds."[5] Shun relinquished the kingdom to Yu as if he were casting off a "worn-out shoe."[6] And yet by calling wealth and status "drifting clouds" [Confucius] only meant to trivialize them; by likening the kingship to a "worn-out shoe," [Mencius] merely meant to disprize it. They did not regard these things as harmful.

Or consider the Daoists, who view wealth and status as so much shit and filth and see rulership as fetters and cangues—their only fear is of not ridding themselves [of such unwelcome troubles] quickly enough. Shit and filth stink, fetters and cangues are burdensome, but they are still not terribly harmful.

---

3. *Analects* 4.8; Legge, *The Chinese Classics*, 1:168.
4. *Analects* 11.22; Legge, *The Chinese Classics*, 1:245. Since Yan Hui still yearned to hear the Way from his master, he could not have died under the circumstances.
5. *Analects* 7.15; Legge, *The Chinese Classics*, 1:200, modified: "The Master said, 'With coarse rice to eat, with water to drink, and my bended arm for a pillow;—I have still joy in the midst of these things. Wealth and status acquired by unrighteousness are to me as drifting clouds."
6. Alluding to *Mencius* 7A35: "Shun looked upon casting aside the kingdom as no more than discarding a worn-out shoe" (modified from Lau, *Mencius*, 303). Given the centrality of the *Mencius* to neo-Confucian education, this anecdote about Shun would have been familiar, but it is not clear that Li here expressly intends to rely on the authority of Mencius.

The Buddha, however, was even more emphatic: he thought we should regard wealth and status as tigers and panthers see pitfalls, as fish and birds view nets, or as people consider the prospect of being boiled or roasted alive—as disasters that leave one able neither to choose death nor to escape. In such vehemence he was unique.

This is how the Confucians, Daoists, and Buddhists differ, and yet they are the same in that their hope of hearing the Way led them to transcend the world. Only by transcending the world can one avoid the suffering of wealth and status.

When Yao proposed to hand the kingdom to Shun, he feared only that Shun would wash his ears [of the offending offer and indignantly refuse].[7] It was a great stroke of luck for Yao to get [Shun as] his replacement, since Shun ought to have refused [the kingdom] and fled: Yao had worried only that he might not get his wish. Shun was no better than Yao at ruling the kingdom, so it wasn't for the sake of the people that Yao relinquished his position. This is most abundantly clear.

When Confucius ate coarse rice and Yan Hui lived in a humble alleyway, were they not one in spirit with Yao?[8] After Yan Hui passed away, Confucius's subtle words were cut short, sagely learning died out, and [genuine] Confucianism was no longer transmitted.[9] This is why Confucius said, "Heaven is destroying me!"[10] Why so? Because even though all his remaining disciples were learned, they didn't regard "hearing the Way" as the heart of their concern, so what was left to prevent them from being led astray by the wealth and status they gained by serving powerful nobles?[11] And having strayed this far, what could have prevented the extrinsic additions of the Han Confucians and the contortions of the Song

---

7. As did the hermit Xu You in a similar circumstance; see *Zhuangzi*, ch. 1.
8. "Coarse rice" again alludes to *Analects* 7:15. "Humble alleyway" comes from *Analects* 6:9: "The Master said, 'Admirable indeed was the virtue of Hui! With a single bamboo dish of rice, a single gourd dish of drink, and living in his humble alleyway, while others could not have endured this distress, he did not allow his joy to be affected by it. Admirable indeed was the virtue of Hui!'" (modified from Legge, *The Chinese Classics*, 1:188).
9. Paraphrasing *Han shu*, *j.* 30, "Yiwen zhi" 藝文志 [Record of arts and letters].
10. *Analects* 11:8: "When [Yan Hui] died, the Master said, 'Alas! Heaven is destroying me! Heaven is destroying me!'" (Legge, *The Chinese Classics*, 1:239).
11. Confucius as portrayed in the *Analects* regarded complete devotion to the ethical ideal of the Way as a prerequisite to any political action. Whether this prerequisite was in actuality met or not, early Confucian disciples sought to serve in administrative and advisory roles. Confucianism became inextricably entwined with political life when it was adopted as the Han state ideology in 136 B.C.E. The "extrinsic additions" Li Zhi objects to here also include the cosmological backing for imperial rule, added by such syncretic Confucians as Dong Zhongshu.

Confucians?[12] And having strayed this much further, what could then have prevented us from making the Song Confucians our paragons and taking their contortions as our compass bearing?[13] People grow ever more base and customs sink ever lower! No wonder we have continued our steady decline to the present, in which people outwardly profess to engage in the Study of the Way and inwardly prize wealth and status; they cloak and gown themselves in Confucian dignity yet comport themselves like dogs and swine!

This age has no dearth of people who have achieved fame, honor, wealth, and status without ever professing the Study of the Way. So why must one profess the Study of the Way in order to gain wealth and status? For no other reason than this: those who achieve wealth and status on their own, without professing the Study of the Way, must be people of learning, talent, achievements, and integrity. To deny such people wealth and status would be futile. But as for those who lack talent and learning, unless they make themselves known by invoking the prestige of the Sage and the Study of the Way, they'll be poor and lowly all their lives. What a shame! This is why people *must* profess the Study of the Way in order to attain wealth and status! Thus today, those with no talent, no learning, no accomplishments, and no insight, who wish to achieve great wealth and status, have absolutely no choice but to profess adherence to the Study of the Way. And those today who *truly* wish to discuss the study of the Way—to grasp the point of the Confucian, Daoist, and Buddhist transcendence of the world and avoid the suffering of wealth and status—have absolutely no choice but to shave their heads and live as monks!

TRANSLATED BY DAVID LEBOVITZ

---

12. The neo-Confucianism of Zhu Xi and the Cheng brothers is here accused of contortion, of literally "drilling holes" in the text, or pursuing refinements of doctrine that distracted from the main point.
13. "Compass bearing" here refers literally to "that which indicates the route back" (*zhi gui* 指歸) and echoes the phrase "lead back" (*gui*) in the title; it could also be rendered as "guide" or "standard."

"AFTER ŚĀKYAMUNI BUDDHA"
釋迦佛後
"SHIJIAFO HOU"

This piece[1] was written in 1600, as Li Zhi reflected on his visit to Confucius's ancestral temple and burial grounds in Jinan, near present-day Qufu in Shandong. Li marveled that the grounds and temple could endure even as cities rose and fell around them. What he would have seen at the "Confucian Forest [Cemetery]," or Kong Lin, was not only the grave mound of Confucius (Kong Qiu) but also the graves of Confucius's son Kong Li and his grandson Kong Ji 孔伋. Kong Ji, also known as Zisi 子思, was an important early Confucian figure in his own right, said to have passed his teaching on to Mencius and to have authored the *Doctrine of the Mean*, one of the Four Books forming the core of the neo-Confucian doctrinal program. The experience gave him a clear sense of Confucius's enduring mark on humanity, or what he calls "the measure of [a person's] insight."

The essay pivots on Li's juxtaposition of the mode of transmission and the model of personhood embodied at the Confucian Forest with the modes and models employed in Buddhist traditions. As a transmitter of Zhou ritual norms, Confucius helped to keep individual, hereditary cults at the center of Chinese ritual life, and he is also known for compiling the textual legacy of the Zhou that subsequently became enshrined as the orthodox canon from the Han dynasty on. In contrast, Buddhists who took the tonsure severed their ties to family, state, and flesh; there was no textual transmission in the generations after Śākyamuni, and Chan likewise deemphasized written traditions in favor of mind-to-mind transmission. In this essay, Li expressly compares the transmissive power of Buddhist robe relics with the transmitted potency that awed him at the Confucian Forest. Although his writings elsewhere indicate that Li saw in Buddhism

---

1. *XFS, j.* 4, in *LZQJZ* 3:291–94.

PART III: MISCELLANEOUS WRITINGS 雜書   283

an indispensible conduit to lost Confucian truths,[2] his experience at Jinan sheds light on his impulse to recover those truths. (DL)

Śākyamuni Buddha lectured on the dharma for forty-nine years and ultimately didn't leave a single written word to Kāśyapa.[3] And it might have remained [wordless] for the thousand years until Bodhidharma came east, [determined] "not to establish written texts."[4] But instead Kāśyapa rashly left Ānanda in charge of compiling texts, and so the religious jargon of the Three Storehouses[5] came into being, befouling the stream of transmission for all posterity. Alas!

When Śākyamuni "handed down his mantle," he didn't hand down his ways—what he transmitted to the next Buddha-to-be was [literally just] his robes, not his dharma teaching. Those who transmitted the robes transmitted them to the next Buddha-to-be, and in all this transmitting of things to the next Buddha-to-be, even if we concentrated a thousand billion aeons into one aeon, or a thousand billion lifetimes into one lifetime—[the sum of what was transmitted] still can't compare with what one man could transmit to his son and grandson within a single lifetime.[6] This being so, how can we ever know the true measure of [Śākyamuni's] insights?

---

2. See "How the Three Teachings Lead Back to Confucianism" and "An Inscription for the Image of Confucius in the Cloister of the Flourishing Buddha," pp. 278–81, 289–90.
3. Kāśyapa is the disciple of Śākyamuni Buddha regarded in Chan as the primary heir to the dharma teaching. After the death of the Buddha, Kāśyapa convened an assembly of arhats to account for the Buddha's words, and he charged another of the Buddha's disciples, Ānanda (known for his superhuman memory), with reciting Śākyamuni's sermons from memory at the First Buddhist Council. See Lopez and Buswell, *Princeton Dictionary*, s.v. "Council, 1st."
4. Bodhidharma (Putidamo 菩提達摩) is known as the founding patriarch of the Zen tradition in China. Bodhidharma came from India in the late fourth or early fifth century. He is known for meditating facing a wall for nine years and for mind-to-mind, rather than textual, transmission. Li Zhi here alludes to the popular Chan idea that "transmission occurs outside the [written] teaching; do not set down written texts." For the saying, see Ma, *Wenxian tongkao* 225.15a.
5. Ānanda's recollection of the Buddha's sermons are linked here to the eventual formation of the Three Storehouses, or Tripiṭaka (Three Baskets), textual canon. The canon collects (1) the sutras, (2) *vinaya* texts (monastic rules), and (3) the *abhidharma* texts (which analyze and interpret Buddhist theory and doctrine).
6. Li alludes to two types of robe transmission. In the first, according to early Buddhist traditions, the dharma taught by the Buddha would degenerate and disappear in cycles that lasted for innumerable aeons. The second signified transmission of the dharma from Zen patriarch to patriarch. Within Chan, the robe was often traced back generation by generation to Śākyamuni himself. The "one man" here who provides the contrastive model of transmission to sons and grandsons is Confucius, who transmitted his wisdom to his son Kong Li and grandson Zisi.

I found myself once on the waters of the Ji [near Jining], and on a whim decided to pay my respects at the Master's temple. I climbed to the Apricot Altar,[7] entered the Confucian Forest [Cemetery], and there I saw junipers and cypresses that crowd the sky—[trees] in which flying birds dare not perch. Stem by stem and trunk by trunk, every flower and tree there is accounted for. No thorns sprout there, nor do weeds grow: clearly, it is the true sagacity of the Sage [Confucius] that keeps the flora so fragrant and fresh and wards off the nesting and chatter of magpies! When a man's ultimate virtue is manifest in his person, rivers and mountains numinously mimic his essence, such that ghosts and spirits naturally come to bless and protect him. Is it just that the crass and impercipient morons who disbelieve this simply have never set foot here? How profoundly blind they are!

Over two thousand years have passed since Confucius's time, but his descendants are still resting peacefully in the glow of his sagely beneficence. What's more, where Confucius's grave mound rises up, flanked by those of his son Li and grandson Ji, the sacrificial platters and goblets have never failed to be brought—ever since the Zhou dynasty, throughout the Qin, Han, Tang, Song, Yuan, and up until today.[8] If it's like this today, it's clear it will carry on likewise for a thousand billion aeons. Isn't this ultimately the measure of a great sage's insight! So what is there [for the Confucians] to envy in Buddhism and Śākyamuni?

Dang Huaiying 黨懷英 (1134–1211) of the Yuan dynasty wrote,

The traces of Lu endure—fallen, faint, and indistinct;
woods and temple alone remain; Licheng lies in waste.[9]
On the temple's plum-wood spine, rosy clouds of dawn alight;
pine portals harbor the lingering beams of spring moons returning.
These ancient cypresses once drank the rain and dew of Zhou
and broken stelae still bear the writings of the Han.

---

7. "The Old Fisherman" (Yufu) chapter of *Zhuangzi* relates an anecdote in which Confucius sits down at the Apricot Altar and strums the zither while his disciples study (Watson, *Chuang Tzu*, 344). The name was later given to a memorial temple rebuilt by the forty-fifth-generation descendant of Confucius and planted with apricot trees. See *LZQJZ* 3:293.
8. For an early account of the grave site, mourning activities, and visits to the site, see Sima Qian, *Shi ji*, ch. 17, "The Hereditary House of Confucius," partially translated in Csikszentmihalyi, *Readings*, 89–93.
9. Licheng designated the area surrounding the temple and woods.

One need no longer ask if this lineage will persist:
So Mount Tai reaches Heaven; so the rivers Wen and Si flow on . . .

Exactly! These words merit reflection: who else has endured through the ages of Zhou, Qin, Han, Tang, Song, and Yuan?

TRANSLATED BY DAVID LEBOVITZ

"DISTRIBUTION OF WORK ASSIGNMENTS IN THE SANGHA"
列眾僧職事
"LIE ZHONGSENG ZHISHI"

This essay[1] strongly suggests that by 1593 not only was the Cloister of the Flourishing Buddha thriving in its ability to attract novice monks but also that this influx of new personnel not fully acclimated to the organizational structure and discipline required of monastic life precipitated its own set of challenges.[2] The essay opens with a discussion of the need for precept masters to better monitor those under their supervision and to distribute work assignments equitably. The redistribution of work assignments carried out by senior monks likely corrected some organizational deficiencies. Li did not participate in this process. However, as this essay indicates, he offered advice. His essay first describes the situation and then adds words of exhortation advocating ways to improve relations among the monks and encourage greater diligence in attention to work assignments.

This essay describes in familial terms the relations among monks. Being celibate, monks cannot honor their filial obligation to continue the family line through marriage and the birth of a son. However, as exhibited in this essay, monastic organizations formed their own "families" and co-opted the language of lineage. For example, the monk Changrong, mentioned in the first paragraph, was a disciple of Wunian Shenyou's, a fully ordained monk. Wunian's

---

1. XFS, j. 4, in LZQJZ 3:300–302.
2. In a 1593 essay, Li claims there are more than forty monks in residence, each of whom had accepted disciples, who in turn had also accepted disciples (Li Zhi, "Anqi gao zhong wen" 安期告眾文 [A notification to the monastic community written during the rain-retreat period], in FS, j. 4, in LZQJZ 2:44–45). In an essay written in 1594, Li says that there are thirty to forty monk disciples and grandson disciples living at the monastery who viewed him as their great father and mother (da fumu 大父母), implying that they accepted him as their master. This claim reinforces the idea that monastic communities mirrored familial ones in both their hierarchical structure and affective relations (Li Zhi, "Qiongtu shuo" 窮途說 [An explanation of difficult circumstances], in XFS, j. 4, in LZQJZ 3:210–11).

disciples all have the word *chang* in their dharma names, signifying that they share the same lineage master. Changrong's older and younger dharma brothers constitute one generation. Each of them likely also accepted disciples. The concern in this essay is with how to maintain good relations among three generations living under one roof. The focus is especially on the grandson disciples of Wunian—that is, the disciples Changrong and his dharma brothers have brought in as their own lineage heirs. Li displays concern over the ways in which these grandsons both treat one another and interact with the monk brothers of their specific lineage master, or what we might call their uncle monks.

A few words are in order with respect to the vocabulary used in this essay. Lineage masters are so called because they formally accept disciples and confer precepts upon them. Lineage masters may also be called preceptors. They further take on the roles of teaching and monitoring their followers. Their disciples would have adopted the ten novice precepts, yet it is unclear from the context here whether any of them were fully ordained monks. (JE)

Our monastic community takes recitation of the name Amitābha Buddha as its primary task. In what concerns all daily tasks, senior monks naturally continue, as in the past, to labor diligently; they are unstinting in their endurance of hard work. In contrast, younger monks,[3] all of whom are the great assembly's disciples and grand-disciples, will not labor tirelessly unless their lineage masters monitor them. As a result, those who eat are many, yet those who toil are few. And even those who desire not to neglect their duties cannot help shirking them. Today the monk Changrong already discussed this with the assembled teachers. He allotted and distributed official duties, which should clear up this problem and lessen the labor of wagging tongues.

However, I would like to emphasize the following: since there are many people here and they all have different preceptors, if the preceptors can

---

3. It was not uncommon in the late Ming for mature men to take the tonsure after having raised a family. Monastic seniority was determined by years since ordination, not age. In this respect, much older men could be novice disciples of younger monks.

strictly control their disciples and show no hint of favoritism toward their own, then when any of the disciples meet the older and younger brothers of their precept master, they will venerate these "uncle preceptors" even more deeply than their own lineage master. Under these circumstances, [the young monks] will naturally come together as one body, united in doing good, without the slightest irregularity.

Those who reside amid the monastery fields endure ten times the hardship of others. The great assembly should especially venerate them. Those monks who lead others when reciting scripture and are renowned for their virtuous conduct—these monks, along with the [administrative] leaders of the monastery, are called monastic treasures.[4]

Hearing of these changes will inspire outsiders' confidence and gentlemen's admiration. When this monastery achieves this level of reform, it will garner greater respect. However, when members of the younger generation completely disrespect other monks, the fault lies with their lineage masters. If they do not understand what is considered acceptable behavior, then how can everyone live together? When it comes to this, the seeds of hell beings are sown and the karma of an animal rebirth is generated—retributions for which one need not wait another day or year. The senior monks at our monastery were not initially inattentive. However, since there are so many monks, we must guard against such problems by explaining the precepts.

There are many monks here, though the monastery is small. From now on the monastery will not permit anyone to accept a single additional disciple or grand-disciple. Should there be those who hear of our reputation and come, "thinking nothing of a journey of one thousand *li*,"[5] I myself can serve as their teacher.

This [list of regulations] is not exhaustive.

TRANSLATED BY JENNIFER EICHMAN

---

4. The term translated here as "monastic treasures" is *sengbao* 僧寶 (literally, "monk treasure" or "monk jewel") and is usually found in the context of the Buddhist list of the Three Jewels, the Buddha, dharma, and sangha. In that context the Three Jewels are objects of veneration and trust. Many Buddhist practitioners regularly profess their trust by formally taking refuge in the Buddha, dharma, and sangha.
5. *Mencius* 1A1.

"AN INSCRIPTION FOR THE IMAGE OF CONFUCIUS IN THE CLOISTER OF THE FLOURISHING BUDDHA"
題孔子像於芝佛院
"TI KONGZI XIANG YU ZHIFO YUAN"

This essay[1] was likely written in 1588, the year Li Zhi's wife died and Li moved to the Cloister of the Flourishing Buddha. Playing on his frequent theme of the need to break free of sedimented customary beliefs, Li captures a seemingly mundane occasion—a gentleman-scholar invited to add an inscription to a commemorative portrait of Confucius—and only in the very last paragraph radically alters our perspective on the meaning of the homage he has just performed. This writing form, the *xiaopin*—an informal, witty, short essay that became popular in the late Ming—is one in which Li Zhi excelled. (PCL)

People all consider Confucius to have been a great sage. I too believe he was a great sage. Everybody believes that Laozi and the Buddha were heretics. I too think of them as heretics. The masses do not really understand the difference between a great sage and a heretic. This is because they have become accustomed to certain ideas by listening to the teachings of their fathers and teachers. But then, fathers and teachers do not really understand the difference between a great sage and a heretic, because these fathers and teachers have become accustomed to listening to the teachings of prior Confucians. Moreover, the prior Confucians did not really understand the difference between a great sage and a heretic. They just based their opinions on what Confucius said.

When Confucius said, "As for being a sage, I am not able to become one," this was because of his modesty.[2] When he said, "Rushing into heretical

---

1. *XFS, j.* 4, in *LZQJZ* 3:309–10.
2. *Mencius* 2A2.

causes is a cause of great misfortune," he was undoubtedly speaking of Laozi and the Buddha.[3]

The Confucians of antiquity interpreted Confucius conjecturally; our fathers and teachers recited these conjectures and passed them down, and young children listen to them as if blind and deaf. When ten thousand mouths all utter the same phrase, none can counter what is said; when for a thousand years there is only a single standard, no one can come to understand the world for himself. Nobody says, "I merely chant the *words* of Confucius." Instead they claim, "I understand Confucius himself." Nobody says, "I distort what I do not know to make it seem as if I know it." Instead they say, "What you know, declare that you know it."[4] So that today, although people possess eyes, nobody uses them.

What kind of a person am I to dare say that I have eyes? I too follow the masses. Not only do I follow the masses and consider Confucius to be a sage, but I also follow the masses and pay respects to him. And so, I follow the masses and pay respects to Confucius in the Cloister of the Flourishing Buddha.

TRANSLATED BY PAULINE C. LEE

---

3. *Analects* 2.16.
4. Ibid., 2.17.

"MASTER LI ZHUOWU'S TESTAMENT"
李卓吾先生遺言
"LI ZHUOWU XIANSHENG YIYAN"

In 1602, suffering from political attacks and weakened by severe illness, Li Zhi sensed that his death was close at hand. From the home of his friend and patron Ma Jinglun, where he had been residing since the previous year, Li composed this testament[1] instructing his disciples precisely how to bury him. The document, which was circulated to Jiao Hong and others, is striking for its level of detail. His insistence on cleanliness and his resistance to any ostentation have led some scholars to ask whether Li's preferences may have been influenced by Muslim burial rituals. There is evidence that at least one of Li's seafaring ancestors married a Muslim woman, and several of Li's relatives professed the Muslim faith; however, Li does not mention Islam explicitly in his writings.[2]

At the end of the testament, Chen Dalai, a printer in Nanjing, appended a historical notice, purportedly at the insistence of Li's acquaintance Tao Shikui 陶石簣 (1562–1609).[3] The notice summarizes the circumstances under which Li Zhi died and confirms that Ma Jinglun buried his friend in compliance with Li's specifications.[4] (RHS)

Since spring I've often been ill and ardently wished to die. Luckily, if I die here, I'll have the privilege of dying in the company of a dear friend.[5] This

---

1. XFS, j. 4, in LZQJZ 3:314–17. For an alternative translation of this essay, see Yu, "Testament," 262.
2. Pei-kai Cheng, "Reality and Imagination," 92. For a more detailed discussion of Islamic culture in late imperial China, see Ben-Dor Benite, *The Dao of Muhammad*.
3. LZQJZ 1:1.
4. For a more detailed description of the plot of land Ma Jinglun prepared for Li's burial, see Li Zhi, "Shu yiyan hou" 書遺言後 [Codicil to my testament], in XFS, j. 5, in LZQJZ 3:296–97.
5. Li Zhi is referring to Ma Jinglun. For more on Ma, see "Written at the End of Yuan Zhongdao's Hand Scroll," p. 268n2.

is what I cherish most. You monks too must appreciate how important it is. As soon as I should die, select a plot of land on a hillside beyond the village and make a pit on the south-facing slope. Let it be ten feet long, five feet wide, and six feet deep. It must be exactly this deep, this wide, and this long. Inside this pit, dig a hollow in which to lay my body to rest: let it be two feet, five inches deep, not more than six and a half feet long, and not more than two feet, five inches wide. Once you've dug two feet, five inches deep, level the floor with five reed mats and lay me peacefully upon them. How could there be the slightest impurity in this? If my mind is at rest [that you have followed these instructions faithfully], I'll be in paradise.

In carrying out these instructions, do not follow common customs or be swayed by what people may say. Do not, in your eagerness to appear respectable, deviate from my original wishes. Even if Ma Jinglun is able to provide an extravagant funeral, it would be better that you put my mind to rest. These words of mine are of the utmost importance. As soon as my vital energy dissipates, prepare the pit in which to rest my remains.

Before you set me in the pit, lay out my body on a plank. Let me be dressed in whatever clothing I am wearing; do not change me into fresh clothes. That would disturb my spirit. But place a veil over my face, rest my head on a pillow as usual, and cover my entire body with a white shroud. Use foot-wrapping cloth[6] to bind me from head to toe.[7] Have four strong men lay me out flat, and as soon as the fifth watch has sounded and the temple door has been opened, carry me silently out to the grave site. Place me upon the reed mats, then return the plank to its owner.

Once my body has been laid to rest, cover the pit with twenty or thirty horizontal beams. On top of the beams, place another five reed mats. Then replace the original earth, and tamp it down flat. On top of that, add a layer of topsoil so as to indicate that here rests the soul of Master Zhuowu. On all sides plant trees, and in front of the grave erect a stone stele inscribed with the words "The Grave of Master Li Zhuowu." Let the inscription be four feet high. You may entrust Jiao Hong with writing the calligraphy. I doubt he will decline.

If you desire to maintain the grave site, put your whole heart into it. If indeed you put your heart into it, then the good Ma [Jinglun] will surely provide for you. Have no doubt! But if you truly wish to have nothing more

---

6. No relation to female foot-binding: men wrapped their feet to provide a protective sock layer under their shoes.
7. The text says literally "to wrap me in the shape of the character 廿."

to do with me, then you may go as you please. In life I did not insist that my family members accompany me; dead, I do not expect them to look after me. This should be clear.

Please do not alter a single word of this testament, written by Zhuowu on the fifth day of the second month. Please follow it! Please follow it!

[Notice:]

It's told that Master Tao [Shikui] said, "In the third month Old Zhuo met with trouble and eventually died in a detention cell. The memorial that had been submitted to the emperor had not yet received a response.[8] Those in attendance [Ma Jinglun and associates] dug a pit and buried him. Its depth, length, and width—even the reed-mat covering—were all arranged exactly according to his specifications. He had planned for every detail. Who could say he lacked foresight?" Please record this so that his intent may be known.

TRANSLATED BY RIVI HANDLER-SPITZ

---

8. For details on Li's imprisonment and death, see the introduction, p. xvi, and Zhang Wenda's memorial, pp. 334–37.

PART IV
POETRY 詩

"ON READING DU FU (TWO POEMS)"
讀杜少陵二首
"DU DU SHAOLING ER SHOU"

I

Du Fu was the first to understand[1]
how to express the spirit:
The instant he felt real homesickness,
he wrote the truth of it.
It's not that all the others
lacked great inspiration,
But even with great inspiration
they still don't startle you.[2]

---

1. *XFS, j.* 5, in *LZQJZ* 3:353–54. Shaoling was one of the style names used by Du Fu 杜甫, one of the greatest poets in Chinese literary history.
2. This line alludes to a famous couplet by Du Fu on his passion for composing poetry: "I'm an eccentric sort of person, captivated by fine lines; / until my language is startling, I'd sooner die than give up" (Jiang shang zhi shui ru hai shi liao duan shu 江上至水入海勢聊短述 [On the river, I came upon waters surging like the ocean: For now, I give this short account]); translated, with commentary, in Cai, *Chinese Poetry*, 184–86.

SELECTIONS FROM *ANOTHER BOOK TO BURN* (*XU FENSHU* 續焚書)

II

Beset, impoverished, indignant, melancholy—
no wonder his sorrow was so deep.
When he opens his mouth to speak,
tears drench his clothes.
His heptasyllabic songs
are rare even among the ancients.
His pentasyllabic sonnets
make the most beautiful music.

TRANSLATED BY TIMOTHY BILLINGS AND YAN ZINAN

WATCHING THE ARMY AT THE EAST GATE OF THE CITY
觀兵城東門
GUAN BING CHENG DONGMEN

How dare these island barbarians[1] provoke the heavenly army?
Today I watch soldiers in fish formation head for the border.

If Zhong You were ever to hear about all this,
He would tie his cap string[2] and run straight into the fray.[3]

TRANSLATED BY TIMOTHY BILLINGS AND YAN ZINAN

---

1. Composed in 1597, this poem is in *XFS, j.* 5, in *LZQJZ* 3:354–55. "Island barbarians" refers to the Japanese.
2. This is an allusion to a story about Zhong You 仲由 (542 B.C.E.–480 B.C.E.), a famous disciple of Confucius's better known by his style name, Zilu 子路. When he received a mortal blow from a halberd in battle, which also cut the string of his cap, he said, "When a gentleman dies, he does not let his cap fall off," then tied his cap string and died. See Sima Qian, *Shi ji*, ch. 67, "Confucius's Disciples," in Nienhauser, *The Grand Scribe's Records*, 7:69. The term "to tie the cap strings" (*jieying* 結纓) has therefore come to signify bravery in battle and fearlessness toward death.
3. The "fray" here is literally "the king's capital" (*wangjing* 王京), the capital city of the imperial state that would become Korea three centuries later (present-day Seoul).

AMITĀBHA TEMPLE
彌陀寺
MITUO SI

I stop my boat to ask someone[1]
The way to Amitābha Temple
Just as a dark haze shrouds the sun
With yellow sand, beyond this willow.

The willow doesn't understand
My thoughts have traveled far ahead
And holds me back as if to show
Its green against my whitened head.

TRANSLATED BY TIMOTHY BILLINGS AND YAN ZINAN

---

1. XFS, j. 5, in LZQJZ 3:355–56. Composed in 1601 in Renqiu in modern-day Hebei province. The implication of the poem is that he has moored his boat to the willow. "Willow" (liu 柳) is homophonous with "stay" (liu 留) and thus often appears in poems of departure.

READING THE RESIGNATION MEMORIAL OF GU CHONG'AN
讀顧沖庵辭疏
DU GU CHONG'AN CISHU

For literary talent and military strategy,[1]
you are a paragon of the age,
But to be honored after thousands of miles,
your luck never came through.

The eaters of flesh have almost always
seen only with eyes of flesh,
So what you've been given now is the chance
to smash to bits a copper spittoon.[2]

TRANSLATED BY TIMOTHY BILLINGS AND YAN ZINAN

---

1. *XFS, j.* 5, in 3:363–64. Composed in 1594 in Macheng. Chong'an was one of the courtesy names of Gu Yangqian 顧養謙 (1537–1604). After proposing a withdrawal of troops fighting against the Japanese in the Korean Peninsula, Gu was forced to step down from his position as supreme commander of the Ji and Liao regions because his opinion was extremely unpopular at court.
2. "Eaters of flesh" derives from *Zuozhuan* (Zhuang, year 10): "The flesh-eaters [i.e., military officials] are poor creatures, and cannot form any far-reaching plans," says a villager contemptuously (and goes on to advise the duke on the battlefield, successfully repelling an invasion by the state of Qi). See Legge, *The Chinese Classics*, 5:85–86. The phrase "to smash a spittoon" (*jisui tuohu* 擊碎唾壺) may suggest either the indignation after a disappointment or, more positively, an enduring zeal for success, as exemplified by the ambitious General Wang Dun (266–324), who would pound spittoons so enthusiastically as he recited the poetry of General Cao Cao (155–220) that he would smash them to bits.

SPRING NIGHT
春夜
CHUN YE

I meditate the whole night long[1]
behind a thin curtain of rain.
I hold a candle and gaze intently—
spring is already lush.

If you have something to say,
just spit it out.
At the fifth watch, a rooster sings:
day is dawning.

TRANSLATED BY TIMOTHY BILLINGS AND YAN ZINAN

---

1. *XFS, j.* 5, in *LZQJZ* 3:364.

LISTENING TO THE CHANTING OF
THE LOTUS SUTRA
聽誦法華
TING SONG *FAHUA*

You can chant *The Lotus Sutra*[1]
three thousand times in full,
But with one word from Cao Creek,
you can forget it all.[2]

It's shameful how these sons grow up
with nothing underneath;
The Buddha's words are in their mouths,
but lies are in their teeth.[3]

TRANSLATED BY TIMOTHY BILLINGS AND YAN ZINAN

---

1. *XFS*, *j*. 5, in *LZQJZ* 3:375–76. Probably composed in 1600.
2. These two lines allude to a story about the seventh-century monk Fada 法達, who studied under Master Huineng 慧能 (638–713), commonly known as the Sixth Patriarch of the Zen sect of Buddhism. Fada claimed that he had chanted *The Lotus Sutra* three thousand times, but Huineng felt that Fada did not yet truly understand it and so helped him reach enlightenment partly through a meditative verse, or *gāthā*. Fada then composed a *gāthā* of his own on the occasion, which contains the lines, "The three thousand times I have chanted the sutra / Are forgotten with a word from [Huineng of] Cao Creek" (McRae, *Platform Sutra*, 59). Cao Creek was a river near the Precious Grove Temple, where Huineng lived and taught, and thus became a metonym for Master Huineng or the Southern school of Buddhism more generally.
3. Literally, "They speak the words of the Buddha, but they lie in their vestments." The translation gives the general idea, but the specifics are difficult to construe. Zhang Jianye argues that clothing (*yishang* 衣裳) refers to the *kāṣāya*, or Buddhist vestments, but the term has a rich range of metonymic senses from officials to the central state and even to the imperial court, any one of which may be at play here despite the obvious attack against the hypocrisy of certain Buddhists. If Li Zhi is satirizing those who only pretend to Buddhist morality while actually pursuing worldly riches as exemplified by their expensive clothing, we may translate the line as "The Buddha's words are belied by their dress."

EIGHT QUATRAINS FROM PRISON
系中八絕
XIZHONG BA JUE

Upon Reviving from My Chronic Illness[1]

I have traveled far and wide,
to the famous mountains, to the great gorges,
Yet this is the one place I had never seen,
the inside of these walls.
Between bouts of illness, I finally realize
I am in prison.
How many times has daylight come and gone?
How many times the twilight?

Floating Tufts of the Flowering Willow

The vital spirits are leaving my body
like horses at a gallop;[2]
Facing two doors, I cannot choose:
the one for life, or the one for death?
The lofting blossoms of the willow enter
the vision of the prisoner;
I'm starting to think the underworld
may have a springtime too.

---

1. *XFS, j.* 5, in *LZQJZ* 3:377–79. This series of quatrains was written in 1602 just before Li's death. Only seven of the eight poems survive, and the last completely disregards all tonal rules for the form.
2. Literally, "The Four Great Elemental Separations [*sida fenli* 四大分離] run like horses." According to Buddhist tradition, the process of death involves the separation or loss from the body of the four fundamental elements of earth, water, fire, and air, resulting in, respectively, brittle bones; bleeding, sweat, and incontinence; chills; and breathlessness.

Bright Moon in the Center of the Sky

For thousands of miles, without a home,
I lodge in villages as I travel,
A lonely soul who, after thousands of miles,
is locked out at the final door.
Lifting my gaze, I rejoice to see
in the dark heaven above
A huge disk of light that can shine even
inside an overturned tub.[3]

Wishing That My Books Be Carefully Read

In the old story, Master Zeng
could either be slain or spared,[4]
Yet if the one on high should pity him,
would he dare to die?
My only wish is that my books
be examined with meticulous care;
And inevitably, fully, it will be understood
they speak the truth.

The Power of Books to Lead Astray

Generations of people have mocked
those who are enthralled by books,
Who pass their lives for no reason
like virgin girls.[5]

---

3. The allusion refers to an injustice for which there can be no redress since light cannot shine inside an "overturned tub" (*fupen* 覆盆). In a hopeful twist, Li suggests that the emperor in his wisdom is capable of doing just that.
4. The allusion to Confucius's disciple Zeng Shen may refer to one of two stories. In one, Zeng submits to a beating by his father for a trivial mistake and dies of his wounds. Confucius criticizes him as unfilial, however, for allowing his father thus to become a murderer. In other words, it would be filial to submit to a beating but not to a lethal beating. In another famous story in the *Zhanguo ce* 戰國策 [Strategies of the Warring States], Zeng is rumored by so many people to have killed someone that even his mother finally begins to doubt his innocence even though he is utterly guiltless of any crime.
5. *Chunü* 處女 refers either to a woman confined modestly to the indoors or to an unmarried or sexually uninitiated girl.

But who in the world
does not read books?
The only thralls to books are those
who read till it brings them death.[6]

Lamenting My Failures in Old Age

The blazing sun fills my window,
but I have not yet risen;
I doze, and the dreams come one after another;
they know me as only a true friend can.
I think to myself: I am lazy. I am old.
And what have I accomplished?
As always before, I read books
and await the judgment of the emperor.

No Hero

"The man of high ideals never forgets
he may end in a ditch;
The man of great valor never forgets
he may forfeit his head."[7]
If I do not die today,
how much longer must I wait?
I yearn for the command soon to send me
back to the world beyond this one.

TRANSLATED BY TIMOTHY BILLINGS AND YAN ZINAN

---

6. The suggestion is that only subversive readers like Li Zhi, whose commentaries have landed him in prison with the threat of execution, can truly be called thralls to books (*shunu* 書奴).
7. These lines are a direct quotation of *Mencius* 3B1. The translation here is based on that by D. C. Lau: "A man whose mind is set on high ideals never forgets that he may end in a ditch; a man of valour never forgets that he may forfeit his head" (Lau, *Mencius*, 106).

SPRING RAIN ON A GREAT HOUSE
樓頭春雨
LOUTOU CHUN YU

The rain falls all night on the roof of the great house.[1]
The guest sighs with pleasure, his host with gratitude.

Imagine the mind of that midlands prodigy
Who could offer such kindness to a wanderer.

Thick clouds seal up the road ahead;
Rainwater tops up a fresh pot of tea.

On the day I head out on the road again
I know there will be a rosy glow at dawn.

TRANSLATED BY TIMOTHY BILLINGS AND YAN ZINAN

---

1. *XFS*, *j.* 5, in *LZQJZ* 3:380–81. Composed in 1601 for Ma Jinglun. In 1600, Li Zhi suffered persecution from Feng Yingjing (1555–1606), the assistant surveillance commissioner of Huguang province, who ordered a mob to destroy his temple lodging and preconstructed tomb at Macheng. Li Zhi fled for his safety and lodged at the Dharma Eye Temple on Mount Huangbo near Shangcheng in Henan province, where he met Ma Jinglun, who was visiting and studying there at the time. The next year, Ma Jinglun accompanied Li Zhi to the suburbs of Beijing. Not long afterward, he would bury Li's body in Tongzhou after his death in prison in 1602. See "Master Li Zhuowu's Testament," pp. 291–93.

MY FEELINGS UPON ASCENDING THE MOUNTAIN AND RECEIVING A LETTER FROM JIAO HONG
入山得焦弱侯書有感二首
RU SHAN DE JIAO RUOHOU SHU YOUGAN ER SHOU

I

As one who is easily moved, I have a lifetime of tears,[1]
But for the unforgettable, I have this letter from my old friend.

Three springtimes pass before the wild goose[2] casts its shadow;
One whole night is spent in my hut reading it over.[3]

The storm rages after a full cup of wine.
The pines seem now as they were once before.

Opening your letter is like seeing you before me,
But it's all just a dream. Or is it?[4]

II

"When true friends exist anywhere in the world,
The horizons themselves are like neighbors."[5]

---

1. *XFS, j.* 5, in *LZQJZ* 3:382–84. Composed in 1581. Ruohou is Jiao Hong's courtesy name.
2. "Wild goose" (*hongyan* 鴻雁) was a conventional metaphor for a letter arriving from afar.
3. Literally, "a night in Ziyun's hut." Ziyun 子雲 was the style name of Yang Xiong 揚雄 (ca. 53 B.C.E. –18 C.E.), whose hut was a conventional metaphor for the humble retreat of a learned scholar who had no desire to seek fame by serving in the imperial court.
4. In this linguistically clever line (*shi mengzhe fei yu* 是夢者非歟), only the word "dream" (*meng* 夢) is a so-called solid word (*shizi* 實字), a grammatical term for nouns, verbs, and adjectives, which have substantive meaning, whereas the remaining four characters are all "empty words" (*xuzi* 虛字)—i.e., syntactical function words such as conjunctions, interjections, prepositions, adverbs, and the like. The distinction between the two is not always precise, but the point is that the learned reader would recognize this line as more "empty" than "solid."
5. This couplet is a verbatim quotation of "Song Du shaofu zhi ren Shuzhou" 送杜少府之任蜀州 [Seeing off District Defender Du, who travels to take a post in Shuzhou], a poem by Wang Bo 王勃 (ca. 649–ca. 675).

The ancients were merely kidding themselves:
These words have never been true.

I study but find so many strange words.
I read but find so few wise masters.

Oh, when will we take up walking sticks again
For a drunken spring day together in old Nanjing?

TRANSLATED BY TIMOTHY BILLINGS AND YAN ZINAN

AFTER THE SNOW
雪後
XUE HOU

The snow has melted, but still no one comes.[1]
It must be the frigid air, the lonely sojourner guesses.

Reading books with a cold eye is easy.
Drinking alone with a troubled heart is hard.

The solstice having passed, I know the nights will shorten,
But when a man is old, he fears winter will linger.

I ought to have a kindred spirit with me.
I tell the boy to boil some snow, and wait.

TRANSLATED BY TIMOTHY BILLINGS AND YAN ZINAN

---

1. *XFS, j.* 5, in *LZQJZ* 3:391. Composed in 1596 in Qinshui in Shanxi province.

SITTING ALONE IN MEDITATION
獨坐
DU ZUO

There's a guest here whose eyes are wide open.[1]
No one is questioning the falling blossoms.

A warm wind spreads a fragrance through the new grass.
A cool moon casts a radiance on the smooth sand.

I've been lodging a long time, but it's all still like a dream.
When friends come, I no longer miss my home.

I have not yet unpacked my zither and books.
I sit alone and send off the evening glow.

TRANSLATED BY TIMOTHY BILLINGS AND YAN ZINAN

---

1. *XFS*, *j*. 5, in *LZQJZ* 3:395–96. Composed in 1589.

A SUDDEN CHILL
乍寒
ZHA HAN

At first, I think I must be falling ill.[1]
At midnight, I rise and pace back and forth.

I hammer the charcoal like young iron for burning.
I rake out the coals from dead ashes for lighting.

Will that icy teapot of the moon ever warm?
For whom does its crystal brilliance shine tonight?

The upright cypress on the plain already knows
A time of bitter cold is on its way.

TRANSLATED BY TIMOTHY BILLINGS AND YAN ZINAN

---

1. *XFS, j.* 5, in *LZQJZ* 3:396–97. Composed in 1596.

EVENING RAIN
暮雨
MU YU

A single torrent of water crashes along the river;[1]
A thousand mountains carry the sound of rain.

Suddenly, I hear a thick confusion of maple leaves;
At once, I shudder at the thinness of my hemp jacket.

Ten thousand volumes of books are hard to get right;
A single spirit sleeping alone is easily disturbed.

The blowing of the autumn wind briefly ceases:
It cannot bear its own desolate moaning.

TRANSLATED BY TIMOTHY BILLINGS AND YAN ZINAN

---

1. *XFS, j.* 5, in *LZQJZ* 3:398. Composed in 1592 in Wuchang in modern-day Hubei province.

WATCHING THE RAIN WITH DAZHI
大智對雨
DAZHI DUI YU

Outside the city, the smoke of habitation is scant.[1]
I live quietly in the northern chambers here.

In the wind and rain, I am dreaming by the third watch.
In the clouds and peaks, I have books to read by the thousands.

A monk comes to ask about difficult passages.
I have no strength left to weed and sweep the courtyard.

It is September. We sit at the south window.
We are free and at ease, you and I.

TRANSLATED BY TIMOTHY BILLINGS AND YAN ZINAN

---

1. *XFS, j.* 5, in *LZQJZ* 3:398–99. Dazhi was a monk from Macheng.

HARD RAIN
雨甚
YU SHEN

Time is something I have no need to recall.[1]
When I miss someone, then I ask the year.

In the third month of last autumn I crossed the Qin River;
In the ninth month of this year I reached the Western Paradise.[2]

A little stream swells in a great surge before me.
Thousands of trees hang in the bleak cold around me.

The mountainsides teem with persimmons and dates.
Eat enough of them, and you become an immortal.

TRANSLATED BY TIMOTHY BILLINGS AND YAN ZINAN

---

1. XFS, j. 5, in LZQJZ 3:399. Composed in 1597.
2. Literally, "western heaven" (*xitian* 西天). The term refers to Sukhāvatī, or the Western Pure Land of Bliss, the home of the Buddha Amitābha according to the Mahayana sect of Buddhism, here used as a metaphor for Li Zhi's new home in the Temple of Bliss on West Mountain in the outskirts of Beijing.

VIEWING THE YELLOW CRANE PAVILION FROM THE RIVER
江上望黃鶴樓
JIANGSHANG WANG HUANGHE LOU

Frosted red maples and snow-blossoming reeds[1]
emerge through the river mist.
Mottled rocks and gliding fish
show clearly and delight.

The masts of merchant vessels
appear in the clouds above.
The towers of the immortals
hang in the mirror below.

In autumn, the shadow of my little raft
extends across the sparkling river;[2]
I hear a flute playing "Plum Blossoms"
falling from the distant sky.[3]

---

1. XFS, j. 5, in LZQJZ 3:411–12. The notoriety of this sensuous poem may be due to an incident in which Li Zhi was accused of heresy by an angry crowd at Yellow Crane Pavilion during a visit there with Yuan Hongdao in 1591. (Li later speculated that the crowd may have been set upon him by Geng Dingxiang; see LZQJZ 26:453–54). It has recently been demonstrated, however, that this poem was almost certainly written by Grand Secretary Zhang Juzhang (1525–1582) and later misattributed to Li Zhi in his posthumous *Another Book to Burn* (1618). For the original title, variants, and biographical details, see Liu Yong, " 'Jiangshang wang huanghe lou.' " Perceptive readers may even recognize the difference in tone and diction from Li's other poems translated here. It is probably but one of several poems in the posthumous collection that are misattributed to him.
2. The "sparkling river" is literally the "bright Han." This line alludes to a famous couplet by Cui Hao 崔顥 (ca. 704–754): "In the bright river—how clear are the trees [on the banks] of the Hanyang! / And the fragrant grasses—how they flourish on Parrot Island!" See "Huanghe lou" 黃鶴樓 [Yellow Crane Pavilion], in *Quan Tang shi*, 1329.
3. This line alludes to a famous couplet by Li Bai 李白 (701–762): "In the Yellow Crane Pavilion, someone plays the jade flute; / In this riverside city, 'Plum Blossoms' fall in the fifth month." See "Yu Shi langzhong Qin ting huanghe lou shang chui di" 與史郎中欽聽黃鶴樓上吹笛 [Accompanying Gentleman of Interior Shi Qin, listening to a flute playing at Yellow Crane Pavilion], in *Quan Tang shi*, 1857.

Like a lone fisherman at the water's edge
with a passion that knows no bounds,
I raise my voice in the depth of night
and pound the gunwale in song.

TRANSLATED BY TIMOTHY BILLINGS AND YAN ZINAN

DRIFTING ON EAST LAKE WITH LI JIANTIAN
李見田邀遊東湖
LI JIANTIAN YAOYOU DONGHU

I have not visited Hangzhou's famous West Lake[1]
for ten autumns now;
When the inspiration arises to set out on the water,
it is easier to come here.
In the vast expanse before our eyes
there is nothing but cold waves and mist;
On the clouded horizon
the jade trees float in the air.
Peach trees bloom along the banks
as our little skiff glides by;
Lights from the vessels in the distant channel
are fishermen mooring for the night at Luzhou.
We travelers, at heart, are but guests in this world
roaming freely at ease like this;
Just think of the bark that carried Li and Guo
and a friendship made famous for ages![2]

TRANSLATED BY TIMOTHY BILLINGS AND YAN ZINAN

---

1. *XFS, j.* 5, in *LZQJZ* 3:413–14. Composed in Wuchang in 1584, this is the first of two heptasyllabic regulated-verse poems (*lüshi* 律詩) with this title.
2. The phrase "the bark that carried Li and Guo" (*Li Guo zhou* 李郭舟) alludes to Li Ying 李膺 and Guo Tai 郭太. The penniless scholar Guo Tai met Li Ying, governor of Henan Commandery, who appreciated his talent and befriended him. When Guo returned to his home village for a visit riding on a bark with Li, people lined the riverbank to see the two together. See *Hou Han shu*, ch. 68, "Guo Fu Xu liezhuan" 郭符許列傳 [The biographies of Guo Tai, Fu Rong, and Xu Shao].

FROM *A BOOK TO KEEP (HIDDEN)* (*CANGSHU* 藏書) (1599)

"INTRODUCTION TO THE TABLE OF CONTENTS OF THE HISTORICAL ANNALS AND BIOGRAPHIES IN *A BOOK TO KEEP (HIDDEN)*"
藏書世紀列傳總目前論
"*CANGSHU* SHIJI LIEZHUAN ZONGMU QIANLUN"

This introduction[1] appears in Li Zhi's *A Book to Keep (Hidden)*, a work modeled in form on the great Han historian Sima Qian's *Records of the Grand Historian* yet deeply subversive in content. The text reproduces Sima Qian's biographical accounts of rulers, ministers, and scholars, among others, but Li interpolates biting commentary—ranging from single words to several lines—to undermine the moral messages encoded in those canonical narratives. Li's unrelentingly unorthodox judgments on historical figures prompted the imperial censor Zhang Wenda to observe that Li's writings "throw men's minds into confusion" (see p. 335). As this introduction shows, the effect was deliberate and premeditated. (PCL)

Master Li [Zhi] said, "Concerning what people view as right and wrong, there is no determined standard. As for people judging others as right or

---

1. *CS*, in *LZQJZ* 4:1–2.

wrong, here too there is no established view. If standards are not determined, then what *this* person views as right and *that* as wrong are both nurtured; they are not in contention. If there exists no established view, then judging this as *right* and that as *wrong* are also simply two views; they do not work against each other.

"And so, as for the judgments of right and wrong presented here, if one would like to say that these are the judgments of just one person—me, Li Zhuowu—that is fine; if one says these are the collective judgments of millions upon millions of generations of great sages and worthies, that is fine too; and if one says that I am turning on their head judgments of right and wrong established through millions and millions of generations and—as I have done before—once again judging wrong what is in fact right, that is also fine. Well then, these views I have of what right and wrong mean, in the end I think they might be just fine.

"As for the earliest three periods of history,[2] I cannot say much. With the later three dynasties—the Han, Tang, and Song—the time spanned is over eleven hundred years, and yet throughout there was no person to set down authoritative judgments of right and wrong. But could it be that these people held no views on what was right and wrong? No. Rather, it was simply that every single person accepted Confucius's views on right and wrong as what indeed was right and wrong; never did anyone pronounce a judgment of right or wrong. So if here *I* praise and censure people—how could one stop with my judgments?

"Disputes about right and wrong are just like the passing of the four seasons or the alternating of day and night; never do these become one. Yesterday it was right, today it is wrong; today it is wrong, and tomorrow it is once again right. Even if Confucius and Zixia were to be reborn again in these times, I am not sure what kinds of judgments of right and wrong they would make.[3] So how can people rashly issue blame and praise based on what Confucius is supposed to have said in the *Spring and Autumn Annals*?

"When I found myself old and unoccupied, I grew fond of looking over the tables of contents of some earlier historical works. I composed my own beginning from the Spring and Autumn period and ending with the Song and Yuan dynasties, separating it into "Annals," "Biographies," and

---

2. Referring to the Xia (traditional dates 2205 B.C.E.–1767 B.C.E.), Shang (traditionally 1766 B.C.E.–1123 B.C.E.), and Zhou (1122 B.C.E.–255 B.C.E.) periods.
3. Zixia, also known as Bu Shang, was one of Confucius's most accomplished and deeply tradition-minded disciples.

"General Surveys." This book is for my own pleasure.[4] I have titled it *A Book to Keep (Hidden)*. Why *A Book to Keep (Hidden)*? It is saying that this book is simply for my own pleasure and not to be shown to others. That's why it is titled *A Book to Keep (Hidden)*. But what am I to do if a few meddlesome friends insistently ask to borrow this book? How am I able to stop them? I only say as a warning: if you read this, judge it based on your own opinions. As long as you do not use it like Confucius's editing of the *Spring and Autumn Annals* to dispense rewards and punishments, then it will be fine."

TRANSLATED BY PAULINE C. LEE

---

4. In contrast, Sima Qian is recorded as saying, "If [my book] may be handed down to men who will appreciate it, and penetrate to the villages and great cities, then though I should suffer a thousand mutilations, what regret would I have?" ("Letter to Ren An," in Watson, *Records: Qin Dynasty*, 236).

LI ZHI ON THE FIRST EMPEROR 秦始皇帝 "*CANGSHU*, 'SHI JI'"
藏書，世紀

Li Zhi's evaluation of the First Emperor of the Qin dynasty,[1] founder of the Chinese imperial system, is expressed in marginal comments to a condensed transcription of the corresponding chapter, "Qin Shihuang benji" 秦始皇本紀 [The basic annals of Qin Shihuang], in Sima Qian's *Records of the Grand Historian*. Rather than reproduce the entire transcription here, we give extracts followed by Li's comments. The reversal of the standard judgments applied to the First Emperor by Confucian historiographers who saw him as wantonly cruel, destructive, and tyrannical was among the "exorbitant, mad, and flagitious opinions" that raised the hackles of Zhang Wenda and other figures at court in 1601–1602. But a careful reading of this historical commentary shows Li Zhi laying the blame for the cruelty and repression of the Qin dynasty on the First Emperor's subordinates, whose unwise policies the headstrong emperor failed to moderate. (HS)

"BASIC ANNALS": THE FIRST EMPEROR OF QIN, WITH AS APPENDIX THE BIOGRAPHY OF HUHAI

[Li's comment:] As a ruler, the First Emperor is unparalleled in all history. Why is the record of Huhai titled "an appendix"?[2] If Huhai were not appended, how could the First Emperor's [uniqueness] become manifest?

---

1. *CS, j.* 1, in *LZQJZ* 4:45–60.
2. The main body of this chapter is Li's free condensation of chapter 6 ("The Basic Annals of the First Emperor of Qin") of Sima Qian's *Shi ji*, for which we have used (with alterations) the translation of Nienhauser, *The Grand Scribe's Records*, 1:127–75. Huhai, one of the First Emperor's younger sons, reigned as Second Emperor for a little over two years.

Liao of Da Liang said, "The King of Qin . . . seldom extends favor and has the heart of a tiger or wolf.³ When in straits, he can submit to others, but when he has his way, he can easily eat you alive. I am a commoner. Nevertheless, when he receives me, he always humbles himself before me. Once he really has his way in the world, the whole world will be held captive by him. One cannot consort with him too long." Then he ran away. When the King of Qin discovered it, he obstinately stopped him, appointed him commandant, and in the end adopted his plans. But Li Si was in charge of affairs.

[Li's comment:] Obviously Li Si is a stand-in for Liao.

In the twenty-sixth year of his reign . . . Qin first unified the world. The king issued an order to the chancellor and the imperial scribes: . . . "The land within the seas has been made into commanderies and counties. Since antiquity it has never been so. Not even the Five Emperors could reach this. . . . [And therefore] I will be called the First Emperor. Later generations will follow with titles ordered numerically."

[Li's comment:] He had it all planned out.

"The Second Emperor, the Third Emperor, and on to the Ten Thousandth Emperor shall follow this rule to infinity." He considered that the Zhou [dynasty] followed the power of fire, and since the Qin had overcome the Zhou, Qin must conform to the power of what Zhou could not overcome. He marked the beginning of the era of the power of water

[Li's comment:] Not wrong.

by changing the beginning of the year: the court would celebrate the new year on the first of the tenth month. . . . He divided the world into thirty-six commanderies, each with a governor, a commandant, and a superintendent.

[Li's comment:] Right.

From the Yong Gate eastward to the Jing and the Wei, the halls and residences [of the imperial palace] were connected by elevated colonnades to the galleries surrounding them.

---

3. Liao, a commander of a peripheral region of Qin, advised the King of Qin (later the First Emperor of China) to bribe and weaken the rulers of the surrounding states so as eventually to overcome them. Li Si, a disciple of the philosopher Xunzi, is usually taken to be the architect of Qin's policies. After the First Emperor's death, Li Si colluded with Zhao Gao to put a younger son, Huhai, on the throne. Zhao Gao organized Li Si's execution soon afterward on grounds of treason.

[Li's comment:] Foolish.

In the twenty-seventh year of his reign, the First Emperor toured the west and the north . . . and built the Palace of Trust on the south bank of the Wei.

[Li's comment:] Foolish.

In the twenty-eighth year of his reign, the First Emperor toured the east. On arriving at Bolang Sands in Yangwu, he was disturbed by bandits.

[Li's comment:] That was fast.

The First Emperor then had Han Zhong, Master Hou, and Scholar Shi seek for the long-life elixirs of the immortals.

[Li's comment:] Stupid.

In the thirty-fourth year . . . the First Emperor gave a feast in the Xianyang Palace. . . . The erudite Chunyu Yue came forward and said, "I have learned that under the Yin and Zhou dynasties, the kings' sons, brothers, and meritorious ministers were enfeoffed as support for the court itself. Now Your Majesty possesses all within the seas, but your sons and brothers are ordinary men. If there were [traitorous] vassals like Tian Chang or the Six Ministers [of Jin], you would lack this support, and who would come to your rescue then?"

[Li's comment:] Exactly right.

The chancellor Li Si said [in response to Chunyu Yue]: "The Five Emperors did not duplicate one another's way of governing, and the Three Dynasties did not inherit them from one another, but each regulated the world in his own way."

[Li's comment:] "Each in his own way" is priceless.

[Li Si continued:] "Now Your Majesty has founded this great enterprise and attained merits that will last for ten thousand generations, which is not the sort of thing an ignorant Confucian can understand. Chunyu Yue spoke of matters concerning the Three Dynasties. Why should they be worth imitating?"

[Li's comment:] "I hate glib-tonguedness, lest it be confounded with righteousness."[4] This judgment applies to Li Si.

"If such [speech] is not banned, the ruler's power will be diminished above, and factions will form below. To ban it is appropriate. I would ask that you burn all the records in the scribes' offices that are not Qin's. If not needed by

---

4. Citing *Mencius* 7B83.

the Office of the Erudites, all copies of the *Odes*, the *Documents*, and the writings of the Hundred Schools that anyone in the world has ventured to keep shall be brought to the governors and commandants to be thrown together and burned. Anyone who ventures to discuss songs and documents shall be executed in the marketplace."

[Li's comment:] Thus it was fitting that [Li Si] was executed and his family extinguished.

Scholar Hou and Scholar Lu conspired with each other: "The way the First Emperor is, he has a disposition to be obstinate and self-willed. . . . Since His Highness has never been informed of his mistakes, he becomes more arrogant daily. . . . We cannot look for an elixir of long life for a person obsessed with power as he is." Then they fled. When the First Emperor heard of it, he was enraged. . . . He had imperial scribes interrogate the various masters. The masters accused and implicated one another to extricate themselves. Those who had violated prohibitions, more than four hundred sixty of them, he had buried alive.

[Li's comment:] And as a result, Confucians are terrified up to the present day.

Fusu, the emperor's eldest son, remonstrated [about the crime of burying scholars alive]. . . . The emperor was angered. He ordered Fusu to leave for the north to supervise Meng Tian in Shangjun Commandery.

[Li's comment:] And this triggers the fall of the Qin.

In the thirty-sixth year . . . a man with a jade disk in his hand stopped an imperial messenger and said, "Give this to the lord of Hao Pond for me." He asked him to transmit the message, "This year the Dragon Ancestor will die." The First Emperor had the Imperial Storehouse examine the jade disk. It turned out to be the one he had dropped into the Yellow River as he was crossing it twenty-eight years before. After this, the emperor had a divination performed and obtained the advice, "Traveling and moving is auspicious."

[Li's comment:] Heaven and Man agree here.

[The First Emperor dies while traveling. Li Si conceals the fact of his death by sealing the body in a coffin and keeping it in the imperial carriage; documents are carried to the "indisposed" emperor and signed on his behalf. Li Si and Zhao Gao send a letter in the First Emperor's name to the emperor's eldest son, Fusu, and Meng Tian, ordering them to commit suicide. They enthrone the young and inexperienced Huhai as the Second Emperor. Huhai's purges and expenditures stir up discontent, his armies rebel, and he ends his own life. A third heir, Ziying, is enthroned and rules for a month. Afraid to attend court functions lest he be murdered by his subordinates, Ziying stabs his prime minister, Zhao Gao, and has his family exterminated. Surrounded by an insurgent army led by Liu Bang, the future Emperor Gaozu of the Han dynasty,] Ziying surrendered and the Qin were done for.

[Li's comment:] Too abrupt!

TRANSLATED BY HAUN SAUSSY

THE HISTORICAL RECORD 史料

"THE LIFE OF LI WENLING"
李溫陵傳
"LI WENLING ZHUAN"

YUAN ZHONGDAO
袁中道

Yuan Zhongdao was the youngest of the three Yuan brothers, who collectively dominated late-Ming literary taste.[1] All three were powerfully affected by their meetings with Li Zhi. Although their advocacy of authenticity over artifice in literary style might seem to indicate an anticonformist streak, they were successful in the examinations and attained official rank early in life. Yuan Zhongdao is best known for his autobiographical writings and travel diaries. (HS)

Li Wenling's name was Zaizhi.[2] He achieved the status of provincial graduate when young, but he did not attend further examinations because the distance to travel was too great. He became a school administrator and

---

1. "Li Wenling zhuan," in Yuan Zhongdao, *Kexuezhai ji*, 2:719–25; reprinted in *LZQJZ* 26:157–61. Yuan Zhongdao refers to Li Zhi by the the sobriquet "Wenling" (Master Warm Springs). For Yuan Zhongdao's recollections of Li Zhi's conversation, see "Zhalin jitan" 柞林紀譚 [Notes from talk in the brush holly grove], ibid., 3:1475–89.
2. Born Lin Zaizhi 林載贄, Li Zhi changed his surname to Li in 1552, the year he sat for the first examination.

stayed in the lower ranks of the official hierarchy. Then he was made prefect of Yao'an [county, Yunnan province]. Inwardly passionate despite his chilly appearance, he was imposing and stern. By nature he was impatient and quick to upbraid people for their faults. He refused to speak to anyone who did not suit his temperament. Forceful and self-willed, he could not be made to do anything against his wishes.

Early in life, he was unacquainted with [philosophical] studies. A master of the School of Principle asked him, "Are you afraid of dying?" He answered, "How could I not fear death?" "Since you have the fear of death, why not study the Way? The study of the Way will free you from matters of life and death." He said, "Is that so?" So he plunged his mind into the mysteries of the Way. After a time, finding in himself a resonance with what he read, he was able to transcend language in a way that those who cling to the outer shell of words cannot reach. As prefect, he issued orders that were clear and simple; he refrained from speech and let things order themselves. He often went to the monastery to judge cases. Occupying the seat of honor, he would have one of the eminent monks placed by his side and discuss with him lofty and abstruse topics once public business had been dispatched. People were astonished at this, but he paid them no mind. Like Lu Ji or Ren Fang of old, he acquired no riches in addition to his official salary.[3] After a time, he grew tired of administration and went to Jizu Mountain with the intention of studying Buddhism there for the rest of his days. The imperial censor Liu Wei was struck by the purity of his behavior and secured special permission for him to retire early.

He was at the time on friendly terms with Geng Ziyong [Geng Dingli] of Huang'an in Huguang province. When he resigned his official appointment, he chose not to return home, saying, "I'm an old man. Having found one or two superb friends with whom to converse intelligently until the end of my days is my greatest happiness, why then should I return home?" So he settled his wife and daughter in Huang'an. In middle age he had begotten several sons, but they did not live.[4]

He was lean of body, tranquil, and obsessively clean. He could not bear to be near a woman, so although he had no son, he refused to take a concubine. His wife and daughter wanted to go home, so he sent them off immediately. He called himself "The Wandering Sojourner." As he had no more

---

3. Lu Ji 陸績, when he left office, carried away only a stone as a souvenir. Ren Fang's 任昉 fortune consisted of a few measures of rice. Li Zhi's official salary was barely sufficient to live on. The meaning here is that he did not take bribes.
4. All but one of Li Zhi's seven children died before reaching maturity.

dependents, he went ahead and cut off all common ties, seeking only to understand the principles of the Vehicle, plumb the depths of his revelation, pare away the skin and see the bone, find the path to utter truth. His published discussions were sharp as a sword's edge, as strong as lions' milk, as assured as an elephant fording a stream;[5] their style was unique, and few dared to challenge their arguments.

After Dingli died, Dingli's brother, Mr. Tiantai [Geng Dingxiang], disliked [Li's] untrammeled ways. Fearing that his own sons and nephews would be led to follow him and cast off their responsibilities, he warned them repeatedly and in no uncertain terms. So Mr. Wenling went to live at Macheng, on the shores of Dragon Lake, in the company of the monk Wunian and Zhou Youshan, Qiu Tanzhi, and Yang Dingjian. They locked themselves up and did nothing but read all day. [Wenling] had a fondness for clean-swept floors and kept several people busy steadily making him brooms. His clothes were clean, as was his person; always scrubbing his face and body, he was as if addicted to water. He did not care for vulgar visitors. If people appeared unannounced, he would greet them briefly and order them to sit far away lest he be sullied by their presence. If he was happy to see someone, he would spend the whole day in conversation and laughter; if not, he would not say a word. Clever remarks fell unceasingly from his lips, sometimes amusing, sometimes caustic. He copied out on fine paper the books he read: tales of the Daoist immortals, Buddhist religious works, the *Li sao* of Qu Yuan, the historical writings of Sima Qian and Ban Gu, the poetry of Tao Yuanming, Xie Lingyun, Liu Zongyuan, and Du Fu, as well as the more remarkable among fictional writings and dramas by famous Song and Yuan playwrights. On snow-white paper, with red annotations, the neatly ordered characters marched down the page between precise margins, original ideas constantly bursting forth. His writing style was not predictable. Brilliant and inimitable, it sprang from his own feelings. He wrote poetry only rarely but always with spirit. He enjoyed doing calligraphy. When he had ground his ink and spread out the paper, he would throw open his clothing, give a shout, and put his brush to work like a hare darting out of the way of a swooping falcon.[6] His more satisfactory efforts are indeed striking: wiry,

---

5. These comparisons are drawn from Buddhist literature and suggest the power of true doctrine.
6. The phrase derives from an essay by Su Che 蘇澈 about the importance of intuition and spontaneity in the arts of the brush: "When one takes up the brush ... it is like the hare's leaping up when the falcon swoops. If it hesitates in the slightest, all will be lost" (Bush and Shih, *Early Chinese Texts*, 207).

forceful strokes and abrupt turns, with a firm wrist and an overall balance, austere on the page.

One day, annoyed by an itching scalp, tired of combing his hair, he had it all shaved off, leaving only his beard.

With his peremptory manner, he was inevitably seen as an eccentric, and as time went on more and more people began to call him a heretic. He fell out with Geng Dingxiang. Their argument, conducted in letters, ran over ten thousand words and probed the very core motivations of the School of Principle. Those who read this passionate correspondence could only admire his acuity, envy his talent, and fear his style.

About this time certain people began to denounce him to the authorities for imaginary misdeeds. The authorities expelled him. Then the magistrate Liu Dongxing welcomed Mr. Wenling to Wuchang and gave him living quarters in the Hall of Master Gai.[7] From that time on Mr. Wenling traveled and returned home several times; Mr. Liu received him in Qinshui [Shanxi province], Vice-Censor Mei [Guozhen] received him at Yunzhong, and Jiao Ruohou [Jiao Hong] received him at Moling. Nonetheless, he still returned to Macheng. Once again, people denounced him for imaginary misdeeds, and the authorities again made the mistake of trusting these accusations, and expelled him. The monastery where he lodged was burned down. Mr. Ma Jinglun, of the Censorate, respectfully received him in north Tongzhou. It was just at this moment that the authorities, wishing to frame a heresy case and reform the style of writing then current, mentioned him specifically. They ordered the guards and marshals to capture Mr. Wenling.

Mr. Wenling had been unwell, and while convalescing revised his *Factors of the Changes* [*Yiyin*], calling it *Jiuzheng Yiyin*. He used to say, "When I finish my *Jiuzheng Yiyin*, death will be near." When the *Yiyin* was finished, the sickness took a turn for the worse. Just then the men came to arrest him. Mr. Wenling asked Mr. Ma why the whole house was in disorder. Mr. Ma said, "The guards have arrived." Mr. Wenling forced himself to stand, took a few steps, and shouted, "You've come for me. Then bring a door panel to take me away!" He lay on top of it and in pain shouted, "Hurry up! If I'm a criminal, I shouldn't linger here." Mr. Ma wanted to go with him. Mr. Wenling said, "The orders won't allow you to follow me all the way to the city, and you have an aged father to look after." Mr. Ma said, "The court thinks you are some kind of demon, and as far as they are concerned, I have been

---

7. Master Gai 蓋 was a Western Han thinker. He advocated a Daoist-inspired style of government that made minimal inroads on the lives of the governed.

harboring a demon. If anyone is going to die, let's die together. In any event, I won't have stayed behind while I let them take you away." In the end Mr. Ma went away with him. When they reached the outskirts of Tongzhou, a letter brought by Mr. Ma's attendants ordered him to stop. Several dozen of his servants came and, weeping, commanded him to stay behind for his father's sake. Mr. Ma would not listen to them. He preferred to stay with Mr. Wenling. The next morning, the leader of the guards interrogated him. (Mr. Wenling's supporters had crept in and spent the night on the steps.) The captain asked, "Why did you write those outlandish books?" Mr. Wenling said, "Your prisoner has written many books. Here they are; they support the sagely teachings and do not harm them." The captain laughed at his self-assurance. A prison was no place for rhetorical displays. Probably no report was made of this rebuttal. After a time the order was given to leave him alone. In prison Mr. Wenling wrote poems and read books quite contentedly. One day, he called to the attendant to come cut his hair. The attendant turned away, and Mr. Wenling seized the razor and cut his own throat. It was a day or two before his life ebbed away. The attendant asked, "Monk, are you in pain?" Mr. Wenling traced with a finger on his palm, "No pain." Again, "Monk, why did you cut your throat?" He wrote out, "What more can an old man of seventy expect?" Then he died. Meanwhile Mr. Ma, thinking that the trial would be postponed, had gone back to see his father but now heard the news and was distressed, saying, "I failed to take adequate precautions and now this has happened. What a loss!" He took Mr. Wenling's body back to Tongzhou and there had a stately tomb erected for him in a Buddhist compound.

Mr. Wenling had no love for authorship. His debates with Mr. Geng were simply transcribed off the cuff; subsequently he collected them in his *A Book to Burn*. Afterward, since from time to time he had written comments on the abstruse meanings of the sages, he compiled the *Shuo shu* [*On the Four Books*]. Afterward, working from his notes and judgments on the *Dynastic Histories*, Mr. Jiao and others had blocks carved in Nanjing and issued *A Book to Keep (Hidden)*. For when Mr. Wenling had leisure to read books, he particularly loved to read the *Histories*. He had a certain insight into the effectiveness of the ancients. He felt that the reasons for order and disorder in the world were to be found in matters more fugitive than a single breath and subtler than a stitch of thread. Through pure luck the small players in history were often able to destroy a kingdom, and the major figures were held back by too many obstacles, too careful of their reputations, too responsible, so that they were prisoners of their situation—as if unaware of the ancients' advice to be detached and free, to refrain from action and act as if without purpose, to stay hidden, endure shame, and act by indirect means in order to get the broadest results. In the absence of this wisdom, the superior man is unable to command the lesser man, and the lesser man is able to put the superior man in place. Seen thus, history is luminous and never confounding. It is turbulent, not peaceful, and often erupts in disorder. But when the Confucian scholars of today look on the traces of the past, they measure them with a uniform standard, unable to reserve their judgment, and so they seek figs from thistles, see the flaws and not the gem, applaud what they should despise, and despise what they should value. By now, they have relayed and echoed one another's voices for so long that their consensus view has sunk into the very marrow of people's bones and can no longer be combated. And so after several thousand years there emerged a new hand and eye: those whom all had long agreed to call great, he would attack for their faults; and as for those whom all agreed to call contemptible, he would not let their good qualities be lost from view. His main purpose was to banish inane writing and seek useful substance. He pushed aside the superficial details in order to capture the essence, discarded vain prattle and stressed human feeling. Although at times he demands too much and can be unbalanced in his judgments, if you will disregard the excesses of invective and sarcasm and read him carefully, the many places where he hits the mark are correctives that the intellectuals of our day should accept. Yet everyone precipitously saw there only an offense to orthodox teaching and objected that [Mr. Wenling] was destroying the sages and rising up against the Way. That was an error.

    The ancient chroniclers Sima Qian and Ban Gu wrote opinionated histories. Sima Qian preferred Huang-Lao[8] teachings over the Six Classics and showed contempt for reclusive scholars and admiration for wandering swordsmen, for which the establishment of the time rejected him; Ban Gu, too, faulted some for their loyalty and scorned others for their forthrightness. When later generations examined the flaws in these two historians, they sifted out their personal opinions and retained the pure vintage, so that today their two works [*Records of the Grand Historian* and *History of the Former Han*] hang above us like the sun and moon. No one can read the historians of the Tang and Song periods to the end. Why then do they make us yawn? Can it not be that personal opinion is the sparkling element in history writing that must not be ground away?

---

8. Referring to the teachings of the Yellow Emperor and Laozi, a combination of Daoist and Primitivist teachings that appealed to many intellectuals in the Han dynasty.

For self-will that casts off all restraint, people say you need look no farther than in *Zhuangzi*; but no one has ever become self-willed and unrestrained through reading Zhuangzi. Self-willed and unrestrained people have no need to read *Zhuangzi*. For harsh and pitiless policy, nothing compares to the *Han Feizi*; but no one ever became harsh and pitiless through reading Han Feizi; harsh and pitiless people do not need to read Han Fei. From the time that those two books first became known, readers of *Zhuangzi* have concentrated their abilities on transcending the externals of fame and advantage, leaving behind the ordinary man; whereas those who read Shen Buhai and Han Feizi secured positions of trust and salaries through employing punishments, whereby their sovereigns became stronger and the courts won awe.[9] Shall we reject and disregard a pure talent like Zhuge Liang, who employed his skills to advance the cause of the last emperor of a defeated dynasty?[10]

The Six Classics and the works of Confucius's school are the meat and grain of our intellectual diet. People who eat too much of this grain and meat may get blocked and suffer from constipation, and the doctor will prescribe a regime of Sichuan soybeans to free up the accumulated matter; only then will the belly be at peace. In a formal dinner for nine guests, chicken, pork, lamb, and fish are brought in successively. Seafood, freshwater scallops, and the like are refreshing as a change from heavy food. So it would not be incorrect to describe Mr. Wenling's books as being of a purgative character. They could also be described as a treasure that one can neither do without nor replace with a substitute. Unfortunately, they were published too early. They did not have enough time to transform the hearts of their readers, and so they led to quarreling and denunciations.

To reflect more deeply on the disaster that befell Mr. Wenling, perhaps it did not arise from his books. For the most part, Mr. Wenling's behavior was hard to explain. A successful degree holder who had renounced his post, he talked about nothing but the art of statesmanship: the affairs of all under heaven, he said, are too important to be left to the management of the typical fame-seeking scholar. Rash, direct, and sharp-tongued, apt to have an effect on people like that of ice and snow, and profoundly repelled

---

9. Shen Buhai 申不害 and Han Feizi 韓非子 were leading thinkers of the Legalist school in the early years of the Qin empire. Legalism advised controlling the people through fear ("punishments") rather than by appealing to their moral or aesthetic intuitions ("ritual," in the parlance of the time).
10. The crafty general Zhuge Liang 諸葛亮 (181–234) served the ruler of the rump state of Shu, the last remnant of the Han imperial house, during the post-Han period of disunity. He is one of the main characters in the *Romance of the Three Kingdoms*.

by puritanism and self-praise, he held that the harm of harsh and unrelenting behavior is inflicted on future generations. He fled sensory pleasures and looked on desire as if it were excrement, but he had a broad capacity for love and greatly enjoyed, and adorned his solitude with, the manifestations of romantic feelings among boys and girls. Hard to please, unable to agree with others about anything, if he fell in with someone who had a special talent, he would voice his admiration and abase himself. Forgetful of the world and his own body, he was a true ascetic, but whenever he read about the death-defying courage of faithful officers and loyal subjects in ancient times, or about the clever escapes of bravos and swordsmen, these legends would make him howl and pound the table, throw back his sleeves, rise, and weep unrestrainedly, with tears streaming this way and that. He was as inflexible as metal or stone and his aspirations were as lofty as the clouds of heaven. If he had something to say, it must come out; his mind was incapable of retreat. Inevitably, he offended those more highly placed than himself.

Kong Wenju 孔文舉 treated Emperor Wu of Wei like a small child, and Xi Shuye 嵇叔夜 looked on Zhong Hui 鍾會 as a slave.[11] You can overturn a bird's nest, but you cannot change a phoenix's beak. You can clip the feathers of a simurgh but not tame its dragon nature. That is why he was bound to be betrayed and imprisoned, like a precious herb or fragrant orchid uprooted. Alas! With too great a talent, too powerful a spirit, he could not conceal himself in foulness as others do, and ended in a prison cell, "blushing before Liuxia Hui 柳下惠 and ashamed before Sun Deng 孫登."[12] How regrettable! What a warning!

Late in life Mr. Wenling studied the *Classic of Changes* and wrote a book titled *Jiuzheng Yiyin*. It shows that he had a deep understanding of the *Changes*, such that he could put aside his haughtiness and enter into humility, but now he has exceeded his years and gone into the beyond! The books Mr. Wenling honored with prefaces, such as the *Yangming xiansheng nianpu* [Chronology of Wang Yangming's Life] or the *Longxi yulu* [Record of Conversations with Wang Ji], are too numerous to be listed here.

---

11. Kong Rong 融 (courtesy name Wenju) was an official and general in the last years of the Han dynasty. For his many rebukes to his nominal superior, Cao Cao, who crowned himself Emperor Wu of the Wei dynasty in 220, he was executed. Xi Kang (courtesy name Shuye) behaved insolently to Zhong Hui, who had been sent to invite him to serve the usurping general Sima Zhao. This resulted in Xi Kang's execution. Both Kong Rong and Xi Kang came to represent the irreverent spirit of the Six Dynasties.
12. Paraphrasing a poem written in prison by Xi Kang, in which the poet reproaches himself both for being an overly loyal officer like Liuxia Hui and for having failed to take the advice of the recluse Sun Deng. See *Wenxuan* 文選 [Selections of refined literature], 23.13a.

Someone once asked me, "Were you ever a follower of Li Wenling's?" I answered, "Although I was devoted to him, I could never be his follower. There are five reasons why I could not be his follower, and three reasons why I would not. First, Mr. Wenling was extremely pure in his actions as an official, and my generation obeys the crowd and does what custom requires. Second, he kept his distance from women and seductive boys, and my generation is incapable of forsaking our passions, indulging endlessly in love affairs. Third, he was deeply learned in the Way and saw it in its greatness, and my generation clings to words without capturing their deeper meaning. Fourth, from his earliest youth to his old age he was exclusively occupied with reading, and my generation is sunk in the dust of worldly ties, unacquainted with the great works of the past. Fifth, he was forthright and fearless, not the sort of man who would bend to suit others, and my generation is spineless, saying yes or no as the crowd demands. He loved confrontation and marshaled his spirit, he was quick to make friends or enemies, and whenever he encountered something unacceptable, he went straight to writing about it—this is one reason I was not willing to follow him. After he retired from office to live as a hermit, he was intending to vanish into the mountains, but he lingered in the world of men, and that is where misfortune tracked him down as his fame grew. Here too I would not follow him. And he was eager for salvation but lax on the rules, careless of minor infractions, guided by his feelings and too quick to say whatever came into his mind: in this, finally, I would rather not follow him. What one is incapable of following, one remains forever incapable of following; what one is unwilling to follow, one simply does not follow. So I say that although I was fond of him, I was not his follower."

Those who spread malicious rumors contend that [Mr. Wenling], after shaving off his hair [and taking monastic orders], still wore the official cap and participated in governing, and at the age of eighty was still subject to lust and ambition—is this possible? As people say, "From a foul toad comes a foul turd"—in their case, through the mouth.

TRANSLATED BY HAUN SAUSSY

"VERITABLE RECORD OF THE MEMORIAL IMPEACHING LI ZHI, SUBMITTED BY SUPERVISING CENSOR ZHANG WENDA ON THE *YIMAO* DAY OF THE SECOND INTERCALARY MONTH OF THE THIRTIETH YEAR OF THE REIGN OF EMPEROR SHENZONG"
神宗實錄萬曆三十年閏二月乙卯禮科給事中張問達疏劾李贄
"SHENZONG SHILU WANLI SANSHI NIAN RUN ER YUE YIMAO LIKE JISHIZHONG ZHANG WENDA SHU HE LI ZHI"

In 1602, while Li Zhi was convalescing from a serious illness at the home of his friend and patron Ma Jinglun, malicious rumors were circulating in the capital about his unorthodox pronouncements and unsavory behavior. In the second intercalary month, the situation came to a head when the imperial censor Zhang Wenda submitted to the throne the memorial[1] translated here, in which he excoriates Li Zhi for writing books that "throw men's minds into confusion." The Wanli emperor responded promptly and issued an edict calling for Li's immediate arrest and the destruction both of all his extant books and of the wood blocks for printing them. According to Ma Jinglun's account, Li Zhi was arrested at his home. Too weak to walk and panting for breath, he was laid half unconscious on a wooden plank and transported to the jail. There he was given to understand that he would be deported to his native province of Fujian.[2] Feeling beleaguered, exasperated, and desperately misunderstood, Li Zhi had no intention of suffering the arduous journey home. When an attendant came to shave him, Li seized the opportunity to grab the razor and slit his own throat. For a full day he remained alive, breathing shallowly, but expired the next day. (RHS)

---

1. *Ming shilu* 明實錄 [Veritable records of the Ming dynasty]; cited in Gu, *Rizhi lu*, *j.* 18.
2. Ma Jinglun, "Yu Wang Tingyi zhushi" 與王廷翼主事 [To Secretary Wang Tingyi]; cited in *XFS*, *j.* 5, in *LZQJZ* 3:317.

THE HISTORICAL RECORD 史料   335

In the thirteenth year of the Wanli reign, in the second intercalary month, on the fourteenth day of the month, the chief supervising secretary Zhang Wenda submitted a memorial of impeachment:

In the prime of his life, Li Zhi served as an official. In his later years he shaved his head. Recently he has written *A Book to Keep (Hidden)*, *A Book to Burn*, *Zhuowu's [Book of] Great Virtue*, and several other books that are in broad circulation and that throw men's minds into confusion.

In these books he considers Lü Buwei 呂不韋 and Li Yuan 李園 wise counselors,³ Li Si 李斯 shrewd,⁴ and Feng Dao 馮道 an official who possessed the moral fiber of a recluse;⁵ he estimates that Zhuo Wenjun 卓文君 excelled in choosing an outstanding mate⁶ and finds laughable Sima Guang's 司馬光 assertion that Sang Hongyang 桑弘羊 deceived Emperor Wu of Han 漢武帝;⁷ he deems Qin Shihuang 秦始皇 the greatest emperor of all time,⁸

---

3. Lü Buwei was chancellor to the First Emperor of China. Sima Qian suggests that he may even have been the First Emperor's biological father. He engineered the promotion of the First Emperor's nominal father to become king of Qin, securing the support of the empress dowager by arranging for her to have an illicit affair with a man whose penis was exceedingly large. Lü's policies were based on the Legalist thought of Han Fei and Xunzi. See Sima Qian, *Shi ji*, ch. 85, "Biography of Lü Buwei," in Watson, *Records: Qin Dynasty*, 159–65. Li Yuan (third century B.C.E.) was originally a protégé of the prime minister of the state of Chu, Lord Chunshen. Li Yuan subverted the royal line by introducing his sister into the palace as a concubine, and after she had had a son by the king of Chu, ordered the assassination of Lord Chunshen. Li Yuan then became prime minister for King You of Chu, his nephew. See Sima Qian, *Shi ji*, ch. 78, "The Lord of Chunshen," in Nienhauser, *The Grand Scribe's Records*, 7:223–32.
4. On Li Si, the prime minister of the First Emperor and architect of many of his most decried policies, see pp. 204–5.
5. On Feng Dao, who served many masters and exhibited no concern for loyalty, see p. 277n9. Li makes the controversial statement that he was a hermit at heart.
6. Zhuo Wenjun (second century B.C.E.) eloped with the poet, musician, and historian Sima Xiangru on the occasion of their first meeting. This was contrary to the rites, which required a matchmaker and parental permission. See Sima Qian, *Shi ji*, ch. 117, "The Biography of Sima Xiangru," in Watson, *Records: Han Dynasty II*, 259–306.
7. Sang Hongyang (152 B.C.E.–80 B.C.E.) served under Emperor Wu of Han (156 B.C.E.–87 B.C.E.). He helped the Han government solidify its monopolies over salt and iron and devised a scheme for replacing taxation with arbitrage, buying commodities in regions where they were plentiful and selling them in regions where they commanded a high price. Emperor Wu's constant wars and high living made such financial wizardry tempting. Sang was assassinated when he came under suspicion for having been involved in a plot to overthrow the emperor (see Ban Gu, *Han shu*, ch. 38). Over a thousand years later, Sang's financial policies were invoked as a precedent by the Song-dynasty reformer Wang Anshi 王安石 (1021–1086), whose arguments the chancellor Sima Guang 司馬光 (1019–1086) rejected as imprudent; see "Sima Guang's Account of a Debate at Court," in Ebrey, *Chinese Civilization*, 151–52). The clause concerning Sang is missing from most reprints of *Rizhi lu*.

and he maintains that Confucius's judgments need not be considered standard. Such outrageous and transgressive judgments are too numerous to count. The majority of them violate norms of propriety, so the books must be destroyed.

Particularly reprehensible is that when he was lodging in Macheng, he gave free rein to his impulses and, together with his unsavory companions, frequented nunneries, fondled courtesans, and bathed with them in broad daylight. Moreover, he enticed the wives and daughters of literati into the nunneries to discuss the dharma. They even went so far as to bring their quilts and pillows and to spend the night there. The situation was out of control.

What's more, he wrote a book called *Questioning Guanyin*. But by "Guanyin," he meant the wives and daughters of literati. Young men took delight in his unrestrained wildness and goaded one another to follow suit. They knew no shame and behaved like beasts, openly stealing money and violating other people's wives and daughters. Recently gentry officials have been clasping talismans and reciting the name of the Buddha; they prostrate themselves before monks and hold rosaries in their hands, all in an attempt to abide by the [Buddhist] prohibitions. Their walls are hung with marvelous images, which they consider holy. Such people, who know not how to respect Confucian household instructions but instead indulge their obsession with Buddhist teachings and monks, are becoming increasingly numerous.

I recently heard that Li Zhi plans to leave Tongzhou. Tongzhou is only forty *li* from the capital. If he should enter the capital and cause a disturbance there, the situation in Macheng will repeat itself. I recommend that an edict from the Ministry of Rites be promulgated by local officials in Tongzhou, that Li Zhi be sent back to his place of origin and punished according to the law. The edict should also be promulgated in both capitals and in every province. Let all of Li Zhi's printed books, together with the unprinted books at his home, be confiscated and completely destroyed. Let them not be passed on to posterity. If this is done, the benefit to society will be great indeed.

IMPERIAL EDICT

Li Zhi has dared to disrupt the Dao, to muddle a generation, and to deceive the people. For this reason, I command that the imperial guards and marshals forcibly bring him to justice. Let them completely confiscate and

---

8. See "Li Zhi on the First Emperor," pp. 320–24.

destroy all his books, printed as well as unprinted, that they may not survive. If any of his disciples should shelter Li Zhi or conceal his books, the bureau in question, along with all other bureaus, will investigate and report the matter so that these collaborators too will be brought to justice.

DISPOSITION

Li Zhi was arrested. Fearing punishment, he refused nourishment and died.[9]

TRANSLATED BY RIVI HANDLER-SPITZ

---

9. This appears to be an attempt to cover up the true cause of Li Zhi's death.

CHRONOLOGY OF LI ZHI'S LIFE

Where dates are in dispute, we have followed the dating suggested by Zhang Jianye.

1527	Born in Jinjiang in Quanzhou, Fujian (Ming period, sixth year of the Jiajing reign).
ca. 1547	Marries Ms. Huang (born 1533).
1552	Passes provincial civil service examination.
1555	Li's first child, a son, dies.
1556	Assumes first post as instructor in Hui county, Henan province. Serves until 1560.
1560	Promoted to the position of erudite in the Imperial Academy, Nanjing. Moves to Nanjing to accept the position. Several months later, he returns home to Quanzhou to mourn his father's death. "Japanese" pirates ransack the city.
1563	Upon the completion of the mourning period for his father, Li and his family return to Nanjing, where Li works as a tutor for ten months while awaiting an official post.
1564	Named erudite in the Imperial Academy at Beijing. Receives notification of the death of his paternal grandfather. Li's second-eldest son too falls ill and dies. Li returns alone to Quanzhou to mourn his grandfather's death. Leaves his wife and three daughters behind, purchasing a plot of land in Hui county for their sustenance.
1565	Unbeknownst to Li, who is still in Quanzhou, two of his three daughters starve to death during the drought in Hui county.

1566	Li returns to Hui county to rejoin his wife and one remaining child, a daughter. The family returns to Nanjing, where Li takes a temporary position in the Ministry of Rites. During this time, Li begins to study the teachings of Wang Yangming and becomes increasingly interested in Buddhism.
1567	(Ming period, Longqing reign, year one)
1570	Assumes the position of secretary of the Ministry of Punishments in Nanjing. He holds this position until 1577.
1572	Meets Geng Dingli.
1573	(Ming period, Wanli reign, year one)
1577	Having been appointed prefect of Yao'an in Yunnan province, Li travels west to assume the post. Passing through Huang'an, he visits Geng Dingli, meets Geng Dingxiang, and leaves his daughter and son-in-law in Huang'an.
1580	Li resigns his post as prefect of Yao'an and travels through Yunnan to visit the Buddhist monasteries of Mount Jizu.
1581	Takes up residence at the Geng household in Huang'an. Meets Zhou Youshan and the monk Wunian.
1582	Begins period of intensive writing.
1584	Death of Li Zhi's soul friend, Geng Dingli.
1587	Sends his wife and daughter home to Fujian. Takes up residence in Macheng at the Vimalakīrti Monastery.
1588	Receives the news of his wife's death in Fujian. Li takes the Buddhist tonsure, shaving off his hair but leaving his long beard intact. Moves to the Cloister of the Flourishing Buddha on Dragon Lake.
1590	Likely date for first publication of *A Book to Burn*.
1591	Yuan Hongdao visits Li at Dragon Lake. The two travel together to Wuchang, where Li is attacked by a rowdy mob while sightseeing at the Yellow Crane Pavilion.
1592	Stays in Wuchang under the protection of Liu Dongxing.
1593	Returns to Dragon Lake.
1595	Huguang Provincial Surveillance Commissioner Shi Jingxian threatens to have Li deported from Macheng for being a danger to public morals.
1596	Seeks refuge with Liu Dongxing in Qinshui, Shanxi.
1597	Travels to Datong.
1598	Visits the Temple of Bliss in Beijing, then travels south to Nanjing with Jiao Hong.

1599	Publishes *A Book to Keep (Hidden)*; meets the Jesuit missionary Matteo Ricci for the first time.
1600	Meets Ricci again. Li's residence at Dragon Lake is attacked, and the grave site he had been preparing for himself is desecrated.
1601	Goes to live with Ma Jinglun in Tongzhou, near Beijing.
1602	Zhang Wenda, the chief supervising secretary in the Ministry of Rites, submits a memorial to the throne impeaching Li Zhi. Li is arrested and commits suicide in prison in Tongzhou. An imperial edict is issued banning his books.
1609	*Another Book to Keep (Hidden)* is published.
1618	*Another Book to Burn* is published.
1625	The edict banning Li Zhi's books is reissued.

BIBLIOGRAPHY

Andersen, Poul. "*Huashu* 化書: Book of Transformation." In Pregadio, *Encyclopedia of Taoism*, 1:517–18.
Araki Kengo 荒木見悟. *Chūgoku shingaku to kodō no Bukkyō* 中国心学と鼓動の仏教. Kitakyūshū, Jp.: Chūgoku shoten, 1995.
Ban Gu 班固. *Han shu* 漢書. Beijing: Zhonghua, 1962.
Ben-Dor Benite, Zvi. *The Dao of Muhammad: A Cultural History of Muslims in Late Imperial China*. Cambridge, Mass.: Harvard University Press, 2005.
Billeter, Jean-François. *Li Zhi, philosophe maudit (1527-1602)*. Geneva: Droz, 1979.
Birdwhistell, Anne. *Transition to Neo-Confucianism: Shao Yong on Knowledge and Symbols of Reality*. Stanford: Stanford University Press, 1989.
Brokaw, Cynthia. *The Ledgers of Merit and Demerit: Social Change and Moral Order in Late Imperial China*. Princeton: Princeton University Press, 1991.
Brook, Timothy. "Rethinking Syncretism: The Unity of the Three Teachings and Their Joint Worship in Late-Imperial China." *Journal of Chinese Religions* 21 (1993): 13–44.
Bush, Susan, and Hsio-yen Shih, eds. *Early Chinese Texts on Painting*. 2nd ed. Hong Kong: Hong Kong University Press, 2012.
Buswell, Robert E., Jr., and Donald S. Lopez Jr. *The Princeton Dictionary of Buddhism*. Princeton: Princeton University Press, 2014.
Cai, Zong-qi, ed. *How to Read Chinese Poetry: A Guided Anthology*. New York: Columbia University Press, 2008.
Campany, Robert Ford. "On the Very Idea of Religions (In the Modern West and in Early Medieval China)." *History of Religions* 42, no. 4 (2003): 287–319.
——. "Tales of Anomalous Events." In *Early Medieval China: A Sourcebook*, ed. Wendy Swartz, Robert Ford Campany, Yang Lu, and Jessey J. C. Choo, 576–92. New York: Columbia University Press, 2014.
Chan, Hok-lam. *Li Chih (1527-1602) in Contemporary Chinese Historiography: New Light on His Life and Works*. White Plains, N.Y.: M.E. Sharpe, 1980.
Chan, Wing-tsit, trans. *Instructions for Practical Living and Other Neo-Confucian Writings by Wang Yang-ming*. New York: Columbia University Press, 1963.

Chang, Kang-i Sun, and Stephen Owen, eds. *The Cambridge History of Chinese Literature*. 2 vols. Cambridge: Cambridge University Press, 2010.

Chang, Kang-i Sun, and Haun Saussy, eds. *Women Writers of Traditional China: An Anthology of Poetry and Criticism*. Stanford: Stanford University Press, 2000.

Chaves, Jonathan. "The Panoply of Images: A Reconsideration of the Literary Theory of the Kung-an School." In *Theories of the Arts in China*, ed. Susan Bush and Christian Murck, 341–64. Princeton: Princeton University Press, 1983.

Cheang, Eng-chew. "Li Chih as a Critic." PhD diss., University of Washington, 1973.

Chen Lai 陳來. *Wuyou zhi jing* 無有之境. Beijing: Renmin daxue chubanshe, 1991.

Chen Rongjie 陳榮捷 [Wing-tsit Chan]. *Wang Yangming Chuanxilu xiangzhu jiping* 王陽明傳習錄詳註集評. Taipei: Xuesheng, 1983.

Cheng, Pei-kai. "Continuities in Chinese Political Culture: Interpretations of Li Zhi, Past and Present." *Chinese Studies in History* 17, no. 2 (1983): 4–29.

———. "Reality and Imagination: Li Chih and T'ang Hsien-tsu in Search of Authenticity." PhD diss., Yale University, 1980.

Ch'ien, Edward T. *Chiao Hung and the Restructuring of Confucianism in the Late Ming*. New York: Columbia University Press, 1986.

Ching, Julia. "The Goose Lake Monastery Debate (1175)." *Journal of Chinese Philosophy* 1, no. 2 (1974): 161–78.

Chou, Chih-P'ing. *Yüan Hung-tao and the Kung-an School*. Cambridge: Cambridge University Press, 1988.

Chu, William. "Bodhisattva Precepts in the Ming Society: Factors behind Their Success and Propagation." *Journal of Buddhist Ethics* 13 (2006): 1–36.

Csikszentmihalyi, Mark. *Material Virtue: Ethics and the Body in Early China*. Leiden: Brill, 2004.

———, trans. and ed. *Readings in Han Chinese Thought*. Indianapolis: Hackett, 2006.

de Bary, Wm. Theodore. "Individualism and Humanitarianism in Late Ming Thought." In *Self and Society in Ming Thought*, 145–247. New York: Columbia University Press, 1970.

———. *Learning for One's Self: Essays on the Individual in Neo-Confucian Thought*. New York: Columbia University Press, 1991.

de Bary, Wm. Theodore, and Irene Bloom, comps. *Sources of Chinese Tradition: From Earliest Times to 1600, Volume 1*. 2nd ed. New York: Columbia University Press, 1999.

Decaux, Jacques. "True Classic of the Original Word of Laozi by Master Guanyin," parts 1 and 2. *Chinese Culture* 31, no. 1 (1990): 1–43; 31, no. 2 (1990): 1–46.

d'Elia, Pasquale, ed. *Fonti Ricciane*. 3 vols. Rome: Libreria dello Stato, 1942–49.

Didier, John. "Messrs. T'an, Chancellor Sung, and the *Book of Transformation* (*Hua shu*): Texts and the Transformations of Traditions." *Asia Major*, 3rd ser., 11, no. 1 (1998): 99–151.

Dumoulin, Heinrich. *Zen Buddhism: A History*. Trans. James W. Heisig and Paul Knitter. 2 vols. New York: Macmillan, 1988.

Ebrey, Patricia Buckley, ed. *Chinese Civilization: A Sourcebook*. 2nd ed. New York: Free Press, 2009.

Eichman, Jennifer. "Intertextual Alliances: Huang Hui's Synthesis of Buddhist and Confucian Paths to Liberation." *T'oung Pao* 100 (2014): 1–44.

Elman, Benjamin A. *A Cultural History of Civil Examinations in Late Imperial China.* Berkeley: University of California Press, 2000.

Fan Ye 范曄. *Hou Han shu* 後漢書. Beijing: Zhonghua shuju, 1965.

Fei, Faye Chunfang, ed. and trans. *Chinese Theories of Theater and Performance from Confucius to the Present.* Ann Arbor: University of Michigan Press, 1999.

Foulk, T. Griffith. "Huixiang 廻向." In *Digital Dictionary of Buddhism*, ed. A. Charles Muller. http://www.buddhism-dict.net/ddb/. Accessed August 8, 2014.

Franke, Wolfgang. "Historical Writing during the Ming." In *The Cambridge History of China, Volume 7, Part 1: The Ming Dynasty, 1368-1644*, ed. Frederick W. Mote and Denis Twitchett, 726-82. Cambridge: Cambridge University Press, 1988.

Fuller, Michael A. *The Road to East Slope: The Development of Su Shi's Poetic Voice.* Stanford: Stanford University Press, 1990.

Gallagher, Louis J., trans. *China in the Sixteenth Century: The Journals of Matthew Ricci, 1583-1610.* New York: Random House, 1953.

Gao Heng 高亨. *Zhouyi gu jing jin zhu* 周易古經今注. 3rd ed. Beijing: Zhonghua shuju, 1989.

Gardner, Daniel K., trans. *The Four Books: The Basic Teachings of the Later Confucian Tradition.* Indianapolis: Hackett, 2007.

Geng Dingxiang 耿定向. *Geng Tiantai xiansheng wenji* 耿天台先生文集. Ed. Shen Yunlong 沈雲龍. Taipei: Wenhai chubanshe, 1970.

Gómez, Luis O., trans. *The Land of Bliss: The Paradise of the Buddha of Measureless Light; Sanskrit and Chinese Versions of the Sukhāvatīvyūha Sutras.* Honolulu: University of Hawai'i Press, 1996.

Gong Duqing 龔篤清. *Mingdai baguwenshi tan* 明代八股文史探. Changsha: Huhan renmin chubanshe, 2006.

Goodrich, L. Carrington, and Chaoying Fang, eds. *Dictionary of Ming Biography, 1368-1644.* 2 vols. New York: Columbia University Press, 1976. (*DMB*)

Graham, A. C., trans. *The Book of Lieh-tzu: A Classic of Tao.* New York: Columbia University Press, 1990.

——. *Two Chinese Philosophers: The Metaphysics of the Brothers Ch'eng.* La Salle, Ill.: Open Court, 1992.

Grant, Beata. "*Da Zhangfu*: The Gendered Rhetoric of Heroism and Equality in Seventeenth-Century Chan Buddhist Discourse Records." *Nan Nü* 10, no. 2 (2008): 177–211.

Gu Yanwu 顧炎武. *Rizhi lu* 日知錄. *Sibu beiyao* edition. Shanghai: Shangwu yinshuguan, 1947.

Haar, B. J. ter. "Newly Recovered Anecdotes from Hong Mai's (1123-1202) *Yijian zhi*." *Journal of Song-Yuan Studies* 23 (1993): 19–41.

Handler-Spitz, Rivi. "Li Zhi's Relativism and Skepticism in the Multicultural Late Ming." *Concentric: Literary and Cultural Studies* 34, no. 2 (2008): 13–35.

Harrison, Paul. "Commemoration and Identification in *Buddhānusmṛti*." In *In The Mirror of Memory: Reflections on Mindfulness and Remembrance in Indian and Tibetan Buddhism*, ed. Janet Gyatso, 215–38. Albany: SUNY Press, 1992.

Hawkes, David. *Ch'u Tz'u: The Songs of the South; An Ancient Chinese Anthology.* Boston: Beacon Press, 1959.

Ho, Ping-ti. *The Ladder of Success in Imperial China: Aspects of Social Mobility, 1368-1911*. New York: Columbia University Press, 1962.
Huang Lin 黃霖. "*Fenshu* yuanben de jige wenti" 焚書原本的幾個問題. *Wenxue yichan* 5 (2002): 89–95.
Huang, Martin W. *Literati and Self-Re/Presentation: Autobiographical Sensibility in the Eighteenth-Century Chinese Novel*. Stanford: Stanford University Press, 1995.
——, ed. *Male Friendship in Ming China*. Leiden: Brill, 2007.
Huang, Ray. *1587: A Year of No Significance; The Ming Dynasty in Decline*. New Haven: Yale University Press, 1981.
Huang Tsung-hsi. *The Records of Ming Scholars*. Ed. Julia Ching. Honolulu: University of Hawai'i Press, 1987.
Huang Zongxi 黃宗羲. *Mingru xue an* 明儒學案. Wanyou wenku huiyao edition. Taipei: Taiwan Shangwu yinshuguan, 1965. (*MRXA*)
Hummel, Arthur W., ed. *Eminent Chinese of the Ch'ing Period (1644-1912)*. 2 vols. Taipei: Ch'eng-wen, 1967.
Hung, Ming-shui. *The Romantic Vision of Yuan Hung-tao, Late Ming Poet and Critic*. Taipei: Bookman, 1997.
Hurvitz, Leon. *Scripture of the Lotus Blossom of the Fine Dharma*. New York: Columbia University Press, 1976.
Hutton, Eric L., trans. *Xunzi: The Complete Text*. Princeton: Princeton University Press, 2014.
Ivanhoe, Philip J., trans. *The Daodejing of Laozi*. Indianapolis: Hackett, 2002.
——, trans. *Readings from the Lu-Wang School of Neo-Confucianism*. Indianapolis: Hackett, 2009.
Jiang, Jin. "Heresy and Persecution in Late Ming Society: Reinterpreting the Case of Li Zhi." *Late Imperial China* 22, no. 2 (2001): 1–34.
Kinney, Anne Behnke, trans. and ed. *Exemplary Women of Early China: The "Lienü zhuan" of Liu Xiang*. New York: Columbia University Press, 2014.
Knechtges, David R., trans. *Wenxuan, or Selections of Refined Literature: Volume 1, Rhapsodies on Metropolises and Capitals*. Princeton: Princeton University Press, 1982.
Kohn, Livia. "Yin Xi." In Pregadio, *Encyclopedia of Taoism*, 2:1169–70.
Lau, D. C., trans. *Confucius: The Analects (Lun yü)*. London: Penguin Books, 1979.
——, trans. *Lao Tzu: Tao Te Ching*. London: Penguin Books, 1963.
——, trans. *Mencius*. London: Penguin Books, 1970.
Lee, Pauline C. *Li Zhi, Confucianism, and the Virtue of Desire*. Albany: SUNY Press, 2012.
Legge, James, trans. *The Chinese Classics*. 5 vols. Hong Kong: Hong Kong University Press, 1960.
——, trans. *The Yi King*. Vol. 16 of *The Sacred Books of the East*, ed. F. Max Müller. Oxford: Clarendon Press, 1899.
——, trans. *The Li Ki*. Vols. 27, 28 of *The Sacred Books of the East*, ed. F. Max Müller. Oxford: Clarendon Press, 1899.
Li Defeng 李德鋒. "Li Zhi 'Cangshu' yu Tang Shunzhi 'Zuo bian' zhi guanxi kaoshu" 李贄《藏書》與唐順之《左編》之關係考述. *Shixueshi yanjiu* 141 (2011): 42–50.
Li Zhi 李贄. *Fenshu, Xu fenshu* 焚書、續焚書. Beijing: Zhonghua shuju, 1975.
——. *Fenshu, Xu fenshu* 焚書、續焚書. Edited and trans. Zhang Jianye 張建業. Beijing: Zhonghua shuju, 2011.

———. *Li Zhi quanji zhu* 李贄全集注. 26 vols. Ed. Zhang Jianye 張建業 and Zhang Dai 張岱. Beijing: Shehui kexue wenxian chubanshe, 2010. (*LZQJZ*)

———. *Li Zhi sanwen xuan zhu* 李贄散文選注. Ed. Zhang Fan 張凡. Beijing: Beijing shifan xueyuan chubanshe, 1991.

———. *Li Zhi wenji* 李贄文集. 6 vols. Ed. Zhang Jianye 張建業 and Liu Yousheng 劉幼生. Beijing: Shehui kexue wenxian chubanshe, 2000.

———. Preface [*Qianyin* 前引] to *Jingtu jue* 淨土決. In *Xinbian wanxu zangjing* 新編卍續藏經, vol. 108, 357.a1–a17. Taipei: Xinwenfeng chuban gongsi, 1983.

Liezi 列子. *Liezi zhu* 列子注. Ed. Zhang Zhan 張湛. Taipei: Taiwan shangwu yinshuguan, 1968.

Lin Haiquan 林海權. *Li Zhi nianpu kaolue* 李贄年譜考略. Fuzhou: Fujian renmin chubanshe, 1992.

Lin Yutang. *Confucius Saw Nancy*. Shanghai: Commercial Press, 1936.

Liu I-ch'ing [Liu Yiqing 劉義慶]. *Shih-shuo Hsin-yü, A New Account of Tales of the World*. Trans. Richard B. Mather. Minneapolis: University of Minnesota Press, 1976.

———. *Shishuo xinyu* 世說新語. Ed. Xu Zhen'e 徐震堮. Beijing: Zhonghua shuju, 1984.

Liu Ts'un-yan 柳存仁 [Liu Cunren]. *Selected Papers from the Hall of Harmonious Wind*. Leiden: Brill, 1976.

Liu Xie 劉協. *Wenxin diaolong xuandu* 文心雕龍選讀. Ed. Wang Gengsheng 王更生. Taipei: Juliu tushu gongsi, 1994.

Liu Yong 劉勇. "'Jiangshang wang Huanghelou' shi zuozhe kaoshi" 《江上望黃鶴樓》詩作者考實. *Wenxian qikan*, no. 3 (2010): 184–86.

Lowry, Kathryn. *The Tapestry of Popular Songs in 16th- and 17th-Century China: Reading, Imitation, and Desire*. Leiden: Brill, 2005.

Lynn, Richard John, trans. *The Classic of Changes: A New Translation of the "I Ching" as Interpreted by Wang Bi*. New York: Columbia University Press, 1994.

Ma Duanlin 馬端臨. *Wenxian tongkao* 文獻通考. In *Wenyuange Siku quanshu*.

Mann, Susan. "Widows in the Community, Class, and Kinship Structures of Qing Dynasty China." *Journal of Asian Studies* 46, no. 1 (1987): 37–56.

Mann, Susan, and Yu-Yin Cheng, eds. *Under Confucian Eyes: Writings on Gender in Chinese History*. Berkeley: University of California Press, 2001.

McRae, John R. "Ch'an Commentaries on the *Heart Sūtra*: Preliminary Inferences on the Permutation of Chinese Buddhism." *Journal of the International Association of Buddhist Studies* 11, no. 2 (1988): 87–115.

———, trans. *The Platform Sutra of the Sixth Patriarch*. Berkeley: Numata Center for Buddhist Translation and Research, 2000.

Mengzi 孟子 [*Mencius*]. In Ruan, *Shisanjing zhu shu*.

Ming shi lu 明實錄. Nangang: Zhongyang yanjiuyuan lishi yuyan yanjiu suo, 1966–1968.

Mizoguchi Yūzō 溝口雄三. "Funsho" 焚書. In *Kinsei zuihitsu shū* 近世随筆集, ed. Iriya Yoshitaka 入矢義高, 275–445. Tokyo: Heibonsha, 1971.

———. "Min matsu o ikita Ri Takugo" 明末を生きた李卓吾. *Tōyō bunka kenkyūjo kiyō* 55 (March 1971): 39–193.

Mote, F. W. "Late Ming Political Decline, 1567–1627." In *Imperial China, 900–1800*, 723–42. Cambridge, Mass.: Harvard University Press, 1999.

Mulligan, Jean, trans. *The Lute: Kao Ming's "P'i-p'a chi."* New York: Columbia University Press, 1980.

Nan Huaijin 南懷瑾 and Xu Qinting 徐芹庭, eds. *Zhouyi jinzhu jinyi* 周易今注今譯. Taipei: Taiwan Shangwu yinshuguan, 1966.

Nattier, Jan. "The *Heart Sūtra*: A Chinese Apocryphal Text?" *Journal of the International Association of Buddhist Studies* 15, no. 2 (1992): 153–223.

Nienhauser, William H., Jr., ed. and comp. *The Indiana Companion to Traditional Chinese Literature*. Bloomington: Indiana University Press, 1986.

Nylan, Michael. *The Five "Confucian" Classics*. New Haven: Yale University Press, 2001.

Owen, Stephen, ed. and trans. *An Anthology of Chinese Literature: Beginnings to 1911*. New York: Norton, 1996.

——. *Readings in Chinese Literary Thought*. Cambridge, Mass.: Harvard University Asia Center, 1992.

Plaks, Andrew H. *The Four Masterworks of the Ming Novel: Ssu ta ch'i-shu*. Princeton: Princeton University Press, 1987.

——. "The Prose of Our Time." In *The Power of Culture: Studies in Chinese Cultural History*, ed. Willard J. Peterson, Andrew H. Plaks, and Ying-shih Yü, 206–17. Hong Kong: Chinese University Press, 1994.

——, trans. *Ta Hsüeh and Chung Yung ("The Highest Order of Cultivation" and "On the Practice of the Mean")*. London: Penguin Books, 2004.

Poceski, Mario. *The Records of Mazu and the Making of Classical Chan Literature*. New York: Oxford University Press, 2015.

Pregadio, Fabrizio, ed. *The Encyclopedia of Taoism*. 2 vols. New York: Routledge, 2008.

——. *The Seal of the Unity of the Three: A Study and Translation of the "Cantong qi," the Source of the Taoist Way of the Golden Elixir*. Mountain View, Calif.: Golden Elixir Press, 2011.

Qian Maowei 錢茂偉. *Mingdai shixue de licheng* 明代史學的歷程. Beijing: Shehui kexue wenxian chubanshe, 2003.

Quan Tang shi 全唐詩. Ed. Peng Dingqiu 彭定求. 12 vols. Beijing: Zhonghua shuju, 1960.

Quan Tang wen 全唐文. 5 vols. Ed. Dong Gao 董誥. Tainan: Jingwei shuju, 1965.

Ricci, Matteo. *On Friendship: One Hundred Maxims for a Chinese Prince*. Trans. Timothy Billings. New York: Columbia University Press, 2009.

Rolston, David L., ed. *How to Read the Chinese Novel*. Princeton: Princeton University Press, 1990.

Rong Zhaozu 容肇祖. *Li Zhi nianpu* 李贄年譜. Beijing: Shenghuo dushu xinzhi sanlian chubanshe, 1957.

——. *Li Zhuowu ping zhuan* 李卓吾評傳. Shanghai: Shangwu yinshuguan, 1973.

Rowe, William T. *Crimson Rain: Seven Centuries of Violence in a Chinese County*. Stanford: Stanford University Press, 2007.

Ruan Yuan 阮元, ed. *Shisanjing zhu shu* 十三經注疏. 1816. Reprint, Taipei: Dahua, 1987.

Sasaki, Ruth Fuller, trans. *The Record of Linji*. Ed. Thomas Yūhō Kirchner. Honolulu: University of Hawai`i Press, 2009.

Sasaki, Ruth Fuller, Yoshitaka Iriya, and Dana R. Fraser, trans. *The Recorded Sayings of Layman P'ang: A Ninth-Century Zen Classic*. New York: Weatherhill, 1971.

Sibu beiyao 四部備要. Shanghai: Shangwu shuju, 1947.
Siku quanshu zongmu tiyao 四庫全書總目提要. 5 vols. Taipei: Taiwan Shangwu yinshuguan, 1983.
Sima Qian 司馬遷. *The Grand Scribe's Records*. Ed. William H. Nienhauser Jr. 10 vols. Bloomington: Indiana University Press, 1994–.
———. *Records of the Grand Historian*. Trans. Burton Watson in 3 vols. as *Qin Dynasty*; *Han Dynasty I*; *Han Dynasty II*. Hong Kong: Research Centre for Translation, Chinese University of Hong Kong; New York: Columbia University Press, 1993.
———. *Records of the Historian: Chapters from the Shih chi of Ssu-ma Ch'ien*. Trans. Burton Watson. New York: Columbia University Press, 1969.
———. *Shi ji* 史記. 10 vols. Beijing: Zhonghua shuju, 1962.
———. *Shiki kaichū kōshō* 史記會注考證. Ed. Takigawa Kametarō 瀧川龜太郎. Taipei: Da'an, 1998.
Sommer, Matthew Harvey. "The Uses of Chastity: Sex, Law, and the Property of Widows in Qing China." *Late Imperial China* 17, no. 2 (1996): 77–130.
Sun Tzu. *The Illustrated Art of War*. Trans. Thomas Cleary. Boston: Shambhala, 1998.
Sunzi 孫子. *Sunzi bingfa* 孫子兵法. Shanghai: Zhonghua shuju, 1936.
Suzuki Torao 鈴木虎雄. "Li Zhuowu nianpu" 李卓吾年譜. In *Li Zhuowu lun* 李卓吾論, ed. Zhu Weizhi 朱維之, 47–143. Fuzhou: Fujian xiehe daxue chubanshe, 1935.
Teiser, Stephen F. "*Heart Sūtra (Xin jing)*." In *Ways with Words: Writing about Reading Texts from Early China*, ed. Pauline Yu, Peter Bol, Stephen Owen, and Willard Peterson, 113–16. Berkeley: University of California Press, 2000.
Van Norden, Bryan W., trans. *Mengzi: With Selections from Traditional Commentaries*. Indianapolis: Hackett, 2008.
Venturi, Pietro Tacchi, ed. *Opere storiche del P. Matteo Ricci, S.I.* Macerata, It.: Giorgetti, 1911–1913.
Wagner, Marsha L. *Wang Wei*. Boston: Twayne, 1981.
Waley, Arthur, trans. *The Book of Songs: The Ancient Chinese Classic of Poetry*. New York: Grove Press, 1996.
Wang Gen 王艮. *Wang Xinzhai xiansheng yiji* 王心齋先生遺集. Shanghai: Guocui xuebao guan, 1912.
Watson, Burton, trans. *The Analects of Confucius*. New York: Columbia University Press, 2007.
———, trans. *The Complete Works of Chuang Tzu*. New York: Columbia University Press, 1968.
———, trans. *The Vimalakirti Sutra*. New York: Columbia University Press, 1996.
Wenyuange Siku quanshu dianzi ban 文淵閣四庫全書電子版. 182 CDs. Shanghai: Dizhi wenhua chuban youxian gongsi / Shanghai renmin chubanshe, 2002.
West, Stephen H., and Wilt L. Idema, trans. *The Moon and the Zither: The Story of the Western Wing*. Berkeley: University of California Press, 1991.
Wilson, Thomas A. *Genealogy of the Way: The Construction and Uses of the Confucian Tradition in Late Imperial China*. Stanford: Stanford University Press, 1995.
Wong, Wai-ying. "The Thesis of Single-Rootedness in the Thought of Cheng Hao." In *Dao Companion to Neo-Confucianism*, ed. John Makeham, 89–104. Dordrecht: Springer, 2010.

Wu Guoping 鄔國平. "Ye tan 'Fenshu' yuanben de wenti" 也談《焚書》原本的問題. *Qinghua daxue xuebao, zhexue shehui kexue ban* 2, no. 19 (2004): 45–50.

Wu, Jiang. *Enlightenment in Dispute: The Reinvention of Chan Buddhism in Seventeenth-Century China*. Oxford: Oxford University Press, 2008.

Wu, Pei-yi. *The Confucian's Progress: Autobiographical Writings in Traditional China*. Princeton: Princeton University Press, 1990.

Wu Ze 吳澤. *Rujiao pantu Li Zhuowu* 儒教叛徒李卓吾. Shanghai: Huaxia shudian, 1949.

Wyatt, Don J. *The Recluse of Loyang: Shao Yung and the Moral Evolution of Early Sung Thought*. Honolulu: University of Hawai'i Press, 1996.

Xiamen Daxue Lishi Xi 廈門大學歷史系. *Li Zhi yanjiu cankao ziliao* 李贄研究參考資料. 2 vols. Xiamen: Fujian renmin chubanshe, 1975.

Ye, Yang, trans. *Vignettes from the Late Ming: A Hsiao-p'in Anthology*. Seattle: University of Washington Press, 1999.

Yu, Clara, trans. "On Reading the Letter to Ruowu from His Mother." In Ebrey, *Chinese Civilization*, 260–61.

———, trans. "Testament." In Ebrey, *Chinese Civilization*, 262.

———, trans. "To Zeng Jiquan." In Ebrey, *Chinese Civilization*, 259–60.

Yü, Chün-fang. *Kuan-yin: The Chinese Transformation of Avalokiteśvara*. New York: Columbia University Press, 2001.

Yuan Hongdao 袁宏道. *Yuan Hongdao ji jianxiao* 袁宏道集箋校. Shanghai: Shanghai guji chubanshe, 1981.

Yüan Hung-tao. *Pilgrim of the Clouds: Poems and Essays from Ming China*. Trans. Jonathan Chaves. Buffalo: White Pine Press, 2005.

Yuan Zhongdao 袁中道. *Kexuezhai ji* 珂雪齋集. Shanghai: Shanghai guji chubanshe, 1989.

Yuan Zongdao 遠宗道. *Baisu zhai leiji* 白蘇齋類集. Taipei: Weiwen tushu gongsi, 1976.

Zeitlin, Judith T. *Historian of the Strange: Pu Songling and the Chinese Classical Tale*. Stanford: Stanford University Press, 1993.

Zhang Yanyuan 張彥遠. *Lidai minghua ji* 歷代名畫記. Taipei: Yiwen yinshuguan, 1965.

Zhang, Ying. "Politics and Morality during the Ming-Qing Dynastic Transition (1570–1670)." PhD diss., University of Michigan, 2010.

Zhu Changwen 朱長文. *Qin shi* 琴史. Taipei: Taiwan shangwu shuju, 1983.

Zhu Guozhen 朱國禎. *Yong chuang xiaopin* 湧幢小品. Shanghai: Zhonghua shuju, 1959.

Zhu Qianzhi 朱謙之. *Li Zhi: Shiliu shiji Zhongguo fan fengjian sixiang de xianquzhe* 李贄：十六世紀中國反封建思想的先驅者. Wuhan: Hubei renmin chubanshe, 1957.

Zhu Weizheng 朱維錚, ed. *Li Madou Zhongwen zhuyiji* 利瑪竇中文著譯集. Hong Kong: Xianggang chengshi daxue chubanshe, 2001.

Zhu Xi 朱熹. *Lunyu jizhu* 論語集注. Taipei: Hansheng chubanshe, 1988.

———. *Sishu zhangju jizhu* 四書章句集註. Beijing: Zhonghua shuju, 1983.

Zhuangzi jishi 莊子集釋. Ed. Wang Xianqian 王先謙. Beijing: Zhonghua shuju, 1961.

Zhuhong 袾宏. *Lianchi dashi quanji* 蓮池大師全集. 1899. Reprint, Taipei: Dongchu chubanshe, 1992.

Zuozhuan chunqiu yizhu 左傳春秋譯注. Ed. Gu Baotian 顧寶田 and Chen Fulin 陳福林. Changchun: Jilin wenshi chubanshe, 1995.

CONTRIBUTORS

TIMOTHY BILLINGS is a professor of English and comparative literature at Middlebury College. His translations include Matteo Ricci's *On Friendship* (Columbia University Press, 2009) and, with Christopher Bush, Victor Segalen's *Stèles* / 古今碑錄 (Wesleyan University Press, 2007).

TIMOTHY BROOK holds the Republic of China chair of the Department of History and Institute of Asian Studies at the University of British Columbia. He has published widely on the social and cultural history of the Ming dynasty.

HUIYING CHEN is a PhD candidate in history at the University of Illinois at Chicago.

DREW DIXON studied comparative literature at Princeton and is a PhD candidate with the John U. Nef Committee on Social Thought at the University of Chicago.

JENNIFER EICHMAN is a religious studies scholar and a research associate at the Centre of Buddhist Studies, SOAS, University of London. Her primary area of expertise is late-Ming Chinese Buddhist traditions, with an interdisciplinary emphasis on the relationship between network and discourse.

RIVI HANDLER-SPITZ is an assistant professor of Chinese language and literature at Macalester College. Her work on Li Zhi analyzes his writings in the context of global early-modern rhetoric and aesthetics.

MARTIN HUANG is a professor of Chinese at the University of California, Irvine. He has published widely on late imperial Chinese literature and gender history. He is working on a project titled *Gender and Memory in Late Imperial China*.

THOMAS KELLY received his BA from Oxford University and is a PhD candidate in East Asian languages and civilizations at the University of Chicago. His research explores the relations between the literary imagination and the decorative arts in early-modern China.

DAVID LEBOVITZ is a PhD candidate in the Department of East Asian Languages and Civilizations at the University of Chicago.

PAULINE C. LEE is an assistant professor of Chinese religions and culture at Saint Louis University. She is the author of *Li Zhi, Confucianism, and the Virtue of Desire* (SUNY Press, 2012), and her current work includes study of changing views of play in China.

HAUN SAUSSY is University Professor at the University of Chicago. His most recent book is *The Ethnography of Rhythm: Orality and Its Technologies* (Fordham University Press, 2016).

ZINAN YAN is a lecturer at Beijing Normal University. He received his MA and PhD in Sinology from SOAS, University of London. His research area is Ming-Qing poetry, with a special interest in the literary culture of the Qianlong court.

INDEX

"Adorned with Every Mark of Dignity" (Wu suo bu pei; Li Zhi), 201–3
"After Śākyamuni Buddha" (Shijiafo hou; Li Zhi), 282–85
"After the Snow" (Xue hou; poem; Li Zhi), 210, 308
"Afterword to *Journeying with Companions*" (Zheng tu yu gong hou yu; Li Zhi), xxix, 158–61
All Men Are Brothers. See *Water Margin*
allusions, xix, xxxiii–xxxv, 3, 138, 204. See also particular works
Amitābha, 13n7; Pure Land of, 178–80, 261, 268, 313n2; reciting name of (*nianfo*), 26, 27, 28, 164, 165, 179, 287. See also Pure Land Buddhism
"Amitābha Temple" (Mituo si; poem; Li Zhi), 298
Analects (*Lunyu*): on adornment, 201, 202n7; on associates, 136n3, 139n6; on Bo Yi, 200n6; and Buddhism, 118n20, 279nn3–5, 280nn8–11, 290n3; and childlike heart-mind, 108n6, 109; and *chuanqi*, 193n4; on cleanliness, 28n26; commentaries on, xx, 4n5; and Geng Dingli, 168; and Geng Dingxiang, 35n8, 38nn14–16, 39n17, 44n26, 46n34, 48n39, 50n44, 51n48, 53nn52–55, 57n66, 58n69, 59nn70–75, 61n81, 62n82; and ghosts, 264n4; and He Xinyin, 85nn5–6, 87n11; and Luo Rufang, 152n5, 155n10, 156nn16–18, 157n20; on Nanzi, 66n7, 67n8; on recluses, 276n2, 277n7; on reputation, 17nn5–6; on rulership, 94n5, 97n19; and self-portraits, 76n9, 83n21; on teachers, 26n22; and Wang Longxi, 147nn3–5, 148n7; and Warring States, 91n12; on wasting words, 27n24; on weapons, 92–98; and women, 30n3, 31n4, 31n7
Ānanda, 283
Annals of Lü Buwei (*Lüshi chunqiu*), 183n11, 236n6
Another Book to Burn (*Xu fenshu*; Li Zhi), xv, xvii, xxiii, xxvii, xxxii–xxxv, 231–316; essays in, 259–93; letters in, 34, 241–57; poetry in, 295–316; prefaces in, 233–40; publication of, 341
Another Book to Keep (Hidden) (*Xu cangshu*; Li Zhi), 146, 341
"Another Reply to Censor Geng" (You da Geng Zhongcheng; Li Zhi), 40–41
"Another Reply to My Old Friend Geng Dingxiang" (Fu Geng tong lao shu; Li Zhi), 47–48
"Appraisal of Liu Xie" (Zan Liu Xie; Li Zhi), 140–41, 247n4
Art of War (*Sunzi bingfa*; Sun Wu), 94n6, 148n10, 251n8
"At a Banquet on a Spring Evening, I Receive the Word 'Lack'" (Chunxiao yanji de kong zi; poem; Li Zhi), 221
Authentic Scripture of Master Wenshi (*Wenshi zhen jing*), 265, 266

authenticity (*shi*), xxix, 3, 67, 234, 235, 245, 325; essays on, 106, 111, 273, 275n9, 278
Avalokiteśvara (Guanyin), xxv, 115n9, 116n12, 249, 251, 336

Bai Juyi, 32n9, 187
"Ballad of the North Wind" (Shuo feng yao; poem; Li Zhi), 215–16
Ban Gu, xxiv, 327, 330
Bao Biao, 91
Bao Qiuzi (Fu Qiubo), 206
"Bidding Farewell to Justice Minister Geng" (Yu Geng Sikou gaobie; Li Zhi), 58–62
biography: in *A Book to Burn*, 75nn1–2, 89–91, 199–200, 209; in *A Book to Keep (Hidden)*, 276, 277n8, 317–19; of Li Zhi, xxxiv, 75–83, 121–24, 185–89, 325–33; of women, 66n7, 67n8
"Biography of Bo Yi" (Bo Yi zhuan; Li Zhi), 199–200
Bo Ya, 158–61
Bo Yi, 59, 60, 138, 199–200
Bodhidharma, 104n16, 283
Book of Documents (*Shang shu*), 31n4, 31n6, 248n7, 323
Book of Rites. See *Records of Ritual*
Book of Transformations (*Huashu*; Tan Qiao), 265, 266
Book to Burn, A (*Fenshu*; Li Zhi), xv, xvii, xxvii, xxxii–xxxv, 3–229, 239, 329; "Author's Preface" to (Zi xu), 3–5; Buddhist petitions in, 172–77; essays in, 75–193, 207; historiography in, xxii–xxiii, 195–208; letters in, 7–74; memorial on, xxiii, 65, 277n9, 293n8, 334–37; poems in, 209–29; publication of, 340
Book to Keep (Hidden), A (*Cangshu*; Li Zhi), 317–24, 329; historiography in, xxiii–xxiv, 320–24; introduction to, 317–19; Li Zhi on, 4, 5; memorial on, xxxiii, 65, 277n9, 293n8, 334–37; publication of, 340, 341
Bowing to the Moon (*Bai yue ting*; Shi Hui), 102, 103, 104
"Brief Introduction to a Selection of Daoist Teachings" (Daojiao chao xiaoyin; Li Zhi), 265–66
"Brief Introduction to *Resolving Doubts About the Pure Land*" (Jingtu jue qianyin; Li Zhi), 178–80

"Bright Moon in the Center of the Sky" (poem; Li Zhi), 303
Buddha Śākyamuni: and Confucius, 279, 282–85, 289, 290; and expedient devices, 270–72; in letters, 19–20, 31, 52–53, 57, 58, 61, 247; and monastic rules, 181, 182–83; on Pure Land, 179n4; syncretic view of, 265, 266
Buddhism, xvi, xxi, xxiv, xxv, xxxiv–xxxv; and Confucianism, 162–65, 178, 278–81, 282–85; in essays, 103n8, 103n13, 114–18; and expedient devices, 270–72; and filial piety, 22, 65, 286; and Geng Dingli, 169n19; and Geng Dingxiang, 35n7, 45n31, 52, 57, 58; hypocrisy in, 301n3; in letters, 12–14, 15, 16n3, 18, 19–20, 21, 22, 26, 242; and Li Zhi, 57, 326, 327, 336, 340; and Luo Rufang, 156; Mahayana, 181, 270n3; and Matteo Ricci, 256; and meat eating, 267–69; monastic discipline in, 181–84, 219, 286–88; nonsyncretic view of, 78n14; in poetry, 209, 219n2, 221n1; purity in, 21, 27–28; supplications in, 172–77; sutras of, 114–20, 172, 173, 175–77, 251n6, 261, 270–72, 273–75; syncretic view of, xxvii, xxviii, xxx, xxxii, 21, 56n62, 129–31, 265–66, 278–81; and Taizhou school, 23n5; taking the tonsure in, xvi, 10n2, 18, 23, 29, 57, 63, 185, 187–88, 228, 236, 251n10, 255, 274, 275, 281, 282, 287n3, 328, 333, 335, 340; Tantric, 242n4; and women, 30, 31, 249; and Yan Shannong, 72–73. *See also* karma; Pure Land Buddhism; Zen Buddhism
bureaucracy, 155, 195–96; corruption in, xvi, xix, xxii, xxvii, xxx, 44n28, 80; and Geng Dingli, 168, 169; and Li Zhi, 63, 64, 77–78, 79, 82, 121, 185–86, 187, 326, 339–40. *See also* examinations, civil service

calligraphy, 327–28
Cao Cao, 211, 299n2, 332n11
Cao Xueqin, xxix
Chan Buddhism, xxvii, 115, 270; and Confucianism, 282, 283; in essays, 147; in letters, 26, 32n12, 33, 51n47, 61; and Li Zhi's behavior, 65, 66, 68–69, 70, 71, 72;

and music, 160; in poems, 301n2; and Pure Land, 178–80
Changrong, 286, 287
Changtong, 175–77
Chen Dalai, 291
Chen Tuan, 277
Chen Yiqing, 188
Cheng brothers (Cheng Hao and Cheng Yi), xviin13, 7, 46n36, 78n14, 130, 130n4, 281n12
Cheng Houtai (Cheng Xueyan), 24
Cheng Lian, 158–61
Cheng-Zhu school. *See* School of Principle
Chi You, 95
"Chrysanthemum Regrets" (Hen ju; poem; Li Zhi), 217
chuanqi (fantastic tales), 109n9, 192–93
Chunyu Yue, 322
Classic of Changes (*Yijing*): and *chuanqi*, 193n4; in essays, 100n4, 101, 103n11, 149n12, 155n11; and ghost stories, 263, 264n3; and He Xinyin, 85n4, 88; in historiography, 202n6; and karma, 260n4; in letters, 24n10, 32n8, 35n3, 71n19, 245–46; Li Zhi on, 245n2, 328, 332; in poems, 224n6; on rulership, 95nn9–10
Classic of Poetry (*Shi jing*): in essays, 95n12, 103n10, 112, 136n2, 154n8, 155n11, 168n13; in letters, 31n5, 74n24
Classified Conversations of Master Zhu (*Zhuzi yulei*), 108n7
cleanliness (*jie*): in essays, 121–24, 137, 202, 291; in letters, 21, 27–28; of Li Zhi, 326–27; and meat eating, 268
Cloister of the Flourishing Buddha (Dragon Lake, Macheng): attacks on, 10, 29, 341; discipline in, 181, 182, 184, 286–88; Li Zhi at, xvi, 20n5, 63, 249, 267, 289–90, 340; and Medicine Buddha, 172, 175n2; monks at, 21, 25n18, 69n16, 255n2; and Ruowu's mother, 164nn5–6
Collected Writings of Mr. Geng Tiantai (*Geng Tiantai xiansheng wenji*), 34
Collection of the Immortal of the Cliff (*Po xian ji*; Su Shi), 20
Commentaries on the Laozi (Jiao Hong), 129
Commentary on the Four Books (*Sishu ping*; Li Zhi), 4n5

Compilation from the Dark Studio (*Anrantang leizuan*; Pan Shizao), 207
"Composed with Joy Upon Arriving at the Temple of Bliss . . ." (Jiu ri zhi Jilesi wen Yuan Zhonglang qie zhi yin xi er fu; poem; Li Zhi), 209, 227
Confucianism, xxxv; and Buddhism, 162–65, 178, 278–81, 282–85; classics of, xvii–xviii; and Confucius, 181; and *Diamond Sutra*, 273; and Five Relationships, 99; and karma, 260; vs. Legalism, 204–5; in letters, 15, 21, 31, 57, 58; Li Zhi's criticisms of, xvi, xix–xx, 330, 331, 336; and Luo Rufang, 155–56; and meat eating, 267–69; nonsyncretic view of, 78n14; in PRC, xxx, xxxi; in prefaces, 235; and Qin Shihuang, 320, 323; and rulership, 92–94, 97, 98; syncretic view of, xvii, xviii, xxx, xxxii, 21, 56n62, 129–31, 265–66, 278–81; of Wang Longxi, 147; on wealth and status, 280–81. *See also* neo-Confucianism; Taizhou school
Confucius: on adornment, 201, 202; on Bo Yi, 199, 200; and *A Book to Keep* (*Hidden*), 318, 319; and Buddha Śākyamuni, 279, 282–85, 289, 290; and childlike heart-mind, 106, 112, 113; and Confucianism, 181; and *Diamond Sutra*, 274; in essays, 139; and Fan Chi, 76–77; on filial piety, 22; and Geng Dingli, 168; and Geng Dingxiang, 35–40, 48–53, 50, 55–59, 61, 62; and He Xinyin, 85, 86; and individualism, xxiii; and Laozi, 130, 265, 266, 289, 290; in letters, 15, 17, 18, 22, 28, 31, 50, 68, 247; Li Zhi's criticism of, xxiii, xxiv, xxv, xxxi, 336; and Luo Rufang, 151, 152, 157; and Matteo Ricci, 256, 257; and Nanzi, 66–67, 70–71; on poetry, 192, 193; on recluses, 276; syncretic view of, xxxii, 265; and Wang Longxi, 147; on wealth and status, 280; on weapons, 92, 93–94; and women, 31
Contemplating My Life (*Guansheng ji*; Geng Dingxiang), 51n47
"Crossing the Sangqian River" (poem; Jia Dao), 12n3
Cui Hao, 314n2

Dang Huaiying, 284
Daodejing: and biography, 75n2; in essays, 98nn24–25, 100n5, 101n7, 119, 120, 265, 266; and Geng Dingli, 167n4; and He Xinyin, 86n9; in letters, 20n3; Li Zhi's commentaries on, xviii, 119, 120; in prefaces, 129–31; on Principle, 100n3; on rulership, 93; and Wang Longxi, 148n9
Daoism, xxiv, xxxiv–xxxv, 327, 328n7; and Buddhism, 270n6; and Confucianism, 278–81; in essays, 101nn7–9, 147, 156, 265–66; in Huang-Lao, 330n8; and karma, 259n2, 260; in letters, 15, 31, 57, 58; and music, 160; nonsyncretic view of, 78n14; and recluses, 277n5; syncretic view of, xvii, xviii, xxx, xxxii, 21, 56n62, 129–31, 265–66, 278–81; and women, 31
Daoquan, 131
Dazhi, 312
Deng Dingshi (Deng Yingqi), 66, 186
Deng Huoqu, 24, 26, 41, 124, 167
Deng Shiyang (Deng Lincai), 7–9, 81, 143, 145, 186n4
Diamond Sutra (*Jingang jing*), 273–75
"Disciplining the Sangha" (Jie zhongseng; Li Zhi), 181–84
Discourses on Salt and Iron (*Yantie lun*), 206
"Discussing Literature with a Friend" (Yu youren lun wen; Li Zhi), 245–46
"Discussion on Husband and Wife" (Fufu lun; Li Zhi), xxvi, 99–101
"Distribution of Work Assignments in the Sangha" (Lie zhongseng zhishi; Li Zhi), 286–88
Doctrine of the Mean (*Zhongyong*), xviii, 4n5, 22n4; and *Diamond Sutra*, 273; in essays, 100n2, 100n5, 282; and Geng Dingli, 166, 168; and Geng Dingxiang, 35n4, 37n11, 42n20, 42n22, 45n33, 51n46, 52nn50–51; in prefaces, 130
Dong Chuance, 188
Dong Zhongshu, 280n11
Dongfang Shuo, 277
"Dragonfly Ditty" (Qingling yao; Li Zhi), 197–98
Dream of the Red Chamber (*Honglou meng*; Cao Xueqin and Gao E), xxix

"Drifting on East Lake with Li Jiantian" (Li Jiantian yaoyou Donghu; poem; Li Zhi), 209, 316
Du Fu, 32n9, 103n9, 105n19, 173n3, 209, 327
Du Guangting, 192

egalitarianism, xxi, xxii, xxvii, xxxii, 23n5, 97n21; in friendship, xxvii, 87n12, 135, 207n2; and Luo Rufang, 150, 156; and women, xxiv–xxvi, xxx
"Eight Quatrains from Prison" (Xizhong ba jue; poem; Li Zhi), 209, 302–4
emotion (sentiment; *qing*), xxviii–xxix, 35, 37, 130, 164, 238; and equilibrium, 168, 170; in music, 158–59; and nonabiding, 273, 275; in poetry, 209
emptiness (*kong*), 8, 9, 114–18, 116n14, 221n1, 306n4
"Encountering Sorrow" (Li sao; *Chu ci*), 201, 327
"Encountering Troops Marching East During a Morning Walk . . ." (Xiaoxing feng zheng dong jiang shi que ji Mei Zhongcheng; poem; Li Zhi), 209, 225–26
Epitome of the Compilation from the Dark Studio (*Anran lu zui*; Li Zhi), 207
essays: in *Another Book to Burn*, 259–93; in *A Book to Burn*, 75–193; in *A Book to Keep (Hidden)*, 89, 92, 320–24; eight-legged, xx, 5, 77, 109, 132–34; informal (*xiaopin*), 289
"Evening Rain" (Mu yu; poem; Li Zhi), 210, 311
examinations, civil service, xx, 233n1, 325; eight-legged essay in, 5n6, 132–34; in essays, 77, 155, 190; in letters, 23, 51; and Li Zhi, xviii, xxv, 339; terms for, 24n16
expedient devices (*upāya*; *fangbian*), 270–72
"Explanation of the Childlike Heart-Mind" (Tongxin shuo; Li Zhi), xx, xxix, xxv, 106–10, 158n2, 276

Factors of the Changes (*Jiuzheng Yiyin*; Li Zhi), 245n2, 328, 332
Fada, 301n2
Fan Chi, 76–77
Fan Zhongyan, 97
Fang Danshan (Fang Yifeng), 122
Fang La rebellion, 126, 127

INDEX 357

Fang Xiaoru, 200n5
Fang Yilin, 167
Fang Zichun, 158–61
Fang Ziji (Fang Hang), 158, 159, 161, 249
Feng Dao, xxiii, 277, 335
Feng Yingjing, 305n1
filial piety, xxviii, 235, 274; and Buddhism, 22, 165, 286; in historiography, 202, 205n5, 206n3; in letters, 21, 22–25, 49, 50–51, 246, 251; in poems, 303n4; and rulership, 97; in self-portrait, 79–80
Five Emperors (Zhuang Xu, Di Ku, Tang Yao, Yu Shun), 95
Five Hegemons, 90–91, 98n27
Five Human Relationships (*wulun*), xxvi; in essays, 87–88, 168, 191, 274; husband and wife in, 99–101; in letters, 8, 51, 53; and rulership, 96, 97
"Floating Tufts of the Flowering Willow" (poem; Li Zhi), 302
Four Books, xviii, 4–5, 239, 240, 257, 282
friendship, xxvi–xxviii, 3; egalitarianism in, xxvii, 87n12, 207n2; in essays, 105, 122–24, 135–37, 138, 142–45, 186, 207–8; in Five Relationships, 99; and Geng Dingxiang, 34, 35, 36, 48, 49, 58, 59, 61; and He Xinyin, 87–88; Matteo Ricci on, 256n3; in poems, 210, 217n1, 306–7, 316; in prefaces, 235; and teachers, 21, 25–27; with women, 13
Fu Xi, 144n7
Fukui Fumimasa, 115n5
Fusu (son of Qin Shihuang), 323

Gai, Master, 328
ganying (action and response), 260
Gao E, xxix
Gao Ming, 102, 103
Gao Yi, 188
Gaozong, Emperor (Song), 126
Geng brothers, xvi, 84
Geng Dingli (Geng Ziyong), xxvii–xxviii, 166–71, 326, 327, 340; in letters, 34n1, 35, 44, 51n47, 58n68, 63, 253
Geng Dinglih, 171, 253
Geng Dingxiang, 162n2, 233n1, 253, 340; conflict with, xxvii–xxix, xxxi, 24n9, 63–74, 138, 166–71, 249, 314n1, 327, 328, 329; correspondence with, 20n5, 34–62; letters from, 36–37, 45, 50–51, 53, 56–57, 58, 61–62
Geng Guyu, 64
Geng Runian (Geng Kenian), 170, 171, 253–54
Geng Rusi, 171
ghosts, 183, 259–64, 268, 284
"Glazed Temple, The" (Liuli si; poem; Li Zhi), 209, 229
Gong'an school, 207, 227n1, 267n1
Gongyang Commentary on the Spring and Autumn Annals (*Gongyang zhuan*), 35n6, 144n11, 152n5
Great Commentary on The Sun Sutra (*Da ri jing shu*), 35n7
"Great Filial Piety" (Da Xiao; Li Zhi), 22–25
Great Learning (*Da xue*), xx, 4n5, 168; and *Diamond Sutra*, 273, 274n7, 275; in letters, 50, 67n9, 68, 241–44
Gu Kaizhi, 83
Gu Yangqian (Gu Chong'an), 299
Gu Yanwu, xxx
Guan Hanqing, 102, 190
Guan Zhong, 90, 98
Guanyin (Avalokiteśvara), xxv, 115n9, 116n12, 249, 251, 336, xxvn41
Guanzi, 49n43
Guo Tai, 316n2
Guo Tuan, 259–60

Hai Rui, 44
Han Feizi, 98n23, 125n2, 204, 331, 335n3
Han Xin, 73n21
Han Yu, 75n1
Han Zhong, 322
"Hard Rain" (Yu shen; poem; Li Zhi), 313
He Liangjun, 142
He Xinyin (Liang Ruyuan), xxvi, xxxi, 24, 25n17, 49, 49n42, 84–88, 167
Heart Sutra (*Bore boluomiduo xinjing*): essays on, 114–18, 119–20
heart-mind (*xin*), 115, 164; childlike, xx, xxix, xxxv, 68n10, 102, 106–13, 147, 158n2, 241, 245, 276; original (*benxin*), 107n4, 112

358 INDEX

Heaven (*tian*): in essays, 93, 99–100, 101, 102, 140, 152, 154, 191; and karma, 260; in letters, 35, 36, 37, 42, 64, 74; Zhu Xi on, 100n2
"Heavy Rain and Snow at the Temple of Bliss on New Year's Day" (Yuan ri Jile si da yuxue; poem; Li Zhi), 209, 228
historiography, xxii–xxiii, xxxiii; essays on, 89, 195–208, 320–24; human nature in, 197–98; relativistic, 132
History of the Former Han (*Han shu*; Ban Gu), 198n3, 330
History of the Later Han (*Hou Han shu*), 12n4
Hong Yao, 31n6
Hongren, 274
"How the Military Strategist Jiang Long Did Away with Deliberation" (*Binglüe Jiang Long qu si ji*; Yang Shen), 197
"How the Three Teachings Lead Back to Confucianism" (San jiao gui ru shuo; Li Zhi), 278–81, 283n2
Huailin, 25
Huainanzi, 90n7
Huan, Duke (Qi), 90, 98n27
Huang Xiang, 22n3
Huang Zongxi, 23n5
Huang'an (Hubei): Geng family in, xvi, 54n56, 58n68, 63, 169, 170, 253; Li Zhi in, 34n1, 119, 120, 122, 135, 253, 326, 340
Huang'an, two monks of (Ruowu and Zeng Jiquan), 21–28, 121, 124
Huang-Lao teachings, 330
"Hub of the *Heart Sutra*" (Xin Jing tigang; Li Zhi), 114–18
Huhai (son of Qin Shihuang), 320, 321n3, 324
Hui Shi, 190, 196n3
Huineng, 274, 301n2
Huizong, Emperor (Song), 125, 126n3
hypocrisy, xx, xxviii, xxxii; in Buddhism, 301n3; and childlike heart-mind, 108, 110, 112, 113; in essays, 121, 138, 140–41; in letters, 12, 13, 18, 247–48; in prefaces, 235

"In Memoriam, Master Luo Jinxi" (Luo Jinxi xiansheng gaowen; Li Zhi), 72n20, 150–57
"In Memoriam, Master Wang Longxi" (Wang Longxi Xiansheng gaowen; Li Zhi), 146–49, 153n6

"In Praise of Four Friends" (poem; Xue Tao), 32
"In Response to Deng Shiyang" (Da Deng Shiyang; Li Zhi), 7–9, 81n18
indigenous peoples, xix, 197–98
individualism, xx–xxii, xxxii, 23n5, 115, 132, 146; vs. orthodoxy, xx–xxi, xxx
innate knowledge (*liangzhi*), xxi, 66, 71, 147, 235n3, 273
inner alchemy, 265, 266nn5–6, 275n8
"Inscription for the Image of Confucius in the Cloister of the Flourishing Buddha" (Ti Kongzi xiang yu Zhifo Yuan; Li Zhi), 283n2, 289–90
"Introduction to the Table of Contents of the Historical Annals and Biographies in *A Book to Keep (Hidden)*" (*Cangshu* shiji liezhuan zongmu qianlun; Li Zhi), 317–19
Islam, xviii, 291

Japanese, 79n16, 297n1, 299n1, 339
Ji Bu, 87
Ji Kang, 195–96
Jia Dao, 12n3
Jia Yi, 205n4
Jiajing Emperor, 182, 204n2
Jiang Long, 197–98
Jiang Shang (Grand Duke Wang), 98
Jiao Hong (Jiao Ruohou), xxviii, xxxii, 20n4, 204n2, 328, 341; and burial, 291, 292; and childlike heart-mind, 106n3; in essays, 154, 158–59, 261; in letters, 51n47; in poems, 210, 222, 306–7; preface by, 233–34; works by, 129, 142
Jiao's Forest of Anecdotes (*Jiaoshi leilin*; Jiao Hong), 142
Jin, state of, 91
Jin Shengtan, xxix
Journeying with Companions (*Zheng tu yu gong*; Li Zhi), 158n1
Juefan Huihong, 270n6
Jurchens, 198

karma, 12, 14, 16n3, 62, 175, 182; essays on, 239, 259–62; and ghost stories, 263
Kāśyapa, 283
Kong Ji (Zisi), 282, 283n6, 284
Kong Li, 282, 283n6, 284

INDEX 359

Kong Ruogu, 75
Kong Wenju, 332
Kong Yingda, 224n6
Korea, 297n3
Kumārajīva, 114n3

"Lamenting My Failures in Old Age" (poem; Li Zhi), 304
"Lantern Festival" (Yuanxiao; poem; Li Zhi), 209, 219
Laozi, 98n28, 156n17, 259n2, 330n8; and Confucius, 130, 265, 266, 289, 290; in letters, 35, 57, 58, 247; on rulership, 92; syncretic view of, 265. See also *Daodejing*
Laozi Explained (Li Zhi), 119, 120
Large Sutra, 114n3
Learning of the Heart-Mind (Xinxue), xx, xxvi
Left Scribes' Record of Deeds and Personalities Through the Ages (*Lidai shi ji zuobian*; Tang Shunzhi), xxiii
Legalism, xxxi, 204–5, 331n9, 335n3
"Letter in Reply to Provincial Officer Liu" (Da Liu Fangbo shu; Li Zhi), 15–17
"Letter in Response to the Claim That Women Are Too Shortsighted to Understand the Dao" (Da yi nüren xue dao wei jianduan shu; Li Zhi), xxv, 29–33
"Letter to a Friend" (Yu youren shu; Li Zhi), xix, 223, 256–57
"Letter to a Friend in the Capital" (Ji jing you shu; Li Zhi), 19–20
letters, xxxiii; in *Another Book to Burn*, 241–57; in *A Book to Burn*, 7–74; chronology of, 34; isolated details (*zhili*) in, 8–9; between Li Zhi and Geng Dingxiang, 20n5, 34–62
Li Bai, 314n3
Li Baizhai (Li Zhi's father), 76–77, 79, 82
Li Fengyang (Li Weiming), 136
Li ji. See *Records of Ritual*
Li Jiantian, 316
Li Mu, 226n3
Li Panlong, 137n5
Li Shilong, 247–48
Li Si, xxiii, 204–5, 206, 321, 322, 323, 335
Li Tao'an, 124
Li Ying, 316n2
Li Yuan, xxiii, 335

Li Yuanyang, 134n4
Li Zhi (Li Wenling; Li Zhuowu): arrest of, 29, 328, 334, 337, 341; attacks on, 10, 29, 63, 314n1, 340, 341; bans on, xvi–xvii, xxx, 341; beard of, xvi, 236, 268, 328, 340; biography of, xxxiii, 325–33; calligraphy of, 327–28; chronology of works by, xxxiii–xxxiv; on classical vs. vernacular language, xxix, 192; death of, xv, xxxi, 3, 238–39, 267, 329, 334, 337, 341; family of, 7, 211, 255, 326, 339, 340; forgeries of works by, xvii, xxx, 233–34, 235–37, 239; historical record on, 325–37; imperial edict against, 336–37; inconsistencies of, xix, xxxiii; memorial on, xxxiii, 65, 277n9, 293n8, 334–37; names of, 325nn1–2; personality of, xix, xxvii–xxviii, xxxv, 326–27, 328; in PRC, xxx–xxxii; and scholarly tradition, xxxi–xxxiii; self-defense by, 65–74; self-portraits by, 75–83, 121–24, 138–39, 185–89; tonsure taken by, xvi, 10n2, 18, 23, 29, 57, 57n64, 63, 185, 186n6, 187–88, 228, 236, 255, 328, 333, 335, 340; wife of (née Huang), 7, 12–14, 57, 61n78, 80–82, 339, 340
Li Zhi, a Herald of Antifeudalism in Sixteenth-Century China, xxx–xxxi
Li Zhi: Rebel Against Confucian Ideology, xxx
Li Zhicai, 78
Li Zhuxuan (grandfather), 79
Lian Po, 226n3
Liang Ruyuan. *See* He Xinyin
Liao of Da Liang, 321
Liezi, 57, 71n18, 103n10
"Life of Li Wenling" (Li Wenling zhuan; Yuan Zhongdao), 325–33
Lingyou, 167n5
"Listening to the Chanting of *The Lotus Sutra*" (Ting song Fahua; poem; Li Zhi), 301
Literary Mind and the Carving of Dragons, The (Wenxin diaolong; Liu Xie), 104n15
Liu Bang (Emperor Gaozu), 324
Liu Dongxing (Liu Fangbo), 15–18, 328, 340
Liu Luqiao (Liu Shishao), 66, 73
Liu Shipei, xxx
Liu Wei, 326
Liu Xiahui, 156
Liu Xiang, 89–91

Liu Xie (Liu Hongyuan), 104n15, 140–41, 247n4
Liu Yiqing, 142
Liu Zongyuan, 327
Liuxia Hui, 332
Lives of Exemplary Women (*Lienü zhuan*), 66n7, 67n8
Lotus Sutra (*Fahua*), 261, 270–72, 301
Lu, state of, 91
Lü, state of, 91
Lü Buwei, xxiii, 183n11, 236n6, 335
Lu Cheng, 273
Lu Ji, 167n9, 326
Lu Jiuyuan, 8n6
Lu Lianzi, 277
Lü Tiaoyang, 188
Lu Xiangshan, xx
Luo Guanzhong, 125, 126
Luo Rufang (Luo Jinxi), xxi, 24, 24n13, 25n17, 72, 150–57
Luo Wenli, 189
Lute, The (*Pipa ji*; play; Gao Ming), 102, 103–4

Ma Jinglun (Ma Chengsuo), 241, 268, 291–93, 305n1, 328–29, 334, 341
Ma Lishan, 241–44
Macheng (Hubei), 340; *A Book to Burn* written in, 3; conflicts in, 253–54; elites in, 29, 63, 140, 186–88, 225n1; essays written in, 21, 99, 121, 138, 142, 143, 146, 150, 162, 199, 201, 221n1; flight from, 305n1; Geng family in, 166, 169n19; and Huang'an, 58n68; letters written from, 7, 10, 12, 65, 70; Li Zhi in, 276, 327, 336; Li Zhi's flight from, 241; poems written in, 221n1; students in, 234n2, 245; threatened deportation from, 249–52; Zhuang Chunfu in, 158. *See also* Cloister of the Flourishing Buddha; Vimalakīrti Monastery
"Master Li Zhuowu's Testament" (Li Zhuowu xiansheng yiyan; Li Zhi), 291–93
Mazu, 33
meat eating, 267–69
Medicine Buddha, 172–77
Medicine Buddha Sutra (*Yaoshi jing*), 172, 173, 175–77

Mei Danran, xxv, 29, 225n1, 249, 251
Mei Guozhen, xxv, 29, 225–26, 249, 328
Mei Zixin, 251n9
Mencius (Mengzi), xviii, 4n5; and childlike heart-mind, 106, 107n4, 108n5, 109, 112, 113; and Confucius, 282; and *Diamond Sutra*, 274n4; in essays, 123n5, 131n7, 138n3, 139nn4–5, 288n5, 289n2; and Geng Dingli, 166, 168; and Geng Dingxiang, 35n5, 36, 37, 38, 42n21, 43, 44, 45n30, 48n40, 50, 51n48, 52, 53, 54n57, 56, 57, 58, 59n73, 61, 62; in letters, 8, 16n2, 247n2, 251n7, 255n3; on Li Si, 322n4; and Luo Rufang, 156n19, 156nn13–15; and meat eating, 268; in poems, 304n7; on rulership, 94nn7–8, 96; and syncretism, 279; and Wang Longxi, 149nn14–15; on well-field system, 93n3
Meng Qi, 192
Meng Tian, 323
Ming Code (Wanli edition), 48n41
Mohism, 62n83
monastic discipline, 181–84, 219, 286–88
"Monastic Seclusion" (Bi guan; poem; Li Zhi), 209, 218
Mr. Li's Discussion of Books (Li Zhi), 92
"Mr. Li's Ten Kinds of Association" (Li sheng shi jiao wen; Li Zhi), 99, 135–37, 207
music, 158–61
"My Feelings Upon Ascending the Mountain and Receiving a Letter from Jiao Hong" (Ru shan de Jiao Ruohou shu yougan er shou; poem; Li Zhi), 210, 306–7

Nan Gongshi, 31n6
Nanzi, 66–67, 70–71
neo-Confucianism, xxiv; criticism of, 280–81; and Daoism, 266n6; in essays, 99, 100n4, 130n4, 279n6, 282; in letters, 7, 84; and Pure Land Buddhism, 178. *See also* School of Principle; Wang Yangming; Zhu Xi
New Account of Tales of the World (*Shishuo xinyu*; Liu Yiqing), 83n22, 142–43
"No Hero" (poem; Li Zhi), 304
"Notes on 'The Hub'" (Tigang shuo; Li Zhi), 114n2, 119–20
Nothingness, 99, 100

obituaries, xxxi; Geng Dingli, 166–71; Luo Rufang, 24n13, 150–57; Wang Longxi, 146–49
"On a Scroll Painting of Square Bamboo" (Fang zhu tu juan wen; Li Zhi), 142–45
"On Friendship" (Pengyou pian; Li Zhi), 99, 207–8
"On He Xinyin" (He Xinyin lun; Li Zhi), 24n14, 84–88, 167n10
"On Loftiness and Cleanliness"(Gao jie shuo; Li Zhi), 27nn24–25, 121–24, 236n7
"On Miscellaneous Matters" (Za shuo; Li Zhi), xxix, 32n10, 102–5, 190, 276
"On Reading Du Fu (Two Poems)" (Du Du Shaoling er shou; poem; Li Zhi), 209, 295–96
"On Recluses" (Yinzhe shuo; Li Zhi), 276–77
On Releasing Life (Fangsheng wen; Zhuhong), 259n3
On Speaking Righteously (Li Zhi), 234
"On the Childlike Mind" (Tongxin shuo; Li Zhi), xxxv, 68n10, 111–13, 147, 245
"On *The Diamond Sutra*" (Jingang jing shuo; Li Zhi), 273–75
On the Four Books (Shuo shu; Li Zhi), 4–5, 234, 236, 239, 240
"On the Letter Terminating Relations" (Jue jiao shu; Li Zhi), 195–96
"On the *Lotus Sutra* Chapter on Expedient Devices" (Fahua fangbian pin shuo; Li Zhi), 270–72
"On the Original Mind" (Tongxin shuo; Li Zhi), xx, xxix, xxxv, 32n10, 68n10, 106–13, 147, 158n2, 245, 276
On the Three Teachings (Li Zhi), 236
"On the Warring States" (Zhanguo lun; Li Zhi), 89–91
"On Weapons and Food" (Bing shi lun; Li Zhi), 92–98
orthodoxy, 132, 282, 317, 334; vs. individualism, xx–xxi, xxviii; in letters, 50, 59–60, 61; and syncretism, 278
Outlaws of the Marsh. See *Water Margin*

painting, 83n22, 136, 142–45, 236n5
Pan Sheng, 188
Pan Shizao, 207, 249

Pang, Layman (Pang Gong, Pang Yun), 32–33
"*Pavilion for Worshipping the Moon*" (Bai yue; Baiyue ting ji; Li Zhi), 190–91
Penglai (Xianshan), island of, 223n4
Peony Pavilion (Mudan ting; Tang Xianzu), xxix
"People of the Song Dynasty Disparaged Xunzi" (Song ren ji Xun Qing; Li Zhi), 206
"Petition of Worship and Recitation to the Medicine Buddha" (Lisong yaoshi gaowen; Li Zhi), 172–74
"Petition Upon Completion of Worshipful Recitation of *The Medicine Buddha Sutra*" (Lisong *Yaoshi jing* bi gaowen; Li Zhi), 175–77
Platform Sutra, 251n6
plays, 32n10, 102–6, 109, 111, 112, 190–93
"'Pleasure of Reading, The,' with a Prologue" ("Du shu le" bing yin; Li Zhi), 211–14
Poems and Their Anecdotes (Ben shi shi; Meng Qi), 192
poetry, xxxiii, 209–29; changing styles of, 133; Confucius on, 192; in essays, 137; essays on, 197–98; introduction to, 209–10; of Li Zhi, 327; recent-style (jinti shi), 209; regulated verse (lüshi), 209, 316n1
"Postface to *The Prose of Our Time*" (Shiwen Houxu; Li Zhi), 5n6, 132–34, 202n8
"Power of Books to Lead Astray" (poem; Li Zhi), 303–4
Prajñāpāramitā (Perfect Wisdom), 114
"Preface to Master Li's *Another Book to Burn*" (Li shi Xu Fenshu xu; Jiao Hong), 233–34
"Preface to *Selections from 'A Record of a Cart Full of Ghosts'*" (Xuanlu kuiche zhi xu; Li Zhi), 259–62
"Preface to Su Che's *Explication of Laozi*" (Ziyou *Jie Lao* Xu; Li Zhi), 129–31
"Preface to the Anthology *Unstringing the Bow*" (Shuo Hu Ji xu; Li Zhi), 263–64
"Preface to *The Loyal and Righteous Outlaws of the Marsh*" (Zhongyi Shuihuzhuan xu; Li Zhi), 125–28
"Preface to the Second Printing of Li Zhi's Writings" (Xu ke Li shi shu xu; Wang Benke), 238–40
prefaces, 332; in *Another Book to Burn*, 233–40, 259–64; in *A Book to Burn*, 3–5, 125–31

Principle (*li*), 7, 100, 107, 108, 110
Prose of Our Time (*Shiwen*), 5n6, 132–34, 202n8
Pure Land Buddhism, 13–14, 26, 27, 28, 178–80, 270

qi (substance), 100, 103
Qi Dan, 168
Qian Dehong, 146
Qian Huaisu (Qian Tongwen), 24
Qianlong emperor, xxx
Qin, state of, 98
Qin dynasty, 92, 204–5, 321
Qin Shihuang, xxiii, xxiv, 73n21, 204–5, 320–24, 335; in PRC, xxxi
Qinzong, Emperor (Song), 126n3
Qiu Tanzhi, 327
Qu Boyu, 67
Qu Yuan, 201, 327
"Questioning Guanyin" (*Guanyin wen*; Li Zhi), xxv, 249, 251, 336

Ran Yong, 38
readers, 19, 304n6; commentaries by, xxix–xxx; and forgeries, 233; of Li Zhi, xvii, xix, xx, xxiii, xxvi, xxviii, xxxiii, xxxv, 104, 138; Li Zhi on, 3–5
"Reading a Letter from Ruowu's Mother" (*Du Ruowu mu ji shu*; Li Zhi), 162–65, 255, 276
"Reading the Resignation Memorial of Gu Chong'an" (*Du Gu Chong'an cishu*; poem; Li Zhi), 299
Rebirth Dhāraṇī (*Wangsheng shenzhou*), 260–61
recluses, xxiii, 17, 155, 195, 269, 330, 333; Li Zhi on, 187, 276–77, 335
"Record of a Cart Full of Ghosts" (*Kuiche zhi*; Guo Tuan), 259–62, 263
Record of Karmic Consequences (*Yinguo lu*; Li Zhi), xviii, 259
"Record of Master Geng Dingli" (*Geng Chukong xiansheng zhuan*; Li Zhi), 130n2, 166–71
Record of Pointing at the Moon (*Zhiyue lu*; Zonggao), 61n79
Records of Ritual (*Li ji*), 22n3, 96n15, 151nn3–4, 202n5; in letters, 29, 30n2, 60n77
Records of Song- and Yuan-Dynasty Scholars (*Songyuan xue'an*), 97n20

Records of the Grand Historian (*Shi ji*; Sima Qian): biography in, 75n1; in essays, 156n17, 265n2; in letters, 60n76, 73nn21–22, 74n23; on Nanzi, 66n7; in poems, 297n2; in prefaces, 239n3; on Qin Shihuang, 320–24
"Red and White Plum Blossoms Flourishing at the Lake . . ." (*Hushang hong bai mei shengkai xi ti*; poem; Li Zhi), 220
"Red Duster" (*Hong fu*; Li Zhi), 192–93
"Reflections on My Life" (*Gankai pingsheng*; Li Zhi), 75n1, 185–89
Ren Fang, 326
"Reply to Censor Geng" (*Fu Geng Zhongcheng*; Li Zhi), 34–40
"Reply to Censor Geng on the Subject of Mildness" (*Da Geng Zhongcheng lun dan*; Li Zhi), 45–47
"Reply to Justice Minister Geng" (*Da Geng Sikou*; Li Zhi), 48–58
"Reply to Li Shilong" (*Fu Li Shilong*; Li Zhi), 247–48
Resolving Doubts About the Pure Land (*Jingtu jue*; Li Zhi), 178–80
"Response to Zhou Liutang" (*Da Zhou Liutang*; Li Zhi), 24n9, 65–74
Return to Antiquity Movement, 89, 132, 137n5
Ricci, Matteo, xviii, 21, 223–24, 256–57, 341
righteousness, 8, 11, 62, 91, 235; and friendship, 207–8
Rites of Zhou (*Zhou li*), 96n17
Romance of the Three Kingdoms (*Sanguo zhi*), 331n10
Ruan Ji (Ruan Sizong), 277
rulership, 19n2, 73, 92–98, 279
"Rules Agreed Upon in Advance" (*Yuyue*; Li Zhi), 185, 249, 250
Ruowu. *See* Wang Shiben

sagehood, 4, 84, 102–3; and childlike heart-mind, 107, 109, 110, 111, 112, 113; and *Heart Sutra*, 115, 118; in letters, 46, 50, 52, 242; and rulership, 97, 98
San Yisheng, 31, 31n6
Sang Hongyang, xxiii, xxiv, 335
Śāriputra, 270, 271

scholar-officials, xix–xx, xxii, 4, 20, 133, 140–41. *See also* bureaucracy
School of Principle (Daoxue; Lixue; Cheng-Zhu school), xvii–xviii, xx, xxx, 7, 199n2, 326, 328; in essays, 99, 140, 188; and Matteo Ricci, 257; and syncretism, 278
School of the Mind (Wang Yangming), xxxi, 65
Seal of the Unity of the Three (*Cantong qi*), 275
Selections from "A Record of a Cart Full of Ghosts" (*Xuanlu kuiche zhi*; Li Zhi), 260
Selections of Refined Literature (*Wenxuan*), 108, 112
"Self-Appraisal" (Zi zan; Li Zhi), 121, 138–39
self-cultivation, xxi, 28, 146, 147; and Buddhism, 178, 273; and individualism, xxi–xxii; and women, 165, 249
"Sending Off Zheng Zixuan, Also for Jiao Hong" (Song Zheng Zixuan jian ji Ruo Hou; poem; Li Zhi), 222
"Sent in Reply to Senior Censor Geng" (Jida Geng Da Zhongcheng; Li Zhi), 41–44
Seven Masters of the Bamboo Grove, 195, 277n6
Shan Tao, 195–96
Shang dynasty, 199
Shang Yang (Lord Shang), 97–98
Shao Yong, 46n36, 47, 78, 105, 187, 277
Shen Buhai, 331
Shen Nong, 200n9
Shi Hui, 102
Shi Jingxian, 249, 253, 340
Shi Nai'an, 125, 126
Shining Lamp of Records of the Antiquity of the Dao (*Mingdeng daogu lu*; Li Zhi), 15n1
Shu Qi, 59, 60, 138, 199–200
Shun (sage-king): in essays, 105, 144; and Geng Dingli, 168, 169; in letters, 8, 36, 42n21, 43, 46, 47, 51, 61; and Matteo Ricci, 256; and syncretism, 279, 280
Sima Geng, 38, 39
Sima Guang, xxiii, xxiv, 187, 335
Sima Qian, xxiii, xxiv, 4n3, 206n5, 317, 319n4, 335n3; on Bo Yi, 199–200; in essays, 104n17, 125, 144n4; and Li Zhi, 327, 330. *See also Records of the Grand Historian*
Sima Xiangru, xxiii, 105n22, 335n6

Sima Yi, 195
Sima Zhao, 332n11
"Sitting Alone in Meditation" (Du zuo; poem; Li Zhi), 210, 309
Six Arts, 96, 97
Six Classics, 91, 257, 330, 331; and childlike heart-mind, 106, 109, 112, 113
Six Perfections (*pāramitā*), 181, 182
"Sketch of Zhuowu: Written in Yunnan" (Zhuowu lunlüe: Dianzhong zuo; Li Zhi), 7, 75–83, 169n19
sojourner (*liuyu kezi*), 186–87
Song dynasty, 125, 126
Songs of the South (*Chu ci*), 201, 237
spirit (*shen*), 142, 144
Spring and Autumn Annals (*Chunqiu*), 318, 319
Spring and Autumn period, 89–91
"Spring Night" (Chun ye; poem; Li Zhi), 209, 300
"Spring Rain on a Great House" (Loutou chun yu; poem; Li Zhi), 305
"Story of Princess Lechang," 192
Story of Red Duster (play; Zhang Fengyi), 192–93
Story of the Western Wing (*Xixiang ji*; play; Wang Shifu and Guan Hanqing), 32n10, 102, 103, 104–5, 190–91; and childlike heart-mind, 106, 109, 111, 112
Strategies of the Warring States (*Zhanguo ce*), 89, 90, 91, 303n4
Su Che (Ziyou), 129–31, 187, 327n6
Su Shi, 20n4, 129, 131, 143, 158, 187, 206n2
Su Xun, 103n12
"Sudden Chill, A" (Zha han; poem; Li Zhi), 210, 310
"Suffering of Old Age" (Li Zhi), 4
Sun Deng, 332
Sun Qi, 57
Sun Shu'ao, 74
Sun Wu (Sunzi), 57, 94n6, 148n10, 251n8
Supplement to "A New Account of Tales of the World" (*Shishuo xinyu bu*; He Liangjun, Wang Shizhen), 142
Sutra on Great Wisdom (*Mahāprajñā-sūtra*), 274

Tai Dian, 31
Tai Si, 31n5
Taigong, 31n6

Taizhou school, xxi, xxvi, xxxvi, 23n5, 129; in essays, 84, 115, 150, 166; genealogy of, 24–25; in letters, 15, 65, 66n5; syncretism of, 21, 278
"Tale of the Curly-Bearded Stranger" (Du Guangting), 192
Tan Qiao, 266n6
Tang (sage-king), 90, 105
Tang Shunzhi, xxiii
Tang Xianzu, xxix
Tao Hongjing, 277
Tao Shikui, 291, 293
Tao Yuanming, 75n1, 217n1, 277, 327
teacher-student relationship, 21, 25–27, 204–5, 206
Temple of Bliss (Beijing), 209, 218n1, 227, 228, 313n2, 341
"Terminating Relations with Shan Juyuan" (Ji Kang), 195
"Three Essays for Two Monks of Huang'an" (Wei Huang'an er shangren san shou; Li Zhi), 21–28, 124n7, 148n8, 167n8, 255n2
Three Jewels (Buddha, dharma, sangha), 288n4
Three Kings (Yu, Tang, Wen), 90, 95
Tian, state of, 91
Tian Chang, 322
"To Geng Kenian" (Yu Geng Kenian; Li Zhi), 253–54
"To Ma Lishan" (Yu Ma Lishan; Li Zhi), 241–44
"To Matteo Ricci of the Far West" (Zeng Li Xitai; poem; Li Zhi), 209, 223–24, 256
"To My Old Friend Geng Dingxiang" (Da Geng chutong; Li Zhi), 47
"To Yang Dingjian" (Yu Yang Dingjian; Li Zhi), 10–11, 63–64, 242n4
"To Zeng Jiquan" (Yu Zeng Jiquan; Li Zhi), 162n1, 255
"To Zhou Youshan" (Yu Zhou Youshan; Li Zhi), 249–52
"To Zhuang Chunfu" (Yu Zhuang Chunfu; Li Zhi), 12–14
Tract of the Most Exalted on Action and Response (*Taishang ganying pian*), 259–62
Transmission of the Lamp (*Chuandeng lu*), 35n7

True Emptiness (*zhen kong*), 8, 9, 116n14
"True Teachers" (Zhen shi; Li Zhi), 25–27
Twenty-four Tales of Filial Piety (*Ershisi xiao*), 22n3

Unstringing the Bow (*Shuo Hu Ji*; Li Zhi), 263–64
Upon Arrival at the Lake (*Chutan ji*; Li Zhi), 142–43, 278
"Upon Reading Old Zhuowu's Writings" (Du Zhuowu Laozi shu shu; Zhang Nai), 235–37
"Upon Reviving from My Chronic Illness" (poem; Li Zhi), 302

"Veritable Record of the Memorial Impeaching Li Zhi" (Zhang Wenda), xxxiii, 65, 277n9, 293n8, 334–37
"Viewing the Yellow Crane Pavilion from the River" (Jiangshang wang Huanghe Lou; poem; Li Zhi), 314–15
Vimalakīrti, 179
Vimalakīrti Monastery (Macheng, Hubei), xviii, 181, 340
Vimalakīrti-nirśa-sūtra (*Weimojie suoshuo jing*), 178, 179n3
Vocation of Younger Brothers and Sons (*Dizi shi*), 49, 50–51

Wan Shihe, 188
Wang Anshi, 335n7
Wang Benke, 233, 234, 236–40, 245
Wang Bi, xxi, 224n6
Wang Bo, 306n5
Wang Bolun, 239
Wang Dun, 299n2
Wang Fuzhi, 100n4
Wang Gen, xxi, xxiv–xxv, 23, 24, 26, 148
Wang Hong, xxx, 217n1
Wang Ji (Wang Longxi), xxi, 82n20, 146–49, 153, 178, 275n13
Wang Shiben (Ruowu), 21–28, 121, 124, 162–65, 255n2
Wang Shifu, 102
Wang Shizhen, 142, 204n2
Wang Wei, 228n1
Wang Xianzhi, 105
Wang Xilie, 188

Wang Xizhi, 105
Wang Yangming, xx–xxii, xxvii–xxix, xxxi, 65, 241n3; on authenticity, 246n3; egalitarianism of, xxiv; in essays, 84, 146, 147; in letters, 15, 23, 26, 52; and Li Zhi, xxiv, 82n20, 340; in prefaces, 129, 235n3; and syncretism, 21, 178, 273
Wang Yi, 189, 201, 202
Wang Zijin (Wang Ziqiao; Prince Ji Jin), 144
Wang Zong, 188
Wanli emperor, xvi, 334
Warring States period, 89–91, 303n4
"Wasting Words" (Shi yan; Li Zhi), 27–28
"Watching the Army at the East Gate of the City" (Guan bing cheng dongmen; poem; Li Zhi), 210, 297
"Watching the Rain with Dazhi" (Dazhi dui yu; poem; Li Zhi), 209, 210, 312
Water Margin (*Outlaws of the Marsh*; *Shuihu zhuan*): and childlike heart-mind, 109, 112; Li Zhuowu edition of, 10; preface to, 125–28
Wei, state of, 91
well-field land system, 93, 95, 97, 202
Wen, King (Zhou dynasty), 31, 32, 60, 90, 144
Wen Zhengming, 137n5
"Wishing That My Books Be Carefully Read" (poem; Li Zhi), 303
Wokou pirates, 79, 198
women: biographies of, 66n7, 67n8; and Buddhism, 30, 31, 249; chastity of, 22n2; and egalitarianism, xxiv–xxvi, xxx; friendship with, 13; letters on, 12–14, 29–33, 249–52; Li Zhi on, xvii, xxiv–xxvi, xxxii, 99–101; Li Zhi's behavior with, 29, 66–67, 69–70, 185n3, 326, 332, 333, 336; and self-cultivation, 165, 249
"Written at the End of Yuan Zhongdao's Hand Scroll" (Shu Xiaoxiu shoujuan hou; Li Zhi), 267–69, 291n5
Wu, Emperor (Han), xxiii, 335
Wu, Emperor (Wei), 332
Wu, King (Zhou dynasty), 22, 31, 60, 105, 199
Wu, Master, 204–5
Wu Qi, 57, 206
Wu Shidao, 91
Wuchang, 328, 340

Wunian (Xiong Shenyou), 20n5, 182, 327, 340; disciples of, 286–87; and Luo Rufang, 150, 153; in poem, 229
Xi Shuye (Xi Kang), 332
Xia (sage-king), 200
Xiang Bo, 87
Xiangyan Zhixian, 161n5
Xiao Tong, 108n8
Xie Dengzhi, 188
Xie Lingyun, 327
Xiong Shenyou. See Wunian
Xu Boshi, 24
Xu Wei, xxix
Xu Yongjian, 56n62, 82n20
Xu You, 280n7
Xuan, King (Qi), 91, 268n6
Xue Tao, 32
Xunzi, 204–5, 206, 321n3, 335n3
"Xunzi, Li Si, and Master Wu" (Xun Qing, Li Si, Wu Gong; Li Zhi), 204–5

Yan Guang, 277
Yan Hui, xxxi, 147, 205; in letters, 17, 18, 35, 38, 55, 57, 59; and Luo Rufang, 152n5, 157; and syncretism, 278, 279, 280
Yan Qing, 44
Yan Shannong (Yan Jun), 24, 65–66, 71, 72
Yang Dingjian, 10–11, 63–64, 266, 327
Yang Qiyuan, 41n19, 42
Yang Shen (Yang Sheng'an), 197–98, 199–200, 201n1, 204–5, 206nn1–2
Yang Xiong (Ziyun), 4n3, 306n3
Yang Zhu, 139
Yao (sage-king), 36, 47, 61, 105, 168, 169, 256
Yao'an (Yunnan), 75, 83n23, 169n16, 189; native peoples in, xvi, 197–98; resignation from, xvi, 135, 166, 169n19
Yellow Crane Pavilion (Huanghe Lou), 314n1, 340
Yellow Emperor (Xuan Yuan), 95, 98, 330n8
"Yellow River Chart" (*hetu*), 144
Yi Jiang, 31, 32
Yi Yin, 36, 139
Yi Zhi, 62
Yin and Yang, 100
yin guo (cause and effect), 260. *See also* karma

Yin Shidan, 188
Yin Xi, 266n5
"Yingying's Story" (Yuan Zhen), 32n10, 106n2
You, King (Chu), 335n3
You Meng, 73
Yu (sage-king), 46, 47, 90, 144n8, 200, 279
Yuan brothers (Hongdao, Zhongdao, Zongdao), xxviii, 207, 267n1, 325
Yuan Hongdao (Yuan Zhonglang), xxx, 63, 227n1, 249, 314n1, 340
Yuan Mei, xxvi
Yuan Yi (Yuan Boye), 211
Yuan Zhen, 32, 106n2
Yuan Zhongdao, xviii, xxxiii, 256n2, 267–69, 325-33
Yuan Zongdao, xviii, 19–20, 250n4, 268

Zai Wo, 61–62
Zen Buddhism. *See* Chan Buddhism
Zeng Gong, 91
Zeng Jiquan, 21–28, 121, 124, 162, 255
Zeng Shen (Zengzi), 59, 60, 151, 205, 206, 303
Zeng Yuan, 60
Zhang Dian, 105
Zhang Fengyi, 192
Zhang Jianye, xxxiii, xxxiv; on essays, 106n3, 134n4, 137n5; on letters, 9n8, 10n2, 37n12, 41n19, 45n32, 47n37, 48n41, 58n68, 251n9; on Li Zhi's chronology, 339; on poems, 222n1, 301n3
Zhang Juzheng, 25, 49n42, 84, 86–87, 314n1
Zhang Nai, 233, 235–37
Zhang Sengyou, 236n5
Zhang Wenda, xv, 317, 320, 341; memorial by, xxxiii, 65, 277n9, 293n8, 334-37
Zhang Xu, 105
Zhang Yanyuan, 236n5
Zhang Yi, 57
Zhang Zai, 78n14, 97
Zhang Zifang (Zhang Liang), 87
Zhao, state of, 226n3
Zhao Dazhou (Zhao Zhenji), 24, 56, 124n9

Zhao Gao, 321n3, 323, 324
Zhao Jin, 188
Zhao Kuo, 73
Zhen Dexiu, 199–200
Zheng Zixuan, 222
Zhong Hui, 332
Zhou, Duke of (Ji Dan), 22, 98, 256, 257
Zhou Dunyi, 78n14
Zhou dynasty, 36, 90–91, 282, 321
Zhou Liutang (Zhou Sijiu), 54–55, 65–74, 249n1
Zhou Youshan (Zhou Sijing), 136, 249–52, 327, 340; in letters, 41n19, 42, 45, 54–55, 64
Zhu Jia, 87
Zhu Jinghua, 131n7
Zhu Xi, xviin13, xviiin14, xxiii, 8n6, 77, 130n4; on Bo Yi, 199nn2-3, 200; criticism of, 281n12; and *Diamond Sutra*, 273–74; on *Great Learning*, 241n3; on Principle, 100n2, 100n4; on rulership, 94n5; as sojourner, 187
Zhu Youcai, 167n3
Zhuang Chunfu, 12–14, 158, 167, 169
Zhuang Rizai, 12
Zhuangzi, xviii, 277, 331; on art, 160n4; and childlike heart-mind, 106, 110n13; on Confucius, 284n7; in essays, 86n7, 101n8, 102nn6-7, 115, 123n6, 149n13, 151n2, 155n9; in letters, 17n7, 57, 68n11; in poems, 223n1; in prefaces, 195, 196n3, 238
Zhuge Liang, 331
Zhuhong, 181n2, 259nn2-3
Zhuo Wenjun, xxiii, 105n22, 335
Zhuowu. *See* Li Zhi
Zhuowu's Book of Great Virtue, 335
Zigong, 55, 92, 136n3, 139, 151n4
Zilu (Zhong You), 70, 71, 297
Zisi (Kong Ji), 282, 283n6, 284
Zixia (Bushang), 147, 318
Ziying (son of Qin Shihuang), 324
Zonggao, 61n79
Zou Leiming, 188
Zuozhuan, 17n4, 31n6, 106n1, 132, 133n3, 155n11, 299n2

TRANSLATIONS FROM THE ASIAN CLASSICS

Major Plays of Chikamatsu, tr. Donald Keene 1961

Four Major Plays of Chikamatsu, tr. Donald Keene. Paperback ed. only. 1961; rev. ed. 1997

Records of the Grand Historian of China, translated from the Shih chi of Ssu-ma Ch'ien, tr. Burton Watson, 2 vols. 1961

Instructions for Practical Living and Other Neo-Confucian Writings by Wang Yang-ming, tr. Wing-tsit Chan 1963

Hsün Tzu: Basic Writings, tr. Burton Watson, paperback ed. only. 1963; rev. ed. 1996

Chuang Tzu: Basic Writings, tr. Burton Watson, paperback ed. only. 1964; rev. ed. 1996

The Mahābhārata, tr. Chakravarthi V. Narasimhan. Also in paperback ed. 1965; rev. ed. 1997

The Manyōshū, Nippon Gakujutsu Shinkōkai edition 1965

Su Tung-p'o: Selections from a Sung Dynasty Poet, tr. Burton Watson. Also in paperback ed. 1965

Bhartrihari: Poems, tr. Barbara Stoler Miller. Also in paperback ed. 1967

Basic Writings of Mo Tzu, Hsün Tzu, and Han Fei Tzu, tr. Burton Watson. Also in separate paperback eds. 1967

The Awakening of Faith, Attributed to Aśvaghosha, tr. Yoshito S. Hakeda. Also in paperback ed. 1967

Reflections on Things at Hand: The Neo-Confucian Anthology, comp. Chu Hsi and Lü Tsu-ch'ien, tr. Wing-tsit Chan 1967

The Platform Sutra of the Sixth Patriarch, tr. Philip B. Yampolsky. Also in paperback ed. 1967

Essays in Idleness: The Tsurezuregusa of Kenkō, tr. Donald Keene. Also in paperback ed. 1967

The Pillow Book of Sei Shōnagon, tr. Ivan Morris, 2 vols. 1967

Two Plays of Ancient India: The Little Clay Cart and the Minister's Seal, tr. J. A. B. van Buitenen 1968

The Complete Works of Chuang Tzu, tr. Burton Watson 1968

The Romance of the Western Chamber (Hsi Hsiang chi), tr. S. I. Hsiung. Also in paperback ed. 1968

The Manyōshū, Nippon Gakujutsu Shinkōkai edition. Paperback ed. only. 1969

Records of the Historian: Chapters from the Shih chi of Ssu-ma Ch'ien, tr. Burton Watson. Paperback ed. only. 1969

Cold Mountain: 100 Poems by the T'ang Poet Han-shan, tr. Burton Watson. Also in paperback ed. 1970

Twenty Plays of the Nō Theatre, ed. Donald Keene. Also in paperback ed. 1970

Chūshingura: The Treasury of Loyal Retainers, tr. Donald Keene. Also in paperback ed. 1971; rev. ed. 1997

The Zen Master Hakuin: Selected Writings, tr. Philip B. Yampolsky 1971

Chinese Rhyme-Prose: Poems in the Fu Form from the Han and Six Dynasties Periods, tr. Burton Watson. Also in paperback ed. 1971

Kūkai: Major Works, tr. Yoshito S. Hakeda. Also in paperback ed. 1972

The Old Man Who Does as He Pleases: Selections from the Poetry and Prose of Lu Yu, tr. Burton Watson 1973

The Lion's Roar of Queen Śrīmālā, tr. Alex and Hideko Wayman 1974

Courtier and Commoner in Ancient China: Selections from the History of the Former Han by Pan Ku, tr. Burton Watson. Also in paperback ed. 1974

Japanese Literature in Chinese, vol. 1: Poetry and Prose in Chinese by Japanese Writers of the Early Period, tr. Burton Watson 1975

Japanese Literature in Chinese, vol. 2: *Poetry and Prose in Chinese by Japanese Writers of the Later Period*, tr. Burton Watson 1976

Love Song of the Dark Lord: Jayadeva's Gītagovinda, tr. Barbara Stoler Miller. Also in paperback ed. Cloth ed. includes critical text of the Sanskrit. 1977; rev. ed. 1997

Ryōkan: Zen Monk-Poet of Japan, tr. Burton Watson 1977

Calming the Mind and Discerning the Real: From the Lam rim chen mo of Tson-kha-pa, tr. Alex Wayman 1978

The Hermit and the Love-Thief: Sanskrit Poems of Bhartrihari and Bilhaṇa, tr. Barbara Stoler Miller 1978

The Lute: Kao Ming's P'i-p'a chi, tr. Jean Mulligan. Also in paperback ed. 1980

A Chronicle of Gods and Sovereigns: Jinnō Shōtōki of Kitabatake Chikafusa, tr. H. Paul Varley 1980

Among the Flowers: The Hua-chien chi, tr. Lois Fusek 1982

Grass Hill: Poems and Prose by the Japanese Monk Gensei, tr. Burton Watson 1983

Doctors, Diviners, and Magicians of Ancient China: Biographies of Fang-shih, tr. Kenneth J. DeWoskin. Also in paperback ed. 1983

Theater of Memory: The Plays of Kālidāsa, ed. Barbara Stoler Miller. Also in paperback ed. 1984

The Columbia Book of Chinese Poetry: From Early Times to the Thirteenth Century, ed. and tr. Burton Watson. Also in paperback ed. 1984

Poems of Love and War: From the Eight Anthologies and the Ten Long Poems of Classical Tamil, tr. A. K. Ramanujan. Also in paperback ed. 1985

The Bhagavad Gita: Krishna's Counsel in Time of War, tr. Barbara Stoler Miller 1986

The Columbia Book of Later Chinese Poetry, ed. and tr. Jonathan Chaves. Also in paperback ed. 1986

The Tso Chuan: Selections from China's Oldest Narrative History, tr. Burton Watson 1989

Waiting for the Wind: Thirty-six Poets of Japan's Late Medieval Age, tr. Steven Carter 1989

Selected Writings of Nichiren, ed. Philip B. Yampolsky 1990

Saigyō, Poems of a Mountain Home, tr. Burton Watson 1990

The Book of Lieh Tzu: A Classic of the Tao, tr. A. C. Graham. Morningside ed. 1990

The Tale of an Anklet: An Epic of South India—The Cilappatikāram of Iḷaṅkō Aṭikaḷ, tr. R. Parthasarathy 1993w

Waiting for the Dawn: A Plan for the Prince, tr. with introduction by Wm. Theodore de Bary 1993

Yoshitsune and the Thousand Cherry Trees: A Masterpiece of the Eighteenth-Century Japanese Puppet Theater, tr., annotated, and with introduction by Stanleigh H. Jones, Jr. 1993

The Lotus Sutra, tr. Burton Watson. Also in paperback ed. 1993

The Classic of Changes: A New Translation of the I Ching as Interpreted by Wang Bi, tr. Richard John Lynn 1994

Beyond Spring: Tz'u Poems of the Sung Dynasty, tr. Julie Landau 1994

The Columbia Anthology of Traditional Chinese Literature, ed. Victor H. Mair 1994

Scenes for Mandarins: The Elite Theater of the Ming, tr. Cyril Birch 1995

Letters of Nichiren, ed. Philip B. Yampolsky; tr. Burton Watson et al. 1996

Unforgotten Dreams: Poems by the Zen Monk Shōtetsu, tr. Steven D. Carter 1997

The Vimalakirti Sutra, tr. Burton Watson 1997

Japanese and Chinese Poems to Sing: The Wakan rōei shū, tr. J. Thomas Rimer and Jonathan Chaves 1997

Breeze Through Bamboo: Kanshi of Ema Saikō, tr. Hiroaki Sato 1998

A Tower for the Summer Heat, by Li Yu, tr. Patrick Hanan 1998

Traditional Japanese Theater: An Anthology of Plays, by Karen Brazell 1998

The Original Analects: Sayings of Confucius and His Successors (0479–0249), by E. Bruce Brooks and A. Taeko Brooks 1998

The Classic of the Way and Virtue: A New Translation of the Tao-te ching of Laozi as Interpreted by Wang Bi, tr. Richard John Lynn 1999

The Four Hundred Songs of War and Wisdom: An Anthology of Poems from Classical Tamil, The Puṟanāṉūṟu, ed. and tr. George L. Hart and Hank Heifetz 1999

Original Tao: Inward Training (Nei-yeh) *and the Foundations of Taoist Mysticism*, by Harold D. Roth 1999

Po Chü-i: Selected Poems, tr. Burton Watson 2000

Lao Tzu's Tao Te Ching: A Translation of the Startling New Documents Found at Guodian, by Robert G. Henricks 2000

The Shorter Columbia Anthology of Traditional Chinese Literature, ed. Victor H. Mair 2000

Mistress and Maid (Jiaohongji), by Meng Chengshun, tr. Cyril Birch 2001

Chikamatsu: Five Late Plays, tr. and ed. C. Andrew Gerstle 2001

The Essential Lotus: Selections from the Lotus Sutra, tr. Burton Watson 2002

Early Modern Japanese Literature: An Anthology, 1600–1900, ed. Haruo Shirane 2002; abridged 2008

The Columbia Anthology of Traditional Korean Poetry, ed. Peter H. Lee 2002

The Sound of the Kiss, or The Story That Must Never Be Told: Pingali Suranna's Kalapurnodayamu, tr. Vecheru Narayana Rao and David Shulman 2003

The Selected Poems of Du Fu, tr. Burton Watson 2003

Far Beyond the Field: Haiku by Japanese Women, tr. Makoto Ueda 2003

Just Living: Poems and Prose by the Japanese Monk Tonna, ed. and tr. Steven D. Carter 2003

Han Feizi: Basic Writings, tr. Burton Watson 2003

Mozi: Basic Writings, tr. Burton Watson 2003

Xunzi: Basic Writings, tr. Burton Watson 2003

Zhuangzi: Basic Writings, tr. Burton Watson 2003

The Awakening of Faith, Attributed to Aśvaghosha, tr. Yoshito S. Hakeda, introduction by Ryuichi Abe 2005

The Tales of the Heike, tr. Burton Watson, ed. Haruo Shirane 2006

Tales of Moonlight and Rain, by Ueda Akinari, tr. with introduction by Anthony H. Chambers 2007

Traditional Japanese Literature: An Anthology, Beginnings to 1600, ed. Haruo Shirane 2007

The Philosophy of Qi, by Kaibara Ekken, tr. Mary Evelyn Tucker 2007

The Analects of Confucius, tr. Burton Watson 2007

The Art of War: Sun Zi's Military Methods, tr. Victor Mair 2007

One Hundred Poets, One Poem Each: A Translation of the Ogura Hyakunin Isshu, tr. Peter McMillan 2008

Zeami: Performance Notes, tr. Tom Hare 2008

Zongmi on Chan, tr. Jeffrey Lyle Broughton 2009

Scripture of the Lotus Blossom of the Fine Dharma, rev. ed., tr. Leon Hurvitz, preface and introduction by Stephen R. Teiser 2009

Mencius, tr. Irene Bloom, ed. with an introduction by Philip J. Ivanhoe 2009

Clouds Thick, Whereabouts Unknown: Poems by Zen Monks of China, Charles Egan 2010

The Mozi: A Complete Translation, tr. Ian Johnston 2010

The Huainanzi: A Guide to the Theory and Practice of Government in Early Han China, by Liu An, tr. and ed. John S. Major, Sarah A. Queen, Andrew Seth Meyer, and Harold D. Roth, with Michael Puett and Judson Murray 2010

The Demon at Agi Bridge and Other Japanese Tales, tr. Burton Watson, ed. with introduction by Haruo Shirane 2011

Haiku Before Haiku: From the Renga Masters to Bashō, tr. with introduction by Steven D. Carter 2011

The Columbia Anthology of Chinese Folk and Popular Literature, ed. Victor H. Mair and Mark Bender 2011

Tamil Love Poetry: The Five Hundred Short Poems of the Aiṅkuṟunūṟu, tr. and ed. Martha Ann Selby 2011

The Teachings of Master Wuzhu: Zen and Religion of No-Religion, by Wendi L. Adamek 2011

The Essential Huainanzi, by Liu An, tr. and ed. John S. Major, Sarah A. Queen, Andrew Seth Meyer, and Harold D. Roth 2012

The Dao of the Military: Liu An's Art of War, tr. Andrew Seth Meyer 2012

Unearthing the Changes: Recently Discovered Manuscripts of the Yi Jing (I Ching) *and Related Texts*, Edward L. Shaughnessy 2013

Record of Miraculous Events in Japan: The Nihon ryōiki, tr. Burton Watson 2013

The Complete Works of Zhuangzi, tr. Burton Watson 2013

Lust, Commerce, and Corruption: An Account of What I Have Seen and Heard, by an Edo Samurai, tr. and ed. Mark Teeuwen and Kate Wildman Nakai with Miyazaki Fumiko, Anne Walthall, and John Breen 2014

Exemplary Women of Early China: The Lienü zhuan *of Liu Xiang*, tr. Anne Behnke Kinney 2014

The Columbia Anthology of Yuan Drama, ed. C. T. Hsia, Wai-yee Li, and George Kao 2014

The Resurrected Skeleton: From Zhuangzi to Lu Xun, by Wilt L. Idema 2014

The Sarashina Diary: *A Woman's Life in Eleventh-Century Japan*, by Sugawara no Takasue no Musume, tr. with introduction by Sonja Arntzen and Itō Moriyuki 2014

The Kojiki: An Account of Ancient Matters, by Ō no Yasumaro, tr. Gustav Heldt 2014

The Orphan of Zhao and Other Yuan Plays: The Earliest Known Versions, translated and introduced by Stephen H. West and Wilt L. Idema 2014

Luxuriant Gems of the Spring and Autumn, attributed to Dong Zhongshu, ed. and tr. Sarah A. Queen and John S. Major 2016

GPSR Authorized Representative: Easy Access System Europe, Mustamäe tee 50, 10621 Tallinn, Estonia, gpsr.requests@easproject.com

www.ingramcontent.com/pod-product-compliance
Lightning Source LLC
Chambersburg PA
CBHW051347290426
44108CB00015B/1914